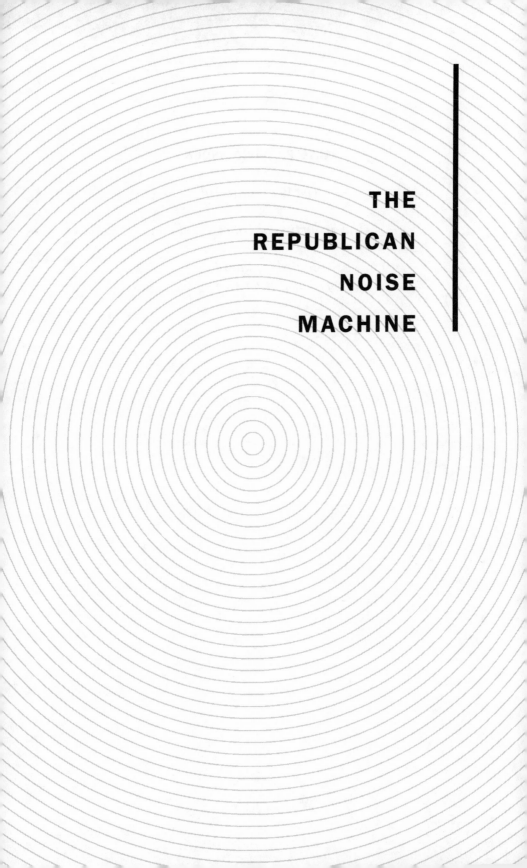

THE REPUBLICAN NOISE MACHINE

ALSO BY DAVID BROCK

The Real Anita Hill

The Seduction of Hillary Rodham

Blinded by the Right:
The Conscience of an Ex-Conservative

THE
REPUBLICAN
NOISE
MACHINE

RIGHT-WING MEDIA AND HOW

IT CORRUPTS DEMOCRACY

DAVID BROCK

Crown Publishers
New York

Published by Crown Publishers, New York, New York.
Member of the Crown Publishing Group, a division of Random House, Inc.
www.crownpublishing.com

CROWN is a trademark and the Crown colophon is a registered trademark of Random House, Inc.

Printed in the United States of America

Design by Leonard Henderson

Library of Congress Cataloging-in-Publication Data
Brock, David, 1962–
The Republican noise machine : right-wing media and how it corrupts democracy / by David Brock.—1st ed.
Includes index.
1. Conservatism—United States.   2. Mass media—Political aspects—United States.   3. Republican Party (U.S. : 1854–).   I. Title.
JC573.2.U6B76 2004   320.52′0973—dc22

2003027381

ISBN 1-4000-4875-3

10 9 8 7 6 5 4 3 2 1

First Edition

To James Alefantis

CONTENTS

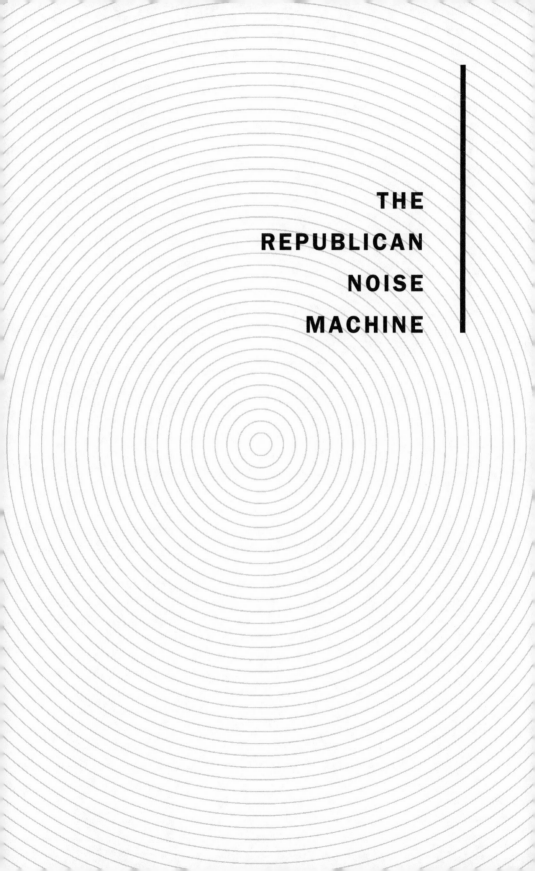

THE
REPUBLICAN
NOISE
MACHINE

INTRODUCTION

THE REPUBLICAN
NOISE MACHINE

INCE DEFECTING FROM THE REPUBLICAN PARTY in the latter half of the 1990s and publishing a confessional memoir in 2002, I've discussed my right-wing past with politicians, political activists and strategists, academic scholars, student groups, fellow writers, and hundreds of readers of my book *Blinded by the Right: The Conscience of an Ex-Conservative.* I'm rarely asked anymore why I changed, or about the baroque intricacies of the anti-Clinton movement, which I once participated in and then renounced and exposed. After a presidential election decided by the Supreme Court, the terrorist attacks on the United States on September 11, 2001, and the war with Iraq, politics has moved to a different place.

Nowadays, when I talk about *Blinded by the Right,* people want to know not how I was blinded by the Right, but how so much of the country seems to be in that position. For the first time since 1929, the Republican Party controls all three branches of government. Fewer people identify with the Democratic Party today than at any time since the New Deal. Conservatism seems the prevailing political and intellectual current, while liberalism seems a fringe dispensation of a few aging professors and Hollywood celebrities. People ask me, a former insider, how the Republican Right has won political and ideological power with such seeming ease and why Democrats, despite winning the most votes in the last three presidential elections, seem to be caught in a downward spiral, still able to win at the ballot box but steadily losing the battle for hearts and minds.

While it is not the only answer, my answer is: It's the media, stupid.

When I say this, in a more respectful way, to folks outside the right wing, I usually get either of two responses. Those who receive their news from the *New York Times* and National Public Radio give me blank stares. They are living in a rarefied media culture—one that prizes accuracy, fairness, and civility—that is no longer representative of the media as a whole. Those who have heard snippets of Rush Limbaugh's radio show, have caught a glimpse of Bill O'Reilly's temper tantrums on the FOX News Channel, or occasionally peruse the editorials in the *Wall Street Journal* think I'm a Cassandra. They view this media as self-discrediting and therefore irrelevant. They are living in a vacuum of denial.

Those who understand what I mean are either members of the media itself, have read media-criticism books or Internet sites devoted to the subject, or are in the political trenches every day dealing with the media. The gap between those who recognize right-wing media power for what it is and those who don't is wide and deep, as if they inhabit parallel universes. The gap is dangerous to democracy and needs to be closed.

When I came to Washington fresh out of college in 1986, I got a job at the *Washington Times*, the right-wing newspaper bankrolled by Reverend Sun Myung Moon, the Korean-born leader of a religious cult called the Unification Church. Though Moon's paper was said to be read in the Reagan White House, nobody paid much attention to it. We were the proverbial voice in the wilderness. Considering that the paper was governed by a calculatedly unfair political bias and that its journalistic ethics were close to nil, this was a good thing. That was eighteen years ago. Today, the most important sectors of the political media—most of cable TV news, the majority of popular op-ed columns, almost all of talk radio, a substantial chunk of the book market, and many of the most highly trafficked Web sites—reflect more closely the political and journalistic values of the *Washington Times* than those of the *New York Times*.

That is, they are powerful propaganda organs of the Republican Party.

For our politics, this development in the media represents a structural change: a structural advantage for the GOP and conservatism, and, I believe, the greatest structural obstacle facing opponents of the right wing. I therefore think it is one of the most important political stories of the era. I have sought to tell this story in *The Republican Noise Machine: Right-Wing Media and How It Corrupts Democracy.*

I know there is a Republican Noise Machine because I was once part of it. From the *Washington Times,* to a stint as a "research fellow" at the Heritage Foundation (the Right's premier think tank), to a position as an "investigative writer" at the muckraking magazine *The American Spectator,* and as the author of a best-selling right-wing book, I forwarded the right-wing agenda not as an open political operative or advocate but under the guise of journalism and punditry, fueled by huge sums of money from right-wing billionaires, foundations, and self-interested corporations.

By the time I said good-bye to the right wing in 1997, what was once a voice in the wilderness was drowning out competing voices across all media channels. The most influential political commentator in America, Rush Limbaugh, and his hundreds of imitators saturated every media market in the country, providing 22 percent of Americans—not only conservatives but independent swing voters—with their primary source of news. Conservatives had changed the face of the cable news business with the establishment of the top-rated FOX News Channel, a slicker broadcast version of the Moonie *Washington Times.* Pundit Ann Coulter and her fanatical ilk topped the best-seller lists, becoming superstars in the world of political punditry. The *Spectator* juggernaut—which had a circulation of three hundred thousand per month at its height in the early 1990s—had been replaced by Internet gossip Matt Drudge, who gets more than 6.5 million visitors to his site every day. Although enormous subsidies were still being pumped into right-wing media that did not turn a profit, right-wing media also had become a multibillion-dollar business, a development that powerfully affected all other commercial media.

The lies, smears, and vicious caricatures leveled against Bill and Hillary Clinton by this right-wing media, and then repeated in virtually every media venue in the country, have now been well documented, not least in *Blinded by the Right.* In that book, I compared the anti-Clinton propaganda to a virus as it seeped off the pages of the *Spectator* into the minds of every sen-

tient American. My memoir ended in 2000; what I did not fully comprehend then, but what is apparent to me now as I have watched the politics
of the last few years unfold, is that the virus was not Clinton-specific. In fact,
it had nothing to do with the Clintons per se; rather, in different strains, it
would afflict any and every political opponent of the right wing, including
Al Gore, Senate Democratic leader Tom Daschle, and the mourners of
Senator Paul Wellstone, every major Democrat seeking the presidency in
2004, *New York Times* columnist Paul Krugman, and the liberal advocacy
group MoveOn.org. What we have here, as a criminal investigator might say,
is a pattern.

In the 2000 presidential campaign, the Republican Noise Machine,
which worked for years to convince Americans that the Clintons were criminally minded, used the same techniques of character assassination to turn
the Democratic standard-bearer, Al Gore, for many years seen as an overly
earnest Boy Scout, into a liar. When Republican National Committee
polling showed that the Republicans would lose the election to the
Democrats on the issues, a "skillful and sustained 18-month campaign by
Republicans to portray the vice president as flawed and untrustworthy" was
adopted, the *New York Times* reported. Republicans accused Gore of saying things he never said—most infamously, that he "invented" the Internet,
a claim he never made that was first attributed to him in a GOP press
release before it coursed through the media. Actually, Gore had said,
"During my service in the United States Congress, I took the initiative in
creating the Internet," a claim that even former House Speaker Newt
Gingrich verified as true.[1]

The right-wing media broadcast this attack and similar attacks relentlessly, in effect giving the GOP countless hours of free political advertising
every day for months leading up to the election. "Albert Arnold Gore Jr. is
a habitual liar," William Bennett, a Cabinet secretary in the Reagan and first
Bush administrations, announced in the editorial pages of the *Wall Street
Journal*. "... Gore lies because he can't help himself," neoconservative
pamphleteer David Horowitz wrote. "LIAR, LIAR," screamed Rupert
Murdoch's *New York Post*. The conservative columnist George F. Will
pointed to Gore's "serial mendacity" and warned that he is a "dangerous
man." "Gore may be quietly going nuts," *National Review*'s Byron York concluded. The *Washington Times* agreed: "The real question is how to react

to Mr. Gore's increasingly bizarre utterings. *Webster's New World Dictionary* defines 'delusion' thusly: 'The apparent perception, in a nervous or mental disorder, of some thing external that is not actually present . . . a belief in something that is contrary to fact or reality, resulting from deception, misconception, or a mental disorder.'"

This impugning of Gore's character and the questioning of his mental fitness soon surfaced in the regular media. The *New York Times* ran an article headlined TENDENCY TO EMBELLISH FACT SNAGS GORE, while the *Boston Globe* weighed in with GORE SEEN AS "MISLEADING." On ABC's *This Week,* former Clinton aide George Stephanopoulos referred to Gore's "Pinocchio problem." For *National Journal's* Stuart Taylor, the issue was "the Clintonization of Al Gore, who increasingly apes his boss in fictionalizing his life story and mangling the truth for political gain." *Washington Post* editor Bob Woodward raised the question of whether Gore "could comprehend reality," while MSNBC's Chris Matthews compared Gore to "Zelig" and insisted, "Isn't it getting to be delusionary?"

The well-orchestrated media cacophony had its intended effect: The election was far more competitive than it should have been—and, indeed, was decided before the Supreme Court stepped in—because of negative voter perceptions of Gore's honesty and trustworthiness. In the final polls before the election and in exit polls on Election Day, voters said they favored Gore's program over George W. Bush's. Gore won substantial majorities not only for his position on most specific issues but also for his overall thrust. The conservative Bush theme of tax cuts and small government was rejected by voters in favor of the more liberal Gore theme of extending prosperity more broadly and standing up to corporate interests. Yet while Bush shaded the truth and misstated facts throughout the campaign on everything from the size of Gore's federal spending proposals to his own record as governor of Texas, by substantial margins voters thought Bush was more truthful than Gore. According to an ABC exit poll, of personal qualities that mattered most to voters, 24 percent ranked "honest/trustworthy" first—and they went for Bush over Gore by a margin of 80 percent to 15 percent. Seventy-four percent of voters said "Gore would say anything," while 58 percent thought Bush would. Among white, college-educated, male voters, Gore's "untruthfulness" was cited overwhelmingly as a reason not to vote for him, far more than any other reason.

Two years after the election, Gore gave an extraordinary interview to the *New York Observer* that could be read as an explanation of what happened to his presidential campaign. Gore charged that conservatives in the media, operating under journalistic cover, are loyal not to the standards and conventions of journalism but, rather, to politics and party. Gore said:

> The media is kind of weird these days on politics, and there are some major institutional voices that are, truthfully speaking, part and parcel of the Republican Party. Fox News Network, the *Washington Times,* Rush Limbaugh—there's a bunch of them, and some of them are financed by wealthy ultra-conservative billionaires who make political deals with Republican administrations and the rest of the media. . . . Most of the media [has] been slow to recognize the pervasive impact of this Fifth Column in their ranks— that is, day after day, injecting the daily Republican talking points into the definition of what's objective as stated by the news media as a whole. . . .
>
> Something will start at the Republican National Committee, inside the building, and it will explode the next day on the right-wing talk-show network and on Fox News and in the newspapers that play this game, the *Washington Times* and the others. And then they'll create a little echo chamber, and pretty soon they all start baiting the mainstream media for allegedly ignoring the story they've pushed into the zeitgeist. And then pretty soon the mainstream media goes out and disingenuously takes a so-called objective sampling, and lo and behold, these RNC talking points are woven into the fabric of the zeitgeist. . . .

True to form, the right-wing media greeted this factual description with yet another frenzy of repetitive messaging portraying Gore as crazy. Speaking of Gore on FOX News, *The Weekly Standard*'s Fred Barnes said, "This is nutty. This is along the lines with, you know, President Bush killed Paul Wellstone, and the White House knew before 9/11 that the attacks were going to happen. This is—I mean, this is conspiratorial stuff." Also on FOX, syndicated columnist Charles Krauthammer said of Gore, "I'm a psychiatrist. I don't usually practice on camera. But this is the edge of looniness, this idea that there's a vast conspiracy, it sits in a building, it emanates, it has these tentacles, is really at the edge. He could use a little help." "It could be he's just nuts," Rush Limbaugh said of Gore. "Tipper Gore's issue is what? Mental health. Right? It could be closer to home than we know." "He [Gore] said it's a conspiracy," Tucker Carlson said on CNN's *Crossfire*. "I actually think he's coming a little unhinged," *The Weekly Standard's* David Brooks, now at the *New York Times,* said of Gore on PBS.

As I write in early 2004, the Republican Noise Machine is primed to run the same campaign of personal vilification in the 2004 presidential election, no matter which Democrat wins the nomination. An op-ed piece in the *Washington Post* by Charles Krauthammer has pronounced former Vermont governor Howard Dean "the Delusional Dean." Krauthammer's "diagnosis" rested on a transcript of a Dean appearance on MSNBC's *Hardball* with Chris Matthews. Through the use of ellipses, Krauthammer doctored the transcript to make his point.[2] As Gore's experience demonstrated, Democrats ignore these attacks at their peril: Not only do such attacks confirm the preconceptions of Republicans but they shape the thinking of undecided voters and even of Democrats. One of the most frightening experiences I have had in recent years in talking with rank-and-file Democrats is the extent to which they unconsciously internalize right-wing propaganda. To add insult to injury, too many Democrats have a tendency to blame the victims of these smears—their own leaders—rather than addressing the root of the problem. For instance, when Senator Daschle made the factual statement that "failed" diplomacy had led to war with Iraq, right-wing media accused him of siding with Saddam Hussein. The ensuing controversy caused many Democrats to think Daschle had put his foot in his mouth.

With the right-wing media now a seemingly permanent and defining feature of the media landscape, if Democrats cut through the propaganda and win back the White House in 2004, they still face the prospect of being brutally slammed and systematically slandered in such a way that will make governing exceedingly difficult. There should be no doubt that the right-wing media's wildings of 1993—which led to Clinton's impeachment four years later—will be replayed over and over again until its capacities to spread filth are somehow eradicated.

●   ●   ●

Ironically, though not coincidentally, this radical transformation of the media has been obscured by conservative charges of "liberal media bias" that are believed by the vast majority of the public, including about half of Democrats. I'm all too familiar with the claim. From my very first days at the *Washington Times,* I was schooled to invoke "liberal bias" to deflect attention from my own biases and journalistic lapses and as a rationale to justify my presence in the mainstream media conversation in the name of providing "balance" or "the other side." We sold a lot of books and magazines and commanded lavish attention for our propaganda outside the right wing by using this cover story. As I showed in *Blinded by the Right,* the truth was that my work as a right-wing journalist and commentator—in particular, my *American Spectator* exposés on Anita Hill and the Clintons—did not deserve the attention they received. I was delivering a truckload of nonfacts, half-truths, and innuendos, not "balance" or "the other side." What I show in *The Republican Noise Machine* is that my experience was not the exception but the rule.

The "liberal media" mantra aside, if one looks and listens closely to what the right wing says when it thinks others may not be paying attention, there should be no doubt that it has made potent political gains not despite the media but *through* it. Rush Limbaugh says his program has "redefined the media" and refers to the "Limbaugh echo chamber syndrome," by which messaging originating on his show drives the twenty-four-hour news cycle. "The radical Left," he says, "is furious that liberals no longer set the agenda in the national media." 'NEW MEDIA' OUTLETS POUND ESTABLISHMENT, the *Washington Times* announced in an op-ed by right-wing publicist Craig Shirley. In a column explaining why the "outing" in the press of the identity of a covert CIA operative by senior Bush administration officials—a possibly criminal act committed to harm a Bush critic—did not spark a major political scandal, Tod Lindberg of the Hoover Institution explained in the *Washington Times,* "The media culture has changed. Conservatives and GOP partisans now have more than adequate means to offer an exculpatory counter-narrative." When CBS announced the cancellation of a biopic that was deemed unflattering toward the Reagans, Matt Drudge appeared on MSNBC, on a show hosted by a former Republican member of Congress, to announce the "beginning of a second media century. . . . It was the Internet, it was talk radio, it was cable that put pressure on CBS, and heretofore, there's never been this kind of pressure applied to one of the big titans, one of the big three." Brian C. Anderson, writing on OpinionJournal.com, a right-wing Web site published by the Wall Street Journal, in late 2003, informed conservatives, "[w]e're not losing anymore" and attributed this fact to a media "revolution." "Everything has changed," he wrote.

In a syndicated column titled "Culture War Signals," John Leo of *U.S. News & World Report* argued that "a corner has been turned" in the "culture wars" with the "rise of a large crop of commentators the left has not been able to match" and "conservative gains in new media" like the FOX News Channel. Conservative *New York Times* columnist David Brooks has written that the conservative media have "cohered to form a dazzlingly efficient ideology delivery system that swamps liberal efforts to get their ideas out." MSNBC's Matthews, interviewing Bernard Goldberg, the author of an attack book on the "liberal media" titled *Bias*, got the author to agree with his view that the cable news industry—whose total news audience is growing while that of the traditional broadcast news networks is declining—is biased all right, though in favor of the right wing. According to Bill O'Reilly, "For decades, [liberals] controlled the agenda on TV news. That's over." In an interview with PBS, Tony Blankley, the former Newt Gingrich flack turned editorial page editor of the *Washington Times* and *McLaughlin Group* panelist, said:

> Starting in 1994, with the Republican election of Congress, I think Limbaugh made the difference in electing the Republican majority. In the following three elections, he made the difference holding the majority. And in 2000, in the presidential race in Florida, he was the difference between Gore and Bush winning Florida, and thus the presidency.

Commenting on the media while interviewing Ann Coulter about her book *Treason: Liberal Treachery from the Cold War to the War on Terrorism,* right-wing radio host Sean Hannity crowed, "We've basically taken over!" Coulter, who has made millions off the charge of "liberal media bias" while maintaining a career as perhaps the most biased right-wing voice in the media, laughed in agreement. A young writer for Rupert Murdoch's neoconservative *Weekly Standard* named Matt Labash—whom I hired into right-wing journalism at *The American Spectator*—was probably laughing, too, when he was interviewed by *Columbia Journalism Review* partner Web site JournalismJobs.com. The interviewer asked, "Why have conservative media outlets like *The Weekly Standard* and FOX News Channel become more popular in recent years?" In his answer, Labash conceded that conservatives reject in their own media the standards of fairness, accuracy, and unbiased coverage that they demand from the "liberal media." He unmasked the hypocrisy at the heart of these endeavors:

> Because they feed the rage. We bring pain to the liberal media. I say that mockingly but it's true somewhat. . . . While these hand-wringing Freedom Forum types talk about objectivity, the conservative media like to rap the liberal media on the knuckles for not being objective. We've created this cottage industry in which it pays to be un-objective. . . . It's a great way to have your cake and eat it too. Criticize other people for not being objective. Be as subjective as you want. It's a great little racket.

Matt Labash's "great little racket" is the subject of *The Republican Noise Machine.* This is a book about the explicitly right-wing media and about how mainstream media, sometimes under the direction of executives who are conservative Republicans, has succumbed to an undue conservative influence and tilt. It is about the right-wing media's history, its reach, its appeal, its practices, its methods, and its financing. It is also about the beliefs of those who populate right-wing media and the beliefs that people derive from it. My conclusion is that right-wing media is a massive fraud, victimizing its own audience and corrupting the broader political dialogue with the tacit permission of established media authorities who should, and probably do, know better.

I argue, moreover, that the creation of right-wing media, and of the strategies by which the right wing has penetrated, pressured, co-opted, and subdued the mainstream media into accommodating conservatism, was not an accident. Once upon a time, right-wing strategists, operatives, and financiers believed that they could never win political hegemony in the United States unless they won domination of the country's political discourse.

Toward this end, a deliberate, well-financed, and expressly acknowledged communications and deregulatory plan was pursued by the right wing for more than thirty years—in close coordination with Republican Party leaders—to subvert and subsume journalism and reshape the national consciousness through the media, with the intention of skewing American politics sharply to the right. The plan has succeeded spectacularly.

The implications of this right-wing media incursion extend well beyond particular political outcomes to the heart of our democracy. Democracy depends on an informed citizenry. The conscious effort by the right wing to misinform the American citizenry—to collapse the distinction between journalism and propaganda—is thus an assault on democracy itself.

The problem is really not so much one of "bias," to use the Right's favored terminology, as it is where bias leads: In the biased right-wing media, among biased right-wing commentators, and in a mainstream media susceptible to right-wing scripting, it leads to verifiable journalistic malpractice, to the publication of misinformation, and to ethical malfeasance. At a deeper level, the existence and influence of the right-wing media as presently constituted is an affront to logic, rationality, and the maintenance of a shared knowledge base from which political consensus and correct public policy choices can be forged.

While the right wing cleverly has achieved its greatest gains in mainstream media sectors that ostensibly present opinion—columns, TV punditry, talk radio, and books—this opinion is predicated on a raft of distortions, misrepresentations, and outright lies presented to readers and viewers as fact. To further confuse the picture, the right wing has funded an array of its own media institutions, including newspapers, magazines, Internet sites, and a cable news channel, that produce a large volume of "news" that is not only offensive and unfair but misleading and often false.

Because technological advances and the race for ratings and sales have made the wall between right-wing media and the rest of the media permeable, the American media as a whole has become a powerful conveyor belt for conservative-generated "news," commentary, story lines, jargon, and spin. It is now possible to watch a lie move from a disreputable right-wing Web site onto the afternoon talk radio shows, to several cable chat shows throughout the evening, and into the next morning's *Washington Post*—all in twenty-four hours. This media food chain moves phony information and

GOP talking points—manufactured by and for conservatives, often bought and paid for by conservative political interests, and disseminated through an unabashedly biased right-wing media apparatus that follows no rules or professional norms—into every family dining room, every workplace, and every Internet chat room in America.

Equally troubling is that the cable and radio talkers who shape the national political conversation have the ability to censor news that does not serve the interests of the right wing. Every day, professional news organizations, primarily in the prestige print press, report facts, across a broad range of subjects, that are essential to an informed view of politics and policy. More often than not, these stories die on the page and never reach most Americans, owing to right-wing command of the new media "echo chamber."

The right-wing drive for media power must also be understood as an overturning of the First Amendment, which posits that good information will drive out bad information given diversity in the marketplace of ideas. As I will show, the Right's premeditated undermining of the media as a public trust in favor of crass commercial values, its coordinated attacks on noncommercial media, and the Republican-led drive for greater consolidation of media ownership have all but wiped out liberal and left-wing views and voices in entire sectors of the American media. Perhaps most ominous, right-wing verbal brownshirts of late have used their mighty media platforms to chill the free speech of their political adversaries and to neuter aggressive journalistic fact-finding that threatens Republican power.

My view is that unchecked right-wing media power means that in the United States today, no issue can be honestly debated and no election can be fairly decided. If California voters recall their governor in the belief that the state budget deficit is four times higher than it actually is, if Americans think Saddam Hussein was behind September 11 before hearing any evidence, if 19 percent of the public thinks it is in the top 1 percent tax bracket, if Americans view criticism of the government's national security policies as tantamount to treason—thank the right-wing media and those who abet it.

I feel it necessary to write a few words about what I am not trying to accomplish in this book. The right wing has spent so many years and so many millions of dollars framing the debate about the politics of the media that this book will inevitably be seen as an attempt to refute charges of "liberal media bias," as if there were no other issue worth discussing. I do address the subject of "liberal bias" in the mainstream media, and how it came to be such a bugaboo, in chapters 1 and 3. While instances of liberal bias—and instances of conservative bias—do exist, I show by examining the available evidence that right-wing claims of systematic liberal bias in the news have never been substantiated. However, as it is a fool's errand to attempt to prove a negative, this book should not be judged on a point that is a distraction from the real matter at hand. The existence of a powerful right-wing media is an incontrovertible fact and a subject fit for examination, quite aside from one's view on the "bias" debate.

It does seem to me a matter of common sense that if the professional media did not do what it is in the business of doing—reporting facts and providing information—it would either have had to change its practices long ago or go broke. Certainly, if CBS News anchor Dan Rather committed the type of willful journalistic malpractice committed night after night by FOX's Bill O'Reilly, who presents his show as a "No Spin Zone," Rather would be out of a job forthwith. That said, I realize that much of bias is in the eye of the beholder, and those who see what they see—on either side of the ideological divide—may never be convinced otherwise. In fact, I have concluded that right-wingers have purposely chosen to make an issue of bias—rather than make their case on the more objective grounds of factual inaccuracy or a breach of standards or ethics—precisely because, as long as there are consumers of news who share the biases of the right-wing media critics, they know that they can never be proved wrong.

This book does not offer a critique of news coverage that is presented as objective and impartial. Unlike conservatives who, willy-nilly, make conspiratorial allegations of bias against professional news organizations, I do not issue the blanket indictment that mainstream news organizations, editors, or reporters secretly harbor conservative biases, nor do I claim they intentionally skew the news to serve conservative ideological ends. This does not mean that there are no instances of conservative bias in news reports, only that I have not sought to document them here. My general feeling and experience has been that ideological bias of any type is the least of the biases prevalent in professional news organizations.

Bias, moreover, is a state of mind. Since, as a general rule, news professionals discuss neither their political views nor the thought processes that go into making the news, charges of personal bias, in whichever direction, require a gift for mind reading that neither I nor the right-wing media critics possess. And with no team of researchers at my disposal to do empirical studies of verifiable patterns in news content, I did not feel it was useful to write a book appraising news coverage that would inevitably be idiosyncratic and, perhaps, more indicative of my own biases than those of the news professionals. (Such studies have been done by credible researchers; where appropriate, I use them in this book.)

Though it is not a subject of this inquiry, I should say that I share the view of many observers that news coverage of the George W. Bush administration has been less aggressive than circumstances warrant. "Any objective person would say that in some ways Clinton was covered too aggressively in some areas, and Bush is not covered aggressively enough," ABC News political director Mark Halperin told *American Journalism Review* in September 2003. The reasons for this sorry state of affairs run a wide gamut, some of them at least indirectly attributable to right-wing intimidation. In an interview with the BBC, Dan Rather explained, "It is an obscene comparison—you know, I am not sure I like it—but you know there was a time in South Africa that people would put flaming tires around the people's necks if they dissented. And in some ways the fear is that you will be 'necklaced' here, you will have a flaming tire of lack of patriotism put around your neck. Now it is that fear that keeps journalists from asking the toughest of the tough questions." A dispatch from Margaret Carlson in *Time* magazine unearthed a more pedestrian concern: "The Cheneys have even dined at the mecca of Georgetown limousine liberals, chez Ben Bradlee and Sally Quinn [of the *Washington Post*]. The Cheneys are the most social of the Bushies, asserts Quinn, which she feels accounts for the relatively friendly press coverage the vice president gets. 'It's harder to trash someone you've had pasta with the night before.'"

I also share with many dismay at the generally shallow level of what passes for political commentary in Washington. However, this is not a book about the state of political punditry overall. Pundits who are not avowedly conservative are not a major part of this story; a few make cameo appearances when right-wing ideology, misinformation, or talking points can be unarguably attributed to them. My purpose here is to examine the authority and weight of the right wing, not to point out examples of pedantry, brownnosing, and idiocy among Washington's chattering classes. This phenomenon, a kind of secondary virus, is not an unimportant subject, but I leave it for another day.

One complaint that I do lodge against the mainstream media and the politically unaligned pundits is their utter failure to expose the right-wing media for the destructive force that it plainly is and to vigilantly police its own ranks against the right-wing raid. Given the amount of ink spilled, and the orgies of self-flagellation, surrounding the cases of serial journalistic fabricators Stephen Glass of *The New Republic* and Jayson Blair of the *New York Times,* I find this laxity curious, to say the least.

As I will show in the pages that follow, there are far more consequential Stephen Glasses and Jayson Blairs on the radio, on television, and in print every day of the week; with the notable exception of a small but hardy band of columnists, authors, and Web loggers, no one says a word about it. The appearance, indulgence, and even celebration of known right-wing dissemblers, extremists, kooks, racists, sexists, homophobes, and anti-Semites in outlets of the mainstream media, including book publishing, is, in my opinion, a disgrace. Some toxic mix of economic and political pressures has caused the guardians of our media to acquiesce in the debasement of our political culture, not to mention of their own integrity and professional standing.

Throughout the narrative, and in the afterword to this book, I briefly describe some new efforts by political opponents of the Right to resist and reduce its influence. Until very recently, progressives appear not to have thought very much about the challenge presented by right-wing media, much less have they done anything to meet it. Today, the questions of whether progressives could or should support a liberal talk radio network, or a liberal FOX News Channel, or a liberal Heritage Foundation, or even a liberal *Drudge Report* are being entertained at a high level by people who are concerned about the malign impact the right-wing media has on American politics. I hope this book will provide further grist for these important conversations and fledgling enterprises.

The issue of my own biases I will address up front. I am an ex-conservative journalist. Having worked closely with them for more than a decade, I hold my former colleagues on the Right in low regard. I have seen, and I know firsthand, indeed from my own pen, how the organized Right has sabotaged not only journalism but also democracy and truth. To stem these ill effects, I believe the current right-wing media ascendancy must be fully understood, exposed, and reversed. It is in this spirit that I offer *The Republican Noise Machine.*

CHAPTER ONE
NIXON'S REVENGE

W HEN JOURNALIST EDITH EFRON died at age seventy-nine in April 2001, Virginia Postrel, the editor of the libertarian magazine *Reason,* for which Efron had been a longtime contributor, published a lengthy remembrance. Postrel celebrated two feature articles Efron had published to wide notice in *Reason* in the 1990s—explorations of the psyches of two famously controversial men she had never met: Supreme Court Justice Clarence Thomas and President Bill Clinton.

While dismissing the sexual harassment laws as an expression of "pure feminist dementia" and ascribing Anita Hill's sexual harassment charges against Thomas to an "emotional disorder," Efron sought to attribute Thomas's own histrionics in his confirmation hearing—he said that he would have rather taken an assassin's bullet than answer Hill's charges—to a deep-seated revulsion to the racial stereotype of "the black man as mythic sexual beast."[1] In her article "Can the President Think?" Efron diagnosed Clinton as suffering from "Obsessive Compulsive Personality Disorder as identified by the American Psychiatric Association" and attention deficit disorder. Clinton, theorized Efron, was "a cognitive cripple," "incapacitated," and "helpless," suggesting that Hillary Clinton literally did his think-ing for him.[2]

Postrel also lauded Efron's 1984 book, *The Apocalyptics: Cancer and the Big Lie,* which charged that the American scientific community, allied with the environmental and consumer movements, had faked a cancer scare as a way of undermining American industry and free enterprise. Although the book was framed as an "impeccably neutral" scientific inquiry, complete with 1,392 footnotes, Efron's "real thrust," concluded the editor of Harvard Medical School's *Health Letter* in a *Washington Post* review, "is political." Moreover, her antiregulatory tract, conceived as an answer to Rachel Carson's groundbreaking book on the environment, *Silent Spring,* was "hardly prophetic" and marred by "unfettered and peculiarly violent rheto-ric," "bizarre metaphors," and "imputation of bad faith." The mountain of footnotes, he concluded, was largely "gratuitous."[3]

Perhaps not seeing the irony in it, Postrel titled Efron's obituary "The Woman Who Saw Through Walls."[4] Oddly, Efron's first book, *The News Twisters,* a *New York Times* best-seller published in 1971, was mentioned only in passing. Yet it was with this purported exposé of "liberal bias" in net-work news that Efron, a writer for *TV Guide*—then published by Republican Walter Annenberg, who routinely used his newspaper and mag-azine empire to advance his political and personal vendettas—made her lasting mark, as the founder of the modern right-wing media criticism industry. *The News Twisters* became its first text.[5]

After inventing what she claimed was a rigorously objective methodol-ogy for detecting bias in the reportage of the three broadcast networks, admittedly derived not from accepted principles of social science but from her own "logic," and then applying it to coverage during the final seven weeks of the 1968 presidential campaign, Efron concluded that the TV media followed "the elitist-liberal-left line in all controversies"—"actively slanting" their coverage against U.S. policy in Vietnam and for the Vietcong; "actively slanting" against the "white middle-class majority" and in favor of "black militants"; and "actively favoring" the election of Democrat Hubert H. Humphrey over Republican Richard M. Nixon and segregationist inde-pendent candidate George Wallace, then governor of Alabama.

A grinning Governor Wallace posed for news photographers holding aloft a copy of *The News Twisters.* At the White House, Richard Nixon, who appointed Walter Annenberg ambassador to Great Britain, was pleased as well. Two years later, testimony before the Senate Watergate Committee revealed that Nixon special counsel Charles Colson took $8,000 from Nixon's reelection committee to purchase copies of *The News Twisters*.[6] Among a long list of dirty tricks, Colson had been charged with planting phony letters to the editor in newspapers to enhance Nixon's image and with entertaining a plot to bomb the Brookings Institution, a Washington think tank the Nixonites considered a symbol of the liberal establishment.[7] During Watergate, Colson was designated to attack news accounts as "a fantasy, a work of fiction," and he ordered up a "butcher piece" on the *Washington Post* staff.[8]

After Nixon's death in 1994, Colson told the story of *The News Twisters* to *Newsweek:* "[Nixon] called me into his office on another occasion and asked me if I had read Edith Efron's book about biased network news coverage. I had. I had also concluded that it was a book destined for obscurity. Nixon then ordered me to get it on the best-seller list. I was used to cryptic instructions, but never one quite like this. After finding the particular stores that the *New York Times* and others regularly checked to determine which books were selling, I enlisted the assistance of some Nixon supporters in New York. We literally bought out the stores."[9] When Nixon aide E. Howard Hunt quit the White House during the Watergate scandal, he left behind several cartons of *The News Twisters*.[10]

Edith Efron was a self-described libertarian and a onetime devotee of Ayn Rand, who advocated free-market fundamentalism and dismantling of the welfare state in her theory of objectivism. Efron believed that "historically . . . liberals . . . have always followed the ideological leadership of the revolutionary left. . . ." Her research was underwritten by a grant from the Historical Research Foundation, established with a bequest from conservative lace importer Alfred Kohlberg. According to a report in *Variety* at the time, Kohlberg was "a close associate of Senator Joe McCarthy, [who] earned the label as 'head' of the so-called China Lobby for his work for Chiang Kai-shek," the authoritarian leader of the Nationalist Chinese government. The institute's "projects chairman" was *National Review* founder William F. Buckley Jr. Buckley hyped *The News Twisters* as "explosive," as did Irving Kristol, godfather of the ideological movement known as neoconservatism, in an essay in *Fortune*. Kristol's magazine, *The Public Interest*, and a second neoconservative organ, *Commentary* (under the editorship of Norman Podhoretz), heaped early praise on the book.

Hitting the best-seller list thanks to Nixon's slush fund, the book broke through in the wider media, where its methods did not survive scrutiny from nonconservatives. It was no coincidence that Efron, whose work over the years betrayed a fascination with the psychological phenomenon of projection, called her tome *The News Twisters*. The *St. Louis Post-Dispatch* editorialized, "The book is no genuine study of TV news performance, but a 1972 campaign document designed to twist network coverage to the right," while the *New York Post* labeled it "right-angled paranoia." Writing in the *Washington Post*, Ben H. Bagdikian called the book "dishonest, inaccurate . . . [a] demonstration on how to doctor evidence."

The reviewers' criticism focused on the fact that Efron's method—taping every broadcast during the period studied and marking the transcripts for "pro" or "anti" bias—was not objective but subjective. Reviewers noted that in Efron's idiosyncratic world, a report on Nixon being met by college hecklers was an example of anti-Nixon bias, while a report on Humphrey being met by college hecklers was listed not as an example of anti-Humphrey bias but as liberal bias: "reporter supports demonstrators." Nor could she explain how her own data tables contradicted her sweeping conclusions, as when she counted the words spoken for and against liberals on the three networks combined and found 20 percent for liberals and 80 percent against.

When CBS News took the extraordinary step of hiring a research firm to do an analysis of the broadcasts Efron cited, it found that she grossly misrepresented the plain meaning of the transcripts. One CBS script that read, "Nixon says he is warning his staff against overconfidence, but he himself hardly looks worried," was listed by Efron as an "anti-Nixon editorial" that "says Nixon is overconfident; suggests he is a liar." Countering Efron's claim that CBS aired sixteen times the amount of anti-Nixon material as pro-Nixon material, the CBS-commissioned study found that 60 percent of all references to Nixon on CBS were neutral, with the favorable and unfavorable references about evenly divided.[11]

In providing a template for what would become a well-organized and well-funded campaign by the political Right to bring the media under its ideological domination, *The News Twisters* was notable not only for the transparent flaws of its central arguments but also for its imperviousness to documentation of those flaws. Efron was not the first conservative author to show that a combination of polemical skills, good timing, and a flair for publicity could carry the day, though she was a pioneer of the technique. A political ideologue, writing for an audience of true believers, could impute to his or her critics a political motive and survive, the facts notwithstanding. This was especially the case on the subject of media bias, in which criticism by the press could be made to look like further proof of the original indictment.

Unbowed and unbound, Efron managed to take her one-woman show before a Senate subcommittee hearing on government regulation of the broadcast industry arranged by President Nixon. She then published a second book, a detailed rebuttal of the CBS report on *The News Twisters,* under the self-dramatizing title *How CBS Tried to Kill a Book.* Had that been the intention of CBS executives, who did not publish their study until six months after Efron's book had become a best-seller, they failed. *The News Twisters* validated abeyant right-wing frustration with the media that dated back to the era when the anti-Communist witch-hunter Joseph McCarthy, whose meteoric rise to power in the Senate was due in part to his talents as a demagogic media manipulator, was exposed as a smear artist by Edward R. Murrow in his CBS documentary series *See It Now.* McCarthy fought back with attacks on Murrow's patriotism, and CBS gave the senator time to air a rebuttal, written by conservative columnist George Sokolsky of the William Randolph Hearst newspaper chain. McCarthy's career, however, did not recover. Twenty years later, sustained by funds from a McCarthy sympathizer, Efron's pseudoscientific claims, and their like, spread like a virus.

The publication of *The News Twisters* in 1971 dovetailed with a political strategy of assaulting and discrediting the journalism profession that had been employed by President Nixon's administration two years before, when White House speechwriter and former *TV Guide* writer Patrick J. Buchanan approached Nixon with the idea of blunting media reports on Nixon's Vietnam War policy by attacking the TV networks as biased in favor of the North Vietnamese and the antiwar movement. When he left the

White House and published his 1973 book, *The New Majority,* Buchanan revealed that his recondite concern was more with media power than with bias. Buchanan flatly stated that the power of the TV networks was an obstacle to conservative Republican governance. "The growth of network power, and its adversary posture towards the national government," he wrote, is "beyond the [American] tradition."

Buchanan would become a central figure in the Right's media strategies over the next thirty years, always working inside the two institutions he attacked relentlessly: "Big Government" and the "liberal media." While plotting his political comeback in 1966, Nixon had hired Buchanan as his sole aide from a job as the youngest editorial writer on a major U.S. newspaper, the ultraconservative *St. Louis Globe-Democrat,* where Buchanan used information fed to the publisher, Richard Amberg, by FBI director J. Edgar Hoover to smear civil rights leaders.[12]

Buchanan grew up comfortably in Washington, D.C., the son of a government accountant in a conservative Catholic household where McCarthy and Spanish Fascist Francisco Franco were revered. Buchanan adopted their authoritarian populism and slashing rhetorical style. He was behind the Nixonian strategy of exploiting race to build political support. In a memo to Nixon in 1971, Buchanan wrote that integration could result in "perpetual friction" owing to what he said were hereditary differences in white and black intelligence. As he rose to political prominence in his own right, Buchanan would be accused of anti-Semitism and of "flirting with Fascism" by his conservative brethren when he praised Adolf Hitler, defended Nazi war criminals, and appeared to deny the Holocaust.[13] When he launched his own bids for the presidency in the 1990s, Buchanan staffed his campaign with people tied to white supremacy and militia groups.[14]

Though politicians of both parties are frequently unhappy with media coverage, Nixon was in a category all by himself. After growing up lower-middle-class in a small town in Orange County, California, attending Whittier College and Duke University Law School, and then getting rejected for jobs by prominent law firms in the Northeast, Nixon nursed status resentments of what he considered to be East Coast elites. Primary among those elites Nixon resented were journalists. His former aide William Safire wrote in his White House memoir *Before the Fall:*

Nixon, who always knew he had a deep and dark rage within him, mastered his temper in just about every other area, but kept "flicking off the scab," in his skin-crawling metaphor, when it came to the quintessential "them," the press. He had contempt for them, as elitist, antidemocratic, lordly, arrogant lookers-down-their-noses at the elected representative of the folks, and he did everything he could get away with to destroy them—becoming, along the way, elitist, lordly, and dangerously arrogant.[15]

Throughout his public life, Nixon believed in his bones that the press was out to avenge his promotion of charges that New Dealer Alger Hiss was a Communist agent and to avenge his slanderous Red-baiting campaign for the California Senate seat against liberal Democrat Helen Gahagan Douglas in 1950—even though the California press, then dominated by conservative Republicanism, was strongly pro-Nixon.[16] Nixon's shifty appearance in a televised presidential debate against Democrat John F. Kennedy in 1960 not only helped seal his loss but also reinforced his fear, and what Safire described as his "hatred," of the media. After losing the race for California governor in 1962, Nixon quit politics, famously saying, "For sixteen years, ever since the Hiss case, you've had a lot of fun. Just think what you're going to be missing. You won't have Nixon to kick around anymore, because, gentlemen, this is my last press conference."

Nixon's retirement lasted six years. By the time he campaigned for the White House in 1968, network news had become a powerful—and, as Nixon saw it, a menacing—medium. Nixon set out to learn how to use television to his advantage, hiring a team of advertising and TV professionals to "package" him, according to *The Selling of the President, 1968* by Joe McGinniss. Joining the Nixon campaign was Roger Ailes, executive producer of *The Mike Douglas Show*, who had met Nixon at the time of his 1967 guest appearance. Ailes was placed in charge of the so-called Man in the Arena segments, regionally televised specials in which Nixon took questions from a carefully selected studio audience hoping to give "the impression to a viewer that Nixon certainly did have charisma," according to McGinniss. The campaign paid for the television time, although the events were choreographed to make them appear more like news than advertising.

As his political troubles mounted in the White House, Nixon became further obsessed with subduing and controlling the "media," a word that the White House insisted on using to describe the press "because [it] had a manipulative Madison Avenue, all-encompassing connotation, and the press hated it," Safire reported. Documents and tapes from his White House years, published by Richard Reeves in his book *President Nixon,* showed a preoccupation "with the type of people who are in the press corps . . . truly a third house supporting the Democratic candidates," Nixon wrote in a memo to top aide H. R. Haldeman. In April 1971, several months before the release of Efron's book, Nixon wrote Haldeman: "We need the kind of attack which will get to their vulnerable spot—their total support of ultra-liberal causes. . . . Naturally the press has a vested interest in seeing the United States lose the war and they are doing their desperate best to report all the bad news and to downplay the good news. As far as the election is concerned, they will be absolutely vicious and violent on that score. . . . I cannot emphasize too strongly my feeling that much more than any single issue that we are going to emphasize, the discrediting of the press must be our major objective over the next few months."[17]

In early 1972, according to Haldeman's diaries, Nixon met in the White House to discuss reelection strategy with the Reverend Billy Graham, a once-obscure evangelist whose career had been secured by favorable publicity in the publications of William Randolph Hearst and in Henry Luce's *Time* magazine. "Either Communism must die, or Christianity must die," Graham maintained, as he became a spokesperson for the worldwide anti-Communist crusade and a public supporter of Joe McCarthy.[18] Of Nixon's meeting with Graham, Haldeman recorded: "There was considerable discussion of the terrible problem arising from total Jewish domination of the media. . . . Graham has the strong feeling that the Bible says that there are satanic Jews and that's where our problem arises. . . ."[19]

Journalists dominated the "enemies list" that Nixon asked his White House counsel, John Dean, to draw up. The telephones of several reporters were wiretapped by the government. And Nixon used telecommunications policy to forward his political aims. During Watergate, Nixon schemed to challenge the *Washington Post*'s broadcast licenses and to convince his supporter Richard Mellon Scaife, an ultraconservative Pittsburgh billionaire, to buy the *Post* outright.[20] Network affiliates were harassed. As Safire reported,

"When the new White House Office of Telecommunications Policy began making noises at local stations to put heat on their networks to stop 'ideological plugola,' that was government intimidation pure and simple."[21]

Nixon and his men had every reason to fear a free and unfettered press corps—and to want to tame it. They had a tenuous hold on power, having won office in 1968 with a razor-slim margin of less than 1 percent of the popular vote over Humphrey, who became the Democratic nominee after the assassination of Senator Robert F. Kennedy. They were criminally minded, determined to "rat-fuck" their enemies by any means, in their parlance. And though Nixon had won office on a pledge that he would end the war in Vietnam, his plans to escalate it would only inflame antiwar protesters and ensure that the TV media would continue to bring right into America's living rooms reports of Americans dying in what already looked like a lost cause. Nixon seemed to know instinctively that if the media did its job—that it served as an alert government watchdog—his administration could unravel. "Sometimes," as Safire put it while explaining that Nixon's hatred of the press wasn't wholly a product of paranoia, "there can be good reasons for secrecy."

The corrupt duo of Nixon and his vice president, Spiro T. Agnew, indelibly tarnished the media's reputation for integrity and professionalism. As reported in Richard Reeves's *President Nixon,* their device was a speech attacking the East Coast media, drafted by Buchanan, edited by Nixon, and delivered by Agnew on national television in November 1969.

According to Safire, Agnew had his own motives for fearing an autonomous media, which had shown him to be a "bumbler" in the 1968 campaign. Agnew would later tangle with the press over the reporting of his racial slurs and bribery allegations; in the face of a bribery inquiry, he resigned his office and pleaded no contest to federal income tax evasion. But before all that, he relished his role as Nixon's pit bull.

Spiro Agnew began his speech by condemning the "instant analysis and querulous criticism" by network newsmen following a major Nixon speech on Vietnam during which the president called on "the great silent majority of my fellow Americans" to help him "end the war in a way that we could win the peace." Agnew excoriated the media for seeking comment on the president's address from Ambassador W. Averell Harriman, President Lyndon B. Johnson's chief negotiator at the Paris peace talks on Vietnam, whom Agnew depicted as a tool of the North Vietnamese. He then blamed the networks for creating a hyped image of the "brutality and violence of merciless police" in their coverage of antiwar protests at the Democratic National Convention in Chicago in 1968—a media event that was thought to have hurt Hubert Humphrey's candidacy, since it played into Nixon's law-and-order themes.

The networks, Agnew suggested, should not air vigorous criticism of government policy, show unflattering images of the police, or be entrusted to cover the news as they saw fit. The network newsmen were reflecting not objective reality in their reportage but, rather, their own distorted views, be they pro-Communist or antipolice. Yet Agnew argued not for neutrality but for the idea that news should reflect the opinions and tastes of the majority of the public, a profoundly antijournalistic sentiment.

Agnew described the newsmen as a "small and unelected elite" who "live and work in the geographical and intellectual confines of Washington, D.C., or New York City . . . they talk constantly to one another, thereby providing artificial reinforcement to their shared viewpoints. . . . The views of the majority of this fraternity do not—and I repeat not—represent the views of America." The vice president continued:

> The American who relies on television for his news might conclude that the majority of American students are embittered radicals, that the majority of black Americans feel non-regard for their country, that violence and lawlessness are the rule. . . . In this search for excitement and controversy, has more than equal time gone to the minority of Americans who specialize in attacking the United States—its institutions and its citizens? As with other American institutions, perhaps it is time that the networks were made more responsive to the views of the nation and more responsible to the people they serve. . . .[22]

Agnew's speech was a sensation. COUNTERATTACK ON DISSENT blared the cover of *Time*. Evidently, Agnew had tapped into a set of emotions that were already roiling a substantial segment of the public. Many Americans were troubled by the political and social tumult in the country that was beamed to them every night by the evening news, from the assassinations of RFK and civil rights leader Martin Luther King Jr., to race riots, to the antiwar protests. A substantial number of Americans sided with government authorities in these controversies. According to a Harris Poll, Agnew was given credit by 67 percent of the public for "having the courage to speak out against radicals, blacks, and students where others don't dare."

Yet there was little evidence that the public embraced Agnew's critique of the media. A majority of those polled by Harris thought the press was objective and professional, not slanted. It would take years of work by the Republican Right to undermine and subvert journalism by painting it as, essentially, an un-American force; but Buchanan had set the process in motion by offering up the East Coast media, the chronicler of unsettling events, as a focus for the public's inchoate concerns, anxieties, and, in some cases, prejudices. Following Agnew's address, East Coast newsrooms reported a flood of hate mail containing words like "eastern snob," "kike," "nigger lover," "homo," "Jew bastard," and "Commie."

Shortly after Agnew's speech, ABC News replaced Frank Reynolds as coanchor of its evening newscast. Reynolds believed he was fired for giving commentaries critical of Nixon. "I paid a price. I was taken off the air," he said.[23] Reynolds's coanchor, Howard K. Smith, who publicly endorsed Agnew's views, was kept on.

Besides chilling the media, the broader political strategy behind the Agnew attack was to build what Buchanan called "the Nixon Counter-Revolution"—a Republican electoral majority—by implicating the media in the racial and cultural tensions of the day. Agnew would go on in future speeches to call the media "pusillanimous pussyfooters," "vicars of vacillation," and "an effete corps of impudent snobs who characterize themselves as intellectuals."[24] Casting the media as the enemy of the "silent majority" was also a way of marginalizing liberalism as a narrow ideology foisted on America largely through a series of orchestrated sound bites and camera angles.

According to Safire, the strategy was a ruse: There never was a "silent majority," only a conservative minority, and Nixon and Buchanan both knew it. The fears and divisions in American society that the Nixon White House sought to exploit were real enough; but, as Safire asked of Buchanan in a skeptical internal White House memo, "How many people think like he does?" Safire wrote that the "silent majority," a construct invented by what Safire called the "intellectual aristocracy" of the conservative movement, represented only a faction within the GOP.

Nor was there much of a "liberal media." From his partisan perspective in the early 1970s, Safire wrote that 90 percent of the media was "enlightened," not politically biased. Buchanan told journalist Martin Schram following the 1972 election, "I think the media was extraordinarily fair and balanced in this election campaign."[25]

In seeking to strike a chord with the "silent majority," it was no accident that Buchanan's attack was tinged with anti-Semitism and nativism. As conservative writer Alan Crawford wrote in his 1980 book, *Thunder on the Right*, revulsion toward the political and cultural institutions of the East Coast, especially those of New York City (which were seen as "cosmopolitan extensions of Europe"), had long been a staple of Far Right populism in the United States. In this view, Crawford explained, the national networks were simply the newest additions to the list of institutions deserving of suspicion and scorn: the government, both political parties, the universities, the big banks, and the American foreign policy establishment.[26] According to Safire, Buchanan understood that he was appealing to base elements, giving the game away by making private cracks about how "the booboisie in the hinterlands" was energized by Nixon's attacks on the media.

It is a paradox of its antimedia stance that the conservative movement "aristocracy," embodied in the future media career of Buchanan, would soon attain media power in its own right. And just as Nixon exemplified the very traits he ascribed to the press, conservatives in the media would do precisely what they claimed liberals did—they used the media to indoctrinate the public into the ideology of their unrepresentative faction.

When Edith Efron began her study in 1968—before Agnew's 1969 TV rant—she was already working against what she called "a backdrop of simmering public antagonism" toward the press. That antagonism, and thus the still diaphanous notion of media "bias," had one primary source: a conviction among segregationists that the media—which had been somewhat slow to record the civil rights movement until it spilled into the streets as a breaking news story—were sympathetic to the forces of desegregation. In what civil rights reporter Pat Watters called a battle "of the sane against the insane," there was little if any openly pro-segregationist sentiment in the major American media.

GOP efforts to stoke and harness this antagonism toward the media for political ends began in the 1964 presidential campaign of Arizona Senator Barry Goldwater, the first movement conservative to be nominated to the presidency and the first Republican to employ the so-called Southern Strategy of appealing to segregationists to win votes that Nixon, on the advice of Buchanan, would later use with much more success. The Republican Right's Southern Strategy, and its antimedia politics, were born in the same historical moment and reinforced each other.

Barry Goldwater had become a leading conservative spokesman and national political figure because of the press—the same press that had buoyed McCarthy and Nixon. As a young and politically inexperienced Senate candidate in 1952, Goldwater's antigovernment, antiunion, anti-Communist platform attracted the crusading support of the powerful right-wing newspaper publisher Eugene Pulliam, who owned *The Arizona Republic* and the *Phoenix Gazette.* Once in the Senate, his conservative salvos won him favorable notices in the Republican newspapers that dominated major print markets nationwide, from the *Chicago Daily News,* to the *Detroit Free Press,* to the *Dallas Morning News,* to Pulliam's papers in Indianapolis, to the *Los Angeles Times.* The East Coast press soon followed, as Goldwater found himself featured in the major national magazines— Henry Luce's *Time,* David Lawrence's *U.S. News & World Report,* and DeWitt Wallace's *Reader's Digest*—under headlines like THE GLITTERING MISTER GOLDWATER. In 1960, Goldwater, who had finished only one year of college, published a ghostwritten book, *The Conscience of a Conservative,* which sold more than one million copies. And he began "writing" a thrice-weekly opinion column that was widely syndicated by the *Los Angeles Times,* which had launched Nixon's career in the 1940s when it was a partisan conservative Republican newspaper under Norman Chandler.[27]

In the 1964 presidential race, Goldwater's glitter wore off. As writer Rick Perlstein details in his Goldwater biography, *Before the Storm: Barry Goldwater and the Unmaking of the American Consensus,* that campaign opened up a political and cultural divide between the Democratic Party and much of the Republican Party on the one side, and on the other Goldwater and his reactionary supporters. The small band of Goldwater militants, who for years had felt alienated, unrepresented, and excluded from the political system, gamed the Republican presidential nominating contest for Goldwater by superior organization. Though their candidate lost many primaries, the Goldwater supporters used explicitly Communist tactics of delegate infiltration in the party caucuses to secure the nomination.[28] One Goldwater adviser favorably quoted Mao Tse-tung: "Give me just two or three men in a village, and I will take the village."[29]

The people around Goldwater were more radical than their standard-bearer. They were both antiestablishment, and anticonservative. Historian Richard Hofstadter called them "pseudo-conservatives," a term borrowed from Theodore W. Adorno's *The Authoritarian Personality*. Rigid moral absolutists who expressed themselves in an apocalyptic style, "they have little in common with the temperate and compromising spirit of true conservatism in the classical sense of the term," Hofstadter observed.[30]

Once he was on the national stage, Goldwater's belligerently militaristic stance toward the Soviet Union; his loose talk about using atomic bombs and invading Cuba; his disdain for the United Nations; his opposition to the 1964 Civil Rights Act; his advocacy of making Social Security voluntary; and his assault on the authority of the Supreme Court ("not necessarily" the law of the land) placed him well to the right of political opinion in both parties. Roundly condemned by his fellow Republicans for advocating "absurd" and "dangerous" national security policies and for exploiting "racist sentiments" in the South to win power, he gained endorsements from members of the John Birch Society, the National Gun Alliance, and the Ku Klux Klan. Meanwhile, his opponent in the race, President Lyndon Johnson, adroitly exploited the extremism and eccentricity of Goldwater and his supporters.[31]

News organizations had a startling story to tell in covering Goldwater's campaign—the extreme positions he took; the racist gaffes (America's cities were crime-ridden "jungles"); the organized effort by renegade conservative activists to seize control of the GOP nominating process; the damning comments from the LBJ campaign and also from his fellow Republicans; the decision to reverse traditional GOP support for civil rights (on the legal advice of William H. Rehnquist and Robert Bork); the refusal of Goldwater delegates to credential black Republicans at their convention while spitting on them and calling them "niggers"; protesters' comparisons of Goldwater to Hitler; and the sudden growth of pro-Goldwater right-wing movements, such as the John Birch Society, fueled by phantom fears of Communist and immigrant subversion.[32] The society's leader, Robert Welch, claimed that a Communist conspiracy had overtaken the American press, labor unions, the Supreme Court, and Congress. Liberals were denounced as "comsymps." Welch even claimed that President Dwight D. Eisenhower was an agent of Communist influence.[33] At the same time, Welch emulated "Communist cells and quasi-secret operation through 'front' groups and preach[ed] a ruthless prosecution of the ideological war along lines very similar to those it finds in the Communist enemy," according to Hofstadter.

Coincidentally, the three major network newscasts had won a sizable national audience just in time to magnify all of this in a way that shocked and frightened many Americans unprepared to see such extremism and paranoia—far outside the mainstream ideological consensus and normal experience—reflected in a national campaign. In 1963, the networks had expanded their evening newscasts from fifteen minutes to a full half-hour, and 1964 marked the first time that more Americans got their news from television than from print sources. Conservative activists of the Goldwater era felt victimized by this newly powerful medium, which was transforming politics into a contest of media techniques; so it became their long-term goal to reverse what they saw as the media forces arrayed against them.

John S. Knight, the editor and publisher of two pro-Goldwater papers, the *Detroit Free Press* and the *Chicago Daily News,* expressed this frustration in a June 1964 editorial:

> I can no longer stand silently by and watch the shabby treatment Goldwater is getting from most of the news media. . . . Of the syndicated columnists, I can think of only a few who are not savagely cutting down Senator Goldwater day after day. Some of the TV commentators discuss Goldwater with evident disdain and contempt. Editorial cartoonists portray him as belonging to the Neanderthal Age or as a relic of the 19th century. It is the fashion of editorial writers to persuade themselves that Goldwater's followers are either kooks or John Birchers.[34]

Knight was one of the few avid Goldwater supporters in the press. As Rick Perlstein documented, while liberal and centrist columnists lined up against Goldwater, so did the conservative media. Goldwater's extreme conservatism had few advocates among even fervently anti-Communist conservative columnists and commentators. He found little support from the country's influential Republican editorial pages or among the conservative national magazines that had puffed him up in the 1950s. These publications usually supported conservative candidates and causes, but they saw in Goldwater's platform and the character of his supporters not traditional Republican conservatism but, rather, the face of the radical, irrational Right. Much of the press, liberal and conservative, was put off because it could not abide Goldwater's racial appeals.

Goldwater was the first Republican presidential candidate since 1940 not to win a majority of endorsements for the presidency from the nation's top one hundred newspapers. The *Los Angeles Times* supported Nelson Rockefeller, the moderate governor of New York, for the GOP nomination; the Luce media empire, the Hearst Corporation publications, and the *New York Herald-Tribune* (a bastion of pro-business sentiment), all backed Democrat Lyndon Johnson for the presidency.[35]

Goldwater's principal support came from a handful of columnists, most of them associated with William Buckley's *National Review,* house organ of the conservative movement, founded in 1955 with funds from the Buckley family's oil fortune. *National Review's* support did little to assuage Republican doubts or to persuade the public of Goldwater's suitability for the presidency. Though Buckley had graduated from Yale and published his magazine in New York City, he wrote and edited several articles defending segregation; in 1959, he justified disenfranchisement of southern blacks based on what he characterized as a lack of education and cultural backwardness.[36] *National Review's* publisher was the Yale-educated William A. Rusher, a self-described "Senate Red hunter," who had been counsel to the Senate investigative subcommittee that gave Joe McCarthy a platform. Because the right wing had little established institutional support, those speaking up for Goldwater on television tended to be members of extremist right-wing groups.

Working in the hinterlands was Phyllis Schlafly, host of a radio show called *America, Wake Up!* and the self-published author of *A Choice, Not an Echo,* which sold six million copies, many of them bought in bulk by

Birch Society millionaires and distributed through political clubs. The book was an exposé on how the Republican political establishment conspired to thwart the party's rank-and-file preferences for true conservative leadership, "perpetuating the Red empire in order to perpetrate the high level of Federal spending and control." According to Schlafly, spinning out a theory widely held on the Far Right, Republican business interests in New York City repeatedly had denied Ohio Senator Robert A. Taft, the son of President William Howard Taft and a midwestern conservative isolationist, the Republican presidential nomination in favor of eastern moderates like Wendell Willkie, Thomas E. Dewey, and Eisenhower. "Vicious and dishonest 'hidden persuaders'" of the East had used the "fantastic propaganda" of the eastern press to take down Taft. The role of the *New York Times,* she charged, was as "chief propaganda organ of the secret kingmakers." The book lit a fire under the Goldwater movement.[37]

On the eve of the GOP convention, Goldwater clashed publicly with CBS News and its anchor Walter Cronkite; Goldwater charged the network with distorting his words, saying, "I don't think these people should be allowed to broadcast." This fury spread onto the convention floor at San Francisco's Cow Palace, where the Goldwater delegates—the western anti-Communist conspiracists, southern segregationists, and others whom Goldwater called "the Forgotten Americans"—flooded the place with lapel pins that said EASTERN LIBERAL PRESS.[38] "The delegates were really hostile and threatening to us," NBC anchor David Brinkley recalled years later. "Threatened us with physical harm. We had to get bodyguards. And we had to sneak into the hotels and sneak out."[39] According to Perlstein's biography, delegates violently shook the supports holding Howard K. Smith's ABC booth high above the convention floor.

When he spoke to the convention, former president Eisenhower tossed out a line that was more like a piece of red meat. A Republican traditionalist who had worried publicly about the "white backlash" that Goldwater was stoking, and who had won the presidency twelve years before with the endorsements of the *New York Times* and the *Washington Post,* Eisenhower nonetheless blasted the media from the podium:

> So let us particularly scorn the divisive efforts of those outside our family, including sensation-seeking columnists and commentators

because . . . these are people who couldn't care less about our party.

The crowd erupted into an unexpected frenzy. Ike continued:

And let us not be guilty of maudlin sympathy for the criminal who, roaming the streets with switchblade knife and illegal firearm, seeking a helpless prey, suddenly becomes, upon apprehension, a poor, underprivileged person who counts upon the compassion of our society.[40]

News reports interpreted the "switchblade knife" phrasing as race-baiting, which for Republicans—who were, at the time, struggling to reposition the party to take advantage of anti–civil rights sentiment in the country by emphasizing social order—seemed to go hand in hand with media-baiting as a new political backlash strategy for riling up the incipient right-wing base of the party. Five years before Buchanan perfected the argument, the media already were officially branded the enemy of the GOP—although not because they were failing to do their job but because they were said not to care about the electoral fortunes of the Republicans. This was the role of propaganda and not of journalism.

A few days after the convention, George Wallace pulled out of the presidential race, calling his candidacy superfluous because the GOP had adopted a segregationist platform. On CBS's *Face the Nation,* Wallace took the media to task for spreading civil rights sentiment: "Today we hear more states' rights talk than we have heard in the last quarter century. . . . The American people are sick and tired of columnists and TV dudes who . . . try to slant and distort and malign and brainwash this country."[41]

In the epilogue to *The News Twisters,* Edith Efron turned her attention to breaking what she called the liberal Left's "intellectual monopoly" over the media—in other words, to making the media more hospitable to movement conservatism.

As the critical reception to *The News Twisters* showed, the Right had difficulty gaining traction for its ideas by the objective standards of journalism. Reviewers decried the book as "political," "inaccurate," "dishonest," and "bizarre." For the right wing to succeed, those standards would have to be undermined; and the journalistic institutions and professionals trained to uphold them would have to be "stopped," as Efron put it.

Efron was thus an early advocate of returning to the ideological approach of journalism that prevailed in the United States before the turn of the century, when newspapers were openly partisan and subjective and spanned a broad range from left to right. Revenue came from loyal subscribers, who chose their newspapers from a variety of offerings in the marketplace with predictable political points of view.

With the rise of mass advertising as a source of revenue and the growth of chain ownership in the twentieth century, newspapers moved to produce more neutral news that would expand their circulation base while offending fewer potential advertisers and readers and ameliorating concerns that newly powerful publishers were dictating the news.[42] In addition to these commercial incentives, "[d]uring the Progressive era, middle-class reformers aimed to bring rationality and high purpose to American life. One of their central tenets was the idea of professionalization, and the press was no exception," media critic Neal Gabler has written. "Schools of journalism were inaugurated and, with them, the novel notion that journalism is a vocation, like medicine or law, with its own rules and standards. One of its highest standards was impartiality. From now on, reporters were to present the news, not plead a case."

Objectivity became the journalistic and business models of such heralded publishers as Arthur Ochs Sulzberger of the *New York Times* and the Associated Press wire service. The goal was by no means flawlessly attained, but journalists were trained to strive for impartiality in their news coverage, to report the news as facts and conditions dictated, without the distortions of personal feelings or prejudices. Objectivity entailed a search for truth, with reporters making judgments, when possible, on conflicting factual claims. They advanced in the profession on their ability to get the story right.

With the notable exception of a few right-wing regional press barons and large-circulation national magazines with a conservative bent, by the 1950s objectivity had become accepted as the gold standard in the news business. The rise of powerful broadcast TV and radio news accelerated this trend. Because the public owned these airwaves, the broadcast media were seen to have special obligations to the public. Network news divisions operated within larger commercial enterprises, but they had higher aspirations than making money; for many years, their programming was not rated.

The broadcasters were regulated by the government to ensure that they operated in the public interest rather than on purely commercial principles. These regulations restricted media ownership to prevent consolidation of power in too few hands and to ensure that factual information and a diversity of views were widely available. TV and radio broadcasters were discouraged from airing biased reports and from propagating their own political viewpoints, and stations were required to air conflicting opinions when they presented controversial subjects.

Efron had different ideas. Efron viewed the media as an extension of politics by other means. In her view, news was not a neutral vehicle for the dissemination of quality information to help people discern their views but, rather, the fulcrum of a broader struggle for political power that the Right was losing. As an ideologue, she believed that *all* news was twisted politically, and she rejected as unattainable the widely accepted journalistic ethic that objectivity should be the goal of news reporting. "Liberal bias" became a way for Efron to brand all journalism as merely opinion.

Because Efron believed that all news was subjective, she advocated the formation of slanted right-wing broadcasts to compete with what she saw as slanted liberal ones. Recalling arguments made by the right wing earlier in the century, Efron wanted to end public ownership of the airwaves, making the TV news product available only for a fee, in one fell swoop of radical privatization. Eliminating public ownership meant scuttling the responsibility of the networks to operate as a public trust and repealing the government regulations that sought to ensure this. The only standard would be what the unchecked market would bear. Such a system would "give the collective public total control over the supply of such commodities by means of the 'dollar vote,'" she wrote.

Efron foresaw that, with the advent of cable television and other new technologies, markets for subjective news would emerge. Pay cable was not regulated the same way as the public airwaves were. And cable's business model was close to that of the old ideologically oriented newspapers, based on attracting a much smaller audience of dedicated subscribers who paid to watch predictable formats appealing to their specialized interests. Viewers would choose their news the way they subscribed to political magazines. Clearly, there was an underserved market niche for right-wing opinion in the millions of people who bought *The Conscience of a Conservative* and *A Choice, Not an Echo*. If their presence were felt in the media market, the media as a whole might change its standards and conventions to stay competitive.

Efron believed that both deregulation and the introduction of pay cable were many years away. Though she said she was a libertarian, she was not beyond using government power to forward ideological ends in the meantime. So, she suggested that the government require the networks to include in their broadcasts less straight news and more of what she considered "a full spectrum of opinion."

Efron was prophetic, too, in seeing that infusing regular news broadcasts with more opinion would fundamentally change the medium, blurring the distinction between news and commentary and giving the organized Right an important opening for the airing, legitimizing, and reinforcement of its views that it could not win through the fact-based filters of objective journalism. By turning public discourse into a matter of highly partisan opinion, the right wing could shatter political consensus and sidestep questions about the veracity or mendacity of its arguments. Opinions can't be false.

The problem for the Right, as Efron correctly described it, was that the conservative opinion then being heard in the TV media was too moderate: It was mainstream, traditional, Republican conservatism. Efron wanted the government to require that the spectrum be expanded to make room for the right wing. Since political struggle is always for the center, she understood that once the Far Right was obliged, with or without the government's intervention, the center of political gravity would inevitably shift to the right, and the United States would become a different place. Or, at least, it would seem that way.

"The solution is . . . spectrum commentary—political analysis and interpretation by intellectuals representing the full spectrum of public opinion . . . in proportions determined by their actual electoral significance. . . ." In this scheme of "proportional representation," she wrote, the "new libertarian right" and "the old right"—the Goldwater coalition from 1964— would be guaranteed commentary slots on the networks. So-called spectrum commentary was not at that time offered by the TV networks, but it was commonplace on radio—enabling Phyllis Schlafly, for example, to air her opinions on CBS radio.

In effect, Efron wanted to make television more like talk radio. On radio, the right wing had been able to find a substantial audience dating at least to the Depression era, when the popular commentaries of Father Charles Coughlin—a fiery Michigan-based populist demagogue and Catholic priest—reached an audience of forty-five million per week, one-third of Americans. During World War II, however, when Coughlin began to scapegoat Jews, intellectuals, and Wall Street bankers for America's economic woes, he lost his audience and was pushed into retirement by the Catholic Church.[43]

Expanding the media spectrum would soon become a key political goal of the Republican Right. But first, the right wing needed to repair its image by creating spokespeople for its causes who appeared serious and reasonable, while at the same time pressing the media, the informal gatekeepers of the bounds of discourse, to give them credence. The Birchers and the Klan, and William Buckley and Phyllis Schlafly, could not accomplish this on their own.

CHAPTER TWO

"GUERRILLA WAR"

THE WRITER EDITH EFRON was not the only conservative in the early 1970s agitating for media activism by the Right. Supreme Court Justice Lewis F. Powell, a Nixon appointee, is perhaps best remembered today as a moderate conservative counterweight on the High Court to right-wing Chief Justice William Rehnquist. Late in life, Powell, a swing vote on the Rehnquist Court, expressed regret over some of his earlier decisions siding with the right-wing bloc. Less appreciated is that Powell, as a wealthy corporate lawyer and board member in Richmond, Virginia, before ascending to the Court, played a galvanizing role in what would become a highly coordinated and lavishly funded effort to shift the country's political zeitgeist to the right and to discredit liberalism through all available media channels.

Three months before the publication of Efron's *The News Twisters,* in a memorandum dated August 31, 1971, and printed in the U.S. Chamber of Commerce's periodical *Washington Report,* Powell, a well-respected former president of the American Bar Association and a conservative Democrat, argued that the American system of free enterprise was under attack by the four institutions that shaped American public opinion: the academy, the media, the political establishment, and the courts. Business needed to "stop suffering in impotent silence, and launch a counter-attack," harnessing its "wisdom, ingenuity and resources" against "those who would destroy it."[1]

With media attention focused on the growing consumer, environmental, civil rights, and feminist movements, a fretful Powell wrote that business was up against saboteurs and propagandists and did not understand how to "assiduously cultivate" political power or "conduct guerrilla war." Worse still, business often was helping to underwrite the "war" being waged against it through corporate giving untied to ideological ends. Business should spend money on propaganda to "inform and enlighten the American people," Powell argued.

Powell then laid out the strategy that the Right would follow in the coming decades, whereby conservative business interests would create and underwrite a "movement" to front its agenda in the media. Under Powell's plan, heavily subsidized "scholars, writers, and thinkers" speaking "for the movement" would press for "balance" and "equal time" to penetrate the media, thereby shaping news coverage, reframing issues, influencing the views of political elites, and changing mass public opinion. These would be the manufactured "intellectuals" referenced by Efron, marketed in the media to "expand the spectrum." They would be housed in new "national organizations" in an effort "undertaken long term" with "generous financial support." Appended to Powell's original copy of the memo was a column by conservative writer John Chamberlain from the *Richmond Times-Dispatch* summarizing the findings of Edith Efron from *The News Twisters.*

While it was well circulated in the business community, the Powell document remained a secret until columnist Jack Anderson wrote about its recommendations for "confrontational politics" in the context of Powell's fitness for the Supreme Court, to which he was nominated shortly after writing the memo and where justices were supposed to be strictly impartial.[2] In the White House, Powell's patron Richard Nixon already had broached the subject of building a privately funded parallel political establishment that could further the conservative ideological cause, and attack his political enemies, while remaining nominally independent of the GOP. According to the diaries of his White House aide H. R. Haldeman, on September 12, 1970, Nixon was "pushing again on [his] project of building

OUR establishment in [the] press, business, education, etc." Buchanan had sent Nixon a memo urging him to establish "a conservative counterpoint to Brookings."

A second major document establishing plans for the Right's media incursion was a memoir by William E. Simon, Nixon's Treasury secretary and a Wall Street venture capitalist who became one of the country's wealthiest individuals by using junk bonds to finance hostile corporate takeovers. Until his death in 2000, Simon also served as chairman of the John M. Olin Foundation, a conservative New York City philanthropy founded on a fortune made in munitions and chemical manufacturing.

A radical free marketeer often at odds with his fellow Republicans in the Nixon and Gerald Ford administrations, Simon represented what was then a minority position in his own party—the Goldwaterism that had triumphed in 1964's nomination struggle but later faded from the scene with the candidate's crushing defeat. Simon, the economic Darwinist, was at war not only with liberalism and the Democratic Party but with traditional Republicanism. He embodied the kind of fevered determination his liberal and moderate adversaries often lacked; that determination would come to characterize a new conservative movement that fought ardently to overturn its minority status within the mainstream political culture. His GOP colleagues called Simon "William the Terrible."

Published in 1978, Simon's *A Time for Truth* pealed the same alarm bell as had Lewis Powell. "The target of the 'consumer' movement is *business,* the target of the 'environmentalists' is *business,* and the target of the 'minorities' at least where employment is concerned, is *business,*" Simon wrote. Business, he argued, was losing politically because it had no intellectual firepower or savvy media spokespeople, the same problem that handicapped Goldwater in 1964. Simon frankly suggested conservatives go out and buy the public debate in a bid to make their ideology look respectable and appealing.[3] So, *pace* Simon, the coal industry would begin funding research to undermine support for environmental regulation, and the financial services industry would pay for a pseudoscholarly campaign to destroy public confidence in the Social Security system.

The ideology of Barry Goldwater and Phyllis Schlafly and William Buckley would now be dry-cleaned for mass media consumption, and along with it came a neolexicon—a language invented by conservative practitioners trained in the use of manipulative, often Orwellian, rhetoric. Agenda items like gutting Social Security, rolling back civil rights protections, and slashing taxes inequitably would be smoothed out with deceptive Madison Avenue–type branding slogans of the kind used to sell commercial products: "privatization," "the new federalism," the "flat tax," and so on. Americans would be told that poverty is a "behavioral" condition, that any advance gained by a member of a minority group amounted to "reverse discrimination," and that providing government subsidies for private and parochial schools while draining resources from public education was to be thought of as "school choice."

Just as objective journalism was an obstacle for the Right, so was objective scholarship. Simon laid out a "blue-print for a counter-intelligentsia"— hired guns who could legitimize and popularize right-wing opinion through the media and do battle in the media on behalf of conservative business interests, the wealthy, and the cultural Right with spokespeople for the consumer, environmental, civil rights, and feminist movements. Under Simon's plan, academic studies that were damaging to right-wing ideological goals and to the imperatives of business were to be countered at every turn by scholarship for sale. Simon advocated "nothing less than a massive and unprecedented mobilization of moral, intellectual and financial resources" with funds "rushing by multimillions" from corporate-backed foundations to a network of pro-business scholars, writers, pundits, and publicists, as well as to conservative book projects, publications, and policy research.

The funds would go exclusively to right-wing ideologues, with no capitulation to "soft-minded pleas for the support of 'dissent,'" Simon advised, thus ensuring that conservatism would have the unwavering message discipline, ideological uniformity, and seeming unity that seemed to go missing in liberalism. The work would carry an air of academic authority and independence, but it would be subject to no peer review or conflict-of-interest safeguards, and it would be carried out covertly in support of "the only party with a philosophical heritage which might permit it to be the Liberty Party in the United States, the Republican Party."

A Time for Truth was published by the conservative Reader's Digest Press, then an imprint of the McGraw-Hill Book Company. It was ghost-written by Edith Efron.

•   •   •

The message machinery that the conservatives built in the 1970s has its roots in the antilabor and anti–civil rights movements of the 1940s and 1950s. The original, model organization was the American Enterprise Institute for Public Policy Research (AEI), founded in 1943 as a business lobby but refashioned as a research institute in the early 1960s by William J. Baroody Sr., a former U.S. Chamber of Commerce staffer and a key member of Barry Goldwater's 1964 brain trust. Thanks to Lewis Powell, the AEI soon had a friendly competitor.

In 1972, after reading the Powell memo, Colorado beer brewer Joe Coors, a Goldwater supporter, notorious union buster, and opponent of minority hiring, donated $200,000 to the forerunner organization that would become the Heritage Foundation, today the Right's premier think tank.[4] Through the Adolph Coors Foundation, the Coors family underwrote a variety of right-wing causes and organizations. Over the years, statements emanated from the family suggesting a dark agenda may have motivated its activism. For instance, William Coors, one of the foundation's principals, told a group of African American businesspeople in a 1984 speech, "One of the best things they [slave traders] did for you is to drag your ancestors over here in chains."[5]

If the genteel Powell represented traditional U.S. Chamber of Commerce–centered business-oriented conservatism, his memo, with its call for radical action, proved an inspiration to, and a unifying force for, the more populist, culturally reactionary southern and western outposts of conservatism. After reading the memo, Coors dispatched an aide to Washington, where he met Paul Weyrich, press secretary to recently defeated GOP Senator Gordon Allott of Colorado.[6] Weyrich's coworker in Allott's office was a young staffer named George F. Will. Weyrich and Will, along with Trent Lott, the future Republican Senate leader then serving as a legislative aide in another congressional office, had formed a "Conservative Lunch Club."

Weyrich had been raised in Wisconsin, the son of German immigrants who admired Robert Taft for his opposition to the U.S. involvement in World War II. He had only a high school education and considered himself a "political mechanic," interested in organizing to attain power rather than in policy or ideas.[7] Weyrich was an organizational genius and also a forbidding demagogue of the pseudoconservative variety, a skill honed in a brief but not inconsequential stint as a broadcast journalist. He had ties to the most extremist groups of the American right wing, dating back to his involvement with George Wallace's American Independent Party. Weyrich and his organizations have had associations with the John Birch Society and the anti-Semitic Liberty Lobby and to Christian reconstructionist Rousas John Rushdoony, a right-wing theologian who taught that "biblical law" allowed segregation and slavery and required the death penalty for homosexuals. A deacon in the Melkite Greek Catholic Church, Weyrich was described as a "demented anti-Semite" by a conservative writer after he wrote that "Christ was crucified by the Jews" in a 2001 Good Friday essay.[8] According to a report by Catholics for a Free Choice, Weyrich's views are "rooted in a kind of populist nativism which often verges on racism," and he "hired convicted Nazi collaborator Laszlo Pastor to staff [one of his organizations]."

In founding the Analysis Research Corporation with a $200,000 check from Coors, Weyrich partnered with Dr. Edwin J. Feulner Jr., who had headed the Republican Study Committee on Capitol Hill. Feulner was an economic conservative and foreign policy rightist who had served in the Nixon administration and then as an aide to Far Right Republican Representative Phil Crane of Illinois. As its chief domestic strategist, Heritage retained Stuart Butler, an architect of Margaret Thatcher's rise in Britain, who called for "Leninist" strategies and "guerrilla warfare" by the American right wing to dismantle the federal government.[9]

Weyrich soon left Heritage, which went on to market the pro-business, antigovernment agenda of the Powell memo to legislators and to the media. Weyrich understood that right-wing economic ideology had little popular support, so he went to work identifying a constituency for it. In building what would become a powerful grassroots organizational network, Weyrich fused the social and cultural agenda of the Right—the antiabortion, anti–civil rights, antigay causes for which there was a significant constituency—with the market fundamentalism of Heritage. With Coors's support, Weyrich went on to charter a host of right-wing advocacy groups, grassroots coalitions, and political action committees (PACs) in the coming decades; foremost among them was the Committee for the Survival of a

Free Congress, which focused on a long-term strategy for wresting congressional control from the Democrats.

"The New Right—and to an extent we're like Communists in this—feels victory is inevitable," Weyrich said.[10]

By 1980, Heritage was positioned to provide the important quasi-academic veneer that Goldwater lacked to the presidential campaign of Ronald Reagan, who had made his political debut in 1964 when he endorsed Goldwater at the Republican National Convention. Upon Reagan's election, Heritage delivered *Mandate for Leadership,* the policy blueprint for his new administration; concurrently, leaders from the burgeoning right-wing think tank network, which by 1980 encompassed seventy organizations, assumed top Cabinet posts—e.g., Attorney General Edwin Meese III (Institute for Contemporary Studies), Interior Secretary James Watt (Rocky Mountain Legal Foundation), and CIA Director William J. Casey (Manhattan Institute for Policy Research).

Also spearheading the Right's p.r. efforts in the mid-1970s was Irving Kristol, a tireless ideologue who called himself a neoconservative. Though Kristol himself was a Republican, the neocons were a group of assorted ex-Communists, ex-leftists, and disaffected liberals who had drifted out of the Democratic Party when the political leaders with whom they had allied themselves failed to gain national power.[11] Kristol's early intellectual history as a follower of Leon Trotsky, the anti-Stalinist Communist military general and writer, brought to conservatism a belief in the paramount importance of disseminating ideology, rather than gathering votes, as the way to win political power. Kristol was interested in ideas not for their own sake, as an academic might be, but for the purpose of influencing public opinion through a "war of ideas."

Though he shared the Right's rigid moralism and pugnacious anti-Communism, Kristol saw that the image of conservatism needed to be overhauled if it was to gain credibility and influence in the media. According to William Buckley, Kristol found conservatism "jejune, and in any event, politically unmarketable." Though he contributed few of his own original ideas to the movement—he has said he lacked the patience to write a book—Kristol was critically important on the sales, fund-raising, and mentoring fronts. As former liberal writers and editors based mainly in New York City, the neocons were conversant with the urban media culture that the "jejune" conservatives found impossible to negotiate.

In a kind of inverted Trotskyism, Kristol adapted to conservatism the Communist style of putting forth an endless series of journals, op-ed manifestos, position papers, public letters, and magazines—founding his own, *The Public Interest*, and helping to secure financing for another, *The American Spectator*, two new subsidized organs for delivering the conservative message.[12] Kristol joined the American Enterprise Institute, where he spent much of his time in the 1970s working to shape the funding strategies of a small group of right-wing, family-controlled foundations and politically conservative corporations. Joining Kristol in these early fund-raising appeals was the AEI's Michael Novak, a right-wing Catholic theologian, who is revered on the Right for his intellect but whose doctoral dissertation was rejected by the Harvard Philosophy Department.[13]

This money financed a colossal new network of multi-issue research and advocacy groups that technically do no lobbying and provide no services, other than the production, marketing, and promoting of conservative ideology to lawmakers, opinion leaders, the media, and the general public. Because the think tanks were multi-issue, their names were popping up routinely in the press, across a broad range of subjects; several groups pushing the same issues, and reinforcing them through repetition of the same jargon, created an appearance of validity and popular consensus and the impression that the Right suddenly was bursting with new ideas.

Edward Crane, president of the Cato Institute, another important right-wing think tank founded in the mid-1970s, described the Republican Right's goal this way: "As we grow, I don't want us to shift toward the mainstream. I want the mainstream to shift toward us, and that's our challenge."

Three decades later, conservatives were crowing openly about the political influence they derived from their think tanks. In a *New York Post* column in January 2003 celebrating the thirtieth anniversary of the Manhattan Institute, novelist Tom Wolfe, a member of *The American Spectator*'s board of advisers, hailed the organization's salesmanship in the media. Wolfe explained that the corporate- and foundation-backed institute was headed by William Hammett, a "tall, movie-star-handsome" libertarian who christened the ideologues on his staff "Senior Fellows" and made their research products "commercial." Hammett "invited journalists and intellectuals with influence in the field of public policy, hundreds of them at a time, for lunch at the Harvard Club. The authors themselves got up and did the show and tell. He held forums where they had the chance to say it again. In 1989, Hammett would create a smartly designed quarterly, *City Journal,* where they said it once more for good measure."

Hammett's first major "triumph," according to Wolfe, came in the promotion of Charles Murray's attack on the welfare system. "Murray's prescription was simple: Get rid of the entire welfare system. The poor would do better left to their own normal instincts," Wolfe wrote. Although the thrust of Murray's theory—that welfare may in some ways hurt those it is designed to help—attracted notice across the political spectrum, his scholarship in the slickly marketed *Losing Ground* was seriously challenged, and his policy recommendations were draconian. They soon became the conventional wisdom in Reaganite policy circles.

A decade later, just as the core of Murray's thesis moved a bipartisan coalition in Congress to tackle welfare reform, Murray, who once burned a cross in high school, found his career derailed with the 1994 publication of *The Bell Curve: Intelligence and Class Structure in American Life* (cowritten with Richard Herrnstein), which misused statistics to argue that blacks are genetically inferior to whites. The Manhattan Institute cut Murray loose rather than endorse this cryptoracist theoretical justification for ending government efforts to help minorities, and he retreated to the American Enterprise Institute, where he has remained. The Right had spent more than $1 million promoting Murray alone.[14]

Next came Manhattan Institute's John M. Olin Fellow Elizabeth McCaughey, who "wrote an article for *The New Republic* on what she discovered in a close reading of the 1,413-page document containing the Clinton Health Care Plan," Wolfe wrote. Though McCaughey's article was predicated on a raft of provably false assertions, "that one article shot down the entire blimp, and Betsy McCaughey became a 35-year-old Cinderella," according to Wolfe. "One of the richest men in America chose her as his wife, and George Pataki made her lieutenant governor of New York." McCaughey, alas, didn't have the temperament for politics, and her husband divorced her: Cinderella turned into a pumpkin at midnight. Though Wolfe didn't mention it, she became a Democrat, took up residence at the right-wing Hudson Institute, and appeared occasionally on the FOX News Channel espousing Republican positions.

Wolfe's list of greatest hits included *America in Black and White,* a sustained attack on affirmative action by Manhattan "Senior Fellow" Abigail Thernstrom. Her distortion of evidence has been exposed by reviewers, her close personal friend and fellow neoconservative Glenn C. Loury among them.[15] Thernstrom "blew up" the notion that "'the system'—or anything else—had prevented economic, social and political progress by minorities," Wolfe wrote. Unable to win academic tenure, she has described herself as "very angry" when she wrote *America in Black and White.* Abigail is married to a Harvard historian and her frequent coauthor, Stephan Thernstrom, who was embroiled in a controversy over a derisive remark about black men he made while he was teaching that some students construed as racist.[16]

Wolfe praised the Manhattan Institute's Peter Huber, who promoted the term "junk science" as a way of undermining scientific work that did not conform to conservative ideology. Huber's book, *Galileo's Revenge: Junk Science in the Courtroom,* was found by legal and scientific scholars to be filled with exaggerated claims and empirical trickery. Kenneth J. Chesebro wrote in *American University Law Review,* "Galileo would attribute the prominence of the book and its author to clever public relations, not merit, and would denigrate it as junk scholarship, not 'junk science.'"

Lastly, Wolfe named mutton-chopped, bow-tied eccentric Myron Magnet, editor of *City Journal* and author of *The Dream and the Nightmare: The Sixties' Legacy to the Underclass,* "the text for George Bush's doctrine of 'compassionate conservatism.'" Among Magnet's proposed reforms was to require unwed mothers either to live in supervised group homes or surrender their children to state-run orphanages. Political strategist Karl Rove passed along the book to George W. Bush, who has said it is second only to the Bible in his pantheon.

A former Heritage official has described this think tank network as "the shock troops of the conservative revolution." By 2000, the National Committee for Responsive Philanthropy estimated that conservatives had spent $1 billion on just their top twenty think tanks out of more than five hundred mini-Heritages that had sprouted up in Washington and throughout the fifty states in the prior three decades. "When it comes to 'winning' political battles, ultimate success results less from who's doing the right thing, and more from whose view of reality dominates the battlefield," said the organization's president, Robert Bothwell. "It doesn't take a rocket scientist to figure out that the millions spent by conservative think tanks have enabled them virtually to dictate the issues and terms of national debates."

In addition to the Olin and Coors foundations, the prime funders behind the effort are the Koch family foundations, run by two brothers who own a huge oil and natural gas firm, Koch Industries, founded by their father, Fred Koch, a charter member of the John Birch Society; the Milwaukee-based Lynde and Harry Bradley Foundation, founded by automotive parts manufacturer Harry Bradley, also an active member of the John Birch Society; and Richard Mellon Scaife, heir to the Mellon banking and oil fortune and a major Goldwater and Nixon supporter. After being bitterly disappointed by Goldwater's defeat and disillusioned by Watergate, Scaife put $350 million alone into building conservative movement organizations to shift the political culture rightward. Along with the Smith Richardson Foundation, funded by the Vicks VapoRub empire, Olin, Bradley, and Scaife are known within the movement as the "Four Sisters."

Run by neocon ideologues, these foundations provide the crucial seed money, and sustained general operating funds, that are critical to successful institution building. Their multimillions are then matched by donations from top corporate foundations, including the Amoco and Alcoa foundations, the JM Foundation, the Rockwell International Corporation Trust, and the Ford Motor Company Fund.[17] The funding strategies of the donors are coordinated by a directorate of top conservative leaders who sit on the Philanthropy Roundtable, while the overall agenda of the movement is loosely set by shadowy organizations of top conservative activists and Far Right politicians, such as the Council for National Policy (a secretive organization of leaders with a religious Right bent) and the Library Court group (named after a small street in the nation's capital and convened biweekly by Paul Weyrich).

Another important coordinating function is performed by conservative activist and Newt Gingrich protégé Grover Norquist, president of an anti-tax group, Americans for Tax Reform. Like some neocons, Norquist took his inspirations on strategy and tactics from Communist thinkers, including Antonio Gramsci, one of the founders of the Italian Communist Party, who wrote that Marxists would come to power by "capturing the culture." Norquist subsidizes his salary at the tax reform group by writing a column for AEI's magazine, *The American Enterprise.*

After he graduated from Harvard Business School, Norquist's first foray into politics was orchestrating a right-wing takeover of the College Republicans, a division of the Republican National Committee that had been led in Washington by moderate Republicans. His plan involved changing the group's constitution to give power in leadership elections to grassroots chapters, which were then infiltrated by the Right and purged of moderates. Years later, Norquist helped Newt Gingrich engineer a purge of House moderates from the GOP leadership in his ascent to the speakership.

Every Wednesday morning in Norquist's Washington offices, the leaders of more than eighty conservative organizations—including major right-wing media outlets and top Bush White House aides—convene to set movement priorities, plan strategy, and adopt talking points. Norquist seems a cross between a Communist Party boss and a Mafia don as he presides over these strategy sessions of his self-styled "Leave Us Alone Coalition," a catchy antigovernment organizing principle that was something of a misnomer in that many of its members wished to impose their ideology through government action or were seeking government favors of one sort or another.

What really united the coalition was savage partisanship and antiliberalism—a desire to roll back the economic and social gains made in the country since the New Deal. "Our goal is to cut government in half as a percentage of the economy over twenty-five years, so that we can get it down to the size where we can drown it in the bathtub," Norquist has said. He has compared the estate tax to the "morality of the Holocaust." "Our goal is to inflict pain," Norquist told *National Journal* in 2003. "It is not good enough to win; it has to be a painful and devastating defeat. We're sending a message here. It is like when the king would take his opponent's head and spike it on a pole for everyone to see."

Now headed by former *Wall Street Journal* editorial page writer and Heritage official Adam Meyerson, the Philanthropy Roundtable guided the giving patterns of the family foundations; meanwhile Norquist served a similar function for corporate donors through his connection to the lobbyists along Washington's K Street. By spearheading what he called the "K Street Project," Norquist placed Republican operatives in the city's top lobbying jobs, brokered legislative deals with the Republicans on behalf of the corporations, and directed substantial flows of corporate money into the coffers of the GOP politicians and advocates who constituted his coalition. "All of the trains run through Grover's office," according to his friend John Fund of the *Wall Street Journal.*

In the 2003 *National Journal* profile, Norquist pointed to the book *Masters of Deceit* as an early inspiration rather than an admonition. The magazine described the book as "a piece of Cold War propaganda written by an FBI agent in 1958 and published under the name J. Edgar Hoover. In an overwrought tone, the book purported to describe the insidious ways that Communism was subverting America." *National Journal* quoted the following passage:

> Communism has something to sell everybody. And following this principle, it is the function of mass agitation to exploit all grievances, hopes, aspirations, prejudices, fears, and ideals of the special groups that make up our society . . . stir them up. Set one against the other. Divide and conquer. That's the way to soften up a democracy.[18]

Because the mission of the think tanks is construed as "educational" under the federal tax code, millions of dollars in, essentially, political contributions are deducted every year as charity. The beneficiaries of this largesse— Heritage, AEI, and a labyrinth of media-focused imitators—began to transform the media landscape for conservatives in the mid- and late 1970s. The debate on government regulation and social spending was being reframed; liberal programs and proposals were targeted for discrediting; and conservative strategies for dismantling so-called Big Government were being widely touted in the press—deregulation, school vouchers, tort reform, supply-side economics, the property rights movement, medical savings accounts, and new military programs like missile defense—all hatched and test-marketed in this sweeping privately funded public relations campaign.

When conservatives sought to justify these ideas empirically, the right-wing think tanks came to resemble flat-earth societies. Among other pearls of wisdom, conservatives were working to convince the public that spending levels bore an inverse relationship to educational progress; that racial preferences were taking away opportunities for whites while hurting minorities; that tax cuts for the very rich would "trickle down" to the lower classes while increasing government revenue; that gun ownership reduced crime; and that "liberal activist judges" had distorted the true meaning of the Constitution in a line of decisions beginning at least with *Brown v. Board of Education,* which desegregated American public schools.

The research "products" were written specifically with the slanting and sloganeering that made good press copy and TV cross talk. The authors of the "products" were credentialed with impressive-sounding fellowships. Rather than publish in intellectually rigorous, established periodicals, the think tanks started their own journals, decked out in scholarly motifs, such as AEI's *Regulation* (once edited by Supreme Court Justice Antonin Scalia), and Heritage's *Policy Review* (once edited by John O'Sullivan, a former speechwriter for Margaret Thatcher and a future *National Review* editor). The Four Sisters foundations poured millions into new publications like *The New Criterion, The National Interest, The Public Interest, The American Spectator,* and *Reason,* freeing them to build friendly relationships with mainstream media outlets and to distribute free copies to opinion leaders, rather than scratching for funds and advertising dollars.[19] The pay scales at the right-wing magazines were substantially higher than at their liberal counterparts, providing attractive employment to a younger generation of writers and editors who could build comfortable careers while never leaving the right-wing network.

Soon, reporters quoted freely from conservative research; editors eagerly ran conservative op-eds; and TV producers sought out conservatives as guests. Crucial to the conservatives' ability to deliver their messages in the media was Lewis Powell's notion of "balance" and "equal time." The right wing turned the media's sense of fair play, and its itch for the quick and easy quote or sound bite, against it.

As the press came under political attack from the Right in the Nixon years and thereafter, in the news business, "objectivity," with its concern for facts and truth, began to give way to "balance"—which in practice often came to mean a purposeful disregard for facts or truth in the name of including "both sides." For the right wing, "balance" was a way of avoiding scrutiny of their arguments. For the media, "balance" became an excuse for its loss of confidence in making judgments about the accuracy of conflicting claims. "I once argued with a former news president that 'balance' is a dangerous word, because you could run a story called *Hitler: Right or Wrong?*" former CBS News president Howard Stringer told the *New York Observer* in 2003. "The job is to go after the objective truth and come to a conclusion."

In the ensuing free-for-all, the Right prospered everywhere. In *The Paradox of American Democracy*, author John B. Judis of *The New Republic* explained that the press "accepted the canard that different views simply reflected different ideologies and that to be fair, both the left and the right, liberal and conservative, had to be represented. Once this concession was made, the conservatives triumphed because in the late 1970s and 1980s, they had far more money than their rivals with which to broadcast, publish, and promote their opinions."[20]

While successfully working the "balance" angle with the mainstream press, by the 1990s the think tank network had become the $1 billion hub in the wheel of newly powerful and deliberately biased conservative media, from talk radio to the FOX News Channel to the *Washington Times,* to the right-wing columnists and pundits who provided a megaphone for all of the content—the policy research and books, the positioning and reframing strategies, and the semantic infiltration—that had been developed in the think tanks in the prior twenty years. The right-wing "products" were dumped directly into this credulous right-wing media with no filtering mechanism whatsoever.

Examining how stories are sourced, and to which experts reporters turn to shape their stories, are fairly precise and objective ways of measuring the slant of news content. For several years now, surveys by Fairness & Accuracy in Reporting (FAIR) have shown that the mainstream media disproportionately relies on conservative think tanks for expertise, and interpretation, of the news.[21] Thus the think tanks are a powerful source of a conservative slant in the news. In 1997, for example, Heritage was cited by the media 1,813 times, and the American Enterprise Institute 1,323 times, as compared with 610 citations for the Urban Institute and 576 for the Economic Policy Institute, the top two progressive think tanks. In each year since, the pattern of con-

servative think tanks getting well more than half the media citations has not
changed appreciably, with the exception of the four months following the
September 11, 2001, terrorist attacks, when progressive think tanks were
cited even less frequently. In 2001—a critical year in which the public's attitudes about the new Bush administration were formed and the American
interpretation of September 11 was set—not one progressive think tank made
it into the top ten most-cited organizations in the print press.

Often, the media does not identify the conservative think tanks as conservative, thereby obscuring their bias to the reader or viewer. For instance,
the *New York Times* has referred to the Manhattan Institute as a "national
policy research organization." Rarer still is disclosure by the media of the
self-interested money behind the research. And almost never does the
media challenge the accuracy or reliability of the information it is spoon-
fed. As Curtis Moore wrote in *Sierra* magazine, "If the voices denying the
existence of global warming or decrying tighter fuel economy standards
were obviously those of the oil, coal, auto, and similar industries, the messages would be seen for what they are—half-truths at best, and outright lies
at worst—and ignored. But when the voices appear to be those of disinterested, public-spirited organizations advocating 'economic freedom,' or
'sound science,' the messages are often accepted uncritically by journalists—and then by the public at large."

The uncritical journalists conferred status and credibility on the Right
for flawed ideas that may have been unaccepted in the academy or by a
more vigilant media. Burton Yale Pines, a former Heritage executive, has
said: "We're not here to be some kind of PhD committee giving equal time."
Cato officials have said they won't print any studies that come out favorably
toward government programs. And right-wing think tank researchers have
been fired for failing to follow the party line. "My contact with [Cato] was
strange," columnist Nat Hentoff has said. "They're ideologues, like
Trotskyites. All questions must be seen and solved within the true faith of
libertarianism, the idea of minimal government."

Trudy Lieberman, an editor at *Columbia Journalism Review,* was able
to write an entire book, *Slanting the Story: The Forces That Shape the
News,* documenting the false claims, shoddy statistics, rigged polling, and
other "clever gimmicks" that outfits like Heritage, the Cato Institute, and
the Competitive Enterprise Institute, among many others, have deployed

to misinform the public through the media on everything from the impact of tax cuts, to the level of support in the medical profession for deregulation of the pharmaceutical industry, to the efficacy of the Head Start program.[22]

According to Lieberman, a 1994 Heritage report on the Clinton tax program claimed that Clinton proposed "the largest tax increase in world history"—a falsehood widely repeated in the media at the time, and one that was still bouncing around the cable talk shows a decade later, cited by, among others, former GOP Representative Joe Scarborough on his MSNBC show and by Sean Hannity on FOX. Heritage was the source of a 1998 study, reported in sixteen major news outlets nationwide, claiming that African American men, because of their relatively lower life expectancy, were being ripped off by the Social Security system. When the Heritage study was definitively debunked by two separate reviews of its data, including one by a prominent Republican, only four relatively small news outlets took note, according to Lieberman.

Lieberman skillfully deconstructed the Cato Institute's campaign to discredit Head Start. In a report written for Cato by John Hood, credentialed as the "research director" of the right-wing John Locke Foundation in Raleigh, North Carolina—one of dozens of Heritage knockoffs in the United States—Cato flirted with eugenics in claiming that "heredity so strongly determines behavior that early intervention is a waste of time," as Lieberman put it. Two months after the study was published, Hood launched it with an op-ed in the *Wall Street Journal*. That same day, the *Washington Post* ran a story titled "As Politicians Expand Head Start, Experts Question Worth, Efficiency." The first "expert" quoted was Hood, who, Lieberman noted, was neither a scholar nor an expert in the field of child development and had done no original research. Hood admitted that he had no expert qualifications to have undertaken the study, which critics said merely strung together the comments of opponents of the program. According to Lieberman, "The [*Post*] paragraph implied that Hood was an academic and that his report revealed new research about the program. The *Post* reporter apparently didn't read the report critically, or discover the holes in it which might have been worth commenting on, or which might have prompted her to question the report's premise to begin with." The *Post* did not see fit to mention Cato's ideological affiliation. From the *Post*, Cato's study dribbled down to the "*Chicago Tribune, Detroit News, Lubbock Avalanche-Journal* and *Youngstown* (Ohio) *Vindicator,*" among other newspapers, where it provided the basis for editorials questioning the program's value at a time when the Clinton administration was seeking more funds for it, wrote Lieberman.

Similarly, writing in *The American Prospect* in May 2002, Aaron Marr Page charted the media attention given a misleading report issued by former Reagan aide Linda Chavez's Center for Equal Opportunity on the use of racial preferences in higher education admissions. The CEO report was fashioned as an exposé on the admissions practices of three partially public-funded law schools in Virginia that take race into account in admissions—affirmative action programs that the institutions do not hide and that are permitted by law, Page wrote. "With the report came the inevitable barrage of press releases, news conferences and op-eds in the *Washington Times* and *National Review,* all of which more or less recited the report's executive summary and most salient findings," according to Page. Launched by right-wing media, the study was then cited uncritically throughout the mainstream press in Virginia.

In an effort to "manufacture outrage," as Page put it, the report relied on "odds ratios" between white and black applicants. "At UVA, the odds favoring a black candidate over an equally qualified white candidate in 1999 were 731 to 1," the report claimed. Yet as Page pointed out, "because of the relatively small number of black applicants, the odds for white students… would rise only by a few percentage points, if at all, in the absence of racial preferences." The report failed to consider other factors, such as preference for athletic achievement and geographic diversity, that could account for some of the disparity. Even with racial preferences in place, 33 percent of white applicants and only 27 percent of black candidates were admitted to that UVA class. "So the image the CEO's much-touted odds ratios paint— hundreds upon hundreds of minority applicants cutting in line—is misleading," Page concluded.

Likewise, conservatives successfully spun the University of Michigan's court-challenged affirmative action program, which assigned 110 points for academic achievement and 20 points for race or socioeconomic disadvantage in making admissions decisions. A factual but misleading talking point—that the university awarded 20 points for race but only 12 points for standardized test scores—was put into the media by the Right to falsely suggest that race counted for more than academic achievement. As traced by Bob Somerby at the Daily Howler Web site, the misleading talking point originated with the Scaife-funded Center for Individual Rights, which fights affirmative action in the courts. The "20/12" comparison was mentioned on CBS News, by Tim Russert on *Meet the Press*, by George Will on *This Week*, by *National Review*'s Joel Mowbray on *Donahue*, by Armstrong Williams on MSNBC's *Nachman*, by David Brooks on PBS's *NewsHour with Jim Lehrer*, by Kate O'Beirne on CNN's *Capital Gang*, and by FOX's Tony Snow, Brit Hume, and James Pinkerton. Pinkerton went one step further, falsely claiming that the Michigan program "awards more points for your skin color than for your academic achievement."[23] When the Supreme Court ruled on the case, former Republican Representative Jack Kemp, now of the conservative advocacy organization Empower America, appeared on FOX's *Hannity & Colmes*. "One point for academic achievement and twenty points for race, I think that was ridiculous," he said.

In addition to underwriting the think tanks, conservative foundations and corporations have poured millions directly into the academy, chartering conservative research centers to advance policy objectives in foreign policy, economics, and the law. In this way, the Right has been able to establish strategic beachheads at a host of elite universities, including Harvard, Columbia, MIT, and Stanford, gaining credibility for ideas that might not otherwise pass muster through the traditional means of judging scholarly merit, then promoting those ideas in the media. University of Virginia Professor Patrick J. Michaels, for example, appears frequently on television, arguing against environmental measures to curb global warming. Michaels is a senior fellow at the Cato Institute and has edited a publication funded by the Western Fuels Association, a coal producer and power cooperative. Those associations are not typically mentioned in the broadcasts.[24]

During the 2000 presidential race, Harvard professor Paul E. Peterson released a study purporting to show that black students who used school vouchers to attend private schools showed significantly increased test scores. Peterson appeared everywhere in the media, from CNN to PBS, with his findings, which were used to attack Al Gore, who opposed vouchers. According to a May 2003 article, Princeton professor and *New York Times* business columnist Alan B. Krueger analyzed the raw data Peterson relied on and concluded, according to the article, "Peterson had it all wrong": There were no gains for blacks.[25] Though the *Times* report did not say so, Peterson's Harvard research was heavily underwritten by the Olin and Bradley foundations.

Heritage is the mother of all think tanks in its single-minded focus on co-opting the media, and its methods have been followed by hundreds of right-wing think tanks. According to the book *Do Think Tanks Matter?* by Donald E. Abelson, "In 1998 Heritage spent close to $8 million, or 18 percent of its budget, on media and government relations." Heritage's public relations program, Abelson reported, is based on a single premise put forth by the foundation: "Make sure journalists never have a reason for not quoting at least one conservative expert—or for not giving the conservative 'spin' in their stories."

According to its highly trafficked Web site, Heritage has eight employees doing p.r. work full-time, runs a 365-day-per-year, twenty-four-hour-per-day media hot line, disseminates to the press a weekly "hot sheet," has its own TV and radio studios in its Capitol Hill offices, and syndicates op-eds through the Knight-Ridder wire service. When Heritage is mentioned in a major publication like the *Washington Post,* it blast-faxes and e-mails the piece to hundreds of smaller newspapers, op-ed editors, syndicated columnists, and talk show producers. An examination of the Web site in spring 2003 showed that Heritage was gaining about forty mentions in just the major print press alone per week.

Another huge outlet for Heritage's "products" is radio: Paul Harvey—a folksy conservative who inveighs against the government, is considered one of the most powerful media voices of the past fifty years, and boasts a weekly audience of twenty-three million—promotes Heritage's "index of economic freedom." Heritage advertises in the trade publication *Talkers* magazine that it will do research for and provide studio time to right-wing radio show hosts when they wish to visit and broadcast from the nation's capital. Laura Ingraham does a nightly nationally syndicated talk radio show from Heritage's studios. In the 1990s, Joel C. Rosenberg, Rush Limbaugh's Washington point man, had his office at Heritage, where Rosenberg was previously employed. Leaving nothing to chance, the "marketing director" of Heritage's "media services" department e-mails Web loggers offering "short notices about significant Heritage studies, publications and events."

Heritage runs the Center for Data Analysis, with a $1 million annual budget, to promote the foundation's economic policies and attacks on government to the mainstream press through data it collects from federal agencies. "The center offers reporters access to raw data and trains them in how to organize and analyze the information, offering to serve as a newsroom's own research department," according to one report. William Beach, the center's director, has said: "Journalists are interested in using data they can source back to, say, a federal agency. They don't have time to prepare a data analysis, put the data back into databases and check for missing data—all the things you have to do before you can even ask a question."[26]

The data center is a project of Heritage's Center for Media and Public Policy, run by Mark Tapscott, a former editor of the *Washington Times*. "There was a time not that long ago when many conservatives believed they were taking a beating in the national news media. And for just as long, many editors, reporters, anchors and producers thought conservatives used them as political punching bags," according to Heritage. The center was founded to "bridge this gulf between conservatives and the media. . . ."

In one case highlighted by Heritage's Web site, the data center was deployed to discredit a program begun by the Clinton administration to put one hundred thousand new police officers across the nation on crime-fighting duty. Heritage's analysis, which purported to show that the program had no impact on violent crime rates, was given to a reporter named Michael Hedges of the Scripps Howard News Service. Hedges is a former *Washington Times* reporter; in addition, the editorial director of the Scripps News Service wrote an opinion column carried regularly in the *Washington Times*. According to Heritage, "Hedges' story was picked up by most of the Scripps Howard–owned dailies in the country, and went out on the Scripps wire to its more than 400 newspaper clients." A subsequent study by two independent academics contradicted Heritage's findings, though Heritage's "spin" had already been distributed nationwide. The Heritage report became accepted wisdom on the Right—repeated by columnist Robert D. Novak among others—and set the stage for Republican efforts to cut the program under the Bush administration.

Through this media center, Heritage conducts "Computer-Assisted

Research and Reporting Boot Camps" for the press. According to its Web site, representatives of fifty-three mainstream media organizations, including ABC News, the Associated Press, MSNBC, *U.S. News & World Report,* and *USA Today,* have attended Heritage training sessions.

Likewise, at the Web site of the Hudson Institute, reporters and TV producers can quickly "find an expert" in eighty-two policy areas. The "press room" at the Cato Institute lists ten communications staffers, while only five employees work in development and three in government relations. Cato has delivered more than one hundred op-eds on privatizing Social Security to organs of the conservative movement, including the *Wall Street Journal,* the *Washington Times,* and *The American Spectator,* as well as to mainstream regional newspapers like the *Chicago Sun-Times* and the *Orlando Sentinel.* When these articles appear, they don't come with a warning label; readers are not apprised of the financial interests behind them.

In just one year, Citizens for a Sound Economy, an antiregulation front group funded by top industrial polluters and headed by the former White House counsel to President George H. W. Bush, C. Boyden Gray, placed 235 op-eds and received coverage in more than four thousand print articles.[27] Cato's David Boaz writes for the *New York Times,* the *Los Angeles Times,* the *Washington Post,* and *Slate,* while Cato's Doug Bandow is a writer for Time Inc.'s *Fortune.* Heritage's Joseph Loconte, "the William Simon Fellow in Religion and a Free Society," is a National Public Radio commentator, as was former Bush speechwriter David Frum, then of the Manhattan Institute and now with AEI, who has written for *National Review* on such subjects as "Is Contemporary Liberalism a Type of Mental Illness?"

The think tanks create the appearance that they are independent of the GOP, though their actions suggest otherwise. According to *The American Prospect,* in late August 2002, press staffers for the National Republican Congressional Committee distributed a memo advising Republican candidates to "educate" reporters to get them to stop describing Republican efforts to privatize Social Security as "privatization" and replace that draconian-sounding word with a softer phrase, "personal accounts." The next week, Cato—which had been at the forefront of the "privatization" initiative—abandoned "Privatization" for "Choice." Soon, prominent journalists such as NBC's Tim Russert were calling "privatizing" Social Security the Democrats' preferred "term" for Republican plans.

The Right uses its think tanks to move its people, as well as its issues, into the media. Before he was discredited, Charles Murray appeared on such prestigious broadcasts as ABC's *Nightline*; Betsy McCaughey took her wares to the *Today* show; and Abigail Thernstrom, now a member of the U.S. Commission on Civil Rights, has been hosted in a genial one-on-one interview by George Stephanopoulos on ABC's *This Week*. Notably, all three launched their careers writing for *The New Republic,* which because of its reputation as a respected, historically liberal magazine, has occupied a special place in the Right's media strategies. McCaughey's anti-Clinton health care diatribe and Murray's *Bell Curve* were published in *The New Republic* under the editorship of British conservative Andrew Sullivan. Thernstrom has been a frequent *New Republic* contributor.

The think tanks provide cushy six-figure sinecures to movement "intellectuals," and to ex–government officials whose role it is to fan out in the media proselytizing for the conservative agenda, providing mainstream and right-wing media outlets with a steady stream of subsidized op-eds and talking heads. These bought-and-paid-for conservative talkers face off in the media in debates that are made possible by right-wing financiers: If conservative special-interest money were to be eliminated from the equation, there wouldn't be much of a conservative "side" to hold up, and there would be few to do the talking.

The paid "experts" secure free media time, moving conservative issues into the mainstream while defining and dominating the debate. Because they are in the employ of a small network of conservative and corporate foundations, they tend to stay "on message"—one of the reasons that conservatism comes through to the public as more clear, confident, and unified than liberalism. While it may appear to readers and viewers that they are hearing hundreds of independent conclusions derived from each journalist's research and reporting, they are really hearing from a handful of right-wing multimillionaires like Richard Mellon Scaife, whose money has gone into more than one-third of the think tanks, and from a few dozen corporations.

Unlike Democrats, Republicans maintain a large class of paid spokespeople, including Judge Robert Bork, former UN Ambassador Jeane Kirkpatrick, ex–Reagan and Bush *père* official William Bennett, Reagan Attorney General Edwin Meese III, former House Speaker Newt Gingrich, former Dan Quayle aide William Kristol, former Reagan Pentagon official Richard Perle, Vice President Dick Cheney's wife, Lynne, and literally hundreds of lesser lights such as Frank Gaffney (Center for Security Policy), Cliff May (Foundation for the Defense of Democracies), Elliott Abrams (Hudson Institute), David Horowitz (Center for the Study of Popular Culture), Michael Ledeen (AEI), Mark Levin (Landmark Legal Foundation), Kate O'Beirne (Heritage), Stephen Moore (Cato), and Dinesh D'Souza (AEI).

They make big money. According to the Web site MediaTransparency, D'Souza, who popularized the term "political correctness," has received $1.5 million in right-wing grants to support his speaking and writing, including money for books apparently never written.

While supported by conservative money, Bennett was hired by CNN; Gingrich and Horowitz by the FOX News Channel; and Kristol by ABC and, later, by FOX. Steven Emerson, who narrated a Scaife-funded documentary titled *Jihad in America* that aired on CBS, is now a "terrorism expert" for MSNBC. The *New York Times* has found Emerson's work to be "marred by factual errors . . . and by a pervasive anti-Arab and anti-Palestinian bias."

Just as right-wing research is undertaken to counter academic studies, these right-wing talking heads are on call to rebut on television every academic, expert, legislator, policy advocate, and lawyer whom the Right wishes to undermine. Thus, professors of law debate right-wing lawyers from the conservative legal centers that are heavily funded by one man, Richard Mellon Scaife; environmental scientists face down industry-backed think tank "fellows"; former UN weapons inspectors are contradicted by ideologues working in subsidized pro-war security centers; and so on, in an endless parade of phony staged-for-cable encounters designed to convey a sense of "balance."

The activities of Irving Kristol's son William are a case study in how the Right's money moves ideas and people into the media. Unlike his father, William earned a PhD; but, like his father, he soon concluded, "I just wasn't cut out to do serious academic work," he told the *Washington Post*. Although he did not serve in Vietnam, while at Harvard he praised Richard

Nixon's Christmas bombing of the North Vietnamese capital as "one of the greatest moments in American history."

The younger Kristol came to Washington in the mid-1980s to work for William Bennett, Irving's protégé, in the Reagan administration's Education Department and went on to serve Vice President Dan Quayle as chief of staff. In the White House, he forged close ties to the Christian Right and was credited as the architect of Quayle's attack on Candice Bergen's TV sit-com character, single mother Murphy Brown. Kristol told Republicans to denounce homosexuality as "the disease it is" and saw overturning *Roe v. Wade* as "the key to conservative reformation."

Out of a job when Bush was defeated by Clinton and relying on the rela-tionships his father, Irving, had forged with the Four Sisters foundations, William played in the 1990s the role his father had played in the 1970s: fixer, agitator, and commissar in chief for the GOP. Backed by the Bradley Foundation and by right-wing media mogul Rupert Murdoch, Kristol set up a small strategy center he called the Project for the Republican Future, headquartered in the AEI building in Washington. Soon he set his sights on wrecking the Clinton plan to reform the health care system by advising Republicans to kill it outright for partisan gain rather than working with the administration to produce a bipartisan bill.

When the reform effort was defeated and the Republicans took control of the House in 1994, Kristol persuaded Murdoch to pony up millions to finance a new magazine, *The Weekly Standard,* which became Kristol's vehicle for continuing the assault on the Clinton administration, while at the same time experimenting with formulas for a Republican comeback. Though Kristol's academic mien provided cover, *The Weekly Standard* began to print scurrilous insinuations about Clinton's private behavior that might have been more fitting for Murdoch's tabloid *New York Post.* According to Nina Easton, author of the book *Gang of Five: Leaders at the Center of the Conservative Ascendancy,* "If not for Kristol's obsessive mar-shalling of the pro-impeachment forces, said a number of conservatives, independent counsel Kenneth Starr's investigation might have petered out, and House Republicans might have allowed the public's disapproval of their course dissuade them from voting to impeach the president." When the strategy came a cropper, causing Republicans to lose House seats in 1998, Kristol disingenuously tried to distance himself from the whole business.[28]

Seeking another strategy to revive GOP political fortunes, Kristol and his senior editor, David Brooks, developed and promoted what they called National Greatness Conservatism, which counseled Republicans to find useful purposes for government and deploy patriotism for partisan ends. For some years after the collapse of the Soviet Union, Kristol had been casting about for a way to politicize national security and thereby resurrect a Republican advantage vis-à-vis the Democrats. He thought he had found an issue in confronting China, but Republican business interests quickly shot it down. (Murdoch has significant holdings in China.) Because there was no appetite among Republicans to use government to solve domestic problems, National Greatness Conservatism needed a foreign policy crisis to work.

With grants from the Bradley Foundation, Kristol established the Project for the New American Century (PNAC), where in the late 1990s the doctrine of American military preemption to project American power around the globe with or without international support and the idea of deposing Saddam Hussein were developed and then road-tested in *The Weekly Standard*. In 1997, a *Weekly Standard* cover story announced SADDAM MUST GO.

While denouncing the press when it suits them (Richard Perle referred to *New Yorker* writer Seymour Hersh as a "terrorist"), Kristol, Perle, and other neocons are renowned for their ability to "work" it. In the run-up to the Iraq war, several think tank neocons, including Michael Ledeen of AEI, employed a Manhattan media booking agency (Benador Associates) to put them on television. Appearing on NPR on September 11, 2001, following the terrorist attacks, Kristol said, "I think Iraq is, actually, the big unspoken sort of elephant in the room today." On September 20, PNAC published a letter to Bush in the *Washington Times*, signed by Perle, Gaffney, Bennett, Kirkpatrick, and columnists Robert W. Kagan and Charles Krauthammer, among others, calling for Saddam's overthrow.[29]

In July 2002, *The Weekly Standard* published a piece titled "The Coming War with Saddam," providing the script for right-wing commentators. In August, George Will wrote a syndicated column pressing the case for war. Krauthammer weighed in with "The Raines Campaign," an attack on the reportage of the *New York Times*, under then–executive editor Howell Raines, which revealed doubts about the war felt by leading

Republicans. For the next seven weeks, Krauthammer beat the war drums in every syndicated column he filed. Also in early August, Kristol's messaging was picked up by Rush Limbaugh ("We want to destabilize the Middle East") and on the FOX News Channel by Bill O'Reilly, who attacked "America's alleged allies."[30]

Once the fighting commenced, Kristol led the neoconservatives in questioning the patriotism of war critics. Appearing on FOX, he said, "I really honestly now believe that a certain chunk of the Democratic Party, a higher chunk of liberal commentators, take a certain relish in the fact when something goes badly in the war. . . . They hate the Bush administration more than they love America." FOX's Brit Hume chimed in, "It's the anti-American stuff. . . . I mean anti-war stuff, I won't say anti-American."

With the Bush administration under heavy criticism for hyping the alleged relationship between Saddam Hussein and the al-Qaeda leader Osama bin Laden, mastermind of the September 11 terrorist attacks, *The Weekly Standard* published a November 2003 cover story under the headline CASE CLOSED that used a memo from a neoconservative Pentagon official to claim that the U.S. government had been in possession of "secret evidence of cooperation." A *Newsweek* investigation of the memo, titled "Case Decidedly Not Closed," called it a "far cry from solid evidence of ongoing cooperation between Saddam and Osama." Even the Pentagon referred to *The Weekly Standard* report as "inaccurate."

The think tanks also have been a vehicle by which the Republican Right created in the media such unrepresentative phenomena as "the black conservative," in a kind of perverse imitation of what the Right perceives affirmative action to be. While black Republicans are a very small minority in the population, a 1992 study of the media visibility of black conservative scholars and black progressive scholars over an eight-year period by Fairness & Accuracy in Reporting found that the top three black conservatives were cited almost ten times as frequently as the top three black progressives over the same period. Beating out two tenured academics was the most frequently cited black conservative, Thomas Sowell of the Hoover Institution, who "received over 400 major paper and magazine citations— in addition to contributing frequently to *Forbes,* the *Chicago Tribune, Newsday,* and the *Washington Times,* while also writing a [nationally syndicated] column for Creators Syndicate."

The original right-wing think tank that funded African Americans to promote an anti–civil rights agenda and deny the existence of racism was the Lincoln Institute for Research and Education, headed by J. A. Parker, who, on the campaign trail for Barry Goldwater in 1964, denounced the civil rights movement as Communist-inspired. Clarence Thomas sat on the board of the institute's journal, *The Lincoln Review,* which opposed affirmative action, abortion rights, and the national holiday for Martin Luther King Jr. During the 1980s, Parker was a paid agent of the apartheid government of South Africa.

In 1993, the National Center for Public Policy Research, funded by the Scaife and Bradley foundations, created Project 21 to espouse "dedication to family and commitment to individual responsibility [that] has not traditionally been echoed by the nation's civil rights establishment." Members of another front group, the African American Republican Leadership Council, are frequently quoted and appear on cable talk shows, particularly on the FOX News Channel, attacking Democrats and praising Republicans. On the council's advisory board are white conservatives Paul Weyrich, Sean Hannity, Grover Norquist, and Christian Right leader Gary Bauer.[31]

Armstrong Williams, a former protégé of GOP Senator Strom Thurmond and Justice Clarence Thomas, is a columnist for the *Washington Times,* a radio show host, and a frequent cable TV pundit. He runs a public relations business in Washington that services the right-wing think tank and advocacy group network. Former Reagan aide Alan Keyes launched two radio shows with money from the Olin Foundation, leading to his own short-lived MSNBC talk show. Walter E. Williams, an Olin-funded economist at George Mason University in the Virginia suburbs of Washington, D.C., advocated the revival of poll taxes in a June 2003 appearance as a guest host for Rush Limbaugh. "If you don't pay taxes, why should you have the right to vote? . . . Or maybe you should get one vote for each dollar in taxes you spend," he said.

Conservative financiers and corporations have created the concept of the "conservative woman" through the Independent Women's Forum, a media booking agency that has promoted radio talk show host Laura Ingraham and *USA Today* columnist Amy Holmes (who is also an adviser to Senate majority leader Bill Frist). The "conservative Hispanic woman," failed Bush Labor secretary nominee and syndicated columnist Linda

Chavez, is given a media platform through the heavily subsidized anti–affirmative action Equal Opportunity Foundation and the Center of the American Experiment. Typical panels on the PBS show *To the Contrary*, a forum devoted to women's issues, pit female journalists from the *Washington Post* and *The Progressive* magazine against a procession of Stepford wives from the Independent Women's Forum and the Heritage Foundation.

After being fired from the editorship of *The New Republic* and then by the *New York Times*, Andrew Sullivan, the "conservative homosexual" who accused Bill Clinton of "pathological recklessness" (while Sullivan sought out unprotected sex despite his HIV-positive status), was reduced to selling a column called "The Dish" to the Moonie *Washington Times* and running a vanity Web log that has taken handouts from a gay Bush supporter, publicist Charles Francis, who, according to the *Washington Post*, set up a fake "citizens" group to front for his tobacco industry clients.

An offshoot of the Right's message machinery is a cluster of organizations that receive millions annually from the Four Sisters foundations and other donors in order to bring conservative messaging to college campuses, recruit students into the conservative movement, and develop conservative "journalists" in college newspapers.

The effort was begun in 1978, when Irving Kristol and Olin Foundation chairman William Simon founded the Institute for Educational Affairs to channel funds to the *Dartmouth Review* and dozens of right-wing campus imitators. The blatantly racist, sexist, and homophobic *Review* launched the careers of Dinesh D'Souza and Laura Ingraham, among others. Rich Lowry of *National Review*, Matt Rees of *The Weekly Standard*, and Dave Mastio (formerly of the *USA Today* editorial board) all got their start in conservative campus newspapers that push the boundaries of civility (for example, referring to "ethnic pimps" and attributing shifts in Clinton policies to the rhythms of Hillary Clinton's menstrual cycle). Young America's Foundation, "the principal outreach organization of the Conservative Movement," pays conservative media figures like D'Souza, David Horowitz, Ben Stein, and ABC's John Stossel to speak to groups of college students. Targeting young women, the Clare Boothe Luce Policy Institute dispatches Ann Coulter, Pat

Buchanan's sister Bay, and AEI's antifeminist Christina Hoff Sommers to college campuses.

The *Christian Science Monitor* described how it works: "YAF sent Dinesh D'Souza to lecture at [Swarthmore]; in the aftermath, YAF collected six enthusiastic conservative students and invited them to its headquarters to plan a yearlong conservative speakers' program; by 1994, YAF boasted that Swarthmore's Conservative Union had swelled from six members to seventy-five, and a new conservative campus newspaper has been started—thanks to $37,000 funneled toward the college from the conservative matrix." According to D'Souza, "The more successful papers are able to shift, however imperceptibly, the center of debate to the right. It makes conservative views more respectable." "Stories" ginned up by the right-wing campus newspapers win national attention from placement in the *Wall Street Journal* editorial page and on FOX News.

Perhaps because they are more interested in politics than in journalism, many young conservatives choose to train at highly ideological media programs—rather than at conventional journalism schools—such as the Intercollegiate Studies Institute's Collegiate Network; the Leadership Institute, headed by Christian Right activist Morton Blackwell; and the National Journalism Center, a project of Young America's Foundation, which has sent more than nine hundred graduates to jobs at seemingly every major media outlet in the country, from the *New York Times* to NPR to CNN.[32] Ann Coulter, reporter Jonathan Karl, and John Fund of the *Wall Street Journal* editorial page are graduates of these programs. Young cable talking head Christine O'Donnell of the Intercollegiate Studies Institute (and founder of the antigay group known as the SALT) advocates what she has called a "nineteenth-century" view of how women should behave.

The Weekly Standard's Fred Barnes directs the Institute on Political Journalism, sponsored by the Fund for American Studies. According to a Columbia University student who attended a two-day workshop for students sponsored by the fund, "Instead of a crash course in writing on economics, the conference turned out to be a seminar on the virtues of supply-side theory. Speakers who dealt with the economy delivered paeans to Reaganomics to unwitting audiences made up primarily of college students who, by and large, had no idea that they were being taught opinion as if it were fact." In addition to *Wall Street Journal* editorial writers John Fund and Susan Lee, speakers included *BusinessWeek* economics editor Michael Mandel and *Newsweek* contributing editor Rick Thomas, who denounced "radical environmentalists" and said *Roe v. Wade* was a "stupid decision."[33]

The Phillips Foundation, whose board includes right-wing columnist Robert Novak and Alfred S. Regnery, the right-wing Washington book publisher, awards annual journalism fellowships to fund topics of interest to the Right. In 2002, recipients included an editor at the Hudson Institute, a reporter for the Moonie newsmagazine *Insight,* an arts editor of *The Weekly Standard,* and, as part of a co-optation strategy, even a writer for the liberal-oriented online magazine *Salon.*

Blackwell's Leadership Institute, which conducts workshops such as "Effective Television Techniques," sent out a fund-raising letter from GOP Representative Dick Armey warning: "While you read this letter, left-wing journalism professors are preparing their new crop of media radicals." But Blackwell appears to be the one turning out radicals. A typical career path is one followed by Bernadette Malone, who switched to journalism rather than joining the U.S. Marines because she wanted to be "a conservative in action," according to the *Christian Science Monitor.* Malone edited a conservative college newspaper, trained at the Leadership Institute, was placed as a reporter for columnist Robert Novak, then became a regular on the archconservative op-ed page of the Manchester, New Hampshire, *Union Leader* before becoming a book editor at Regnery. Major Garrett of FOX News has been a Leadership Institute presenter.

According to YAF's National Journalism Center, which runs a special wire service for right-wing campus newspapers suggesting "story ideas," its graduates have worked at the *Washington Post,* the *Wall Street Journal,* CBS, CNN's *Larry King Live,* and *Newsweek.* The Journalism Center's most famous graduate is Ann Coulter, who told the *Christian Science Monitor,* "Ideology was not taught. Reporting was taught; do research and get your facts right." If Coulter's notoriously error-filled best-selling book *Slander: Liberal Lies About the American Right* is any indication, what is taught in these programs is neither research nor reporting. *Columbia Journalism Review* concluded that *Slander* "misreads history, selectively (and deceptively) presents facts, and misquotes the media. . . ."

•   •   •

When they started Heritage and its spin-offs, Paul Weyrich and his fellows believed that they were setting up what he called "mirror organizations" that could match the organizational and media prowess of contemporary liberalism. But the conservatives knew nothing of liberalism, and they did not imitate it. The architects of the conservative movement had learned their craft either by consciously imitating Communist tactics to take over the GOP in 1964 or by direct involvement in various Communist sects. In Weyrich's case, the impulse seems to have sprung from an odd mix of Germanophilia and theological fanaticism.[34] The right-wing Council for National Policy, the secret directorate of religious Right leaders, bears no resemblance to the Council on Foreign Relations, the foreign affairs debating society on which it is modeled. Nor is the right-wing Philanthropy Roundtable, with its strategic dictates, an analog to the group it is supposedly copying: the nonpartisan Council on Foundations. The conservatives built the kind of machinery they thought they were up against but never were.

Unlike the conservative movement, the liberal "movement" was a collection of genuinely broad-based social and political grassroots movements that sprang up independently of a Daddy Warbucks like Joe Coors or Richard Mellon Scaife. As small-d democrats, they rarely acted in top-down unison and were for the most part organized around single issues, not around broader ideological work or sustained critiques of conservatism. Many of them, like consumer advocate Ralph Nader, had immense media flair, especially in the 1970s. Yet because they did not conduct their issue advocacy behind the walls of think tanks, the liberals stood accused by the Right of representing "special interests" over the public interest, in a complete inversion of reality.

Perhaps because they felt their research was self-evidently valid, liberals did not adopt the techniques of advertising, marketing, and p.r. to change the thinking of Americans in a period when politics was driven increasingly by mass media, especially television. Liberals do not have access to the subsidized media "booking agency" operations that pitch right-wing pundits to television and radio for every news cycle. For many liberals, the gimmickry and distortion of the Right became another reason to resist concise, effective communications in the new media age.

Liberal foundations do not strategically coordinate their philanthropic giving for political ends. The liberally oriented Pew Charitable Trusts, for example, funds research to foster debate, providing support to scholars and advocates on both sides of an issue. When not funding both sides, liberal foundations tend to support impartial policy analysis, minus the ideological topspin, slick packaging, and easily digested talking points of the Right. Once the budget cuts of the Reagan administration began to fray the social safety net, money available for promoting liberal ideas dried up as liberal foundations gave smaller, single-year, highly circumscribed grants to the work of direct service charities, like domestic violence prevention programs, or to undertake legal and community action to defend rights that were under attack by the right wing.

The liberal foundations generally eschew partisan politics, and many shy away from anything that might be construed as advocacy—partly as a vestige of chilling Republican attempts, beginning in the Nixon administration, to attack and delegitimize the legal ideological advocacy of nonprofits that received some federal grants for their charitable services work, in a right-wing strategy known as "defunding the Left." The Capital Research Center was set up by the Right to monitor and harass the nonconservative nonprofit sector, even as the Right exploited the law by conducting political advocacy through nonprofit charities.

Then, too, the large foundations with a liberal cast, like Ford and Rockefeller, draw their boards from the cautious and conservative-minded business community. Liberals lack the patient and fearless investment capital aimed at shaping the political culture provided by the Right's Four Sisters. Scholars estimate that think tank, research, and ideological advocacy groups on the Right outspend their liberal counterparts by a factor of four to one.[35]

With liberal professors in the universities completely detached from Washington politics, the few multi-issue D.C.-based think tanks that can be identified as liberal and can match the resources of Heritage, for example the Brookings Institution, are far less partisan, dogmatic, and media-driven than their ideological competitors. During the Clinton presidency, the head of Brookings, which is largely corporate-funded, was a Republican.[36]

As liberal institutions made concessions to bipartisanship—the American Civil Liberties Union (ACLU), for example, hired former Far

Right Republican Representative Bob Barr as a spokesman—conservative financiers used their money to further infiltrate organizations that are considered to represent mainstream opinion, while seeing to it that right-wing think tanks employed no liberals and did not entertain nonconservative ideas. Robert W. Kagan, an architect of Reagan's Nicaragua policies and co-founder with William Kristol of the Project for the New American Century, became a fellow at the liberal Carnegie Endowment for International Peace. Former *Wall Street Journal* editorial writer Max Boot brought Olin money into the Council on Foreign Relations, where he was named a fellow and wrote *The Savage Wars of Peace: Small Wars and the Rise of American Power.* Boot has lauded American "imperialism" and said that the United States should impose its views globally "at gunpoint." When the Aspen Institute opened its Washington offices under the leadership of former *Time* managing editor and CNN chairman Walter Isaacson, it threw a book party for the discredited former Speaker of the House Newt Gingrich, author of a novel that posits a Confederate victory at Gettysburg.

The once-vigorous alternative left-leaning press fell on hard times. As media historian Robert W. McChesney has observed, all successful social and political movements, whether salutary or malign, develop and produce their own media. Lenin had his radio broadcasts for "mass persuasion"; Socialist Party publications were once well circulated in the United States; and, according to McChesney, by 1940 the American labor union movement was publishing eight hundred papers.[37] Franklin Delano Roosevelt took to the radio airwaves to counterbalance the largely GOP-controlled newspaper industry.[38] The feminist movement got a lift from the founding of *Ms. Magazine.* Buckley understood this as early as 1954 when he staffed his magazine, *National Review,* with ex-Communists and paid them with his family's fortune.

Twenty years hence, alternative right-wing publishing was flourishing. Millions in right-wing funds were freed up for dozens of magazines and newsletters in all shapes and sizes. *Imprimis,* a newsletter published by conservative Hillsdale College, had a circulation of five hundred thousand, while *Commentary* won enormous influence with only a twenty-seven-thousand circulation base. While the new right-wing magazines pursued a common agenda, were well integrated with the Republican Right's political establishment, and had millions in cash reserves, left-liberal publications like *The Nation, The Progressive, Mother Jones,* and *In These Times* were ideologically splintered, genuinely independent of partisan politics, and received less than 10 percent of what their political competitors did in foundation support.[39]

Meanwhile, the "concession" that the media made to the right wing in the 1970s and 1980s, as described by John Judis, didn't just happen spontaneously. It was wrung out of the media, by another well-financed pressure campaign, run by the Right in tandem with its think tank "guerrilla war" and aimed directly at them.

CHAPTER THREE
THE BIG LIE

THOUGH MOST OF LEWIS POWELL'S 1971 memorandum to American business leaders concerned the building of a conservative counterestablishment, Powell also proposed a second track through which "the movement" would directly harass the media into conforming to its ideology. The subsidized right-wing ideas and spokespeople could not compete in the media marketplace without a subsidized pressure campaign to make it happen.

Business, Powell advised, should underwrite "monitoring" of the media—particularly the broadcast networks—to enforce its demand for "equal time" for right-wingers. "The movement" would play a coordinated double game, seeking to co-opt the media, while at the same time scorching it as biased against conservatism and conservatives. The latter tactic would enforce the former. "These staffs of [media] experts," Powell wrote, should commence a "constant examination of the texts of adequate samples" of TV programs, newspapers, magazines, and books; such systematic scrutiny and criticism of the media would provide "incentives" to "induce" the media to put the heavily subsidized pro-business commentators in print and on the air.[1]

When Powell wrote the memo, he was likely unaware that a quiet effort launched in Washington in 1969, the year in which Spiro Agnew delivered his attack on the networks, was already under way, doing what he was proposing. Just as Paul Weyrich had little in common with Powell, the men involved in the Right's first media monitoring project may not have been the kind of media "experts" the establishmentarian Powell had in mind, but they would get the job done.

Accuracy in Media (AIM) was the brainchild of Reed Irvine, then an economist at the Nixon Federal Reserve Board, who had begun writing letters to the editors of major publications complaining of alleged pro-Communist bias, particularly in coverage of Nixon's policies on the war in Vietnam. If the letters were not published, Irvine bought ad space in those publications in which to place the letters. Like Irving Kristol, Reed Irvine was once a Communist sympathizer who brought agitprop techniques to the conservative cause. "In my youth, I was on the Far Left, but I realized that Marxism in any form causes grief, not good. I decided to fight back against the constant stream of lies and distortions," Irvine said. Irvine fought back with lies and distortions.

In its first incarnation, the Right's media monitoring had strong echoes of McCarthyism. Irvine was associated with the Council Against Communist Aggression, a Red-baiting group founded in 1951 to combat what it saw as a campaign of Communist "subversion" and "insidious propaganda campaigns" within the United States to "confuse our people and undermine our determination to contain and shrink the Communist empire."[2] He was later a member of the United States Council for World Freedom, an American affiliate of the World Anti-Communist League, a Far Right group of former military and intelligence officers, Latin American death squad assassins, assorted Fascist and Nazi terrorists, war criminals, and prominent Moonies from around the globe.[3]

One book published by AIM, *Target America: The Influence of Communist Propaganda on the U.S. Media,* by James L. Tyson, a former government official with the Office of Strategic Services (the forerunner organization of the Central Intelligence Agency), specifically recommended a government reactivation of Joseph McCarthy's Red-hunting investigative techniques. Tyson wrote that the Russians were pursuing a "massive secret propaganda campaign" through four thousand journalist-agents strategically placed throughout the American media. Tyson urged that the Federal Bureau of Investigation, and the internal security committees of the U.S. Congress that had been at the center of the Red scare, investigate "Communist agents in the media" under the Espionage Act. Journalists were to be targeted for government investigation not only if their work contained "falsehoods" but also if it failed to include "anti-Communist truths." He recommended that government monitors be placed in the TV networks to oversee editorial policy in disregard of First Amendment constitutional protections. "In a word, TV news has become much too important a matter to be left to TV newsmen," Tyson wrote.[4]

Irvine was joined at AIM by Abraham Kalish, who taught communications at the U.S. Army's Defense Intelligence School, and Bernard Yoh, a professor of psychological warfare at the U.S. Air Force University.[5] The notion of "liberal bias" in the media, which is today part of the conventional wisdom across the political spectrum, owes much to the activities of this small but dedicated trio, two of whom had been propaganda experts for the U.S. military during the Vietnam War. Irvine had met the pair while he was working in military intelligence.

Irvine claimed that his group was working for "fairness, balance, and accuracy in news reporting" and denied that it had an ideological agenda, though on its face the effort was political. AIM's original aim was to discredit the media as pro-Communist in the eyes of the public—part of a deliberate strategy to build political support for Nixon's Vietnam policies, for the Pinochet military coup in Chile, and more broadly for an aggressively militant U.S. posture toward the Soviet Union. AIM advocated that domestic protesters of the Vietnam War be charged with treason under the Alien and Sedition Act (used by the Federalist Party in the late eighteenth century to silence criticism from Republican newspaper editors). And it was an ally during Watergate of the Nixon White House, which already understood that accusing the media of being "liberal" was a way of deflecting damaging reports, encouraging the media to self-censor, and training it to be less aggressive in covering conservatives and Republicans. "In a sense, AIM and Agnew's speech were on the same track; there was a lot of discontent with the way the media was behaving," Irvine said.

Irvine wanted the press to behave differently. Through AIM's newsletter, through a column that would eventually be syndicated in 100 newspapers, and through a daily radio commentary on 250 stations by the mid-1980s, Irvine's approach was to attack particular anchors, editors, and reporters as dupes of the Soviet Union—"comsymps"—with reckless and false allegations designed to damage their careers. He suggested that Walter Cronkite had been "recruited" as a Soviet agent during his tour of duty in Moscow in the 1940s. He charged the *New York Times* with repeating Fidel Castro's "disinformation." And he attacked the Corporation for Public Broadcasting (CPB) for underwriting a documentary on the life of Nelson Mandela, which Irvine called "a glorification of an African terrorist."

AIM's research was sloppy; its reporting was phony; and its facts, when checked, were shown to be flat wrong. In AIM's campaign to discredit *New York Times* correspondent Raymond Bonner, Irvine, citing two unnamed sources, charged that Bonner had been affiliated with two left-of-center organizations: the Institute for Policy Studies and Pacifica News Service. The *Times* investigated and reported that Irvine was wrong on both counts. Targeting the *Washington Post*'s Karen DeYoung, Irvine reported a rumor that she had stepped out of her role as Central America reporter and hand-carried a diplomatic letter to Maurice Bishop, the Marxist prime minister of Grenada. DeYoung had not carried the letter and told Irvine so before he published the false item.[6]

Typical AIM reports included "Peter Jennings Distorts the Facts," "How Bryant Gumbel Manipulates Guests," "A Mike Wallace You Won't Like," and "What's Wrong with Dan Rather? Plenty." Irvine attacked TV programs critical of J. Edgar Hoover, Joe McCarthy, and the nuclear power industry. After the fall of the Soviet Union robbed him of an issue, he charged that the media hyped "chicken little science scares" and championed the "homosexual agenda." During the Clinton era, he vigorously promoted crackpot theories suggesting the death of White House lawyer Vincent Foster was something other than suicide. Though the connection to media criticism was unclear, AIM called for the use of napalm against guerrillas fighting the military junta in El Salvador; during the Persian Gulf War in 1991, Irvine advocated the use of nuclear weapons against Iraq.[7]

Media monitoring was a new strategy for the Right; and although his analysis echoed nothing so much as the conspiracism of the John Birch Society, Irvine, a former Fulbright scholar, was a gifted polemicist with a flair for publicity stunts, such as buying small amounts of stock in media companies and creating a ruckus at shareholder meetings. Errors are par for the course in journalism, and Irvine proved adept at packaging these routine errors to create the appearance of systematic bias. After a belligerent Irvine got ABC to correct some mistakes in a program on the arms race, AIM landed on the front page of the *Wall Street Journal* in 1973.[8]

Whether or not he realized it, Irvine, who knew nothing about journalism and cared for it even less, was trying to replace the neutral and impartial view of journalism with a subjective conservative view of the world. In the guise of attacking "liberal bias," he was attacking the fact-finding ethic of journalism and the editorial independence of news organizations.

With its notice in the *Journal*, the organization's fledgling operation was off and running and was soon incorporated by the right-wing message machine, which recognized its political potency. Public intimidation and defamation of the media by the organized Right had the potential to make it not only more timid in confronting the powerful but also more conservative. Ultimately, the role of Irvine, his cadre, and their offspring was to make the accusation of being "liberal" the newsroom equivalent of the Hollywood blacklist of the 1950s.

Having propelled itself into the spotlight, AIM won financial backing from Richard Mellon Scaife and the Coors Foundation, as well as from Mobil Oil and Union Carbide; the latter two corporations Irvine publicly defended against damaging media revelations. Mobil also pursued its anti-media campaign directly, distributing free op-ed style columns to local newspapers, and locally broadcasting commercials attacking the press.[9] AIM would soon operate with well over $1 million annually; joining its board were prominent conservatives such as Admiral Thomas H. Moorer, the chairman of the Joint Chiefs of Staff under Nixon; former Republican Representative Clare Boothe Luce, the spouse of Henry R. Luce, owner of *Time;* Dr. Edward Teller, father of the hydrogen bomb; the writer and anti-Communist activist Midge Decter; and William Simon.

Simon's role was especially telling. In his book *A Time for Truth,* he revealed that he did not believe in a free, unfettered, and fair press operated by independent journalists but, rather, wanted a press that reflected right-wing, pro-business interests and that was controlled and censored by business owners. Describing a plan for "mobilization" against the media, Simon wrote, "Finally, business money must flow away from the media which serve as megaphones for anti-capitalist opinion and to media which are either pro-freedom or, if not necessarily 'pro-business,' at least professionally capable of a fair and accurate treatment of pro-capitalist ideas, values, and arguments. The judgment of this fairness is to be made by businessmen alone—it is their money that they are investing."

Though he said he dealt only in facts, Irvine was never able to establish anything remotely resembling a factual case that the media was systematically biased. The media was "liberal" because Reed Irvine hung out a shingle and said it was, and he just kept on saying it to anyone who would listen.

Even with financial backing, Irvine might have been dismissed as a crank without the indulgence of his target: the media. Irvine built a network of about thirty thousand AIM members, many of whom inundated news organizations with tens of thousands of letters on a single issue; AIM also threatened advertiser boycotts, working with Phyllis Schlafly's Eagle Forum and the Reverend Jerry Falwell's Moral Majority, to spike broadcasts it didn't like. One such censorship campaign, run against an ABC News program on nuclear war called *The Day After,* failed to keep the show off the air but succeeded in inserting right-wingers into a discussion panel broadcast after the show to accommodate right-wing criticism. Later, ABC aired *Amerika,* a fictionalized account of a Soviet victory over the United States that was heavily promoted by the right wing.

Irvine was practicing a form of jujitsu. Seeing itself as a public trust, the media was responsive to calls for accountability and was highly susceptible to criticism. Understandably, a well-funded public campaign and well-orchestrated threats made news executives jittery. Arthur Ochs Sulzberger, publisher of the *New York Times,* instituted regular meetings to hear Irvine's complaints as a means of neutralizing him, reported author Michael Massing in *The Nation.* Yet there was no appeasing Irvine, who claimed credit when Raymond Bonner was reassigned off the Central America beat, even though the *Times* said the move was unrelated to Irvine's attacks. In 1977, *Washington Post* ombudsman Charles Seib, who won acclaim for his role in the Heritage Foundation's *Policy Review,* wrote, "It sticks in my craw, but I'll say it: Irvine and his AIM are good for the press." At an annual meeting, ABC News president Roone Arledge told Irvine, "I have great respect for you and your organization," Massing reported. Newspapers ran Irvine's column and quoted his reports. ABC's *Nightline* hosted him.

Eventually, ABC created a show called *Viewpoint*, aired occasionally in the *Nightline* slot and hosted by Ted Koppel, which gave conservative media critics, among others, a regular platform for the airing of their grievances.

Even when he drew scornful retorts from media executives brushing aside his slanderous allegations, Irvine spun them as victories. "ABC News Panics," one typical AIM report announced. The media empowered Irvine by engaging him in a battle it could not win.

In choosing to entertain Irvine and his ilk at all, the media gave credence to a nonfactual attack from ideological zealots who showed their disdain for journalistic values by lying, distorting, and advocating censorship by government and business. Political liberals, meanwhile, did nothing to defend a free press from this right-wing onslaught. Perhaps because these First Amendment stalwarts believed the media ideally should be an open forum free from outside pressure, they did not organize, or conduct credible research, to hold the media accountable. With only one ideological side monitoring the media, the scales tipped predictably.

As AIM and Irvine were attacking the media from the front lines with a bazooka, another group of conservatives, through their think tank network and their corporate-subsidized, small-circulation yet influential opinion journals, was beginning to craft a more sophisticated line of attack as part of a deliberate strategy to infiltrate, and ultimately capture, the media. Media bashing was something on which the old Goldwaterite Right, and the neoconservatives, could agree, though Reed Irvine and his "jejune" cohort needed the abstractions and finesse that the godfather, Irving Kristol, offered.

The Watergate scandal—which *Commentary* editor Norman Podhoretz called a media "coup d'état"—and the withdrawal of the United States from the Vietnam quagmire, a policy failure wrapped in government lies that conservatives wishfully blamed on media coverage, provided powerful reinforcement throughout the conservative movement for the view already held both by Pat Buchanan and by Kristol: The media, as much as the Democratic Party, was a threat to Republican rule.

Kristol began to attack the media as early as 1967, in an essay in his magazine *The Public Interest* called "The Undeveloped Profession." In a subsequent piece endorsing the theories of Edith Efron, he averred that "ideological bias on television newscasting" was not a "malicious invention" of Spiro Agnew. Daniel Patrick Moynihan, an aide in the Nixon White House, weighed in with "The Presidency and the Press" in *Commentary* in 1971. In 1972, Baroody's American Enterprise Institute published a volume called *Press, Politics, and Popular Government.* Among its contributors were Kristol on "Crisis for Journalism: The Missing Elite" and Robert L. Bartley, the young editor of the *Wall Street Journal* editorial page, on "The Press: Adversary, Surrogate, Sovereign, or Both?" The book was edited by Kristol protégé George Will, who was then writing for *National Review* and *The American Spectator.*

At this time, a second important conservative theorist, Kevin P. Phillips, published a book on the media, which he predicted would become the center of political conflict in the United States. For his 1968 book, *The Emerging Republican Majority,* Phillips had been credited with defining Nixon's Southern Strategy of using racial appeals to win votes. A voting trends analyst in the Nixon campaign, Phillips dedicated the book to the "new majority and its two principal architects: President Richard M. Nixon and Attorney General John N. Mitchell." Phillips's book was distilled into campaign strategy memos, and he joined the White House staff.[10]

In 1975, Phillips published *Mediacracy: American Parties and Politics in the Communications Age,* an analysis of the power of new national communications companies that Phillips posited were supplanting the role of the old American aristocracy, or the conservative business elite, and the regional right-wing press barons, as the arbiters of political power. "Effective communications are replacing party organizations as the key to political success," Phillips wrote.[11]

According to Kristol and Phillips, the media constituted a social and educational elite, in Kristol's words a "new class," or "an adversary culture," whose views were said to be hostile to "work, patriotism, and traditional values." Phillips identified the "mediacracy" as a "cultural-geographic media axis" that, he asserted, functioned as a "spokesman" for "pro-integrationist" forces and "interest-group liberalism." The "axis," a "multibillion-dollar social engineering industry," was centered on the East Side of midtown Manhattan in the broadcast TV networks and the *New York Times.*

Also in 1975 came William Rusher's *The Making of the New Majority*

Party. Rusher concocted a theory of class conflict that pitted the struggle for political power as one of the "producers"—manufacturers, blue-collar workers, and farmers—against the "non-producers," "chiefly members of the knowledge industry, the major news media, the educational establishment, the federal bureaucracy, the foundations and research centers—and a semi-permanent welfare constituency."[12] Singled out for special scorn were the "verbalists" of the media, of which Rusher was one, even if he didn't recognize it. Contrary to conservative belief in unregulated markets, he argued for vigorous use of the antitrust laws to "bust-up" "liberal" media conglomerates.[13]

A fourth right-wing writer, Samuel T. Francis, sounded anti-elitist themes in attacking the press. A Heritage Foundation analyst and future editorial writer at the *Washington Times* who had worked for Far Right Senator John East of North Carolina (elected by Jesse Helms's political machine), Francis wrote of the "increasingly alienated and threatened strata of Middle America" and referred to the American government as a "regime." He celebrated the southern Confederacy and the segregationist movement, and he advocated a "white pride" philosophy. He cited the media as one of the "power preserves of the entrenched elite whose values and interests are hostile to the traditional ethos and which is a parasitical tumor on the body of Middle America." Francis concluded: "These structures should be leveled."[14]

Though the idea of the media as an alien, unpatriotic, and even un-American "elite" would become the basis of a sustained attack on the media by the Republican Right and a widely accepted critique even in media circles, the mix of theories that lay underneath it all made for a strange ideological stew, while the common ingredient appeared to be the class or status envy of the authors. Rusher had been considered an odd duck at *National Review* long before he retired to San Francisco. Francis bounced from job to job in the outer margins of the right wing—likely the consequence of his racism, though he blamed his disappointments on yet another elite: a conspiracy of neoconservatives to marginalize traditional rightists like Francis. Francis's faux pas was open racism. "A dinner with Sam Francis is less tinged with snickers and winks about the behavior of people of color than a dinner in the New York neocon world," according to conservative writer and editor Scott McConnell, a former editor of the *New York Post.*[15]

For their part, the "New York intellectuals" who had formed the neo-conservative movement began to feel apart from and even penalized by the intellectual class they had tried so determinedly to join, an angst expressed publicly not so much by Kristol as by Norman Podhoretz in his four memoirs. Though they attacked their enemies for hostility to "the work ethic" and assailed public welfare, one of the self-interested motivations of those who built the think tank network was their failure to earn a living within established institutions. Kristol, who like many of his class and generation attended the City College of New York because it was free, and who had no graduate degree, was able to arrange for himself an Olin Foundation chair at the business school of New York University in addition to his AEI sinecure. Upon his retirement from *Commentary,* a magazine underwritten by the American Jewish Committee, Podhoretz was put on the payroll of the Hudson Institute, a right-wing think tank where his wife, Midge Decter, was a trustee.

Kristol's "new class" critique comes from the 1957 book *The New Class* by Milovan Djilas, who offered it as an explanation for the way Communist bureaucrats controlled their countries.[16] Kristol also seemed informed by the work of sociologist C. Wright Mills, who was a student of the Marx-influenced social theorist Max Weber. In his 1956 classic, *The Power Elite,* Mills argued that government, corporate, and military sectors manipulated and controlled the American masses; he recommended diversification of the media and strengthening representative democracy as a response. Many of the arguments between the Leninists and the Trotskyites during Kristol's youth revolved around the power of bureaucratic elites.

Kristol seemed to appropriate these arguments and apply them through sheer assertion to American society, as an explanation for supposed liberal political domination. Meanwhile, Kristol was working busily on the project of constructing a new class or elite of conservative "intellectuals"—William Simon's "counterintelligentsia"—to win political victory through penetration of the media. Kristol had doubts about democracy, and his writings on the media were not concerned with fostering a wider debate or with better informing the electorate. For Kristol, it seemed, the problem with the "liberal elite" was the liberal part, not the elite part.

As Walter and Miriam Schneir explained in *The Nation,* Kevin Phillips's theory of competing elites was similarly revealing. Born to a lower-middle-class family in the Bronx and educated at Harvard and the London School of Economics, Phillips adopted the fierce radical populism of the cultural Right, with pointed enmity reserved for Manhattan. "The traditional Populist constituencies of the South and West are clearly up in arms," Phillips wrote in *Mediacracy*. The question he posed was whether the "traditionalist coalition" had "the intellectual capacity to turn things around."

As the Schneirs observed, Phillips's analysis seemed to owe a debt to elite theory as set forth in the writings of early-twentieth-century sociologists Vilfredo Pareto and Gaetano Mosca. They argued that every society is ruled by a small ruling class of a few men, an elite minority, who control the majority of the citizenry. The struggle for power in such a hierarchical authoritarian system is a struggle among elites, much the way Phillips described America. The work of Pareto and Mosca, the Schneirs wrote, was an inspiration to Mussolini and to early Italian Fascists.[17]

Phillips questioned democratic ideals. In an article published in the Far Right weekly *Human Events* in 1973, Phillips argued that the First Amendment was "obsolete." "The Public's 'right to know' is a code for the Manhattan Adversary Culture's desire to wrap the First Amendment around its attack on the politicians, government and institutions of Middle America," he wrote.[18] Notably, in varying degrees, Reed Irvine, William Simon, Irving Kristol, and even Lewis Powell had advocated government or business censorship of nonconservative views in the media.

For political liberals, the idea of seeking power through the antidemocratic means of media dominance, subversion, and suppression by political elites was antithetical; as they stood by, right-wing elites ensured that Phillips's 1975 prediction came to pass: They would make the media the center of political conflict in the United States.

By 1981, the charge of liberal media bias had been in circulation for more than a decade, but no one had tried to prove it since Edith Efron in 1971. That task fell to a trio of researchers who printed their findings in *Public Opinion*, a magazine published by the American Enterprise Institute, just as Ronald Reagan took office. Their findings were summarized in the right-wing newspaper *Human Events*, in *National Review*, and in Irving Kristol's *The Public Interest*. The article was expanded and appeared as a 1986 book,

The Media Elite: America's New Powerbrokers. Here were the intellectuals, with their conscious reference to C. Wright Mills, who, in Kevin Phillips's words, had the capacity to turn things around.

The authors were S. Robert Lichter, then a research professor at the George Washington University; his wife, Linda S. Lichter, a sociologist; and Stanley Rothman, a government professor who held an Olin Foundation–funded chair at Smith College and later became president of the right-wing National Association of Scholars, a group founded to combat "political correctness." The Lichters' and Rothman's work was financed by the Institute for Educational Affairs, the boutique think tank founded by Irving Kristol and William Simon primarily to fund right-wing campus newspapers, and by the Olin and Scaife foundations. "I don't think I'm as conservative as Dick Scaife," Rothman said, "but I'm a conservative."[19]

Shortly before the book was published, the Lichters founded their own high-toned, quasi-academic media monitoring organization, the Center for Media and Public Affairs, supported by the same right-wing foundations that underwrote Reed Irvine. The center's fund-raising letters were signed by Ronald Reagan, Pat Buchanan, Edwin Meese III, and Reverend Pat Robertson.[20] Like Irvine, the Lichters claimed to be nonpartisan; though unlike him, they managed to convince the mainstream media that they were. Many references to the organization in the press call it "nonpartisan," even "independent." Robert Lichter was widely quoted as a credible press critic while on the payroll of the FOX News Channel as a contributor.

The Media Elite employed a method that was "empirical and systematic rather than impressionistic and anecdotal," according to the authors. The first section was an "ideological profile" that compared the voting habits and personal beliefs of 238 working journalists at the nation's top three news-papers and newsmagazines, and the three TV networks, to those of CEOs and other top executives at six Fortune 500 companies. The findings that headlined the study were that the media voted more Democratic than the country on the whole and that on a battery of questions measuring eco-nomic and social views, the "media elite" was to the left of the "business elite."

The revelation that most reporters surveyed voted Democratic, even in years of Republican landslides like 1972, was one from which the media's reputation for objectivity probably never recovered. Most people are not trained journalists. They either don't know, or don't believe, that the profession aspires to impartiality. They have little idea of how competitive and commercial concerns, pressure to conform, deference to power, a desire to avoid being labeled "liberal" by right-wing critics, and myriad other biases can influence a story at the expense of any personal political beliefs. They *do* know that news stories are not churned out by a computer and that personal judgments must enter into the equation somewhere along the line; they presume that politics naturally does, too. For many, this one statistic about how workaday reporters and editors tend to vote, and the attendant presumption that voting habits determined any bias in their work, closed the case before the subject of the voting patterns of media owners, executives, and top editors could even be broached. That was a question, among many others, that *The Media Elite* hadn't bothered to ask.

The Lichters used a very small sample to reach their sweeping conclusions. The study relied on the voluntary responses of 238 print and broadcast journalists out of 210,000 editors and reporters and 47,000 TV journalists then working in the field.[21] And the Lichters' ideological profiling was slippery. By choosing the "business elite," a traditionally conservative group, as a point of comparison, rather than, say, teachers, or truck drivers, or even a sampling of general American public opinion, the authors seemed predetermined to make the media appear more liberal and out of touch with mainstream values than it actually was.[22]

Nevertheless, the majority of the media was *conservative* on five of six economic questions. For instance, 63 percent of the media favored less regulation of the economy. The book made the media look liberal on this question only in relation to the business elite, which favored deregulation by 86 percent.

On seven social questions, the study established that the majority of the media favored liberal positions down the line. The media were "strong supporters of environmental protection, affirmative action, women's rights, homosexual rights, and sexual freedom," the authors wrote. Yet the Lichters coded the responses in such a way as to make the media appear more liberal than it was. For example, one question asked whether the government should regulate people's sex lives—something most liberals *and* most conservatives would likely oppose, although this view was treated as solely liberal. Nine of ten Americans consider themselves environmentalists, a "liberal" position, perhaps, but one that is held by most Americans.

Indeed, though the researchers strongly implied it, they did not assert that the media's liberal social views were out of sync with those of most Americans, which, after all, was the whole point of designating the media as an "elite" in the first place. The plain fact is that, even accepting the Lichters' data as representative of the media as a whole, the personal views of media professionals—favoring racial and sexual equality, working toward a clean environment, tolerating diversity—are shared by most Americans. In the mid-1980s and even more so today, these social views are thoroughly mainstream. In addressing this point, the authors could say only that the media's social views made them "natural opponents of the Moral Majority."

A deeper chasm, as the authors went on to describe it, was not one of partisan politics, or even ideology, but one of culture. "Working-class parochials" went into "culture shock" when exposed to "New York and Washington styles and modes" on television. Reporters of a bygone era were working-class and not highly educated; but in the TV era, "[t]he combination of unprecedented affluence and intellectual and cultural sophistication produced a cosmopolitan sensibility that clashed sharply with the verities of small-town America," as the authors put it.

The Lichters' analysis suggested that the "parochials" were suspect of the media not because of biased reportage but because of reportage itself. They associated the media with their fears of modernity. The right-wing ideologists—all of them based in New York and Washington, affluent, and intellectually inclined—preyed on this authentic "culture shock" and the sense within the Moral Majority constituency that news was "biased" if it introduced them to social realities that differed from their own. The elite right-wing media critics put this social and cultural division, frustration, and misunderstanding into the service of their political effort to influence, infiltrate, and subdue the media. "Liberal bias" was a handy rallying point that the Lichters failed not only to prove, but to even charge.

Though the book's reviewers suggested the opposite, the authors concluded that the media was *not* liberally biased—a concept the authors defined as calculatedly unfair. They stated flatly that the media's social liberalism did not manifest itself in coverage of Democrats or Republicans, of legislative debates, or even of liberals and conservatives. They pointed to great ideological diversity within news organizations, claiming that the *Washington Post* was more "pro-environment" but far more economically conservative than the *New York Times*. Many years later, in a 1997 interview with the Moonie magazine *Insight,* Robert Lichter said: "Conservative columnists all over the place were saying that we proved that there was a liberal bias in the press, which at the time we had not."

Still, the authors sought to make the case that the media's "partial views of social reality," or underlying assumptions, were evident in the overall trend of coverage of "long-term social controversies," even as they conceded that culture or personal ideology was not a determining, or even necessarily a defining, factor in shaping coverage.

To prove that reporters' personal views played *some* role in their stories, the researchers analyzed media coverage of nuclear power, school busing, and the oil industry, using a putative empirical device known as "content analysis." While significant differences among the news organizations suggested that the media was hardly an ideological monolith—*U.S. News & World Report* was "pro-nuclear"; the *New York Times* was "balanced"; and the TV networks were "anti-nuclear"—overall the authors claimed to find a pattern: Media sympathies were with nuclear safety and busing to achieve integration and against price gouging by the oil industry.

The Lichters did not say why these so-called biases were objectionable. But in any case, the authors were unable to prove the truth of their claim, as the methodology they employed was dubious. For example, the survey was conducted during the Three Mile Island nuclear accident. With the authors counting every story on reactor safety during the period as biased against the nuclear power industry, the results were predictable. In the case of busing, they found the media slightly favorably disposed to busing at the beginning of the survey period and trending against it toward the end. As critics noted, if true, this was more plausibly ascribed to the fact that opponents of busing became more vocal over time than to any personal biases on the part of reporters.[23]

At several points in the book, the authors knocked down entirely the idea that the media's "ideological profile" biased its coverage. For example, they wrote: "When leading journalists confront new information, they usually manage to process it without interjecting their own viewpoints." When the book was published, and its scientific claims were challenged, the authors backed off further. "The findings that should be understood tell us only about the backgrounds and attitudes of journalists as individuals. They do not tell us about the content of the news they present, nor indeed

whether the content is affected by their personal views at all," Robert
Lichter and Stanley Rothman wrote in the *Washington Post*.

Though the Right artfully reversed the presumption, the burden of proof
that the media is liberally biased ought to have been on the right-wing critics. *The Media Elite* was the best shot conservatives had taken—and would
ever take—at proving the connection between reporters' personal politics
and their work. It failed. At the end of the day, all that had been established
in *The Media Elite* was that reporters tend to vote Democratic and that on
matters of race and sex, the media held personal views that were more liberal than those of the Christian fundamentalist right wing. The relationship
between these personal views and the news, if any, remained murky.

Studies of political bias in the media by nonconservatives have found no
connection between journalists' personal views and their reporting.
Researcher David Croteau of Virginia Commonwealth University concluded in a June 1998 study, "Content analysis of the news media have, at
a minimum, shown the absence of any such systematic liberal/left tilt; some
studies have found a remarkably predictable press usually reflecting the
narrow range of views of those in positions of power, as well as a spectrum
of opinion that tilts toward the right."[24] The respected nonpartisan media
analyst Kathleen Hall Jamieson has written, "Content analysis has failed to
demonstrate a systematic liberal bias in press reports on politics."[25]

Surveys of the Washington press corps have found editors and reporters
to be more centrist than they were characterized by the Lichters. A 1981
study by Stephen Hess of the Brookings Institution showed 58 percent of
the Washington press corps identified as "middle of the road" or "conservative." The Croteau study found, "Of the minority who do not identify with
the center, most have left leanings concerning social issues and right leanings concerning economic ones." Judging the journalists' views against those
of the general public, Croteau found that their economic priorities, views
of corporate power, and preferred tax policies were well to the right of the
public's, while the one area where they were slightly to the left of the public was the environment.

The Lichter survey did not include the views of top media executives—
a subject conservative media critics avoid because it undercuts their argu-

ment. "Most media are owned by Republican conservatives," Louis Boccardi, the former chief executive officer of the Associated Press, said in 2003. A week before the 2000 elections, *Editor & Publisher* asked newspaper executives about their personal political views. "The nation's newspaper editors and publishers strongly believe the Texas governor will beat Al Gore in Tuesday's election for president," the magazine found. "By a wide margin, they plan to vote for him themselves. And, to complete this Republican trifecta, newspapers endorsed Bush by about 2-to-1 nationally."

According to Jamieson, "Unrecognized [in the media bias debate] are the number of studies that suggest that endorsements affect the favorable coverage of the candidate who receives the paper's nod—in three different studies, it was the ideological disposition of the editors and publishers that predicted bias. . . ." As for why reporters' personal political views are not reflected in their coverage, she wrote, "One might hypothesize instead that reporters respond to cues of those who pay their salaries and mask their own ideological dispositions."

Two independent studies of press coverage of the 2000 election campaign found that the regular media was biased toward Bush and against Gore. "Early on journalists and political scientists argued that character, rather than the issues or ideological questions, would be the decisive factor in the presidential campaign," according to a survey of 1,786 news stories in seven newspapers, 218 Internet stories on two sites, and 400 TV and radio broadcasts or cablecasts that was conducted by the nonpartisan Project for Excellence in Journalism. "While the most common Bush theme studied was positive—he is a different kind of Republican—the most common Gore character themes in the press have been negative—that he is scandal-tainted and that he lies and exaggerates. Fully 42 percent of statements asserted he was scandal-tainted, and another 34 percent asserted that he stretched the truth."

Though one might conclude that these results merely reflected objective news reports of charges against Gore by the Bush campaign, the survey concluded that "journalists themselves, rather than outsiders or candidates, were the most common source for the assertions, suggesting the subjective and analytical nature of much of the campaign coverage." And Gore could do little to get out from under the characterization—even when it proved false. "[E]ven though some of the reports about Gore's exaggerations have been based on misquotations and other faulty evidence, only 2% of the character assertions about Gore refuted that he was a liar."

A less scientific survey of the media in *Columbia Journalism Review* by Jane Hall, a former media reporter for the *Los Angeles Times*, found that "the underlying message of all of these stories was clear: Al Gore is a lying politician who will do anything to get elected. . . . Gore's motives are frequently questioned, frequently framed in the most negative light—even in the lead straight-news stories from some of the most respected and influential news organizations . . . [while Bush has] often been given the benefit of the doubt on subjects where he could be vulnerable." Hall singled out for criticism stories by *Washington Post* reporter Ceci Connolly and the Associated Press's Sandra Sobieraj, among others, that cast Gore, unfairly, as a "phony."

In the same year that *The Media Elite* was published, liberals founded their own research group, Fairness & Accuracy in Reporting, to identify conservative bias in the media. Its methods were more straightforward and far less subjective than those of the right-wing monitoring groups. FAIR often used simple counting surveys to demonstrate that the media disproportionately relied on conservative-leaning sources in their reporting. A well-publicized survey of ABC's *Nightline*, for example, documented that government, corporate, and military sources far outnumbered dissenting voices. Yet FAIR did not have the high profile of the right-wing watchdog groups, nor did it have their financial resources.

From the Lichters' findings, conservatives discerned the proof they had been waiting for ever since Edith Efron's *The News Twisters* imploded in 1971: Most reporters voted Democratic, and, at least socially, they were liberal. As during Vietnam and Watergate, the accusation of "liberal bias" in the media seemed tailor-made for a moment when President Reagan's proxy war in Central America was embroiling the administration in the Iran-contra scandal. Fifteen years of right-wing attacks on the media, originating with Nixon supporters, helped the Reagan administration survive the political storm of Iran-contra in the face of mounting evidence of criminality. On *NBC Nightly News,* anchor John Chancellor said, "Nobody wants another Nixon."[26]

The Media Elite was trumpeted far and wide, from the pages of *Fortune* to *Guns & Ammo.* Irving Kristol beat the drums on the *Wall Street Journal* editorial page. Significantly, even the usually reliable *New York Times* seemed influenced by the book and the mood it created. A writer named John Corry, appointed *New York Times* TV critic by the paper's executive editor, A. M. Rosenthal, appropriated the theme in his sharp attacks on the supposedly pro-Communist bias of PBS in his articles in the *Times* and in his own book, *TV News and the Dominant Media Culture,* which was underwritten by the Olin Foundation. Corry would later leave the *Times* and find a home as media critic for *The American Spectator.*

"From that point forward," wrote *National Review* publisher William Rusher, "the Lichter-Rothman findings were a staple in the armory of conservative critics of the media," not least in Rusher's own armory; in 1988, he published *The Coming Battle for the Media: Curbing the Power of the Media Elite.* Though ostensibly concerned with media bias, Rusher described his true worry: "We are dealing here with the fundamental problem of the distribution of forces within American society." Fondly recalling the days prior to the 1960s and before the dominance of the TV networks when the media was "overwhelmingly conservative," he proposed four strategies to reverse right-wing fortunes. Rusher recommended "jawboning," the relentless assertion by the Right of "liberal bias"; "internal monitoring," the placement within news organizations of ombudsmen, who could then be pressured by the organized Right; "external monitoring" of the type done by Irvine and the Lichters; and, finally, "outright takeover." Within one decade, all four of Rusher's strategies would be in place.

Another significant development at this time came in a speech by Terry Dolan—conservative activist, closeted homosexual, and founder of the National Conservative Political Action Committee (NCPAC)—at the National Press Club in Washington. NCPAC financed more than $1 million in attack ads questioning the patriotism and moral values of six Democratic senators in 1980. One ad asserted, "Crime continues to rise . . . our nation's moral fiber is weakened by the growing homosexual movement, by the fanatical ERA pushers (many of whom publicly brag they are lesbians), by leftist-produced movies and television programs that are often indecent and full of sex." Four incumbent Democratic senators were defeated as the Republicans won Senate control that year.

Citing the findings of Rothman and the Lichters at the press club, Dolan announced a $1 million campaign to brand and publicize "liberal bias in the media." Dolan, who also headed the nonprofit National Conservative Foundation (NCF), NCPAC's "educational" arm, told reporters: "We believe that the media acts as if it were a wholly owned subsidiary of America's liberal establishment. We are trying to have the American people know that this bias exists. We want them to do nothing more than to take what you in the media say with a grain of salt." According to a report on Dolan's remarks in the magazine *Broadcasting:*

> The NCF plans to spend a minimum of $250,000 on television, radio and newspaper ads and on distribution of a bumper sticker that reads: "I don't believe the liberal media." It has earmarked money—$10,000–$20,000 per issue—for a newsletter to be sent to its members, other conservative organizations, Capitol Hill and the media. It plans to hold seminars on media bias, and has established a scholarship program to aid promising "conservative writers." To alert the public to media bias, the organization has developed two, 60-second television commercials. The first, "Brokaw," begins with a shot of the "I don't believe the liberal media" bumper sticker, and an announcer who urges: "If you're fed up with the anti-Reagan liberal bias of the media, call 1-800-228-1800."[27]

Dolan's right-hand man in the media attack was a young organizer as fiery as the red-orange hair atop his head. L. Brent Bozell III's deep ties to the conservative movement were yet another illustration of the fact that the people who were professionally engaged in convincing the public that the press had a liberal bias were either right-wing conservatives or in their pay. Usually, they were both.

Bozell's father, L. Brent Bozell Jr., had been a speechwriter for Joe McCarthy and Barry Goldwater, and he was the ghostwriter of Goldwater's *The Conscience of a Conservative.* Bozell Jr. married William Buckley's sister, Priscilla, and all three worked for *National Review.* He founded an ultraconservative Catholic magazine called *Triumph* and organized the first antiabortion rally in the capital in 1970.

Like his father, L. Brent Bozell III was more than a conservative; he was an accomplished activist. Under his direction, the Right's campaign against the media became an explicitly acknowledged strategy in forwarding the conservative movement's broader agenda. Unlike Irvine and the Lichters, Bozell loudly announced his conservative partisanship. "The most powerful adversary of the conservative movement is the leftist media," Bozell said. He compared the media to "cornered rats lunging at the jugular of conservatism." Though he claimed to be "neutralizing the propaganda that comes across as news to the American people," in a 1992 speech to the Heritage Foundation, Bozell laid out an openly propagandistic vision for the American media:

> Imagine, if you will, a future wherein the media willfully support the foreign policy objectives of the United States. A time when the left can no longer rely on the media to promote its socialist agenda to the public. A time when someone, somewhere in the media can be counted to extol the virtues of morality without qualifications. When Betty Friedan no longer qualifies for "Person of the Week" honors. When Ronald Reagan is cited not as the "Man of the Year," but the "Man of the Century."

When Terry Dolan died of AIDS shortly after announcing the media attack campaign, Bozell took the helm at the heavily indebted NCPAC; in 1987, he resigned and raised more than $300,000 to establish what would become the Right's premier media monitoring operation: the Media Research Center (MRC). In his Heritage speech, Bozell explained that the organization was not seeking to pressure the media to be objective, a standard based on facts and truth by which the conservatives could come up short. Its goal was "balance," a standard that required the reportage of differing views in equal measure with no regard for their veracity.

While appearing widely in the mainstream media, where he was more or less accepted as a credible critic, Bozell continued his partisan political activities. At the same time that he founded the Media Research Center, Bozell chartered the World Freedom Foundation, a lobby for the anti-Communist guerrilla wars being financed by the Reagan administration in the developing world. He was on the board of the Emergency Project to

Support Colonel [Oliver] North's Freedom Fight in Central America. Bozell was executive director of the Conservative Victory Committee, a political action committee that produced smear ads against Democratic senators during Clarence Thomas's 1991 Supreme Court confirmation battle. In 1992, Bozell served as finance chair of Pat Buchanan's presidential campaign. He was on the board of the American Freedom Coalition, a "traditional values" advocacy group founded with money from the Reverend Moon's Unification Church. And he advised the National Right to Life Committee.

To celebrate the inauguration of George W. Bush in 2001, Bozell joined Jerry Falwell in hosting a mock funeral for Bill Clinton, complete with a casket and flowers. "Yes, Virginia, the vast right-wing conspiracy did exist all along!" Bozell exclaimed to the crowd of five hundred conservatives. "And [there are] two more days to revel in the politics of personal destruction!"[28] At an anniversary dinner for the MRC in 2003, Bozell proclaimed that the organization was engaged not in dispassionate media analysis but in a "war for public opinion."

Founded with the use of Reed Irvine's AIM mailing list, the MRC would soon dwarf AIM in resources, reach, and influence. Like any political strategy, the "liberal media" effort would now be lavishly funded, professionalized, and closely coordinated. Bozell was a master fund-raiser, having raised millions for NCPAC from ultrarightist donors like Nelson Bunker Hunt of Dallas. By 2002, the MRC had more than sixty employees and an annual budget of more than $6 million—six times what AIM spent— from corporations, the Scaife and Olin foundations, and wealthy individual donors like Roger Milliken, a textile manufacturer, and oil magnate T. Boone Pickens.[29] Bozell paid himself more than $225,000; for the conservative movement, he was worth every penny.

Unlike the scattershot Irvine and the pseudoscholarly Lichters, Bozell realized that the war on journalism could be effective only with a constant supply of ammunition, backed by the kind of savvy marketing pioneered by the Heritage Foundation. "Liberal bias" would become just another right-wing "product," sold like the "flat tax" and "school choice."

The Bozell organization created an electronic database through which it catalogs and scrutinizes major print and TV news reports. Bozell works in real time, trying to skew every news cycle in a conservative direction. Using direct quotes from the media, labeling studies, and content analysis, the MRC packages and aggressively markets its materials via a newsletter, *MediaWatch*, a Web site, and e-mail alerts to more than five thousand journalists in the mainstream media, as well as to the conservative press. *Notable Quotables,* an attention-getting, twice-monthly publication, provides "a compilation of the latest outrageous, sometimes humorous, quotes in the liberal media." A curious committee comprising Watergate co-conspirator G. Gordon Liddy, Iran-contra convicted felon Oliver North, Marvin Olasky (author of the book *Prodigal Press: The Anti-Christian Bias of the American News Media,* which advocated that journalists "follow the Bible" in crafting their reports), and the ubiquitous Midge Decter, among others, makes frequent "awards" to the press, such as "Hypocritical Media Hatemongering" and "Good Morning, Morons."

Armed with transcripts from his database, Bozell claimed that he could move media criticism out of the realm of the subjective. What he did was create the appearance of black-and-white objectivity in the service of ideology. When the MRC purported to demonstrate that the media devoted far more coverage to government death squads by rightists in El Salvador than by leftists in Nicaragua, it failed to supply the context that the horror of death squads was far more widespread in El Salvador.[30] A content survey that charged CNN was "Castro's megaphone" by failing to cover the dictator's human rights abuses looked only at the main network, not at Headline News or CNN International, which carried many more such stories.[31] As one critic noted, the MRC chose to examine TV news coverage of guns during a period that included the massacre at Columbine High School and, not surprisingly, found more "anti-gun" than "pro-gun" stories. The "news" that reporters were "anti-gun" ricocheted from the *Washington Times,* to the Associated Press, to Oliver North's syndicated column, to the *Chattanooga Times,* to the Sunday *Oklahoman.* To get the answer it wanted in a labeling study—that conservatives were disproportionately labeled as such by the media when compared with liberals—the MRC didn't count politicians' sound bites. "So a network can choose to run a string of clips with Republicans calling Democrats 'tax-and-spend liberals,' and not get dinged, but if they describe Bush as a 'compassionate conservative,' that counts as bias," writer Mark Weber noted.[32]

Founded almost twenty years after AIM, the MRC benefited mightily from a burgeoning right-wing media in the late 1980s, mostly on radio, that played to the cultural prejudices of the minority of Americans who felt disenfranchised by the regular media; a new and substantial presence of conservatives in the wider media, especially on cable television; and a mainstream press cowed into treating partisan and inaccurate right-wing media criticism seriously. In 1993, the MRC reported:

> The MRC produces a twice-weekly column distributed by the Creators Syndicate to newspapers across the country. Special articles from the MRC have appeared in *The Wall Street Journal*, *Chicago Tribune*, the *Cleveland Plain Dealer*, *Los Angeles Times*, *National Review* magazine, and other publications. MRC spokesmen regularly appear on radio talk shows and have appeared on numerous television programs, including ABC's *Good Morning America*, NBC's *Today*, CNN's *Crossfire*, *Reliable Sources*, and *Sonya Live*, CNBC's *The Real Story* and *Business Insiders*, The Family Channel's *700 Club* and *The Fox Morning News*.

In this era of new conservative media, the "liberal media" campaign was not only a political battering ram to make the regular media more conservative but also a powerful marketing tool for the new right-wing media. The MRC provided an ongoing rationale for conservatives in the mainstream media to justify their presence and for building the market for the right-wing media outlets. If the mainstream media wasn't marked as "liberal," there would be no need for an influx of conservatives to balance it or for alternative right-wing media. At the same time, the new right-wing media was a way for the MRC to deliver its "products" to the public. The relationship between Bozell and the conservative media was a perfect symbiosis.

The right wing flogged Bozell's products so reflexively that both Rush Limbaugh and William Rusher were caught in embarrassing hoaxes when, without checking them independently, they cited MRC reports that distributed fake media quotes. Rusher expressed outrage that *Newsweek* supposedly blamed Reagan's economic policies for the deaths of eighty-seven Hispanics in a Bronx social club. The MRC falsely claimed *Newsweek* had reported, "Reagan-era budget cuts . . . left Hispanics too poor to frequent downtown Manhattan bars, which operate within fire codes." In fine print at the bottom of the report, the MRC revealed it was all just an April Fool's Day joke, though the result was more like a sting operation. Rusher apologized.[33] Limbaugh, who repeated the false story, said he "fell victim."[34]

In his lecture to the Heritage Foundation in 1992, Bozell admitted something that seemed to contradict MRC's public line. The "monopoly" liberals held on the media had been "broken" by the "conservative network." Bozell revealed that the MRC wasn't only a media watchdog but also a device to propel conservative views and their "appropriate mouthpiece" into the news. "We have learned that many in the media are quite open to the conservative perspective if it is presented properly," Bozell said. "We provide journalists with the conservative argument on a given issue, lead them to the organization expert in it, and recommend qualified spokesmen. . . . It is amazing how very receptive some journalists are to this assistance. . . ."

Bozell explained that "more often than not, you won't see the MRC name on much that appears on the subject of media bias." He then made the astonishing claim that the MRC instigated the vast majority of stories about "liberal media bias" in the press. "Indeed, I will go so far as to warrant that 90 percent of the stories in both the electronic and print media which deal with the political bias in the industry have their origins in the Media Research Center," he said.

Bozell boasted that ABC's John Martin, a frequent MRC target, had been the keynote speaker at MRC's annual board meeting. The MRC won another feather in its cap when *Washington Post* ombudsman Joann Byrd wrote a column recommending an MRC book, *How to Identify, Expose, and Correct Liberal Media Bias*, to the *Post*'s readers.[35] The book was a how-to guide for conservatives in the hinterlands to replicate the methods of the MRC on a local level. Among its suggestions, including buying reporters free meals while proselytizing for the conservative cause, was to "take advantage of the ombudsman."

During the Clinton administration, the MRC's role was to pressure the media to cover the so-called Clinton scandals. Occasionally, Bozell let slip that he was quite pleased with his handiwork. In 1996, he said that both the *Washington Times* and the *Washington Post* had been "very good" on Whitewater, a GOP-generated "scandal" in which the Clintons were fully exonerated after years of negative press and a $70 million federal investigation that proved no wrongdoing by either Clinton. In 1998, Bozell said, "Since [October 1996] you cannot fault the *Los Angeles Times*, the *New*

York Times, USA Today. You cannot fault them with a media bias in favor of Bill Clinton."

With George W. Bush in the White House, the MRC moved from press critic to censor. After September 11, 2001, the MRC adopted a strategy of questioning the patriotism of TV networks that it saw as insufficiently supportive of Bush's war aims. According to *Columbia Journalism Review,* Bozell sent out a fund-raising letter declaring: "We are training our guns on any media outlet or reporter interfering with America's war on terrorism or trying to undermine the authority of President Bush." While Rush Limbaugh insisted "the mainstream press never reports what the Media Research Center is saying," the article continued:

> In terms of mainstream media exposure, the center has enjoyed significant success in its new role, often framing the discussions of journalistic objectivity. Between September 11 and December 31, MRC reports and staff members were quoted eighty separate times by major news outlets in the Nexis database. This included eleven interviews and citations on Fox News, CNN, and CNNfn. Bozell even made it onto *Imus in the Morning* in February.

According to the article, the MRC targeted ABC's Peter Jennings for special criticism after he observed that "Americans respect different views of patriotism." The MRC said: "Unlike Jennings, who is still a Canadian citizen, we are Americans." The journalism review concluded:

> While the center's direct impact on those [television] newsrooms is difficult to measure, television coverage has been far more supportive of the Bush administration's policies than have newspapers reports. In November, for instance, a new study by the Project for Excellence in Journalism found that 54 percent of broadcast segments "entirely" supported official U.S. viewpoints, compared with 23 percent of applicable newspaper coverage.
>
> At CNN, NBC, MSNBC and ABC, reporters and producers said that while they are aware of the center's criticisms, they keep partisan assaults from influencing their news judgment. Still, says Tom Nagorski, the foreign news editor at ABC, "I suppose in a subtle way it's in back of your mind."[36]

Writing about the same MRC campaign, the *New York Times* reported:

> Much of the criticism comes from a group of conservative media voices and outlets, including Rush Limbaugh's radio talk show, the *New York Post*'s editorial page, the Drudge Report, and some commentators on the Fox News Channel. Much of the information for their critiques has been assembled by a conservative media watchdog organization called the Media Research Center, which hires full-time monitors to watch the network newscasts. . . .
>
> "Any misstep and you can get into trouble with these guys and have the Patriotism Police hunt you down," said Erik Sorenson, president of MSNBC. "These are hard jobs. Just getting the facts straight is monumentally difficult. We don't want to have to wonder if we are saluting properly. Was I supposed to use the three-fingered salute today?"

The article went on to describe a speech given by ABC News president David Westin at Columbia University's journalism school in which he was asked if the Pentagon was a "legitimate military target" for terrorists. Westin declined to answer, saying as a journalist he should give no opinion. The MRC spun this innocuous no-comment into treason. According to the *Times:*

> [The MRC] was the first to report Mr. Westin's comments to the journalism students, in an email report it sends out to its supporters. From there, the item was picked up by the editorial page of the [*New York*] *Post,* on Oct. 31. That day, it appeared on the Drudge Report on the Internet and on Mr. Limbaugh's radio show.

Apparently to appease his critics, Westin promptly apologized and asked the MRC to include his apology in an amended report.[37]

If it were possible for a media critic to be more intemperate and less trustworthy than Brent Bozell, David Horowitz fit the bill. In the 1960s, Horowitz had been an editor of *Ramparts,* one of the most violently radical organs of the New Left. Horowitz was the author of a book, *The Free World Colossus,* an influential New Left text indicting U.S. foreign policy. His thinking was shaped by his friend and mentor Isaac Deutscher, a Marxist historian and a biographer of Leon Trotsky.

Like Irving Kristol, Horowitz was an extremely effective publicist and media manipulator. He seemed to share with Kristol the view that established cultural institutions such as the news media and academia were to be infiltrated to gain ideological and then political power in what German New Leftist Rudi Dutschke had called "the long march through the institutions."

When *Ramparts* failed in the mid-1970s, Horowitz hooked up with Black Panthers leader Huey P. Newton, wrote for his newspaper, and raised money for a school for the children of the Black Panther Party. In 1975, a woman whom Horowitz had recommended for a bookkeeping job with the Panthers was found murdered; though no charges were ever brought, Horowitz was not alone in his suspicion that the Panthers were implicated. Feeling personally responsible for the tragedy, Horowitz sank into what he called a "really clinical depression." Hugh Pearson, author of a history of Huey P. Newton and the Black Panther movement, believed this emotional trauma caused Horowitz to go "berserk with regard to the left-liberal community."[38]

A few years later, Horowitz reemerged on the public stage, launching a bitter attack on his former friends and colleagues on the Left and announcing, with much fanfare, that he had voted for Ronald Reagan. He then wrote a book, *Destructive Generation: Second Thoughts About the Sixties,* which sought to blame contemporary social ills on the 1960s. In 1987, Horowitz was recruited to do work for the Reagan administration, and he wrote speeches for Senator Bob Dole in the 1988 presidential campaign. So began Horowitz's incendiary second career as another highly paid shock trooper for the Republican Right that would lead to accusations from *Time* columnist Jack E. White that he was a "real, live bigot" and that would bring him, by 2000, into the circle of Bush adviser Karl Rove.[39]

A frequent cable talking head, op-ed columnist, and until 2002 a contributor for *Salon,* Horowitz was yet another mouthpiece for the same band of conservative funders—Scaife and Bradley, among others—who supported an array of his political projects, mostly under the umbrella of the Los Angeles–based Center for the Study of Popular Culture, which focuses on attacking "political correctness" and affirmative action. He runs several Web sites featuring the rants of Ann Coulter and Andrew Sullivan, among others; a right-wing legal arm specializing in "reverse discrimination" claims; a book-publishing imprint; the Wednesday Morning Club, which brings speakers like Dick Cheney, Newt Gingrich, George Will, and Christopher Hitchens to Hollywood; and the Matt Drudge Defense Fund, set up to support the Internet gossip against a libel claim filed by the writer Sidney Blumenthal, whom Drudge had smeared with a false item. Horowitz's Web magazine, *FrontPage*, is a vehicle for smearing leading Democrats. In a "story" picked up by Rush Limbaugh, *FrontPage* described Democratic presidential candidate General Wesley Clark as a "traitorous, opportunistic, grandstanding, self-promoting egotist and 4-star jack-ass."

To move the debate on college campuses to the right, Horowitz founded a magazine called *Heterodoxy*, which exposes liberals to childish ridicule. The magazine "is meant to have the feel of a *samizdat* publication inside the gulag of the PC university," an expression of Horowitz's apparent belief that American liberalism is really a dictatorship. But it was Horowitz, the ex–radical leftist, who seemed to want to squelch political dissent. During the debate over American policy in Iraq, he impugned the patriotism of antiwar protesters as a "regrouping of the Communist left, the same left that supported Stalin and Mao and Ho." And he accused war critic Noam Chomsky of treason. His eagerness to make accusations of treason seemed related to Horowitz's anguished belief that he himself committed "actual treason" by publishing classified government information while editing *Ramparts*.[40]

His handling of racial issues is more controversial still. Horowitz's book *Hating Whitey*, in which he made controversial claims about the incidence of rape of white women by black men, was rejected by his publisher, the conservative Free Press. Horowitz has argued that blacks benefited from slavery, and he calls the NAACP's Kweisi Mfume a "racial ambulance chaser." Horowitz wrote in *Salon* that Americans suffer from "group psychosis" and "collude with demagogic race hustlers in support of a fantasy in which African Americans are no longer responsible for anything negative they do, even to themselves." After reviewing the column on race, *Time*'s Jack White called it "blatant bigotry" and concluded that Horowitz was a "real, live bigot."[41]

In addition to his role as aging campus agitator and inflamer of racial tensions, Horowitz is a sometime Republican Party strategist, running a Web site called the War Room that depicts his angry visage presiding over a battalion of army tanks. Though he called Clinton a "sociopath," Horowitz professed to admire what he considered the president's strategy of triangulating between left and right; in campaign 2000, he urged Republicans to imitate it. "Republicans lose a lot of political battles because they come off as hard-edged, scowling, and sanctimonious," he wrote in his book *The Art of Political War and Other Radical Pursuits*. "A good rule of thumb is to be just the opposite." He continued, ". . . [d]on't forget that a soundbite is all you have . . . keep it short—a slogan is always better. Repeat it often. Put it on television. . . . In politics, television is reality."[42]

Americans, Horowitz wrote, side with the underdog; so in order to win, Republicans were going to have to make it look as if they did, too. The Republicans had to be "repositioned" as the "party of the underdog." To this end, he suggested the term "compassionate conservative" as a new branding slogan for the Republican Right. But Horowitz himself was not so compassionate, agreeing with Vladimir Lenin's tenet "not to refute your opponent's argument, but to wipe him from the face of the earth."[43]

Horowitz's manifesto was little noticed otherwise, but it was a hit with Republican operatives. Karl Rove, who had already asked candidate George W. Bush to read Horowitz's memoir, *Radical Son*, wrote a jacket endorsement for *The Art of Political War*: "It's a perfect pocket guide to winning on the political battlefield from an experienced warrior."[44] Thirty-five GOP state chairs endorsed the book; the Heritage Foundation distributed 2,300 copies to key activists; and House majority whip Tom DeLay sent it to every GOP member of the House.[45]

Along with Myron Magnet of the Manhattan Institute and Newt Gingrich protégé Marvin Olasky, Horowitz became part of a triumvirate of right-wing thinkers advising the Bush campaign, and Bush himself, behind the scenes. Everything from the symbolic presence of blacks at the 2000 GOP convention to Bush's claim to be a new kind of conservative seemed to come straight from Horowitz's playbook. "I do think [the media] are biased against conservative thought," Bush told *National Review* in 1999. "And the reason is that they think conservative thinkers are not compassionate people. And that's one of the reasons I've attached a moniker to the philosophy that I espouse, because I want people to hear a different message."

Long before he played media strategist to the Bush campaign, Horowitz teamed up with Senator Dole as the architect of an attack on the Public Broadcasting System. In 1970, Dole had become a Nixon favorite after telling the president that his nominee for the Supreme Court, G. Harrold Carswell, who was rejected by the Senate because of his history as a racist, instead had been done in by the "liberal media." Horowitz, too, received praise from Nixon in the form of a fan letter he displayed on the office wall of his Center for the Study of Popular Culture.[46]

In 1988, while advising the contras at the behest of Reagan State Department official and future Iran-contra scandal figure Elliot Abrams, Horowitz founded the Committee on Media Integrity (COMINT), to monitor PBS programming, with seed money from the Richard Mellon Scaife foundations. One of the first subjects COMINT tackled was a PBS *Frontline* episode on the Iran-contra affair that Horowitz found displeasing. After Horowitz made a stink, PBS aired a pro-contra broadcast, *Nicaragua Was Our Home,* funded by a Moonie front group called CAUSA, which raised money for the contras after Congress terminated funding.

In a microcosm of the overall right-wing media strategy, the same group of conservative funders now underwrote a two-track strategy to move PBS to the right: threatening PBS funding and seeking to stigmatize as biased and censor programming it did not approve of, while concurrently flooding PBS with heavily subsidized right-wing opinion masquerading as journalism. The coordinated campaign against PBS drew together all four right-wing media monitoring groups—Irvine, the Lichters, Bozell, and Horowitz, the latter of whom served as name-caller in chief, attacking individual producers and reporters as "propagandists" and "intellectual low-lifes."

The Corporation for Public Broadcasting was created in 1967 by an act of Congress as a private but in part publicly funded system devoted to providing an alternative to commercial broadcasting on television and radio. From the beginning, the idea of noncommercial journalism, unfettered by the pressures of the market, was resisted by the right wing because corporate interests would exercise no control over it. Public broadcasting was free to be more objective, and to maintain higher standards, than the profit-seeking media. Almost immediately, the Republican Right set out to destroy it.

CPB ran afoul of the Richard Nixon administration, which blocked its funding in controversies over investigative documentaries that Nixon opposed.[47] Pat Buchanan wrote a memo calling for a "thought-out program for cleaning out public television of that clique of Nixon haters."[48] Though public funding continued, CPB began to seek corporate support as a hedge against government censorship, impinging on the purpose of having independent noncommercial media.

Nixon also decentralized the Public Broadcasting System. "That move, quite brilliant, not only shifted the power of public television to local powers around the country—usually businessmen, not journalists—but also crippled PBS marketing and advertising because there were no longer guarantees that shows would run on the same day and hour everywhere in the country," according to historian Richard Reeves.[49] In 1975, Reed Irvine claimed that CPB was in violation of a statutory requirement that it maintain balance in its programming and sued to bring CPB under the political control of the Federal Communications Commission (FCC). The suit failed; but in the late 1980s, in their bid to have it sold to the private sector or have its federal funds cut drastically, conservatives resurrected the claim that CPB's "leftward" drift was illegal.

During the Nicaraguan contra war, the Reagan State Department had characterized National Public Radio as "Radio Managua on the Potomac." After Reed Irvine complained about a PBS documentary titled *Vietnam: A Television History*, PBS allowed Irvine to produce a one-hour rebuttal hosted by conservative actor Charlton Heston. With the founding of COMINT, the campaign reached fever pitch. According to Horowitz, "PBS has become a subsidiary of the Democratic Party . . . has produced incredibly one-sided programming from the far-left . . . has served the Clinton agenda. . . . NPR has hyped the Black Panthers. . . . NPR's sympathies are so much on the left side of the spectrum. . . . There are no senior figures at NPR who are conservative. . . . PBS programs regularly attack whites. . . . CPB for 25 years has been run by Democrats and liberals. It needs to change itself or go down."[50]

Like clockwork, the Lichters released a study, funded by the Smith Richardson Foundation, charging PBS with liberal bias. According to a critique of the study by FAIR editor Jim Naurekas, the Lichter study examined only PBS documentary programming. It left out newscasts like *The*

NewsHour with Jim Lehrer and talk shows like William Buckley's *Firing Line,* John McLaughlin's General Electric–funded *McLaughlin Group* and his *One on One, Tony Brown's Journal,* and *American Interests* with Morton Kondracke—thus neglecting a substantial conservative presence on PBS. Documentaries, of course, offer the perspectives of the filmmaker and are not presented as straight newscasts—and it was precisely these handful of public affairs documentaries like *Frontline* that the conservatives set out to discredit.

In their study, the Lichters identified only what they called "thematic messages," or explicit statements of opinion or evaluation, Naurekas reported. Since these constituted a minuscule portion of the overall reports, often less than 2 percent, they were not a reliable way of measuring the overall content of the broadcasts; if anything, the fact that there were so few "thematic messages" seemed to demonstrate how little opinion was contained in the broadcasts.

Naurekas also found the Lichters' coding of messages as liberal or conservative to be highly misleading. A section on how PBS treated the Constitution counted all messages in favor of free speech and freedom of the press as liberal, though one would expect broad bipartisan support for these rights. Whether they came from conservative or liberal sources, all messages saying "Religion should advocate social change" were construed to show liberal bias. FAIR found that any statement that described racial discrimination as a condition of American society was coded as "liberal," even when it came from a segregationist. The Lichter study accused PBS of bias against apartheid by pitting opponents of the practice against "extreme," rather than moderate, proponents, as if there were such a thing as a moderate proponent of apartheid. Once again, the Lichters proved nothing except their own excellent sense of political timing.[51]

The Lichter survey powered the propaganda offensive by Horowitz, who took his case to Washington, which then provided about 40 percent of CPB's budget. In the Capitol, he found an eager audience in Bob Dole and Newt Gingrich, two very different GOP politicians who nonetheless shared a Nixonian propensity to lash out at the "liberal media." In the final days of his failing presidential campaign in 1996, Dole announced, "The country belongs to the people, not the *New York Times.* . . . Don't read that stuff! Don't watch television! You make up your mind! Don't let them make up your mind for you!" He attacked the *Times* as "the biggest apologist for Bill Clinton in the world" and "an arm of the DNC." "We are not going to let the media steal this election," he said. (Kathleen Hall Jamieson observed, "If there was a bias in the amount and prominence of reporting in the *New York Times,* it was pro-Dole.")

Gingrich believed that if the public did not trust the information it got from the professional media, the Right could win more influence. Shortly after becoming Speaker of the House in 1994, Gingrich told a group of corporate executives that American newspaper editorial boards were filled with "socialists," and he implored them to use their economic power to force the papers to adopt more conservative views.[52]

Instigated by Horowitz, congressional hearings on "balance" at PBS were convened; Big Bird from *Sesame Street* came under attack; and funding was cut—although the bid to privatize PBS faltered. The right-wing offensive was a spectacular success, however, in getting PBS to "expand the spectrum," getting more conservative-produced shows on the air, and making PBS executives less secure about green-lighting progressive-oriented programming in the face of a well-funded right-wing harassment campaign.

The Scaife, Olin, and Bradley foundations became cofunders with PBS of a barrage of programming clearly biased by right-wing ideology and rife with conflicts of interest. "An informal scan through PBS public-affairs offering from 1992 to the present turns up at least 17 instances in which a single program or continuing series underwritten or co-funded by [three right-wing foundations] served as a platform for the views of [the three right-wing foundations'] grantees and their organizations," journalism professor and former CBS and ABC newsman Jerry Landay wrote in *Current* magazine in 2001.[53] These right-wing shows include American Enterprise Institute fellow Ben Wattenberg's weekly *Think Tank* series; a show called *Peggy Noonan on Values,* hosted by the former Reagan and Bush speechwriter; and even a program called *The Conservatives,* as if, after eight years of Reagan in office, viewers needed further introduction.

Another series originally called *Reverse Angle* and later renamed *National Desk* was a heavily subsidized collaboration between two conservative columnists, Fred Barnes and Morton Kondracke, and Lionel Chetwynd, a conservative Hollywood producer and cofounder with Horowitz of the Wednesday Morning Group. Horowitz was hired as a consultant. As

Landay reported, the series flouted established journalistic practices as it promoted the conservative agenda on school vouchers, "traditional morality," and deregulation—with such hosts as conservative columnist Charles Krauthammer and Larry Elder, a right-wing African American radio talk show host who almost lost his show owing to charges of racism until Horowitz raised $500,000 for a campaign to keep him on the air.

As Jennifer L. Pozner reported in *Extra!*, typical was a three-part series on the "gender wars," which posed the question of whether "advancement of women" comes at the expense of men. The program—which appeared to be based on the widely disputed Scaife-funded work of American Enterprise Institute scholar Christina Hoff Sommers, author of *Who Stole Feminism?: How Women Have Betrayed Women* and *The War Against Boys*—attacked pay equity, affirmative action, and Title IX (the federal antidiscrimination law in education). Advocates of something called "the boys' rights movement" asserted that equality was leading to "feminized" boys and high rates of young male suicide, and they predicted "gender Armageddon." Conservative economist Walter Williams, whose post at George Mason University was underwritten by Olin and who is one of Rush Limbaugh's substitute hosts, declared that "mental differences" between the sexes rendered women unfit for military service. The series was cohosted by Laura Ingraham.[54]

The *Frontline* documentaries aspire to standards of objectivity and fairness in their execution, and they are produced and reported by independent documentary filmmakers. The conservatives play a radically different game. The conservative pressure tactics saw to it that the professional *Frontline* broadcasts were now "balanced" by grossly biased programs, like *National Desk,* that were funded, produced, and reported by right-wing mouthpieces.

In this way, Horowitz's COMINT was able to move PBS in the direction of the corporate-controlled media. Right-wing talk show hosts Ben Wattenberg, William Buckley, John McLaughlin, and Tony Brown filled the PBS schedule. In 2003, PBS announced that conservative pundit Tucker Carlson of CNN would be awarded his own show. *The NewsHour with Jim Lehrer* was flooded with "experts" from the right-wing message machine, and it gave permanent berths to ideologues like the *Wall Street Journal's* Paul Gigot and David Brooks of *The Weekly Standard*, which launched false attacks on PBS's Bill Moyers in an effort to silence him.

Though the Lichters' methodological mumbo jumbo is not reliable, by their own reckoning *NewsHour* was more pro-Bush in 1992 than were any of the three major networks or CNN; and in 1996, they claimed it was more pro-Dole than any network except CBS. "My impression is that PBS saw [the bias charge] as a problem and moved to correct this," Robert Lichter told the *Boston Globe*. Lichter, perhaps, was being overly modest.

Thirty years after the appearance of Edith Efron's *The News Twisters*, the Right had a pair of bookends. Former CBS news reporter and producer Bernard Goldberg did not need a slush fund from Richard Nixon to hit the best-seller charts.

For thirty years, the right wing had spent tens of millions of dollars on its "liberal media" campaign. Though no evidence had been adduced to support the charge, the Big Lie took hold. The media was widely distrusted as an institution. Not only did upward of three-quarters of Republicans say they believed the media was liberally biased, so too did 47 percent of Democrats. A vast Republican Noise Machine had been established, as both the beneficiary of the claim and its chief propagator. For the most part, the mainstream media still resisted the claim as invalid but, nonetheless, seemed to internalize it and sometimes succumb to its pressures—compromising objectivity and relaxing standards to appease the right wing. Certainly, rather than vigorously defending itself against false, politically motivated attacks, the mainstream media had become a primary vehicle through which the Right successfully publicized its "liberal media" claims. Few argued the contrary case, and those who did were seldom heard.

Bernard Goldberg had a preconditioned market. He had something else as well, a selling point that all the authors and media monitors and conservative pundits and Republican politicians before him did not have: He was a media insider. Before Goldberg, everyone in the business of branding the media "liberal" was either a professional conservative or funded by the Right. It was as if the Raelians had funded a campaign to tell the world the media was biased against them—and the world took them at their word.

Goldberg's book was called *Bias: A CBS Insider Exposes How the Media Distort the News*. Presumably, his résumé as a former CBS news reporter and producer for twenty-eight years gave him unique authority to validate the Right's claims. Goldberg had been one of *them*. He portrayed himself as a courageous industry whistleblower and a disaffected Democrat.

He also was very angry, a trait shared by many books that sell to the right-wing audience. In 1995, in an act of public defiance, Goldberg had taken his complaints about CBS News directly to the right-wing camp, splaying them across the opinion page of the *Wall Street Journal*. Dan Rather, whom Goldberg had considered a friend and mentor, was unhappy. Goldberg's colleagues gave him the cold shoulder. Though he had violated the terms of his employment contract by failing to get clearance for outside writing, he was not fired. Still, he felt put out to pasture. He licked his wounds on CBS's dime. When his pension kicked in a few years later, Goldberg resigned and took his revenge.

In his book, he portrays CBS as a "mafia," a dictatorship, and a prison, headed by "the Dan." CBS executives and producers are "Dan's bitches." Goldberg wrote that he imagined himself in a Witness Protection Program. *Bias* sold more than a half-million copies. President George W. Bush was photographed carrying a copy under his arm.

The success of *Bias* was evidence against its thesis. It sold not despite the media but because of it. Though no one mentioned it, the book had conservative backing: It was published by Regnery, a right-wing Washington house that filled the best-seller lists in the 1990s with a slew of largely fictional anti-Clinton tracts packaged as nonfiction. Goldberg hawked it through the newly powerful right-wing talk radio network and all over cable television. "Here's a guy who says what I would venture 70 percent of the American people agree with—that the press is liberal—and he's in huge trouble," Rush Limbaugh bellowed. "I like guys who put their balls on the line like you do," Chris Matthews told Goldberg during an hour-long *Hardball* love fest on MSNBC. (The special broadcast was done for the paperback edition of *Bias*—which was published simultaneously with media critic Eric Alterman's *What Liberal Media?*, a book that argued the opposite case yet was not afforded the same opportunity on *Hardball*.)

Bias was sold by the right-wing press, from *National Review* to the *Wall Street Journal*. It was sold by conservatives in the mainstream press, like John Leo of *U.S. News & World Report*. And it was sold by the "liberal" press. "*Bias* should be taken seriously," said a review in the *New York Times*. "Mr. Goldberg has done real homework. . . . He asks questions that are worth asking." As the book climbed the *Times* best-seller list, that quote was pasted onto its cover. On FOX News, Goldberg crowed, "I would say 90 percent of what I've heard and read about the book has been positive."

Goldberg's case against the media followed a now-familiar conservative line. The "liberal media" boiled down to ABC, NBC, CBS, and the *New York Times*—perhaps the four most highly regarded journalistic institutions in the country. Unlike the right-wing media, these media aspired to the universal standards of objective, nonpartisan journalism. Though they duly reported on conservative views and carried conservative opinion, they were not smothered by right-wing punditry or "products" from the right-wing message machinery.

Like the Lichters, Goldberg says that liberal bias is neither overt nor covert; it's subconscious, a convenient assertion because it is impossible to prove. "What happens is far worse because it's more insidious," he explained. "The liberal elites live in places like Manhattan and Washington. They go to cocktail parties and dinner parties. . . . They mingle with their smart, hip sophisticated liberal friends." "The Dan" attends such parties, wearing Savile Row suits that Goldberg improbably claimed cost more than Goldberg's home.

Notably, Goldberg averred, as did the Lichters, that this subconscious bias does *not* much affect issues of partisan politics. According to Goldberg and other conservative media critics, the media is not biased in favor of Democrats or against Republicans. By and large, conservatives are happy with the coverage of politics. Their anxiety boils down to the "social issues."

Goldberg's complaint seems a product of his own conservative cultural views and resentments. The people who go to the East Coast cocktail parties have attitudes on race and sex that don't agree with his. The media elite are charged with favoring civil rights, women's rights, and gay rights. They are too "sensitive" in their portrayal of ethnic minorities, women, and gays on television. "White producers are very sensitive to what black colleagues feel," Goldberg revealed conspiratorially. They don't often enough quote "mainstream" women like Phyllis Schlafly who "say that it's more important for more women to spend more time with their children, and not bring home a second income." "Even Sam Donaldson, one of the toughest reporters in all of television journalism, turns into a sniveling wimp when it comes to challenging feminists." These biased liberals allowed a producer with AIDS to work on a documentary about AIDS. The documentary failed to ask AIDS victims, "How did you get it?" The liberals are "victims of America correspondents." They are "compassionate." They are pawns of the "gay lobby," the "homeless lobby," and the "AIDS lobby." They call Indians "Native Americans." They call the handicapped "disabled." They are plagued by "white guilt." Goldberg referred to "American Racial Sin" as if it hadn't existed. Of affirmative action, Goldberg asked:

> Why should the children of Jesse Jackson or Colin Powell or Diana Ross get some kind of racial preference when they apply to college or go out for a job, but no "affirmative action" is given to the child of a white Anglo-Saxon Protestant coal miner for West Virginia?

According to Goldberg, the liberal media is not only "pro-" minorities, women, and gays; it is anti-white-heterosexual-male. In a strange chapter titled "Targeting Men," Goldberg criticized a tongue-in-cheek Father's Day story that asked, "Do we live better with men or without them?" Goldberg wanted to know if a story could be run asking, "Do we live better with blacks or without them?" Harry Smith of CBS once joked on the air that most men are "putzes." Goldberg wondered if he could have gotten away with saying, "I'm under the assumption that most black people are putzes." Katie Couric once asked an abandoned bride if she had thought about castration. An abandoned groom, Goldberg raged, would never be asked about chopping off breasts! Meredith Vieira of ABC's *The View*, interviewing baseball player Mike Piazza, asked him, "Let's talk about bats. Who has the biggest wood on the team?" Goldberg took offense at what he considered a sexually suggestive remark. Goldberg imagined Piazza firing back with, "Hey, Meredith, who has the biggest ta-tas?" If Piazza had fired back, a "snarling pack of post-feminists" would have "rip[ped] his mustache off by the bristles, right?"

Goldberg was so furiously letting off steam about seeing social trends he doesn't like reported in the media that he forgot to write about liberal bias in the media. When he moved beyond derisive character descriptions of his "politically correct" former colleagues, and his own disturbing hypothetical analogies, his examples did not demonstrate liberal bias.

Again and again, Goldberg complained that the TV news "dresses up reality" by showing heterosexual women as AIDS victims, rather than "reckless" gay men or drug-addled prostitutes, and by portraying homelessness as a problem of "blond-haired, blue-eyed" all-American families rather than of criminals and the mentally ill. While Goldberg may have been on firmer ground here, he attributed these biases to the fact that the TV news audience is overwhelmingly white and middle-class: They want to see people like themselves when they tune in.[55] The villain is ratings, not liberal bias, he concluded. He also railed against NBC for treating its parent company, General Electric, with kid gloves. That isn't liberal bias, either.[56]

Once in the book Goldberg attempted a verifiable empirical claim. He argued that conservatives are more often labeled than liberals. "In the world of the Jennings and the Brokaws and the Rathers, conservatives are out of the mainstream and have to be identified. Liberals, on the other hand, are the mainstream and don't have to be identified," he wrote. He did no research to establish the assertion.

Stanford researcher Geoffrey Nunberg checked the numbers and published his results in *The American Prospect* in 2002. Nunberg designed a database search of twenty major U.S. dailies, choosing ten well-known politicians, five liberals, and five conservatives. "[T]he average liberal legislator has a better than 30 percent *greater* likelihood of being given a political label than the average conservative does," Nunberg concluded. He replicated the same results by changing the names of the politicians and limiting the search to only three—all presumably "liberal"—newspapers, the *New York Times,* the *Washington Post,* and the *Los Angeles Times.* "If the media wind up labeling liberals somewhat more than conservatives, that's chiefly an indication of how phobic they've become about charges of bias from the right," Nunberg wrote.

When challenged during his TV appearances, Goldberg invariably replied that since so many Americans believe the claim that the media is liberal, he couldn't be wrong. But as Nunberg pointed out, this logic has a circular quality to it. "In newspaper articles published since 1992, the word 'media' appears within seven words of 'liberal bias' 469 times and within seven words of 'conservative bias' just 17 times," he wrote. "If people are disposed to believe that the media have a liberal bias, it's because that's what the media have been telling them all along."

Yet while Goldberg was a beneficiary of the organized Right's deliber-

ate "liberal media" strategy, he wrote with such raw emotion that it is difficult to consider him a knowing part of it. While Goldberg failed to prove his
"bias" case empirically, he clearly believes what he wrote; millions agree
with him, and not only because they've been conditioned by a relentless
barrage of right-wing propaganda making the case for decades. Like Spiro
Agnew before him, Goldberg hit a nerve; his book had genuine appeal, and
it revealed, perhaps unintentionally, certain truths.

Goldberg seemed to give voice to many Americans who see as "liberal
bias" reporting on social and cultural values, particularly on matters of race
and sex, that do not comport with their own. In the Lichters' vernacular
from the mid-1980s, these news consumers were the "parochials" and the
"Moral Majority constituency." Twenty years previous, in the Goldwater
era, they were the people who were angry with what they saw as media support for the civil rights movement. The perceived "bias" seems to be more
on the part of the ideologically charged viewer than of the media.

Almost by definition, the sensibilities of those who hold views that are
outside the mainstream, whether on the right or the left, will be offended
by some of the reporting, images, and attitudes they are exposed to in what
is called, for good reason, the mainstream media. The cultural Right's genuine antipathy toward the mainstream media seems a reflection of the fact
that, despite its impressive ability to direct political discourse through the
media, the cultural Right remains a minority in the United States and therefore does not agree with a lot of the social content it sees and reads in the
media.

To Goldberg and his audience, mainstream media treatment of women,
minorities, and gays really does seem "liberally biased"; to those outside the
right wing, it seems unprejudiced. To these cultural rightists, an "unbiased"
media might be implicitly or even explicitly sexist, racist, and homophobic—
precisely the stances struck in Goldberg's *Bias*. Such a media might be skeptical toward working women, scapegoat minorities, regard homosexuality as
an abomination, treat the downtrodden without compassion, or caricature
environmentalists. To those outside the right wing, this sort of media would
look reactionary and intolerant.

There never was a "liberal media elite"—imposing a rigid ideological
agenda and strict party line on the conservative American majority in a ruth-

less propaganda campaign—that Reed Irvine, Irving Kristol, Kevin Phillips, William Rusher, Samuel Francis, Bernard Goldberg, and eventually the entire conservative movement and broad swaths of the country, imagined. But the conservative media elite created ostensibly to supplant it was quite real.

When Spiro Agnew spoke in 1969, right-wing media was a fringe phenomenon. When *Bias* was published in 2001, political talk radio, Christian broadcasting, the FOX News Channel, a parade of TV talking heads, widely syndicated op-ed columnists, and major best-selling authors all reflected Goldberg's cultural biases. Through a process something like osmosis, the values of this right-wing media were bleeding into the regular media; but as Goldberg's complaint showed, never fast enough to please the right wing.

CHAPTER FOUR
THE FIFTH COLUMNISTS

N THE MIDST OF THE BURGEONING Watergate scandal in 1973, Meg Greenfield, the deputy editorial page editor of the *Washington Post*, attended a symposium at Kenyon College in Ohio on relations between the press and politicians. The venomous attack on the press that had been unleashed by the Nixon White House and its supporters spilled over into the proceedings. Robert Novak, whose column, co-written with Rowland Evans, was syndicated by the *Chicago Sun-Times* and picked up by the *Post*, delivered a searing indictment of the press for liberal bias, becoming one of the first journalists to credit the idea being promulgated by Reed Irvine.[1]

When they began writing their column together in the early 1960s, Evans and Novak were considered nonpartisan shoe leather reporters; but in the early 1970s, as antiwar protests heated up, the columnists targeted the American Left, and the Democratic Party, with polemical attacks. Crossing the line from analysis and insider tips into rank partisan slogan-eering, Evans and Novak, who were nicknamed "Errors and No Facts" by Washington insiders, put in print the false and inflammatory slogan that smeared Democratic presidential candidate George McGovern as favoring "acid, amnesty, and abortion." Testimony in the Senate Watergate hearings showed that officials from the Nixon reelection committee were leaking memos "on plain bond" to Evans and Novak.[2] The Republican p.r. department now had a voice in the mainstream press, and it would soon have a multitude of others.

The duo began to specialize in taking dictation from Republican sources. In the 1970s, they relied on Nixon Defense Secretary Melvin Laird and Capitol Hill aide Richard Perle to attack the policy of détente with the Soviet Union. Novak took personal credit for Ronald Reagan's adoption of the then-unorthodox supply-side economics theory—which posed that government receipts increase as taxes are cut—through heavy promotion in his column. The theory was flawed, but ensuing deficits became a conservative rationale for slashing federal spending. In his memoir *The Triumph of Politics*, Reagan budget director David Stockman referred to the Evans and Novak column as his "billboard." During the 1980s, a front-page story in the *Wall Street Journal* knocked the pair for "openly plugging their friends and opposing their enemies for top jobs in government." *The New Republic* reported that newspapers were dropping the column over its exaggerated claims of Soviet expansionism and its reflexive defense of right-wing dictatorships. A *Washingtonian* magazine poll of the Washington press corps revealed that Evans and Novak were its "least respected" members.

Novak had a financial interest in the economic policies he promoted. His personal money manager was Richard Gilder, a wealthy investment adviser who founded the Political Club for Growth, a PAC that pushed supply-side economics, slashing the capital gains tax, and privatizing Social Security. Gilder was able to devise an investment strategy based on anticipation of the changes in public policy that he was lobbying for through the PAC and that Evans and Novak were plumping in their column. Gilder attended the annual conferences sponsored by Evans and Novak, where the well-off subscribers to their newsletter mingled with GOP bigwigs, who in turn doubled as the columnists' sources.

Though they were writing an op-ed column, the pair continued to refer to themselves as journalists, yet they hid behind the "opinion" designation when, as often happened, they got stories wrong. In a 1985 libel suit filed against the columnists by Bertell Ollman, a Marxist professor who claimed that an Evans and Novak column falsely describing him as having no stand-

ing in the profession caused him to lose an academic appointment, the U.S.
Court of Appeals for the District of Columbia ruled by a margin of six to
five for the columnists. Judge Robert H. Bork, who was in the majority,
wrote that the mix of fact and opinion in the column made it "rhetorical
hyperbole" and, hence, not actionable.[3]

Though Evans is now deceased, Novak still churns out prodigious
amounts of tendentious copy that, despite its journalistic flaws, roils the
political waters by virtue of being published in major newspapers. In summer 2003, a Novak column identifying the wife of a Bush administration
critic as an undercover CIA operative plunged the Bush administration into
a political crisis and triggered a criminal investigation into the leak.
According to subsequent news accounts, Bush officials eager to harm their
critic shopped the secret information to six reporters who declined to print
it before Novak did. Clumsily trying to spin the scandal for an administration that he had wounded, Novak made a series of dubious claims (the identity of the operative had never been "much of a secret") and contradicted
his own original reporting (the undercover "operative" was now just an
"analyst"). Apparently, neither Novak's newspaper, the *Chicago Sun-Times,*
nor the op-ed editors at the hundreds of papers that carry Novak's column
flagged the column as problematic.

Rather than suffer professional sanction for being complicit in a political smear campaign that might have endangered U.S. intelligence assets
through the agent's exposure, Novak was hailed by respected professionals
with whom he has rubbed elbows as he successfully inserted himself, and
his brand of reporting, into the journalistic mainstream. "All of us who know
Bob Novak know he's one of the best reporters in the business and has been
for nearly half a century," said Novak's CNN colleague Wolf Blitzer.

Also on the dais in 1973 at Kenyon College was a thirty-year-old speechwriter for conservative GOP Senator Gordon Allott and a sometime contributor to *National Review* and *The American Spectator:* George Will. A
protégé of Irving Kristol, Will had edited the American Enterprise Institute's
1972 media-bashing book. It was the persnickety Will, not the bulldog
Novak, who intrigued Greenfield.

According to a *Washington Post* profile in the mid-1980s, Will, the son of a liberal midwestern academic, had honed his rhetorical style by playing intellectual big fish in the small pond of Trinity College, where he headed Students for Kennedy, and was remembered as a prototypical white-socked nerd. He returned from a stint at Oxford as a Tory conservative and a Barry Goldwater booster.[4]

Greenfield made an inquiry and learned that, since Allott had been defeated for reelection despite Nixon's landslide, Will was about to leave the Senate staff to become *National Review's* "Washington editor." Returning to Washington, she saw to it that Will, who wrote for the right-wing publications and think tanks that would soon form a powerful pipeline into the mainstream media, began contributing columns to the op-ed page, even as he moonlighted as a speechwriter for Senator Jesse Helms of North Carolina, who had been elected to the Senate in 1972 on the strength of his racist appeals.

The overture to Will came at a time—after Agnew's assaults on the press and Nixon's 1972 landslide victory—when both the *Post* and the *New York Times* were seeking a pro-Nixon voice as a defensive maneuver and were competing for the services of William Safire. Unlike Will, Safire had not apprenticed in the right-wing press. A former p.r. man, his credentials were as a Republican operative and wordsmith, who, in the Nixon White House, helped carry out Nixon's attacks on the media, including on the *Times* itself. Safire had penned Spiro Agnew's infamous characterization of the press corps as "nattering nabobs of negativism."

Now Safire was poised to benefit directly from those attacks, from which he would later distance himself in his memoir *Before the Fall*. In a move that *Time* called a "peace offering" to the Nixon administration, Safire went to the *Times*. Upon Safire's appointment, the venerable journalist David Halberstam wrote to the publisher that Safire was "not a Conservative . . . but a paid manipulator. He is not a man of ideas or politics but of tricks."[5]

In what looked like an attempt to live down or even to avenge Watergate, Safire became preoccupied with unearthing scandalous material to damage Democratic political figures; two decades later he was still at it, publishing in the *Times* phony allegations of criminality among top Clinton White House aides and publishing false suggestions of an imminent indictment of First Lady Hillary Rodham Clinton. Yet no matter how hard he tried to force the analogy, Safire was never able to find a Democrat who came close to rivaling the crookedness of his old boss Nixon.

Will, meanwhile, became the *Post's* in-house conservative, writing a nationally syndicated op-ed column for the paper and another column in the *Post*-owned *Newsweek,* where he would rotate on the back page with his patron, Greenfield. Though his manner suggested otherwise, Will never really transcended the role of congressional staffer. His attempt at writing a serious work of political philosophy, *Statecraft as Soulcraft,* was risible. His column was mainly a way of popularizing the work of other conservatives who toiled in the Right's propaganda mills. Will's reputation for erudition would later be tarnished by a disheveled Georgetown bookworm named Timothy Dickinson, who told the *Wall Street Journal* that he supplied Will with many of his literary and historical references. The revelation was spoofed in Garry Trudeau's *Doonesbury* comic strip.

Though he wished to be viewed as above the fray, Will was every bit the dishonest attack dog that Novak was. In a column titled "Not Like Ike," on the presidential candidacy of General Wesley Clark, Will recycled a false story from Rupert Murdoch's *Weekly Standard* charging that Clark had given conflicting accounts of how he learned that the Bush administration had sought to tie Saddam Hussein to the September 11 terrorist attacks. To counter Clark's statement that he received the information on White House intentions in a call from a Middle East think tank based in Canada, Will wrote, "There is no such institution." But there is such an institution, which Clark later identified as the Montreal office of the Begin-Sadat (BESA) Center for Strategic Studies.

As it happened, 1973 turned out to be a banner year for the mainstreaming of right-wing views into the prestige print press. Over at the *Wall Street Journal,* the largest-circulation newspaper in the country, thirty-three-year-old Robert L. Bartley took over the editorial page upon the sudden death of Vermont Royster, a more traditional conservative. Bartley was another Kristol protégé, a student of his *Public Interest* magazine, and a collaborator with Kristol and George Will on the AEI book. With the imprimatur of Dow Jones & Company, the newspaper's publisher, Bartley turned the page into a rabidly partisan and indispensable appendage of the fledgling conservative movement. (His first act was to hire Will, who left for the *Post*, and the small Washington fish pond, soon thereafter.)

Joining the paper's board of contributors, Kristol worked with Bartley to popularize supply-side economics, devising a strategy to attack the media's objective reporting on the economy in order to increase coverage of the theory. "I was not certain of the economic merits but quickly saw its political possibilities," Kristol conceded in a book of essays, *Neoconservatism: The Autobiography of an Idea*. Perfecting Kristol's antimedia strategy, the *Journal* would be an influential showcase for a variety of equally doubtful "products" from the right-wing think tanks.

Still defending the discredited supply-side theory after Reagan left office, Bartley published a book, *The Seven Fat Years*, in which he measured the "prosperity" of the Reagan years by leaving out the recession of the early 1980s.[6] During the second Bush administration, the *Journal* popularized the notion that low-income people who do not make enough money to pay federal income taxes but pay other taxes—"lucky duckies," in *Journal*ese—should be made to bear more of the tax burden "to get his or her blood boiling with tax rage." Soon, the line that low-income workers who "pay no taxes" should get no tax relief was passing from the lips of everyone from Republican leader Tom DeLay to Robert Novak to FOX's Sean Hannity.

The *Journal* constituted an ideological training ground for a new generation of young conservative writers and editors who then dispersed into the rest of the media. For example, David Asman became a news anchor at FOX; David Brooks went to *The Weekly Standard*, PBS's *NewsHour with Jim Lehrer*, *Newsweek*, and finally to the *New York Times* op-ed page; while Max Boot used his Olin fellowship at the Council on Foreign Relations to publish op-eds for the *New York Times* and the *Washington Post*. John Fund, ghostwriter of Rush Limbaugh's error-filled book *The Way Things Ought to Be*, spent time dispensing political advice to Newt Gingrich and his close friend Grover Norquist and appearing on MSNBC's *Hardball*.

Bartley did not believe in the traditional journalistic standard of objectivity and worked to destroy it. In a 2003 column, he wrote, "I think we're coming to the end of the era of 'objectivity' that has dominated journalism over this time. We need to define a new ethic that lends legitimacy to opinion, honestly disclosed and disciplined by some sense of propriety."[7] After stepping down as the *Journal's* editorial page editor in 2003, Bartley became "senior editorial adviser" of *The American Spectator.* He died a few months later.

Unhappy with the objective news coming from the *Journal's* news department, Bartley trained his staff to compose "reported" editorials that purported to bring to light new facts that were implicitly hidden or ignored by the "liberal media." The idea of possessing special knowledge had historically appealed to a certain type of right-wing mentality; although before Bartley came along, that psychic need had been filled largely by self-published books, crank newsletters, talk radio, and other marginalia. More often than not, Bartley's "facts" turned out to be lies, half-truths, and innuendos. The *Journal* perpetrated the hoax that the Soviet Union was poisoning its adversaries by dropping "yellow rain" in Southeast Asia. The mysterious substance turned out to be bee feces. During the 1984 presidential campaign, the *Journal* suggested that vice presidential candidate Geraldine Ferraro's father-in-law had mob ties; the man was deceased, so he could not defend himself.[8]

In the 1990s, Bartley's page was a repository for virtually every wild anti-Clinton smear and rumor in circulation, from drug running to murder. Former White House counsel Vincent Foster, who was the target of personal innuendo from the *Journal* editorial page before and after he committed suicide, mentioned the editors' "lies" in his suicide note. The *Journal* published five books of anti-Clinton editorials covering more than 2,500 pages on the Whitewater scandal, which came to nothing. Paul Gigot, who replaced Bartley in the job in 2001, said of Clinton, "He was great for my career. He was great for business."

Bartley used the fact that he ran an opinion page as cover for injecting right-wing "news" into the wider media. In a strategy broadly adopted by right-wing columnists and magazine and Web site writers, the conservatives, calling themselves, as Bartley did, "opinion journalists," were able to have it both ways: reporting "stories" that would never meet the journalistic standards of legitimate news organizations, while relying on their status as "opinion writers" to avoid the scrutiny reporters must withstand.

Perhaps the most egregious instance of the *Journal's* war on journalism came in 1999, when *Journal* editorial writer and TV critic Dorothy Rabinowitz broke a "story" that accused President Bill Clinton of a heinous criminal felony: rape. Over the years, the allegation had been rejected by several professional reporters and news organizations because it was unverified and uncorroborated. The accuser, Juanita Broaddrick, had previously sworn in an affadavit that she had not been raped. The credulous *Journal* piece put news organizations under pressure to air their own versions of the story that had been held back for journalistic reasons. For weeks before an NBC News interview with Broaddrick aired, conservative activists had bombarded NBC with demands that the network "free Lisa Myers," the NBC reporter who had conducted the iced Broaddrick interview. When the *Journal* published the allegations, NBC aired the interview. In a textbook case of character assassination instigated by right-wing media, the unproven rape story was broadcast around the world, leaving the public to play the role previously entrusted to professional news organizations: discerning whether there was anything to the charges or not.[9]

One current *Journal* columnist, former Reagan and Bush *père* speechwriter Peggy Noonan, is not content simply to breach journalistic rules and stretch the truth. Her political columns often adopt a fictional form. Noonan has written up her dreams, her daydreams, her visions, and her apparitions. Life, she has written, is "an illusion," "a shadow," "a story," and "a madness." She has imagined herself to be Hillary Clinton, conducting an unhinged interior monologue. She has pretended to be Senator Paul Wellstone speaking from the grave. And she has even channeled God, as he tells us, "You're all in a heap of trouble." In 2003, Noonan's exposure in the *Journal* earned her a slot as a "prime-time commentator" on MSNBC and a contributor to NBC News, where she works the values beat, identifying the Republican Right and its leaders with God and goodness, while stigmatizing Democrats as un-American and abnormal. During the 2000 ballot recount in Florida, Noonan compared the Republican battle against Democrats to the United States' war with Nazi Germany. "The triumph of the normal" was how Noonan described GOP gains in the November 2002 elections on MSNBC.

Yet it was conservative influence at the *Washington Post,* the most widely circulated newspaper in the nation's capital and once considered a beacon of liberalism, that has been perhaps the signal achievement of the Right in print media. The incursion was largely the handiwork of Meg Greenfield, herself something of a neoconservative—a "1950s Democrat," as she put it. Greenfield tended to be a foreign policy hawk and an economic and social moderate. She came to the *Post* in 1968 from *The Reporter*, a cold war liberal magazine, once edited by Irving Kristol, which folded when its readers would no longer countenance its strident support for the Vietnam War.

Unusual for an editorial page editor, Greenfield thought of herself as anti-ideological. In disposition, she was certainly not "a cause person," as she once said, making her an early skeptic of the women's movement. IF LIBERATED, I WILL NOT SERVE, announced a plaque adorning her office. Greenfield's view was that she had "made it" on her own before the women's movement came along, explained *Post* matriarch Katharine Graham in her memoir, *Personal History.*[10] Greenfield's approach suited Graham, who called herself a "centrist" and once said, "Papers that want to serve and keep their readership cannot afford to be eccentric or extreme."[11] In 1979, Graham removed Greenfield's more liberal boss, Philip Geyelin, and appointed Greenfield in his place.

Whether she set out to shape the times or merely reflected them, more than perhaps anyone in mainstream print journalism, Greenfield moved the political center to the right. While her columns unabashedly criticized the Democrats' partisanship, critics observed that she hired a long line of right-wing partisans to write for her editorial page. The shift at the *Post* had a tremendous impact on the entire class of Washington-based liberal and centrist pundits, for whom the *Post* editorial page was and remains to this day the center of gravity. During the Reagan years, the paper supported aid to the Nicaraguan contras (a defining ideological issue), and the *Post* waited to gently oppose the nomination of Robert Bork to the Supreme Court until it was already dead.

What Greenfield considered open-mindedness, the conservatives considered an opportunity. During her editorship, Greenfield joined Graham at long lunches with Nancy Reagan, a relationship that Mrs. Reagan revealed years later in a memoir. Greenfield also held weekly Saturday lunches with George Will, who had helped brief Reagan in the presidential campaign; he then praised Reagan's performance on television. Will threw an inaugural party to introduce Reagan to Washington; Will's first wife, Madeleine, was appointed to a post in the administration. Joining the two at lunch was *New Republic* neocon Charles Krauthammer, a trained psychiatrist whom Greenfield also recruited to the paper. Like Will, Krauthammer struck an intellectual pose but had done no significant intellectual work. In his columns, he has misused his psychiatric training to "diagnose" Democrats as mentally ill, writing of Senator Edward M. Kennedy's "derangement" and referring to Bush critics such as PBS's Bill Moyers as "pathological." For his labors, the Bradley Foundation, in an imitation of the liberal MacArthur Foundation's "genius" awards, gave Krauthammer a $250,000 award in 2003. Greenfield called the lunch bunch "the Tong"—a reference to a secret fraternal society of Chinese in the United States once known for gang warfare.[12]

Casting her net further right, Greenfield brought on R. Emmett Tyrrell Jr., of *The American Spectator* and Michael Kelly from *The New Republic;* the latter's work was widely touted by Rush Limbaugh. She published a weekly contribution from Robert Samuelson, whom Limbaugh calls one of his "favorite newspaper columnists." Greenfield filled the op-ed page with regular contributions from former Republican officeholders and neocon ideologists such as Henry Kissinger, Jeane Kirkpatrick, William Bennett, William Kristol, and Robert Kagan; Kagan became a regular columnist. In 1997, Colman McCarthy—then the only in-house columnist as far to the left as Novak, Will, and Krauthammer were to the right—was fired. Concerned that McCarthy's syndication numbers were sliding, the *Post* said it was taking "a cue from the marketplace."

After two decades at the helm, Greenfield died in 1999. In an appreciation in Murdoch's *Weekly Standard*, conservative writer Michael Barone, whom Greenfield had brought to the *Post* editorial page staff in 1982, wrote, "Meg Greenfield, the editorial-page editor of the *Washington Post*, who died May 13, was one of the great patrons of conservative ideas over the last 25 years. . . . Meg Greenfield was not just responding to the intellectual marketplace, she was also transmitting them, in her writing and in the writers she put before the public. 1990s conservatives owe a lot to this 1950s liberal."

Greenfield was replaced by *Post* foreign correspondent Fred Hiatt. As *Washingtonian* magazine described it, under Hiatt the *Post* became "the nation's most hawkish newspaper," endorsing President George W. Bush's hard line on Iraq. "Its editorial pages have expressed an over-the-top preemptive enthusiasm, arguing the case as repetitiously as Bush and nearly as cockily as [Donald] Rumsfeld," according to *Post* veteran William Greider.[13] Media critic Todd Gitlin found that between December 1, 2002, and February 21, 2003, as the United States debated the wisdom of war with Iraq, the op-ed page published thirty-nine hawkish commentaries and only twelve dovish ones.[14] While the page is by no means uniformly conservative, on Hiatt's watch *Washingtonian* noted strong support for right-wing Bush judges like Miguel Estrada and Priscilla Owen and enthusiasm for school voucher schemes.

Among those working under Hiatt as staff editorial writers was Anne Applebaum, who grew up in privileged liberal environs in Washington but moved abroad, making a name for herself in British journalism as an editor and columnist for two Tory publications, the *Daily Telegraph* and *The Spectator.* After following the 1994 senatorial campaign of convicted felon Oliver North, she decided the Senate would be elevated by his presence. Applebaum is married to Radek Sikorski, a disciple of Richard Perle and Jeane Kirkpatrick at the American Enterprise Institute. The couple has a "reputation for politically incorrect social mischief," according to the *Post.*

Benjamin Wittes, who writes on legal affairs, frequently proffers the same views as the Federalist Society, a powerful network of right-wing lawyers and judges who seek ideological dominance for the Right through the courts. On a critical dividing line of the 1990s, the *Post* editorial page, and Wittes in particular, consistently defended Federalist Society stalwart Kenneth Starr and his investigations mauling the Clintons. Wittes is the author of the book *Starr: A Reassessment,* an attempt at revising the history of Starr's investigation by portraying Starr as a truth-seeker, "more sinned against than sinning." An outside reviewer in Wittes's own paper said that while "Clinton bashers may enjoy Wittes's visceral disgust" for Clinton, Wittes paid insufficient attention to evidence of Starr's political motives and accepted Starr's false explanations at face value.[15] Wittes has done outside writing for *The Weekly Standard.*

Although the *Post* treated the Clintons' 1978 Whitewater land deal as the second coming of Watergate, when a scandal about Bush's business dealings emerged in 2002, the *Post* rushed to put it down, running an editorial called "The Harken Energy Distraction," arguing that the scandal should be dismissed because "the Harken story took place years ago."

Conservatives applauded. Terry Eastland, former publisher of *The*

American Spectator and current publisher of *The Weekly Standard*, enthused, "The *Post* cannot be called liberal. I like it better than the *Wall Street Journal.*"

In the 1970s, the op-ed page itself was a relatively new phenomenon in print journalism. The vast majority of newspaper editorial boards in the country, controlled by individual owners and publishers, were historically Republican and conservative-leaning. The editorials were offset with mostly conservative local political columns and/or a few regular nationally syndicated columns by giants of the genre like Walter Lippmann, Joseph Alsop, and Joseph Kraft, all of whom shared the more or less centrist-liberal anti-Communist consensus of both the Democratic and the Republican mainstream that the reactionary right wished to supplant.

With space to fill on the new opinion pages, newspapers sought out right-wing voices in the 1970s, partly in reflection of the conservative bias of the newspaper editorial boards, which remained that way even as essentially apolitical media conglomerates like Knight-Ridder, Hearst, and Gannett—which had been quite conservative under founder Frank E. Gannett—acquired the independently owned papers. At the same time, the consolidation of newspaper ownership and the drive for greater profits were drastically reducing competition and diversity in the industry. As a result, once the newly syndicated right-wing columnists achieved prominence, their views would come to dominate entire metropolitan areas that, increasingly, were served by only one daily newspaper. And it is to local newspapers like the *Detroit News*, the *San Diego Union-Tribune,* and the *Indianapolis Star,* rather than those circulated nationally, that most readers turn to for information.

Many smaller chains and regionally influential papers stayed under the direct control of the right wing even in the period of consolidation. Among other things, these p.r. sheets for the GOP are captive markets for conservative columnists. The Freedom newspaper chain, for example, describes itself as a "libertarian-owned media company" and now publishes more than two dozen papers with a combined daily circulation of about one million. It is owned in part by Harry Hoiles, a major backer of the Cato Institute, and includes such newspapers as the *Orange County Register,* a force in

Southern California politics that has used its news pages, as well as its editorial columns, to forward its political agenda. That description also fits the *Oklahoman,* the largest-circulation daily newspaper in the state. Under the ownership of Edward Lewis Gaylord, it was "turned into a partisan bully," according to *Columbia Journalism Review.* The editorial page was run for many years by Patrick McGuigan, a former aide to Paul Weyrich, who refused to feature any liberal columnists on the op-ed page.[16]

Even if they didn't know it, the newspapers may have been recruiting conservatives in reaction to the mythology of the mid-1970s that the "liberal media" had brought down a Republican president and lost the Vietnam War, as well as to the concerted right-wing political attacks by Accuracy in Media and others. While there was no wholesale shift to the right in the public at this juncture, the media shifted to the right. Now joining William Buckley, a voice in the wilderness when his column was first syndicated in 1962—the same year that right-wing writer Westbrook Pegler lost his column for what the writer H. L. Mencken called "Ku Kluxery"—were right-wingers Safire, Will, Evans, Novak, *National Review's* William Rusher and Jeffrey Hart, James J. Kilpatrick, M. Stanton Evans, Phyllis Schlafly, Pat Buchanan, Kevin Phillips, and John Lofton, among others. Included in the group was former actor and radio announcer Ronald Reagan, who followed Barry Goldwater's path of becoming a syndicated columnist after leaving the governorship of California and preparing for a presidential run. Reagan was featured in about 175 newspapers and gave commentaries on more than 200 radio stations.

While the bow-tied Will set himself apart with a fusty Anglophilic bearing, most of the newcomers followed a variant of resentful right-wing populism and fiery cultural conservatism that was well to the right of mainstream public opinion, even in the Republican Party. They were pseudoconservatives. In 1976, even as they lambasted the media for being ideologically out of step, Buchanan, Rusher, and Phillips supported drafting for the national ticket George "Segregation Forever" Wallace, whom Buchanan described favorably as representing the "angry, white working man."

Whatever Buchanan, an improbable graduate of the Columbia School of Journalism, and his fellow Ivy League populists knew of the working class was gleaned from loftier heights. While inflaming and pandering to what

Buchanan had called "the booboisie in the hinterlands," the conservative media elite got rich and famous, earning ten and twenty times the salaries of the ink-stained newsroom workers whom they denounced as elitists. On the side, Evans, Novak, and Phillips sold lucrative political newsletters to the East Coast business and political elite. Evans lived and socialized in Georgetown; Buchanan bought a mansion in McLean, Virginia; and Phillips, a trade protectionist, tooled around in a Jaguar.

The Lippmann tradition of detachment and impartiality was contravened by the conservatives. With the exception of Evans and Novak, who left reporting for the more gainful field of punditry, none of the new conservative movement columnists had worked as truth-seeking journalists or academics before they began opining. Rather, they were trained in polemics in the right-wing propaganda mills or came from the hardball world of political campaigns. Yet while they had never worked in newsrooms, their central rhetorical and marketing technique was a running attack on how journalistic professionals did their jobs. United Feature syndicated columnist John Lofton, for instance, had gotten his start editing the Republican National Committee's *First Monday,* a magazine he used to launch attacks on journalism at the instruction of Charles Colson.[17]

Many of the conservative columnists, including Buchanan, Rusher, Phillips, and M. Stanton Evans, wrote books in this period that were undisguised strategy memos for the Republican Party. In *The Future of Conservatism, Los Angeles Times* syndicated columnist and CBS Spectrum radio commentator Evans wrote:

> Conservatives can win, but they will have to make their negative presentation superior to that of the Democrats. They must make their version of the bad things that will happen to the country under Democratic rule prevail over the Democrats' version of the bad things that will happen to the country under Republican rule.[18]

Twenty years later, the conservative publishers, editors, columnists, and writers had forfeited their independence altogether and been fully integrated into the sophisticated right-wing political network. *Forbes* magazine editor in chief Steve Forbes, a failed presidential candidate, sat on the boards of Heritage and of William Kristol's Project for the New American

Century. *National Review* publisher Thomas Rhodes was a director of the Club for Growth, a political action committee founded to drive the GOP further to the right, which its president, Stephen Moore, has called a "political terrorist organization." Walter Williams was a syndicated columnist, *Nightly Business Report* commentator, and frequent guest on *Nightline, Face the Nation,* and *The NewsHour with Jim Lehrer.* He also was a sometime substitute host for Rush Limbaugh and served on the boards of Citizens for a Sound Economy, co-chaired by former Republican House majority leader Dick Armey, the Hoover Institution, the Landmark Legal Foundation, the Pacific Legal Foundation, the Family Security Foundation, the Alexis de Tocqueville Institute, and the Institute for Research on the Economics of Taxation. The National Center for Policy Analysis wrote the tax plans in Newt Gingrich's Contract with America and popularized "Tax Slavery Day" and the "death tax" in studies released by GOP members of Congress; it also "sponsored" the op-ed columnists of its "senior fellows," former Delaware governor Pete du Pont (Scripps Howard) and former Reagan economics adviser Bruce Bartlett (Creators Syndicate). Robert Novak sat on the board of the right-wing Phillips Foundation.

Conservative media turned out in full force for the weekly strategy meetings convened by right-wing activist Grover Norquist—Peggy Noonan and John Fund of the *Journal,* representatives from *National Review* and the *Washington Times,* and a researcher for Bob Novak all checked in. The right-wing writers considered themselves members of the conservative movement "team," as Norquist put it. William Safire dispensed private political advice to Newt Gingrich. *National Review* founder William Buckley has written of "an off-the-record meeting of 20 right-wing editors, writers and diverse others . . . to inquire how enthusiastically should American conservatives labor for the election of George W. Bush." Kate O'Beirne, of *National Review* and CNN's *Capital Gang* and a former Heritage Foundation lobbyist, hosted regular lunches where conservatives like Andrew Sullivan could hear from Bush *fils* White House adviser Karl Rove. In New York, right-wing columnists and editors mingled with political activists at the Fabiani Society, named in honor of former Clinton aide Mark Fabiani, who had drawn attention to the right-wing media-political nexus in the mid-1990s. Before major Bush initiatives were announced, pundits went on conference calls to get their points down. On FOX's

Hannity & Colmes in January 2003, William Bennett referred to one such "phone call," the evening before his appearance, regarding Bush's tax cut proposals. Bennett called the proposed cuts a "bold stroke" and a "big, bold step." Bold, bold, bold, reverberated through the media for weeks thereafter.

The presence in the mainstream media of a vocal conservative "Tong" that reinforced one another's positions, was always on the attack, and didn't play by the rules of journalism couldn't help but skew the media playing field, the Republican Party, and, thus, politics overall, in a conservative direction. Political scientists have found that news commentary has a very high impact on public opinion.[19] By achieving prominence in the print opinion sector, the right wing had found a way to substantially direct political discourse. When Goldwater's heir campaigned for the presidency in 1980, Reagan's views would be well represented on the op-ed pages, giving his platform, which was not much different from Goldwater's, a measure of plausibility.

The contours of what would become a permanent right-wing attack campaign carried out in the free media and reinforced by paid political attack ads were starting to take shape that year. Scurrilous misinformation on Jimmy Carter was published in the mainstream media. William Safire pounded on what he called the "Billygate" scandal, by which he sought to falsely charge that the president's brother, Billy Carter, had improperly influenced administration policy on Libya; Evans and Novak falsely reported that White House counsel Lloyd Cutler had reached a secret handshake deal with emissaries of the Iranian government for the release of U.S. hostages held in that country.[20] The columns of James Kilpatrick, author of the book *The Southern Case for School Segregation*, were fodder for Reagan's famously hyperbolic anecdotes about "Big Government" spending.

"Not even the media—those 'sensation seeking columnists' of 1964—feel any wave of hate, though a few ripples of resentment remain," William Safire observed on the eve of Reagan's election.

The influx from the conservative movement into the media was balanced by no equivalent force of ideological warriors from the Left. The nearest approximation to the role played by the *Journal,* at least as conservatives claim to see it, is the *New York Times.* While the *Journal* has a higher circulation and deeper national reach, the *New York Times* is a special irritant to right-wingers, who resent its influence, and their failure—minus a few exceptions like Safire and David Brooks—to penetrate it. Yet the *Times* editorial page is not a liberal version of the *Journal's.* Nor is there any other liberal daily playing an attack-dog role.

The *New York Times* editorial page is consistently liberal on the issues; but it is not especially partisan or even political (it regularly endorses Republicans, such as Governor George Pataki); and it is rarely, if ever, intemperate.[21] It treats its opponents with respect and usually steers clear of attacks on the character, motives, and morality of Republicans. While liberals and liberalism are shredded every day in the *Journal,* conservatives and conservatism not only are spared this treatment in the *Times* but also are regularly given the benefit of the doubt. For instance, during the 2002 contretemps over the pro-segregationist comments of former Senate majority leader Trent Lott, the *Times* wrote that "no one could question President Bush's commitment to racial healing," overlooking the race-baiting campaign Bush ran in the 2000 presidential primary against GOP Senator John McCain and his nomination of anti–civil rights judges to the federal judiciary. By the same token, while the *Journal* always acts politically, deflecting charges leveled against conservatives, the *Times* has been known to publish sternly critical editorials on what it considers to be the ethical shortcomings of leading Democrats. (As with other right-wing media, the *Journal* will criticize Republicans when it benefits conservatism and will very occasionally tweak conservatives if it benefits the GOP.)

Like other major liberal metropolitan dailies, the *Times* tends to staff its editorial page with former reporters and editors, who take that training and sensibility with them to the opinion pages. They write subjectively but compose their arguments from facts. The difference between such liberal-leaning writers and their right-wing counterparts is not so much one of "ideology, but of technique," as the writer Anna Quindlen has observed. Unlike the *Journal* editorial writers, liberal editorialists are not professional ideologues, reliable partisans, or serial fabricators.

The difference in approach and tone could be seen during the Florida fiasco in 2000, when the liberal *Times* ran editorials with headlines like

TOWARD AN ORDERLY END, while shortly before succeeding Robert Bartley as editor of the *Journal,* columnist Paul Gigot lauded the "bourgeois riot" staged by Republican operatives to stop the counting of ballots with Bush very narrowly ahead. In May 2002, the Republican National Committee issued an "e-mail alert" citing editorials in the *New York Times* and the *Washington Post* both defending the Bush administration's handling of pre–September 11 intelligence reports and warning Democrats against recriminations. The Democratic National Committee found no succor in the *Wall Street Journal.*

An extensive July 2003 study of the partisan nature of four leading editorial pages, the *New York Times,* the *Washington Post,* the *Wall Street Journal,* and the *Washington Times,* proved the point. Sponsored by the Joan Shorenstein Center on the Press, Politics, and Public Policy at Harvard University and conducted by *American Prospect* editor Michael Tomasky, the study found that "while the pages are more or less equally partisan when it comes to supporting or opposing a given presidential administration's policy pronouncements, the conservative pages are more partisan—often far more partisan—with regard to the intensity with which they criticize the other side. Also, the paper finds, conservative editorial pages are far less willing to criticize a Republican administration than liberal pages are willing to take issue with a Democratic administration." (For purposes of the study, Tomasky counted the *Washington Post* as "liberal.")

Tomasky found that the liberal papers criticized President Bill Clinton 30 percent of the time, while the conservative papers criticized President George W. Bush only 7 percent of the time. The conservative papers praised George W. Bush's administration 77 percent of the time, while the liberal papers praised the Clinton administration only 30 percent of the time. The liberal papers criticized Bush 67 percent of the time, while conservative papers criticized Clinton 89 percent of the time.

"The study finds that there was often a striking difference in tone between the two sides as well," Tomasky wrote. "The Clinton administration had barely unpacked its bags when the *Wall Street Journal* referred to administration figures as 'pod people from a "Star Trek" episode . . . genetically bred to inhabit the public sector.' That sort of language does not appear on the liberal pages. In sum, the two sides define partisanship quite differently and envision the roles they play as political actors very differently as well. . . . In sum, the distinction is between a traditional view of journalism as detached, independent, and unaffiliated (or at least less affiliated) with a particular party, which is the liberal papers' conceptions of themselves; versus a more activist-oriented journalism that envisions itself as being part of a cause, and sharing that cause with a political party."

Another critical difference in approach is that while liberal opinion writers for the most part are content to let the right wing have an unobstructed say in the marketplace, the right-wing media works to narrow the spectrum of opinion by chilling and intimidating their opponents. When *Times* columnist Paul Krugman issued a sustained critique of Bush administration policies and delineated its pattern of lies, he was targeted and ridiculed by the right-wing media machine as payback. According to CNN's Tucker Carlson, who was trained as an editorial writer in the right-wing editorial apparat under Paul Greenberg at the *Arkansas Democrat-Gazette,* and then at *The Weekly Standard,* Krugman, a Princeton economist who is considered a future Nobelist, is a "partisan" with "no credibility." Carlson—who quoted General Wesley Clark on *Crossfire,* saying that the general had complimented the leadership of George W. Bush, when in fact Clark had been referring to Bush's father—berated Krugman while claiming to be "an objective observer" himself. Andrew Sullivan calls Krugman an "ideologue" and a "fraud." Sullivan's Web site has posted such items as a photo of Tom Daschle saluting the flag with his left rather than his right hand, an Internet smear circulated by right-wing hoaxsters that Sullivan presented as true before later disavowing it; and Sullivan has admitted making false accusations against General Clark because he was "writing off" the Drudge Report. Rush Limbaugh, who has spoken on the air of receiving directives from the Bush White House by e-mail, called Krugman "a daily regurgitation of the Democratic Party fax machine." *National Review Online* runs a "Krugman Truth Squad," headed by a California investment consultant named Donald Luskin. "I have looked evil in the face," Luskin wrote after trailing Krugman at a book signing. "I've been in the same room with it. I don't know how else to describe my feelings now except to say that I feel unclean, and I'm having to fight being afraid." According to *The New Yorker,* "Krugman occasionally receives death threats"; in fall 2003, he "started turning ominous e-mails over to the FBI."[22]

Rounding out the top five newspapers in the United States are the *Los*

Angeles Times and *USA Today*, the latter of which is published by Gannett. The liberal *Los Angeles Times* editorial page seems to go out of its way to accommodate conservative views, no matter how bizarre or incoherent: It instituted a "column left" and "column right" feature, which seemed a contrived device to expand the spectrum rightward, pairing established liberal journalists with people such as Norah Vincent, a self-identified pro-life libertarian lesbian whose syndicated column is riddled with non sequiturs. The pattern of ritualistic genuflection to the right wing's demands for "balance" is followed at virtually every major newspaper in the country. Antifeminist writer Cathy Young, who took right-wing foundation money for her book *Gender Wars* while at the Cato Institute, is a columnist at the *Boston Globe*, while *Newsday* columnist Raymond J. Keating is "chief economist at the Small Business Survival Committee," a Washington antitax group that has received Olin cash.

USA Today's editorial page is decidedly moderate and nonideological, taking up issues on a case-by-case basis, never veering far from the center. The paper follows the unusual practice of dubbing its editorials "Our View" and balancing them with equal space devoted to an "Opposing View" written by a freelance contributor. An unscientific sampling in spring 2003 suggested that the paper's moderate views are more often "balanced" by contributors from the Right than from the Left, providing a regular landfill for "products" from places like Cato and Citizens for a Sound Economy, whose funding sources are never revealed to readers, and from recycled GOP partisans like Newt Gingrich and Dick Armey, both of whom are now also supported by the right-wing think tank network.

USA Today has a board of contributors who fill the op-ed page, and its membership is a good reflection of what the media as a whole considers acceptable discourse nowadays. Learned academics like the liberal economist Lester Thurow and the neoliberal sociologist Amitai Etzioni share space with Michael Medved, a right-wing radio show host who branded Al Gore "delusional"; right-wing "comic" and *American Spectator* "diarist" Ben Stein; and Independent Women's Forum types Laura Ingraham and Amy Holmes.

Former Democratic campaign operative Susan Estrich is one voice that might be expected to match these conservative partisans, though Estrich is now a FOX News contributor, and in that role she seems to go out of her way to disparage Democrats and defend Republicans. On FOX, she has spoken of her "friendship" with Matt Drudge and with Ann Coulter. During the California gubernatorial recall vote in 2003, Estrich appeared on FOX's *Hannity & Colmes* to join Republicans in lambasting the *Los Angeles Times* for running an exposé on sexual harassment allegations against Republican candidate Arnold Schwarzenegger. Even though the *Times* said it had not been ready for publication until a weeks-long investigation was complete, Estrich played to right-wing charges of liberal bias, insisting the charges should have been published earlier in the campaign.[23] Estrich frequently expresses the view that the Clintons should "go away" and harshly appraises the Clintons' marriage, although she knows nothing about it. On *Hannity & Colmes,* Estrich exclaimed, "If somebody said to me [Bill Clinton] . . . had oral sex I would say where was [a female Clinton aide who had never been romantically linked to the President] that day?" Though Estrich provided no evidence for this innuendo, Hannity has called her "an intellectually honest Democrat."

Unlike the conservative "Tong," the widely syndicated liberal columnists of the 1970s and today include in their ranks many former reporters and editors. In general, they are more careful, more skeptical of all sides, and quieter; moreover, they are less reflexively ideological, less partisan, and less prone to cutting journalistic corners than are their conservative foils. Even in the midst of a column eviscerating Ann Coulter's book *Treason* for its manifest dishonesty and racial bigotry, liberal *Washington Post* columnist Richard Cohen felt obliged to write, "Fairness compels me to say that Coulter scores some reasonable points." The Coulters of the world would never return the courtesy.

When legendary CBS anchor Walter Cronkite came out of retirement to write a syndicated column in 2003, he expressed what could be considered the liberal credo: "I would call myself a liberal, but I hope I don't lose my ability to be dispassionate. I would think I would use reporting to say things with intelligence, as I see it, but not let ideology get in the way. . . ."

Unlike the conservatives, the liberals are unmoored to any cohesive political movement, and they have no symbiotic relationship with politicians. No liberal columns in wide syndication are "sponsored" by partisan think tanks or subsidized by opinion magazines. The liberals either make it in the market or they don't, while the so-called free marketeers are on the dole. Nor are the liberal writers known to attend weekly closed-door strategy meetings to forward the agenda of the Democratic Party. They are truly independent columnists and, therefore, a much less potent fighting force when going up against the right wing, which plays a different role in the media wars.

The spectrum of opinion itself is out of balance. Ideologically, left-wing voices that were the true polar opposites of those of the right wing—anticapitalist, anticorporate, populist, or pacifist—long ago had been all but expunged from the nation's editorial pages as the print media became increasingly corporatized and reliant on advertising.[24] Liberal and left-wing columnists with fervid ideological and moral convictions—and sharper knives—who tend to apprentice in opinion journals, alternative news outlets, and politics, don't seem to be prominently featured in major papers or sought after by the newspaper syndicates.

Even if these writers were more widely distributed, their impact on politics would not be the same as the conservatives'; most liberal writers even in the opinion journals consider themselves more loyal to journalism than to politics, as any comparison between the party-line *National Review* and the unpredictable *New Republic* attests. If they aspire to punditry, the young liberals naturally follow the example of the fair-minded liberals who already have made it in the big leagues.

Many young liberal writers aim to leave the poorly paying opinion magazines and make careers in newsrooms, which further constrains their partisan advocacy; meanwhile, their conservative counterparts, relying on the lucrative cradle-to-grave jobs program of the right-wing network, generally aim only to spread their views into the mainstream. Even so, coming from the notoriously partisan *American Spectator* hasn't hampered the mainstream careers of Andrew Ferguson of *Time* and the Bloomberg News Service, or Sam Dealey, who was hired by the Capitol Hill newspaper *The Hill* and assigned to cover the 2004 Democratic presidential candidates.

Liberal advocacy is further tempered by the reality that counterintuitive thinking and criticizing one's own political bedfellows are valued and even celebrated in liberal journalistic circles. By contrast, independence is looked on as disloyalty in the conservative media, which ironically prizes "political correctness." As *The American Prospect*'s Michael Tomasky has noted, "[Liberals] bend over backward to 'prove' their 'independence.'" He continued:

> Here's an example. Maureen Dowd [of the *New York Times*]: Liberal columnist, right? She's not a right-winger, so at least she's a liberal by default. So you'd expect that during the last election, she tossed most of her darts at George W. Bush, right? She didn't. I counted. Between Labor Day and Election Day 2000—when it mattered—she wrote about twice as many columns having sport with Gore (and Clinton) as with Bush. This is the sort of thing that constitutes the liberal side these days.[25]

The conservative tilt is also the result of the fact that moderate Republican voices failed to attain the prominent media platforms commandeered by the Far Right. Moderates in the GOP, whose public face and internal orientation were transformed in part by the right-wing presence in the media in the mid- and late 1970s, seemed disinterested in, or unable to make, careers in the media.

One prominent exception to this rule was David Gergen, the centrist-conservative former Nixon aide and future aide to both Reagan and Clinton. In an interview published shortly after Reagan's election in 1980, Gergen, who edited the American Enterprise Institute's journal *Public Opinion* during the Carter administration, told the magazine: "In terms of syndicated columnists, if there is an ideological bias, it's more and more to the right."

By 1985, Dinesh D'Souza—an alum of the *Dartmouth Review*, where he had acquired the moniker "Distort D'Newsa"—could announce in the pages of the Heritage Foundation's *Policy Review*, "Newsrooms are full of liberals, but conservative columnists now dominate the Op-Ed pages of newspapers across the country."

Newspaper syndicates closely guard their circulation figures, but there is no doubt that conservative columnists today appear across the country in regional and local papers with far more frequency than do liberals. In 1999, *Editor & Publisher* commissioned a survey of the syndicates asking how many papers each of their columnists appear in. Of the top ten columnists, carried in papers with a combined circulation of over ten million, six were conservatives, three were liberals, and one was a centrist. The top two columnists, James Dobson of the right-wing group Focus on the Family, and Cal Thomas, a former official of the Moral Majority, present Christian Right views in more than five hundred newspapers each, while the Christian Left has virtually no voice in the American media. Robert Novak and George Will came next, followed by Ellen Goodman, the sole liberal in the top five.

These figures tell only part of the story. Far more dogmatic and mono-chromatic, the conservative columnists constitute a powerfully unified echo chamber that liberals don't match. Art Buchwald, a humorist with a liberal bent whose columns run near the funny pages, was number six, though his dedication to politics can hardly be compared to that of right-wingers like Mona Charen, a former speechwriter for Nancy Reagan and Jack Kemp, or Hoover's Thomas Sowell, who ranked seventh and tenth, respectively. Two top liberals, Goodman and Buchwald, are independents removed from movement politics; only Molly Ivins, who ranked ninth, writes from a con-sistent ideological point of view, yet even Ivins says she "ain't the left . . . I'm Molly Ivins."

The reach and approach of Ellen Goodman, who has a moderate, com-monsense style, cannot be said to balance out the fiery extremism of James Dobson, who controls a multimillion-dollar media empire of which his col-umn is just a small part. At the Web site of Dobson's Colorado-based group, an umbrella organization for eighty Christian ministries nationwide, a con-venient e-mail form is provided through which users may contact their local newspapers "to bring Dr. Dobson's advice to your hometown."

Other top syndicated columnists include conservatives such as Safire and Buckley and liberals such as Maureen Dowd of the *New York Times* and Clarence Page of the *Chicago Tribune*. Moving down the charts, one finds a sprinkling of liberal names, like Arianna Huffington and Mark Shields, and then a seemingly endless list of conservative relics and munchkins, writ-ers of little renown and even less distinction, who nonetheless have been propelled into punditry by right-wing media groups, conservative news-paper editorial boards—and, increasingly, subsidized right-wing Web sites.

By the mid-1990s, with more newspapers folding and syndication opportunities dwindling, it was openly acknowledged in the industry that the remaining opinion "niches" were for African American and female conservatives, who could be created, groomed, and fed by the right-wing network. In 1995, the president of the *New York Times* syndicate said, "There are very few competitive markets left and fewer newspapers," but added that there was still space for "conservative columns by minorities or women."[26]

Most of the B-list right-wing columns are circulated in power centers like New York and Washington and pop onto the mainstream media radar screen because they are rolled out like toilet paper every day over commentary pages in two right-wing money pits that subsidize them: Rupert Murdoch's *New York Post* and the Moonie *Washington Times*. On its Web site, the *Times* lists twenty-four syndicated columns it runs regularly, from Bruce Bartlett to Walter Williams, in addition to ten in-house staff columnists.

One random summer day, June 24, 2003, found the following columns, among others, in the *Washington Times*: Jay Ambrose, "chief editorial writer for Scripps Howard News Service"; Stephen Moore, "senior fellow at the Cato Institute, distributed by Scripps Howard News Service"; Armstrong Williams, "a nationally syndicated columnist"; Henry I. Miller, "a fellow at the Hoover Institution"; Gregory Conko, "director of safety policy at the Competitive Enterprise Institute"; Frank J. Gaffney Jr., "president of the Center for Security Policy"; Michelle Malkin, "nationally syndicated columnist"; Paul M. Weyrich, "chairman and CEO of the Free Congress Foundation"; and Jonathan V. Last, "online editor of the *Weekly Standard*."

These columns then become fodder for nationally syndicated right-wing radio talk show hosts and are calling cards for cable talk show producers. Right-wing talk show hosts, in turn—even ones who can barely write, such as FOX's Bill O'Reilly—have won newspaper syndication deals based on their TV and radio visibility.

Many of the unexceptionable right-wing columnists have enormous national reach. Joseph Perkins, a former Dan Quayle aide and *Journal* editorial page writer, is syndicated through the conservative *San Diego Union-Tribune*. About 250 papers carry the column, which reaches seven million readers with its highly eclectic views— particularly considering Perkins is African American—such as a defense of Trent Lott's pro-segregationist comments. Until 2001, Ben Wattenberg of the American Enterprise Institute was still carried in about 250 papers. The column was cowritten by his son Daniel, formerly of *The American Spectator*. In addition to Buckley, three *National Review* staffers, Rich Lowry, Jonah Goldberg, and Joel Mowbray, are syndicated nationally, while the Reason Foundation's *Reason* magazine is home base for Jacob Sullum. Like Sullum, dozens of others— including Linda Chavez, president of the Center for Equal Opportunity; Maggie Gallagher, president of the Institute for Marriage and Public Policy; Paul Craig Roberts, "John M. Olin fellow at the Institute for Political Economy, research fellow at the Independent Institute, and Senior Research Fellow at the Hoover Institution"; and Deroy Murdoch, former Steve Forbes aide and Atlas Economic Research Foundation "senior fellow"—write columns from think tank perches, an important means of support, as syndicated columns don't pay well unless they are very widely circulated. Donald Lambro is nationally syndicated by virtue of his post as the *Washington Times*'s "chief political correspondent." Oddballs like Ann Coulter, Michelle Malkin, Betsy Hart, former Reagan aide Lawrence Kudlow, former Clarence Thomas aide Armstrong Williams, and Rush Limbaugh's parasitic brother David, among many, many others, round out the list.

Heritage's Townhall Internet portal lists sixty-one such right-wing columnists and is by no means exhaustive. The output of each columnist is carefully archived, biographical and e-mail contact information is provided for reporters, TV producers, and fans, and viewers may purchase the columnists' books. Heritage reported 14.4 million visitors to Townhall in 2001. By typing in your ZIP code, you are fed the e-mail address of your local daily newspaper and told to "urge them to carry your favorite conservative columnist!"

In October 2003, Townhall columnist Kathleen Parker reprinted in her syndicated column a letter from a "friend" saying that the Democratic presidential candidates should be "lined up and shot." Townhall removed the column and altered the text—purported to be a direct quote—to read "lined up and slapped."

A stable of more gifted liberal writers from publications like *The Nation*, *The American Prospect*, *Salon*, and the *Washington Monthly* don't find easy syndication deals (nor is there a liberal equivalent of Townhall). When liberal columnists do get a foothold despite the odds, their jobs may be imperiled regardless. Since the Iraq war, several American antiwar columnists have lost their jobs, including Dan Guthrie in Oregon, who had received an award as the state's top columnist; Tim McCarthy, editor of a weekly New Hampshire paper, who had been named "Editorial Writer of the Year" by the New Hampshire Press Association; Salim Muwakkil, an op-ed columnist at the *Chicago Tribune;* and Brent Flynn of the Star Community Newspapers in Texas.

In fall 2002, the *San Francisco Chronicle* fired columnist Stephanie Salter from her longtime left-of-center, twice-weekly op-ed column, which was syndicated by Hearst and Scripps Howard. Salter said she was told that her liberal, feminist views "didn't resonate" with a new publisher.[27] Meanwhile, the *Chronicle,* generally considered a liberal paper, publishes in-house conservative Debra J. Saunders, who wrote in one column, "When mainstream journalists report both sides of racism—pro and con with equal weight—or both sides of having a free press in America, then I'll believe that American media don't take sides on issues, and that there is at least a rationale for American media not rooting for U.S. troops to win in Iraq. But that day will never come."

Through their domination of the newspaper opinion columns, the conservatives created a demand for their views in highly circulated mainstream national magazines. *Time* has had on its roster neocon hawk Charles Krauthammer, Andrew Sullivan, and *American Spectator* and *Weekly Standard* writer Andrew Ferguson; *Newsweek* has had George Will and David Brooks of *The Weekly Standard.* At *U.S. News & World Report,* Michael Barone, CNN's Lou Dobbs, and John Leo (exposed by *The American Prospect* for relying on a mythical anecdote to fill an "anti-P.C. screed") are conservatives; in the middle or on the right, depending on the subject, *U.S. News* features publisher Mortimer Zuckerman, who was caught in an embarrassing flap when he repeated fabricated stories about supposedly frivolous lawsuits that circulate in the right wing, Washington wise man David Gergen, and Meg Greenfield protégé Jodie Allen. Apparently, no liberals need apply at *U.S. News.*

Forbes, an influential business magazine, is soaked with right-wing opinion. And the magazine once considered to epitomize the American heartland, *Reader's Digest*, has for years been run in Washington by right-winger William Schulz as a gravy train for conservative writers like Fred Barnes and Michael Barone, who subsidize their other work with the *Digest's* fat fees.

As Eric Alterman observed in *What Liberal Media?*, even magazines that cater to nonconservative audiences have been tainted by the Right. While *The New Yorker* remains immune to most conservative noise, it succumbed to anti-Clinton hysteria in the mid-1990s when editor Tina Brown replaced writer Sidney Blumenthal with Clinton basher Michael Kelly as the magazine's Washington correspondent; Brown also published lengthy Clinton "scandal" pieces by Peter J. Boyer, the author of a mash note to Bernard Goldberg reprinted in *Bias*. (Curiously, Boyer had previously published a book, *Who Killed CBS? The Undoing of America's Number One News Network*, in which he wrote, "The idea of CBS News as an organ of the left was a caricature of the grossest sort. . . . CBS News was about as left-wing as the Cedar Falls Chapter of the American Legion.")

In November 2003, *The New Yorker* published Boyer's profile of Wesley Clark. In *The American Prospect*, Matthew Yglesias noted that while Boyer's charges "have been percolating in the conservative press for months . . . it is surprising to see them appear in the level-headed, liberal *New Yorker.*" Yglesias described Boyer as someone who has made "something of a career for himself as a conservative interloper at otherwise liberal media outlets." According to Yglesias, Boyer authored a 1992 *Vanity Fair* profile of Rush Limbaugh that Brent Bozell's Media Research Center described as "fair" and was the correspondent on several *Frontline* episodes that voiced unfounded allegations against various members of the Clinton administration. Also in *The New Yorker*, Yglesias noted, Boyer was the author of a profile of Al Gore that "became a source of the largely hostile storyline into which the media fit future Gore coverage during the 2000 campaign" and a "sympathetic" article defending actor Mel Gibson against charges of anti-Semitism.[28] Writing in the *New York Times*, columnist Frank Rich showed that the Boyer article included a false quotation that appeared designed to minimize statements by Gibson's father denying the Holocaust.

Elsewhere, gay basher P. J. O'Rourke, the "Mencken fellow" at the Cato Institute, works for *Rolling Stone*, which stopped publishing the respected liberal reporter William Greider; *Esquire* publishes Tucker Carlson. When publisher Mortimer Zuckerman sold *The Atlantic Monthly* to Washington entrepreneur David Bradley, Michael Kelly was installed as editor; he inserted writers from *National Review* and *The Weekly Standard.* Kelly also imported conservative columnists to Bradley's small-circulation, but highly respected, nonpartisan policy magazine, *National Journal.* Microsoft's *Slate,* founded by liberal Michael Kinsley and now edited by liberal Jacob Weisberg, showcases the Web log of Mickey Kaus, who says, "I like attacking Democrats more than I like attacking Republicans," while the liberal-oriented online magazine *Salon,* perhaps as part of a diabolical plan to discredit the Right, has hired as columnists Camille Paglia, David Horowitz, and Andrew Sullivan.

Even an explicitly liberal opinion magazine like *The New Republic,* often mistaken as a counterpoint to right-wing magazines like *The Weekly Standard* or *National Review,* has been a major springboard for conservative writers and their views. Like the *Post* op-ed page, *The New Republic* used its liberal reputation during the Reagan era to legitimize aspects of the right-wing agenda on foreign policy and affirmative action; in so doing, it became the hottest magazine in the capital. Conservatism had become so predominant in the opinion industry that one surefire way for increasingly marginalized liberals to gain prominence was to track right. Morton Kondracke of *Roll Call* and FOX News, Fred Barnes of *The Weekly Standard* and FOX News, and Charles Krauthammer of *Time* and FOX all came from *The New Republic* shop of that era.

In the 1990s, under the editorship of Andrew Sullivan and then Michael Kelly, the magazine continued its rightward drift. Sullivan published an article containing breathless allegations of nefarious doings at Little Rock's Rose Law Firm, where Hillary Clinton had been a partner before becoming First Lady. The author of the article, promoted on the *Wall Street Journal* editorial page, conceded that he fabricated a key section. Sullivan published an excerpt of Charles Murray's infamous book, *The Bell Curve.* And Sullivan hired the serial fabricator Stephen Glass, who was then promoted by Kelly. Glass got his start in journalism at the University of Pennsylvania, where he inflated a campus controversy over hate-speech codes to launch an inaccurate attack—on the "politically correct" university administration—that subsequently spilled into the national press. Before joining *The New Republic,* Glass had worked at the Heritage Foundation's *Policy Review.*

In 2002, longtime owner Martin Peretz sold controlling interest in *The New Republic* to Roger Hertog, the chairman of the Manhattan Institute and investor in the right-wing *New York Sun* daily newspaper, and Michael Steinhardt, a major financier of the centrist Democratic Leadership Council and the Progressive Policy Institute. In a profile of the magazine in February 2003, Howard Kurtz of the *Washington Post* wrote, "The *New Republic* sees the Democratic Party these days as an assortment of duplicitous, racially hypersensitive war wimps." Kurtz described editor Peter Beinart as a "full-fledged talon-bearing hawk." While Beinart criticizes all sides in his own pieces, and continues to publish a roster of strong liberal staff writers like John Judis, another staff writer is Lawrence F. Kaplan, a former editor at Irving Kristol's *National Interest* and coauthor with William Kristol of the book *War over Iraq*, published by the right-wing Encounter Books. Kurtz raised the prospect that *The New Republic* might endorse Bush for reelection in 2004, suggesting such a repositioning might help the magazine recapture its glory days in the Reagan era.

Liberal writers, by contrast, seldom appear in conservative-oriented magazines. *The New Republic* can accommodate a Kaplan and move editorially in the direction of *The Weekly Standard,* which in 2003 the *New York Times* described as having transformed itself from an "outré journal of the right to the Boswell of the new global agenda"; the reverse alchemy somehow never happens.

CHAPTER FIVE

SCANDAL SHEETS

CONSERVATIVES WERE NOT CONTENT simply to embed themselves in the established press through the widely syndicated columnists and the *Wall Street Journal's* editorial pages and to publish the higher-toned "intellectual" reviews aimed at elite opinion. Accepted standards of discourse, intelligibility, and common decency were keeping a sizable segment of right-wingers outside the mainstream conversation. To remedy this, the conservative movement needed to build a second-tier, separate media—an alternative media netherworld—to reach what the conservative writer Alan Crawford, in his 1979 book *Thunder on the Right,* called the "primitive right-wing activists" who comprised a substantial and growing base of the GOP.

Alternative media long had been a device used by the Far Right to communicate to its members the racist, anti-Semitic, and fringe views the regular media wouldn't publish. In his 1967 book, *The Farther Shores of American Politics,* George Thayer listed innumerable examples of this right-wing alternative media.[1] In the 1940s, the *Beacon Light Herald* carried this headline: IMPEACH ROOSEVELT AND REPEAL THE TALMUD INSPIRED NEW DEAL LAWS. The *White Sentinel* and the *Winrod Letter* were racist; the *Rockwell Report* was pro-Nazi; the *Free American* was "the battle organ of racial fascism"; and the *Thunderbolt,* published by the National States Rights Party, announced that "we favor the burning of beatniks." The racist, anti-Semitic Liberty Lobby's *Liberty Letter,* 175,000 subscribers strong, published a "confidential Washington report," *Liberty Lowdown,* which assailed civil rights laws, the United Nations, and "socialized medicine." An "emergency" *Liberty Letter* advised: "Final Death Notice: Civil Rights Passage Would Insure Dictatorship." The pro-Goldwater Conservative Society of America considered itself "the agitprop of the conservative wing." *Tax Fax,* its newsletter, carried articles like "Treason on Campus" and "The Income Tax Can Be Repealed."

According to Thayer, subscribers to these publications were told that they were based on facts, "proofs," careful analysis, and truth. The anti-Semitic *Cross and Flag* considered itself "the only purveyor of truth in the U.S." The *Review of the News* and *Public Opinion* were the work of John Birch Society founder Robert Welch, who claimed to be a "true scholar" but believed that "knowledge is a one-way street." The publications were written in a journalistic style. The Liberty Lobby's tabloid pamphlets included *LBJ: A Political Biography* (which compared Johnson to Hitler and to Mussolini and reached ten million people before the 1964 election), and an assault on the patriotism of a prominent Democratic senator and Vietnam War critic, *J. William Fulbright: Freedom's Judas Goat.* And they contained attacks on the professional press as both a rhetorical and a marketing device. *Common Sense,* "the nation's anti-Communist newspaper," which attacked the press as Jewish-controlled, had ninety thousand subscribers in the early 1960s. Welch's publications alleged that the *New York Times* took its line from Communist Party publications. Kent Courtney of the Conservative Society of America accused the media of "mass Pavlovian brainwashing every day."

As a prelude to the Reagan era, a new set of alternative right-wing magazines, newspapers, and newsletters began to thrive outside the structures and strictures of the regular press and mostly beneath its radar screen, reintroducing into conservatism the kind of paranoid conspiracism, scurrilous "reporting," and hysterical calls to political action that fueled the earlier publications. These new vehicles, focusing heavily on racial and sexual issues, were the forerunners of what would become a powerful right-wing alternative media in the United States.

Many of the new publications were sold through a direct-mail fund-raising apparatus that the right wing was pioneering to transform American politics in the new era of the political action committee. Under a landmark 1976 Supreme Court decision, political committees were permitted to spend money in unlimited amounts to elect favored candidates, as long as the contributions were not given to the candidates but, rather, were spent "independently" on the candidates' behalf. The rise of corporate PACs and so-called independent expenditure committees immediately began benefiting the Republican Party, which picked up seats in both the House and the Senate in 1978.

Republicans were quicker than Democrats to use these independent expenditure committees, raising money mostly through slick direct-mail operations, with prospect lists culled from old records from the Goldwater insurgency, to elect their candidates. A coterie of Far Right direct-mail wizards and PAC fund-raisers went into business raising money for groups like the American Conservative Union (formerly the Draft Goldwater Committee), the Conservative Caucus, the Moral Majority, Paul Weyrich's Committee for the Survival of a Free Congress, the Conservative Victory Fund, and the National Conservative Political Action Committee. Independent expenditures from groups like NCPAC and the Fund for a Conservative Majority were critical to Reagan's success. Altogether, groups favoring Reagan spent more than $12 million in 1980 on independent expenditures, while less than $50,000 was spent by groups favoring Carter's reelection.

These direct-mail hucksters and PAC staffers became part-time publishers to provide an echo effect for their paid political ads and to keep the PAC money flowing in. The popularity of the publications suggested there was an audience, if not yet a substantial market, for communicating in a new form—not only opinion but a kind of faux conservative movement news.

In 1979, Alan Crawford, a former editor of *New Guard,* a publication of the right-wing campus group Young Americans for Freedom, published *Thunder on the Right,* in which he chronicled, from a critical perspective, the rise of the radical Right in his party. "The New Right has no positive program but flourishes on backlash politics, seeking to veto whatever threatens its vision of its way of life—busing, textbooks, women's liberation, abolition of capital punishment, gay rights, gun control, loss of the Panama Canal," the book jacket claimed. "Not conservative, it feeds on social protest and encourages class hostility. Its heroes are rugged frontiersmen of the new Old West; its enemies are moderates, liberals, and true conservatives of whatever party."

Crawford described the astonishing growth of "the New Right's Fourth Estate" in the late 1970s and lamented that the more intelligent conservatism of William Buckley, and even of newer entrants like George Will and William Safire, was being overshadowed by the new rabble-rousers:

The American Right now has an active, vigorous battery of publications and publicists, ranging from the eminently conservative William F. Buckley and *National Review*—not strictly New Right at all—to the neopopulist monthly *Conservative Digest. Human Events,* a Washington-based news weekly part conservative, part New Right, provides in-depth coverage of Capitol Hill and political campaigns. *Washington Weekly,* a tabloid distributed in the Capitol area, reprints syndicated right-wing columnists and staff-written editorials focusing on the lapses of the established *Washington Post* and *Washington Star,* all served up in sensationalist and hard-hitting style. Richard A. Viguerie, the New Right fundraiser, publishes *Conservative Digest,* a slick magazine geared to Wallacites, and *The New Right Report,* a twice-weekly newsletter for right-wing political activists. Outside of Washington, right-of-center newspapers like the *Manchester* (New Hampshire) *Union Leader,* the *Richmond* (Virginia) *News-Leader,* the *Arizona Republic,* and the *Santa Ana* (California) *Register* provide a "movement" perspective for local readers. Their editors sometimes contribute to the national rightist publications. These magazines and newspapers, taken together with such non–New Right establishment publications as *The Wall Street Journal, The Saturday Evening Post,* and *U.S. News and World Report,* ensure that conservative views are well represented in the national news media.

The aim of the new publications—in addition to millions of direct-mail hit pieces known as "panic" letters written in a yellow journalism style and warning of a takeover of America by "anti-life Baby Killers," "radical anti-family forces," "cruel atheists," "Godless politicians," and the "socialistic" United Nations—was explicitly right-wing proselytizing, movement building, and fund-raising. The conservatives were capitalizing on underlying social and political reaction against the pace of modern American society, challenges from abroad, and the failures, real and perceived, of government policies; their publications were agitprop for a movement attempting to win political control by convincing troubled people that conservatism was an elixir for their woes.[2] Their media provided the conservatives a calming sense that they were not alone, that their extreme views were the views of the "average American."

Publications like *Conservative Digest* and a cascade of others, including the *Pink Sheet on the Left,* the *Phyllis Schlafly Report,* and the *Right Woman,* were sold to subscribers as "a breath of fresh air cutting through the liberal media," according to the *Digest.* "Direct mail has allowed conservatives to by-pass the liberal media, and go directly into the homes of conservatives in this country," Viguerie was quoted by Alan Crawford. "There really is a silent majority in this country, and the New Right now has learned how to identify them and communicate with them and mobilize them." The material was written to "make them angry" and "stir up hostilities," said NCPAC's Terry Dolan. An unidentified New Right leader told Crawford that the goal of these communications vehicles was to "capture the culture" and, ultimately, the presidency.

The immediate political effect of the proliferating newspapers and newsletters, which encouraged a previously dormant activist cohort to take direct political action, such as flooding his congressional office with letters, was to suggest that right-wing sentiment existed on a scale that it did not. As Crawford put it, there was still no "silent majority" but, rather, "a small percentage of the electorate," mobilized by right-wing media, that was beginning to win "a disproportionately high degree of political power."

Crawford, who had worked at *Conservative Digest,* wrote that the magazine and others like it appealed to distrustful right-wing readers who, unlike liberals apparently satisfied with the facts provided by objective journalism, eagerly patronized a partisan press that they could be sure was on their side and that fed them only "facts" that fit their worldview. The marketing pitch, Crawford revealed, was more psychological than political. The target audience comprised "those threatened by upward mobility of blacks and others" and readers who were "insecure due to lack of respect to their values by upper-class 'prestige givers.'" Describing what he called the hankering for "macho politics" among this group, Crawford wrote:

> They are suspicious, slightly intimidated individuals who, wishing they had greater control over their lives, harken back to the days when men like John Wayne could take control; they are people looking for a leader like him. . . . They seek victory to regain lost status, to embarrass or humiliate their enemies in the Eastern liberal establishment, and to gain control of the culture. It is a politics that is almost wholly reactionary.

Crawford traced these impulses back to their political manifestation in the McCarthy era. Quoting the essayist Peter Viereck, Crawford wrote that McCarthyism was "an effort to embarrass Eastern liberal intellectuals in the universities and government. They acted out feelings of inferiority and resentment of those better-educated and more prestigious than they."

As Crawford described them, the new publications were expressly anti-intellectual; editors and writers at *Conservative Digest,* which had a circulation of 130,000, were instructed to "use small words," to boil down complexities, and to suggest simple answers to policy challenges. One aim of the publications was to smear President Carter and Senate Democrats up for reelection in 1978 and 1980 with recklessly false allegations, Crawford reported.

The Washington weekly *Human Events* had been published since the mid-1940s as the voice of conservative isolationism but came to more prominence in the mid- and late 1970s. Nonsensically, it claimed to be both objective and biased. "In reporting the news, *Human Events* is objective; it aims for accurate presentation of all the facts. But it is not impartial," its masthead proclaimed. "It looks at events through eyes that are biased in favor of limited constitutional government, local self-government, private enterprise and individual freedom." "Stories" included "Senator Kennedy's Right to Loaf Bill," "Public Enemy Number One—Taxes," and "Communism: A False Religion."[3]

According to a 1980 article in the *Washington Post,* one editor at

Human Events, Thomas S. Winter, a Harvard Business School graduate, sat on the board of the American Conservative Union and was treasurer of the Conservative Victory Fund. Another editor, Allan Ryskind, had grown up in Hollywood as the son of a Socialist who had fought to rid the entertainment industry of Communist influence. "They call themselves 'advocacy journalists,' a profession that requires an almost continual state of outrage," the *Post* reported, continuing:

> Those who call it strident may be referring to items such as a picture that ran in the May 24 issue of two women holding signs that said "I love this woman with all my heart." Although the picture was from the National Women's Conference in Houston in 1977, it was used with a story about the White House Conference on Families, and the caption read, "Thanks to a benign Carter Administration scenes such as the one above . . . will almost certainly return."

The *Post* reported that one of *Human Events'* most "faithful readers" was Ronald Reagan, who, along with Paul Harvey and J. Edgar Hoover, had been an occasional contributor. "People in the campaign have told us that what we've said [in the paper] often comes back from him verbatim," Ryskind bragged to the *Post.* While investigating the weekly, Alan Crawford answered an ad in *Human Events* for "Confederate and KKK memorabilia"; he received in the mail an application for Klan membership.

Human Events is owned by Eagle Publishing, which also owns the right-wing book-publishing company Regnery; although Winter remains "editor in chief," the current "editor" is Terry Jeffrey, a former aide in Pat Buchanan's presidential campaigns and former editorial writer for the *Washington Times.* Though its editorial policies remain unchanged, Jeffrey, who has said he vents his "anger" through his work, has far more visibility in the regular media than did his forebears, a result of the sliding standards of new media outlets on cable and radio. Jeffrey is a nationally syndicated columnist and a very frequent guest on MSNBC's *Hardball,* where he once conceded, "I think Hillary is a threat." His publication has specialized in pseudoinvestigations of Democrats such as Linda Daschle, wife of the Senate Democratic leader, which are in turn picked up by megaphones like Limbaugh, who featured on his Web site the "Linda Daschle Project." Ann Coulter is the *Human Events* "legal affairs correspondent."

Conservative Digest and *Human Events* routinely trafficked in the sort of rumormongering that one could not find even on the *Journal* editorial page (until the Clinton era). So did the *Washington Weekly*, a new tabloid that billed itself as the conservative alternative to the *Post* and the *Star.* The paper carried a steady diet of the nationally syndicated right-wing colum- nists but specialized in "sex scandals and sensational items," Crawford wrote. It was owned by John P. McGoff, publisher of a chain of forty con- servative newspapers throughout the country, including a string of papers in California in which he was part owner with Richard Mellon Scaife. McGoff, whose Panax Corporation had ties to the apartheid government of South Africa, used one of his Michigan newspapers to spread the story that "President Carter condones sexual promiscuity on the part of his male staffers," according to Crawford. Featured as well was an interview with a psychiatrist who "reveals [Carter's] secret plan to install [his wife] Rosalynn for vice president in 1984."

Richard Mellon Scaife, who did more than any single individual to fund the right-wing think tank network, was interested in publishing as an additional means to propagate his views. The Pittsburgh-based scion of the Mellon banking and oil fortunes, Scaife publishes a newspaper in his hometown, the *Pittsburgh Tribune-Review*, which he ordered to destroy any photo of Nixon not smiling during his 1972 reelection campaign. Also during the early 1970s, at the behest of the CIA, Scaife subsidized a London-based news service called Forum World Features, which disseminated CIA pro- paganda around the globe. British intelligence officers charged that the service planted false personal allegations against British Labour Party mem- bers to help the conservative cause.[4] The *Tribune-Review* is known for race baiting and the revelations of the "sexcapades" of its political foes.[5]

Scaife became an important means of financial support for *The American Spectator*, the right-wing monthly that had its start on the cam- pus of Indiana University in the late 1960s. In 1986, the magazine moved its offices to Washington; though its circulation remained small, its essays and criticism became an important part of the debate within post-Reagan conservatism, helping to bridge the divide between the neoconservatives and the traditional right wing. During the presidency of Bush Sr., the mag- azine began to carve out a niche as a muckraker against liberals and

Democrats, notably targeting women such as Anita Hill ("The Real Anita") and Hillary Clinton ("The Lady Macbeth of Little Rock"). These dubious exposés, framed as an antidote to what editor in chief R. Emmett Tyrrell Jr. called the "one party press," attracted the attention of Rush Limbaugh, who promoted them on the air. With the advent of the Clinton administration in 1993, the magazine's circulation would soar tenfold to well over three hundred thousand.

In 1993, Scaife substantially boosted his subsidy to the magazine, which for a time became the leading anti-Clinton smear factory for the right wing. With more than $2 million from Scaife's family foundations, the magazine set up the "Arkansas Project," a dirt-digging expedition trained on the First Family that touted the personal and political scandals of the era, ranging from Whitewater, to Travelgate, to Filegate, to allegations of sexual impropriety against both Clintons, to charges of drug abuse, drug trafficking, and even murder. Whether by the independent counsel, congressional committees, the courts, or the "sources" later discrediting their own accounts, the Clinton "scandals" were shown to be a masterful campaign of innuendo, baseless assertion, and outright lies manufactured by the right wing, most of it traceable to Scaife's money.

With the exception of Clinton's private consensual affair with a White House intern, the Clintons were never shown to have done anything wrong. Yet by 1998, the "stories" fomented, generated, and publicized by the *Spectator* and other right-wing media earlier in the decade had penetrated every media channel in the country and created a political crisis culminating in Clinton's impeachment by a party-line vote in the GOP-controlled House of Representatives and his acquittal in a Senate trial.

Ironically, around this time, the *Spectator* itself imploded in the midst of a Justice Department investigation into whether it had corruptly sought to influence government investigations by paying off anti-Clinton witnesses. In a fit of pique, Scaife, who had spent millions to promote false theories linking the suicide of White House counsel Vincent Foster to foul play, balked at the publication by the *Spectator* of a negative review of the book *The Strange Death of Vincent Foster* by notorious Foster conspiratorialist Christopher Ruddy. Ruddy's work was so slipshod that even Rupert Murdoch's *New York Post* fired him, and Ann Coulter referred to his book as a "conservative hoax." He was hired as a "reporter" at Scaife's *Tribune-Review*.

When Scaife learned of the *Spectator* review, he pulled all funding from the magazine, leaving it in desperate financial straits as circulation plunged after the failed impeachment gambit. It was sold for a pittance to right-wing economist and investor George F. Gilder, who failed to make a go of it and handed it back to editor Tyrrell, who in the meantime had become an "adjunct scholar" at the Hudson Institute and started a Web site, the American Prowler, to continue the *Spectator's* smear campaign on the Internet. Limbaugh frequently mentioned the new site. In 2002, Alfred Regnery Jr. of Regnery Publishing took over as *Spectator* publisher, and Robert Bartley of the *Wall Street Journal* became "senior editorial adviser."

Scaife was not finished as a benefactor of right-wing propaganda, becoming in the late 1990s the third-largest shareholder in a magazine-publishing and Internet venture called NewsMax. By this time, much of the think tank network that Scaife financed had established an active Internet presence, such as the Heritage Townhall portal, built at the cost of more than $1 million, linking hundreds of right-wing organizations, print media, and talk show hosts in one online forum.

Like talk radio, the Internet offers editorial content unchecked by journalistic authorities; therefore, it offers an unvarnished view of what kind of media right-wing audiences seek out as an alternative to professional media outlets. Asked in September 2003 by the *Baltimore Sun* to account for the "sea change" in American journalism during the 1990s, Ann Coulter identified "the Internet: victory for America" and predicted that with "the alternative media, the dailies will wither away, a good thing."

The climate that the *Spectator's* scandalmongering had ushered in—wherein the story lines of the Far Right fringe press had come to shape mainstream discourse during the Clinton era—made NewsMax appear to many as a relatively normal enterprise. Installed as editor was none other than Christopher Ruddy, whose work had been discredited not only by such professional news programs as *60 Minutes* but even by the *Spectator.* After the *60 Minutes* debunking, Ruddy produced a video, *The 60 Minutes Deception,* funded partly by Accuracy in Media. According to the NewsMax Web site, Ruddy is a "media fellow" at the Hoover Institution. In 1999, *Newsweek* named Ruddy "one of America's top 20 media personalities." The *Wall Street Journal* editorial page has hailed him as "relentless."

NewsMax claims to be "America's news page" and "the leading conservative news agency in the country." On the NewsMax homepage in

September 2003 were such "stories" as "Senator 'Osama Mama' Murray Exploits 9/11"; "Teddy Kennedy vs. Poor Black Children"; and "O'Reilly: Elite Media Are Out to Destroy Mel Gibson" (written off his FOX show "Talking Points Memo," in which he defended the actor against charges of anti-Semitism). Other "stories" were from press releases from right-wing organizations funded by Scaife, such as Judicial Watch, which files lawsuits and ethics complaints primarily to harass Democrats. According to NewsMax, its "veteran investigative journalist," Phil Brennan, formerly wrote the "From Washington Straight" column for *National Review* and "in 1964 during the Goldwater campaign he organized the GOP Truth Squad and served as its PR director."

The site features a long list of columnists, including Paul Weyrich, Michelle Malkin, the former feminist turned right-winger Tammy Bruce (who, although she is openly gay, defended Dr. Laura Schlessinger, who said that homosexuality is a "biological error"), radio show hosts Steve Malzberg and Barry Farber, Gary Aldrich (author of *Unlimited Access,* a discredited tale from inside his FBI perch in the Clinton White House), and Bill O'Reilly. It sells right-wing books, including Ann Coulter's *Treason* and Carl Limbacher's *Hillary's Scheme* ("If you love to hate Hillary . . . there's plenty in this book to make your blood boil") and top-seller *How to Conquer Negative Emotions.*

Visitors to the site can purchase a monthly magazine, *NewsMax;* "desert camouflage hats" and "USS *Ronald Reagan*" Navy caps are also for sale. Viewers can sign up to receive the "Insider Report" and e-mail alerts. NewsMax markets decks of playing cards on which "controversial figures are skewered," according to a report by the Scripps Howard News Service. During the war in Iraq, a "Deck of Weasels" picturing "the 54 worst leaders and celebrities who opposed America" brought in more than $1 million. NewsMax paid for a *New York Times* ad urging a boycott of some eighty French products, while on his site Ruddy was urging that the use of nuclear weapons be considered.

A "Deck of Hillary" cards was released by NewsMax on the day Hillary Clinton's memoir, *Living History,* was published. "As the Pentagon proved with its Most Wanted Iraqis, there's no better way to 'out' the enemy than to depict it on a deck of cards. . . . Move over, Saddam, Hillary is the new Ace of Spades," NewsMax announced. The cards were promoted by Sean

Hannity on his radio show. "I didn't know she talked like this," Hannity said in mock horror as he read off racy quotes attributed to Senator Clinton by now-discredited sources. The site launched the "Counter Clinton Library," which it said would be the "headquarters of the Stop Hillary Now campaign."

NewsMax sells taped interviews as part of its "Off the Record Club." Among those who have sat for NewsMax "exclusives," according to the Web site, are Bernard Goldberg; former CIA director R. James Woolsey, a neo-con Iraq war hawk; and Dick Morris, who resigned as an adviser to Bill Clinton in a call-girl scandal and now attacks his former boss for a living. September 2003 brought "a sensational new audio program exclusive to NewsMax.com [in which] Lucianne Goldberg reveals the inside scoop on the Monica Lewinsky case, Bill & Hillary, and what's really going on in New York and Washington." Goldberg, "one of the best informed people in America," was interviewed by right-wing radio show host Barry Farber. According to the site, the hour-long interview revealed "the real Hillary Clinton, the one Barbara Walters won't tell you about; Lucianne's inside take on Hillary's presidential plans; the secret rivalry between Hillary . . . and her own husband Bill; the real story about the Democratic candidates, including Lucianne's take on Joe Lieberman, Al Sharpton, and the other dwarves; Michael Moore—and how he tried to photograph Lucianne in her bedroom; and how the president's personal faith really matters."

Goldberg has her own Web site, Lucianne.com, on which she links to and comments on various news reports, as do her readers. About a report that Chelsea Clinton had the flu, one reader posting said: "The mutt most likely had a herpes flare-up given to her by that serial rapist she knows so well." When Democratic Senator Paul Wellstone died in an airplane accident, some postings were:

"Good riddance WellScum You TraitorCrat."

"Burying Wellstone is a waste of fertilizer. Take him to the nearest cornfield and plow him into the rows. That's where all Democrats belong. They serve no other useful purpose on this earth. One down and 49 to go."

Mickey Kaus links to Lucianne.com on his Web log on *Slate,* Microsoft's online magazine, potentially driving traffic to Goldberg's site and giving it mainstream exposure. (Michelangelo Signorile in the *New York Press* suggested that Kaus takes right-wing positions and links to right-wing writers to boost traffic to his own site.) Still in 2003, Goldberg (who in the *New York Post* accused Clinton of "finger-fucking" his daughter) was bringing her insights on the Clintons to MSNBC's *Hardball* and the FOX News Channel. She has her own daily syndicated radio show, too.

NewsMax's connection to the old *Washington Weekly* tabloid is direct: its star correspondent, Carl Limbacher, got his start there. Limbacher "specializes in the news the mainstream media overlooks," according to NewsMax. Limbacher has broken "stories" such as "Hillary Snubs Gold Star Mothers," charging that the New York senator—referred to as "the Queen herself" and "the Hildebeast"—refused to meet with the mothers of sons killed in military combat. The Gold Star Mothers story reached untold millions via talk radio, though Clinton had met with the group in the past; the women had no appointment with Clinton; she was not in her office when they stopped by unannounced; and the Gold Star Mothers renounced the characterization of events given by NewsMax. Limbacher was the author of "stories" claiming a "government cover-up" in the death of Clinton Commerce Secretary Ron Brown; before the *Wall Street Journal* editorial page weighed in, his "stories" on the Juanita Broaddrick case ignited the right-wing pressure campaign on NBC News to broadcast her unverified and self-contradicted charges.

In April 2003, Ruddy told the *Fort Lauderdale Sun-Sentinel* that the site draws eight million hits per month and boasted that Rush Limbaugh mentions it on the air frequently. According to Amazon.com's site Alexa.com, it ranks twenty-fifth among favored "news" sites, ahead of CBSNews.com and the Associated Press. NewsMax contributors like Tammy Bruce; Dick Morris; James L. Hirsen, author of *Tales from the Left Coast;* and "prairie pontificator" Diane Alden, "a recognized critic and analyst of radical environmentalism," blanket the radio airwaves across the country courtesy of a NewsMax pundit directory. Ruddy has gotten the kind of TV exposure that *Conservative Digest* writers could never have imagined two decades before. He has been a guest on CNN, MSNBC's *Buchanan and Press* and *Scarborough Country,* and PBS's *Tony Brown's Journal.*

According to NewsMax, Limbacher's "stories have been picked up by conservative media stars Rush Limbaugh and Sean Hannity and his scoops are regularly covered by the *New York Post* and even the *Washington Times* editorial page. . . . He was a recent guest on Bill Maher's *Politically*

Incorrect." "Read all about it—NewsMax.com! We check out the site every morning 'cause you always have the stuff a day early," says FOX News Channel's *FOX & Friends* morning show host, Steve Doocy. Sean Hannity says Limbacher is "one of the best reporters in America—I read him every day." Limbacher has appeared on MSNBC and CNN. When the host of MSNBC's *Scarborough Country* went on vacation in August 2003, NewsMax columnist Steve Malzberg sat in for him.

On the company's board of directors are Arnaud de Borchgrave, the former editor in chief of the Moonie *Washington Times;* former Navy admiral Thomas Moorer of Accuracy in Media; Lord William Rees-Mogg, a columnist for Murdoch's *Times* of London; Jeff Cunningham, the former publisher of *Forbes;* and James Dale Davidson, president of the Scaife-backed National Taxpayers Union and author of the book *The Story of a One-Term President,* which claimed that Vincent Foster's suicide was an "extra-judicial execution" and a "sign of incipient fascism." On its "international advisory board" is former Reagan Secretary of State Alexander M. Haig Jr., a frequent *Hannity & Colmes* guest on the FOX News Channel.

NewsMax unsuccessfully attempted a public offering of stock in 2002. According to an analysis of papers filed by NewsMax with the Securities and Exchange Commission by Terry Krepel on his Web site, ConWebWatch.com, which tracks right-wing Internet sites, although NewsMax has claimed that *NewsMax* magazine has "more than 300,000 paid readers. . . . We have just surpassed almost every conservative publication in America," NewsMax informed the SEC that its paid circulation was "approximately 59,395." In a 2000 interview with Wired.com, Ruddy falsely claimed that NewsMax had become profitable, according to Krepel. Since its inception, Krepel calculates, the company has lost about $11 million of right-wing investor money, principally that of Scaife and former Dallas real estate investor Michael Ruff.[6]

Scaife is tied to a second high-traffic right-wing "news" site called WorldNetDaily (WND), run by Joseph Farah, co-founder with James H. Smith (former publisher of the *Sacramento Union*), of the Scaife-funded Western Journalism Center. The center was founded in 1994 primarily to publicize and support Christopher Ruddy's work on the Vincent Foster case. While Ruddy was writing on the subject for Scaife's Pittsburgh newspaper, the center took out full-page ads in major newspapers reprinting the articles so that they would circulate nationally. The center provided Ruddy with money for travel, publicity, and legal fees. In 1997, just as Scaife was cutting off the *Spectator*, WorldNetDaily was begun as a project of the center and later spun off as a for-profit subsidiary, though it does not appear to turn a profit.[7]

The site bills itself as a "fiercely independent news site committed to hard-hitting investigative journalism" and "your independent online intelligence source." Among the "scoops" listed on its site are stories quoting unnamed "FBI officials" blaming the Clinton administration for the September attacks; about "a pro-life research organization says data collected as a result of an ongoing investigation into teen pregnancy show that the number of underage girls being 'sexually exploited' by adult men has reached 'epidemic' proportions in the U.S. and that Planned Parenthood facilities are knowingly concealing such sex-abuse crimes"; and about a "new study" purporting to show that "child molestation is an integral part of the homosexual movement." The "study" was written by Steve Baldwin, president of the right-wing Council for National Policy, and published in the "law review" of Pat Robertson's Regent University. WorldNetDaily featured an article in September 2003 titled "Satanic Schwarzeneggerians."

An article in *Newsday* reported that Farah, who helped Rush Limbaugh write his book *See, I Told You So*, "spends much of his time and virtual ink lambasting Muslims and 'secular humanist' supporters of gender and sexual equality. In his world view, the Islamic threat joins a panoply of devils that includes uppity women, promiscuous gays and even union members." Columnists featured on the site include Pat Buchanan, Ann Coulter, Michelle Malkin, David Limbaugh, Walter Williams, Larry Elder, William Rusher, Dr. Laura Schlessinger, and radio show host Neal Boortz ("The Hildabeast Stirs: Hillary Clinton Is Fundamentally Dishonest").

WorldNetDaily claims five million unique visitors per month and more than forty million page views. According to the site, "WorldNetDaily.com consistently ranks as the 'stickiest' news site on the Internet, meaning readers spent more time on it than on any other—including against CNN, MSNBC, and ESPN. WorldNetDaily.com often ranks at the top of the news pack in number of page views per user and minutes per page—two other important categories measured by Internet ratings agencies." The site is "habit-forming," Farah says.

According to Farah, "The prime source of support for the website" are books (*The Case Against Darwin*), videos ("Videos Expose Arafat as Father of Middle East Terror"), and *Whistleblower* magazine, which in September 2003 featured an issue on "The End of Marriage?" which included articles titled "Ain't Nothin' Like the Real Thing," written by a "former homosexual"; and "Marriages Made in Heaven—and Hell," an exploration of the "mystery between men and women becoming 'one flesh.'" WND publishes books, in partnership with the Dallas "Christian" book publisher Thomas Nelson. Titles include the best-selling *Savage Nation,* by gay basher Michael Savage; *Journalistic Fraud: How the New York Times Distorts the News and Why It Can No Longer Be Trusted* by Bob Kohn; and Farah's own *Taking America Back: A Radical Plan to Revive Freedom, Morality, and Justice,* in which he argues that "pro-life activists" begin to "question the legitimacy" of the U.S. Supreme Court.

"Turn the bums out," Farah has exhorted his readers. "Stir the pot. Make political history. Cause a revolution. Don't do it because the Republicans represent a great alternative—they don't. Do it because the Democrats—far too many of them—are evil, pure and simple. They have no redeeming social value. They are outright traitors themselves or apologists for treasonous behavior. They are enemies of the American people and the American way of life."

An article in *Columbia Journalism Review* about Farah's journalistic ethics while he was editor of the *Sacramento Union* concluded that he had none. The 1991 article, written by a former *Union* reporter, said:

> One of the first things Farah did was issue memos prohibiting reporters from using the words "gay," "assault rifles" and "women's health center." These were replaced by "homosexual," "semi-automatic rifles," and "abortion clinics." He edited a story by one of the paper's state bureau reporters so that the National Organization for Women was defined as a "radical feminist group" and former Supreme Court Justice William J. Brennan was described as having "consistently struck down all legal protections of the unborn."

Things are far worse at WorldNetDaily, which as Terry Krepel has charged, has plagiarized stories from the Associated Press; reworked press releases from right-wing organizations into articles; and recycled false

National Enquirer exposés on Democrats. Yet in a manifesto printed on the site, Farah upbraided the professional media as if they were his peers. "In this tumultuous era for the press—which has changed in one generation from having been dominated by the *Washington Post, New York Times* and 'the big three' networks to offering today a multitude of news choices—the so-called 'Old Media' are having a little trouble accepting the 'New Media.' . . . WND has garnered at least 14 Associated Press citations for stories it's broken—by far the most of any independent news site on the Internet—which is more proof that the old establishment media are having to take our reporting seriously," he wrote. "Sometimes we get credit for our work, and sometimes we don't. But we always have an impact."

In the 2000 election campaign, WorldNetDaily published a series of conspiratorial "stories" in the Bircher style attacking Al Gore's integrity that were broadcast widely through Gore's home state of Tennessee by right-wing talk radio hosts. These included "Gore Plays Fixer to 'Crooked' Uncle"; "Al Gore Protects Local Corruption?"; "CIA Official: Gore Compromised by Secret Past"; "Experts Fear Russia to Blackmail Gore"; and "Gore Protected Military Thieves?" According to Nashville radio host Phil Valentine, "Thanks to talk radio and sources like WorldNetDaily getting out the truth, I believe it tipped the state to Bush. They [the WND stories] stayed under the radar nationally, but around here they were on everyone's lips." The *Decatur County Chronicle,* a weekly independently owned newspaper, ran a WorldNetDaily series on Gore's "corruption." According to the paper's editor, "We sold out of every edition that carried those stories. People literally drove in from hundreds of miles away to buy twenty-five, fifty, one hundred copies, whatever they could afford, to take back with them." (The series prompted a multimillion-dollar defamation suit against WorldNetDaily by a top Gore fund-raiser in Tennessee. To defend itself, WorldNetDaily directed donors to the U.S. Justice Foundation, a right-wing legal group with ties to *The Welch Report,* named after the John Birch Society founder.)

In a 2003 interview with the *Seattle Times,* Farah declared that the liberal media monopoly had been broken by right-wing organs such as his site, which he said was a commonly used bookmark by right-wing radio show hosts around the country. The site provides "a highly qualified cadre of inspiring, knowledgeable speakers who are available to address your group or broadcast audience." Among those listed in the "Speaker's Home" are Jerry Falwell, Larry Klayman of the Scaife-funded Judicial Watch, Howard Phillips of the Conservative Caucus, Heritage official Rebecca Hagelin, and ABC's John Stossel, host of the network's *20/20* news broadcast. It has featured the Clinton accuser Kathleen Willey, who was judged by an independent counsel investigation to be an unreliable witness. Hagelin told readers in one NewsMax column, "It takes organizations such as the Heritage Foundation and WorldNetDaily to provide the other side of the story—the side not spun by President Bush's avowed enemies."

Apparently providing "the other side of the story," Farah has appeared on MSNBC's *Buchanan and Press* and *Hardball*, on FOX's *Hannity & Colmes,* and on CNN's now-defunct *TalkBack Live.* Hannity endorsed Farah's "side of the story"—his claim that environmentalists were responsible for the *Columbia* space shuttle disaster.

In the age of the Internet, the right wing quickly found a new means of transmitting "news" not only to its own members but also into increasingly porous mainstream media channels. "Anyone who knows anything about the Net is aware of the professional influence of conservative sites," according to *The Note,* ABC's widely read insider political report. "The Internet's most powerful effect has been to expand vastly the range of opinion—especially conservative opinion—at everyone's fingertips," Brian C. Anderson wrote on OpinionJournal.com, a right-wing Internet site published by the *Wall Street Journal.* "The Internet helps break up the traditional cultural gatekeepers' power to determine (a) what's important and (b) the range of acceptable opinion," according to Virginia Postrel, former editor of the libertarian *Reason* magazine.

The Internet is the fastest-growing news source for Americans. "The 'blogosphere,'" wrote *U.S. News & World Report* columnist John Leo, "tilts strongly to the right." Conservatives also use the Internet to skew online public opinion surveys. According to a survey by the Pew Internet and American Life Project, half of Republicans, but only 28 percent of Democrats, used the Internet to register political opinions in the 2002 election cycle.

Perhaps because the Internet relies on written communication, and is

therefore closer to the logical imperatives of print than is broadcast journalism, liberals maintain an active presence on the Web. Of those who say
they get their news online, up to 40 percent are self-described liberals. The
liberal sites are chock-full of news and commentary ignored by the mainstream press; but the sites are not lavishly subsidized, and they cannot drive
a news cycle because they do not have access to anything like the talk radio
and cable outlets of the right wing; nor are they devoted to pushing misinformation into the rest of the media.

The right-wing sites, by contrast, have financial resources and a powerful distribution network at their disposal that move right-wing messages and
misinformation into the mainstream. A popular site maintained by *National
Review*—and given huge nationwide play through frequent Rush
Limbaugh mentions—confines itself to disseminating twisted opinion, such
as racist columns by John Derbyshire advocating that public sector workers
be disenfranchised; smears against progressive groups as "pro-Saddam";
and paeans to the "political virility" of Defense Secretary Donald Rumsfeld,
"almost a riot of manliness," according to editor Jay Nordlinger.

However, other sites, such as that of the Murdoch-funded *Weekly
Standard,* attempt journalism—with unfortunate results. During the controversy over the nomination of openly gay Episcopal Reverend Gene
Robinson to be the bishop of the church's New Hampshire diocese, on the
eve of a final vote by the House of Bishops, Robinson's opponents circulated
charges that he was "linked" to an Internet porn site and had engaged in
inappropriate touching with a male parishioner. The porn "story" had been
shopped to news organizations, like CNN, which had passed. But it was
picked up by Fred Barnes and posted to the *Weekly Standard* site. Barnes
then took the "story" to FOX News, where he is a contributor; from there,
it made front-page headlines across the country.

Barnes is on the board of the Institute on Religion and Democracy, a
right-wing Scaife-funded orthodox-Christian group that opposes "radical
forms of feminism, environmentalism, pacifism, multi-culturalism, revolutionary socialism [and] sexual liberation." Its "Episcopal Action" arm fought
Bishop Robinson's elevation and fights gay unions. These facts were not disclosed in the Barnes dispatch or by FOX News.

The vote on Robinson was put off while the church investigated both
charges, which were found to be without merit. There was no link to

pornography on the Web site maintained by a gay youth group that Robinson had not been involved with for several years. The "touching" "story"—communicated in a private e-mail—turned out to be a touch on the forearm and back of an adult male. While Robinson's reputation was tarnished from coast to coast by Barnes and by FOX, only a handful of media outlets, including the editorial page of the Minneapolis *Star Tribune* and Michelangelo Signorile in the *New York Press,* connected the ideological dots, revealing what the *Tribune* called "The Anatomy of a Smear."

The Barnes/FOX smear took flight into the rest of the press via the Drudge Report, the Internet gossip site maintained by Matt Drudge, an uneducated and professionally untrained former sales clerk at a CBS Entertainment gift shop. In the mid-1990s, Drudge started a Web site on which he posted Hollywood gossip that he said he gleaned at the gift shop. In other interviews, he has intimated that he snooped through executive offices. It didn't take long for the right wing to find Drudge and use his site as a dumping ground for "news" driven by a political agenda. Much of the "news" was false, such as his 1996 report of an imminent indictment of First Lady Hillary Clinton. Drudge has said his postings are 80 percent accurate. An investigation of his claim by the magazine *Brill's Content* found that ten of thirty-one Drudge "stories" were true. "Screw journalism," Drudge has said. "The whole thing's a fraud anyway."[8]

Amid the gossip, Drudge's site provided convenient links to newspapers, magazines, and syndicated columns and highlighted articles from the regular press of interest to news junkies on both coasts. He attracted a substantial following during Clinton's impeachment, in which he was as much participant as observer. When anti-Clinton operatives were unable to plant smears and rumors against the Clintons in the regular press, they leaked frequently to Drudge, who became known for these spoon-fed "scoops" and "exclusives."

As traffic to his site swelled, Drudge gained the following: a contract with AOL, giving him a much wider audience; a weekly interview show on the FOX News Channel (since canceled); invitations to speak at the National Press Club; appearances on CNN, MSNBC, and even *Meet the Press;* a radio talk show first on the ABC Network and then on a division of Clear Channel Worldwide—Premiere Radio Networks, which syndicates the Limbaugh show; and a book deal. In *Drudge Manifesto,* dedicated to

Linda R. Tripp, who betrayed her friend Monica Lewinsky in the White House sex scandal, Drudge wrote, "With a modem, a phone jack, and an inexpensive computer, your newsroom can be your living room, your bedroom . . . your bathroom, if you're so inclined."

By 1999, Drudge was getting more than 240 million hits to his site annually. He received 1.4 billion hits in 2002. Today, Drudge gets approximately 6.5 million visitors each day and is ranked number 242 in overall Web traffic by Alexa.com. It is the sixth most popular "news" site, following CNN, BBC News, and the *New York Times,* but ahead of the *Washington Post, USA Today,* and ABC News. In September 2003, Drudge told the *Miami Herald* that he makes $1.2 million per year from his combined Web and radio ventures. Though Drudge has taken right-wing money to defend himself against libel charges, the site is advertiser-supported. Ads are sold through Intermarkets, a Virginia-based agency that works package deals and cross-promotes *Human Events* online, NewsMax.com, *The American Spectator,* and other alternative "news" sites.[9] The Scaife-supported NewsMax and Rupert Murdoch's FOX Sports are among Drudge's frequent advertisers.

The Drudge Report is by far the premier transmission vehicle for right-wing media. He is able to filter and then link to "news" from outlets such as the *Washington Times,* the *New York Post, The Weekly Standard,* British tabloids, right-wing columnists, book authors, and far more obscure right-wing Web sites and to project this "news" and its authors onto talk radio and across all cable channels—thereby providing the organized Right with a priceless national and even international platform for its propaganda. Columnists highlighted on the site skew to the Far Right, including Brent Bozell, Larry Elder, Suzanne Fields of the *Washington Times,* David Limbaugh, and Marvin Olasky. Drudge links to WorldNetDaily, Lucianne.com, and Far Right publications like *Jewish World Review* and Pat Buchanan's *American Conservative.*

Drudge claims to be a two-man operation, working with a longtime associate, Andrew Breitbart, from his Miami Beach condominium, selecting from the thousands of news stories in the legitimate press each day— often from regional or local newspapers or wire services that others do not read—the handful of stories that will drive the right-leaning radio and cable TV media into a frenzy in any given news cycle. According to a September

2003 report in the *Miami Herald,* "Many radio hosts check The Drudge Report before starting their air shifts just to make sure they know what's going on." Drudge told the newspaper: "Once I was listening to Michael Savage's [syndicated radio] show and he opened by reading The Drudge Report on the air, story by story—in order—without once mentioning he was looking at my site." Savage has one of the top five nationally syndicated radio shows in the country, reaching more than six million listeners.

Whether these stories are true or false, they typically forward the agenda of the conservative movement and disparage Democrats and liberals. Drudge's own politics and personal relationships may play a role—at various times he has said he is a libertarian, that he supported Pat Buchanan for the presidency, and that he is "a pro-life conservative who doesn't want the government to tax me." Of Rush Limbaugh, Drudge has said, "He is our voice, he is our brain, in so many respects, those of us who believe in less taxes and smaller government." Bizarrely, Drudge accompanied his friend Ann Coulter on her book tour for *Treason,* claiming that she needed protection when entering network news buildings. When the two appeared together on Sean Hannity's radio show, Coulter had to correct Drudge's lurid exaggerations of what had transpired behind the set of ABC's *The View,* which hosted Coulter as a guest.

Drudge has a keen sense of what the dominant media channels want. Rush Limbaugh refers to "my old pal Matt Drudge." Sean Hannity salutes Drudge on the air for "the great work you're doing giving the elites a hard time." On the day Hillary Clinton's *Living History* was published, Pat Buchanan, hosting his MSNBC show, referred to a conversation he had with Drudge earlier in the day about the book; he then gave Drudge's absurd take on Hillary as his own, comparing her to the fictional character Sue Ellen Ewing on the 1980s prime-time soap opera *Dallas.* On a later MSNBC broadcast, Drudge revealed, to Buchanan's obvious discomfort, that he and Buchanan have an intense AOL "instant message" Internet dialogue. Often without attribution, Brit Hume's FOX News broadcast includes Drudge items on a regular basis.

"Almost daily, stories that originate on the Web make their way into print or onto TV or radio," Brian C. Anderson wrote on OpinionJournal.com. "Fox and Rush Limbaugh, for instance, often pick up stories from [David Horowitz's magazine] FrontPage and OpinionJournal—especially those about the antiwar left. Fox News's Sean Hannity surfs the net up to eight hours a day, searching sites like Drudge and the hard-right news site WorldNetDaily for stories to cover." Anderson pointed out that the phrase *Axis of Weasel,* used to disparage the French and German governments during the debate over Iraq policy, originated on the humor Web log ScrappleFace, was picked up by the *New York Post,* then moved to talk radio, FOX, and CNN.

Drudge reaches far beyond the right wing. Network producers e-mail him ratings information. Perhaps because there is nothing remotely like a liberal Drudge Report either in content or traffic, liberal authors secretly hope he will tout their work, as he does virtually every fallacious Regnery book that rolls off the presses, propelling them up the best-seller charts. According to ABC's *The Note,* Drudge is "every [TV] booker's homepage." Among other mainstream newspapers, he was cited with some frequency in the *Washington Post* during the time Lloyd Grove wrote the paper's "The Reliable Source" column. (In August 2003, Grove left the paper for the *New York Daily News.* His going-away party was hosted by, among others, right-wing pundette Kellyanne Conway and CNN's Tucker Carlson. In attendance was Grove's girlfriend, right-wing columnist Amy Holmes.)

Drudge is far from a two-man operation. Rather, he is deployed by Republican political operatives who are doing the dirt-digging and the culling of vast public sources for him, e-mailing him their rumors, tips, and findings—all timed for maximum political impact. Before the 2002 election, Drudge carried an eleventh-hour item claiming that Democratic Senate candidate David Pryor had employed an illegal immigrant. According to an Associated Press dispatch, Pryor, who said the story was false, responded to "an item on the Drudge Report Web site of Internet gossip columnist Matt Drudge." According to the Web site Spinsanity, Drudge falsely accused the Democratic Socialists of America of "sending people to [Minnesota] to illegally vote for [Senator Paul] Wellstone." The false report was repeated by Rush Limbaugh, Brit Hume, and the *Wall Street Journal* editorial page.

A particularly egregious example of how the Republicans use Drudge came in spring 2003, after ABC News aired a report by Jeffrey Kofman on morale problems among some U.S. troops in Iraq. Drudge carried an item noting Kofman was Canadian and linked to an article about Kofman, who is openly gay, in a gay magazine. Drudge told the *Washington Post*'s Grove that the Bush White House had "tipped" him to the story about the gay Canadian reporter in an apparent effort to undermine Kofman.

Drudge was enmeshed in other right-wing efforts to misinform the public about the progress of the war in Iraq. In August 2003, Drudge linked to stories from WorldTribune.com, which reported that weapons of mass destruction had likely been located, buried in Lebanon's Bekaa Valley. Limbaugh ran with the "story," which he wrongly said came from a "paper" in the United Kingdom, and it was discussed that evening on FOX's *The O'Reilly Factor.* As *The New Yorker* magazine later reported, WorldTribune is a Web site run in his off hours by Robert Morton, "assistant managing editor" of the *Washington Times.* The site was conceived, Morton told the magazine, while he was serving as a "media fellow" at the Hoover Institution. Morton's contributors are a murky network of mostly anonymous informants. Though he told *The New Yorker* that "we emphasize newspaper standards to counter the half-baked unfiltered content of some on-line sites," there was no truth to the weapons-in-Lebanon dispatch, among other baseless stories the site has posted. Traffic to WorldTribune.com is about one million hits per month.[10]

The Drudge Report has been at the forefront of smears—often trivial, but then used by the Republican Noise Machine to suggest deeper character defects—of Democratic opponents of Bush. In December 2003, he ran the shock headline HOLLYWOOD DEMS GATHER FOR "HATE BUSH" MEETING AT HILTON, falsely claiming that the gathering of Democratic activists was billed as "Hate Bush." Apparently, an e-mailed invitation forwarded from the host that did not use the phrase "Hate Bush" had been dispersed widely, and someone unconnected to the event put a "Hate Bush" header on the e-mail, which eventually reached Drudge. The "Hate Bush" story was all over radio and cable within hours, and the host of the event, Laurie David, the wife of *Seinfeld* creator Larry David, received a torrent of hate e-mail—including at least one laced with anti-Semitic messaging. "Welcome to the wonderful world of the Internet," Drudge told Lloyd Grove, who moved his gossip column to the *New York Daily News* in 2003.

The right-wing media specializes in these "death by a thousand cuts" attacks, the accumulation of which are meant to paint unattractive portraits of leading Democrats in the public mind. In early 2003, Drudge published a false report claiming that Senator John Kerry pays $150 to have his hair cut at an exclusive downtown Washington salon; the false report was repeated on CNN.

In August 2002, Drudge linked to a report by Roger Friedman of FOXNews.com claiming that Tipper Gore had tried to get free tickets to a Bruce Springsteen concert for "the entire Gore staff." The "story," which was meant to make Tipper Gore look as though she were taking advantage of her position as ex–Second Lady, was attributed to "sources" close to the Gores and Springsteen. One "source" claimed that when Tipper Gore was asked to pay for the tickets, she declined. "And you know, that's why Gore isn't president, in a nutshell," the FOX piece concluded, framing the item for the rest of the right-wing media. Drudge linked to the piece, Limbaugh jumped on it, and so did the FOX News Channel.

Especially when these "stories" are of small import, the right-wing media is able to paint its victims into a corner. To leave false items uncontested is to acquiesce in smears. Contesting them involves furthering the story, looking petty or churlish, and never really undoing the initial misimpressions. Though he was informed by Gore's staff that the FOX story was "100% wrong," Lloyd Grove ran it in the *Washington Post,* suggesting the controversy was a "speed bump" for Al Gore's political comeback plans.[11]

The Springsteen organization denied the FOX account. FOX corrected it. Though he busted Drudge on the "Hate Bush" hoax, Grove never let his *Post* readers know the Tipper Gore story was wrong.

Many readers are rightly skeptical of what they see on the Internet. Newspapers, however, are typically ranked as highly trusted sources of news. Once something appears in newsprint, people believe it, and the information exists in perpetuity, cited over and over again in subsequent accounts. That is why, long before the Internet came along, the right wing was willing to lose hundreds of millions of dollars to seize control of or start their own newspapers in the media power centers of New York City and Washington, D.C.

CHAPTER SIX

TOILET PAPERS

N THE LATE 1970S AND EARLY 1980s, Keith Rupert Murdoch, the Australian-born newspaper-publishing heir, went on a buying spree in the United States, purchasing papers in San Antonio, New York City, Boston, and Chicago. American journalism was never the same.

Murdoch was the personal embodiment of the right-wing libertarian philosophy espoused by Edith Efron in *The News Twisters*. He believed that journalism was a business just like any other, with no responsibilities other than to make a profit. Anathema to him were decades of bipartisan laws, regulations, and court decisions undertaken to ensure competition, public accountability, and diversity in the media.

"His editorial or journalistic policy was oriented toward the market," William Shawcross wrote in his biography *Murdoch: The Making of a Media Empire*. "His papers tended to be grey broadsheets or racy tabloids. Neither attracted excellent journalists. The ethos of News discouraged independent investigation or troublesome journalism."[1] Criticizing the Watergate investigation started by the American media, Murdoch, who befriended Richard Nixon after his resignation, said, "I differ from the vast majority of my peers in this country in that I believe the new cult of adversarial journalism has sometimes been taken to the point of subversion."

Murdoch's idea of journalism was to cater to working-class tastes with a formula of titillating tabloid fare and the populist, ostensibly antiestablishment politics that he inherited from his raffish father. Like Nixon, Murdoch— who would be named by *Time* magazine in 1995 as the fourth most influential American, behind the president of the United States, the chairman of the Federal Reserve Board, and Bill Gates of Microsoft—saw himself as at war with journalistic and cultural "elites," whom he felt looked down on him and on his readers.

As he worked his way through American, Australian, and British newspaper publishing, the commercial pressures he brought to bear on his competitors invited the lowering of standards. His success in London with the tabloid *Sun,* denounced as a "shit sheet" by the *New Statesman,* caused the competing *Mirror* to "abandon its more serious pages," according to Shawcross. Murdoch's *New York Post* drew similarly scathing reviews from American journalistic professionals. *Washington Journalism Review* said the *Post* was filled with "S curves of sex, scandal, sensation and screw the facts." According to *Columbia Journalism Review,* "The *New York Post* is no longer a journalistic problem. It is a social problem—a force for evil."[2]

Murdoch stood squarely outside the twentieth-century American journalistic tradition of objective and impartial reporting. He had no respect for the wall that had been erected by common accord over those years to separate and protect American journalists from the capricious whims of owners. Unlike other media moguls in the United States, Murdoch had personal control over his vast holdings in his media company News Corp., and he unabashedly used his media outlets to advance his commercial, ideological, and partisan agendas. While denouncing the "once powerful media barons," he was actually a throwback to the age when powerful media barons produced news that couldn't always be trusted. Like them, he published opinion and misinformation not only on the editorial pages but also in the news columns.

No such liberal partisans have ownership over major American news outlets that reach millions. Whereas the right-wing press of long ago was balanced by less powerful but still feisty crusading liberal publications, in reviving the long-abandoned style of partisan ideological journalism in the United States, Murdoch had a monopoly. No major executive in American journalism behaved as he did, using his media to communicate a political point of view and to dump dirt on his opponents.

Murdoch's goal as a media mogul—to expand his wealth and power by producing a vast supply of media content and owning the means to distribute it—would be facilitated by conservative support for the deregulation of the telecommunications industry. Over the next two decades, Murdoch's News Corp. became a worldwide media force in entertainment, newspapers, TV news, magazines, and book publishing. He publishes forty million newspapers per week that dominate the market in Great Britain, Australia, and New Zealand. Major holdings in the United States now include the FOX broadcasting network; dozens of U.S. TV stations; FOX News Channel; the film and TV production studio Twentieth Century–Fox; magazines, including *TV Guide;* and HarperCollins Publishers. In December 2003, by a 3–2 vote, the Federal Communications Commission gave Rupert Murdoch's News Corp. permission to buy control of DirecTV, the largest satellite operator in the United States, giving it a platform to launch new cable channels reaching eleven million subscribers.

In London, Murdoch had turned his Labour-oriented tabloid toward Margaret Thatcher, pushing her to power. For years until Murdoch acquired it in 1977, the *New York Post* had been "owned by Dolly Schiff, an ardent New Dealer . . . [and] the paper represented a readership shaped by immigration (especially Jews), Depression, war and Cold War: fiercely pro-Israel, and strongly liberal. In the 1950s, the *Post* broke the stories about the Nixon slush fund that led to Tricky Dick's famous 'Checkers' speech," wrote *American Prospect* editor Michael Tomasky. In 1980, Murdoch's *New York Post* broke with longtime precedent and gave a front-page endorsement to Reagan for president; Reagan carried the state.

"Murdoch had used the *Post* ruthlessly to promote his favored politicians and to savage their opponents," Neil Chenoweth wrote in *Rupert Murdoch: The Untold Story of the World's Greatest Media Wizard.* "The long list of victims and beneficiaries goes from former New York Mayor Ed Koch, whom the *Post* backed; to one-time vice presidential nominee Geraldine Ferraro, whom the *Post* crucified; to [Rudy] Giuliani, whom the *Post* ferociously supported; to Hillary Rodham Clinton, whom the *Post* described as a 'rejected wife,' a perpetrator of a 'veritable crime wave in the White House,' who 'couldn't find the Bronx unless she had a chauffeur, and couldn't find Yankee Stadium without a seeing eye dog.'"[3]

The Oxford-educated Murdoch had started out in life on the political Left, and his closest university friend was an open homosexual; but in time

"Murdoch came to reject almost every aspect of life that Oxford represented," wrote Chenoweth. Sexual libertinism appeared to be among the
rejected views. "It was not only his politics that would become more conservative. His views on other people's sexuality would also change. It would
be reflected in his newspapers' growing homophobia, and the zeal with
which they would 'out' public figures," Chenoweth wrote. In 1998,
Murdoch himself would be "outed," when his wife of thirty-two years,
Anna, filed for divorce after discovering he was having an extramarital affair
with News Corp. employee Wendi Deng, whom Murdoch soon married.
Murdoch was "ruthless" toward his former wife, Anna Murdoch said.[4]

Cultural resentment seemed a cornerstone of Murdoch's media properties and also of his employment practices. In the 1960s, the "unofficial
employment policy" at the Murdoch papers in Australia was, according to
Chenoweth, "no blacks, no poofters, no suede shoes." There was a notable
dearth of female executives welcomed into News Corp.'s higher echelons,
and Murdoch's *New York Post* was criticized for inflaming racial tensions in
the city. "The Murdochs have always believed in the superiority of their own
genes," Chenoweth reported. "In December 1999, Rupert Murdoch made
a speech in Oxford where he emphasized the importance of IQ and genetic
inheritance."

Beginning in the Reagan years, many of Murdoch's speeches were quietly written by his close adviser, Irwin Stelzer, an economist who linked
Murdoch's media world to the world of the right-wing think tank network,
which would come to supply a good deal of the content for his print and TV
"news" divisions. Stelzer had been the "director of regulation" at AEI
before joining the Hudson Institute. According to Chenoweth, Stelzer's
"consultancy with News Corp was worth a million a year" in the late 1980s.
Stelzer was published widely throughout the world in Murdoch publications, including in *The Weekly Standard*, William Kristol's neocon sinkhole.
Stelzer arranged lucrative writing assignments for other think tank
denizens, including Charles Murray, whose theories linking intelligence to
genetics Stelzer supported. Murray called Stelzer "the Godfather."[5]

Murdoch himself later joined the boards of the Cato Institute and the
Hoover Institution, but his journalistic endeavors had a less scholarly pretense. In 1977 Murdoch hired Steve Dunleavy as editor of the *Post*. A veteran of Murdoch properties in Australia and England and a sometime

contributor to *Conservative Digest*, Dunleavy, who had only a ninth-grade education, was described in a *Newsweek* profile as "at once populist and rabidly right-wing," a "notable boozer and brawler," and an admirer of Richard Nixon and G. Gordon Liddy. Dunleavy was also the author of a rumor-filled book, *Those Wild, Wild Kennedy Boys. Newsweek* reported that he wrote it in one weekend after courting a purported Kennedy hanger-on who had no idea he was a reporter, getting her drunk, falsely professing his love, and then betraying her in print.

Soon after Dunleavy's arrival, respected journalists began to flee the *Post*. Robert Lipsyte, a columnist who quit, told *Newsweek*, "Steve is dedicated to wringing out emotion and whipping up frenzy. His prose is not orderly, measured, or intelligent, and I can't see what his stories have to do with truth, beauty, or even what the public needs to know." While liberal-oriented newspapers published conservative columnists, liberals were not accorded the same freedom by Murdoch. The esteemed liberal columnist Murray Kempton left the *Post* in 1981.

Murdoch, who has poured millions into the coffers of the Republican Party, had an odd business model—he operated the *Post* at a heavy loss as a way of buying influence in American political, financial, and media circles to further extend the reach of his commercial holdings. Twenty-five years after Murdoch took control, the *New York Post* is still a money-loser, unable to support itself through circulation or advertising. It doesn't quite have the respect of the journalism world; but by virtue of being published in the media capital of the world, it can't help but affect the media ether. (He applies the same model in Washington, where *The Weekly Standard,* which pays editors Kristol and Fred Barnes well into six figures, costs him more than $1 million per year to underwrite.)

The *Post* is a force in New York politics, running hit pieces on Democrats, cheerleading for Republicans, and publishing a motley crew of uniformly conservative columnists—who frequently and without irony bash competing publications for bias—including Steve Dunleavy, John Podhoretz (son of Norman), disgraced former Clinton adviser and FOX News "analyst" Dick Morris, and Deborah Orin, who doubles as the *Post*'s Washington bureau chief. (At normal newspapers, reporters and editors may move on to roles as columnists but don't typically play both parts simultaneously.)

Attacking Al Gore in the news pages during the 2000 election, the *Post* cover screamed LIAR, LIAR. During the Iraq war, which Murdoch strongly supported, the *Post* led the right-wing media's effort to blacklist performers who had expressed opposition to the war as "appeasers" of Saddam Hussein. DON'T AID THESE SADDAM LOVERS, blared a March 2003 headline.

One of Murdoch's most poisonous smears was aimed at Senator Hillary Clinton in the midst of her heated race for the New York seat in 2000. It began with the release of a book written by Jerry Oppenheimer and published by Murdoch-owned HarperCollins, titled *State of a Union: Inside the Complex Marriage of Bill and Hillary Clinton*. The press release promised revelations that would "impact" Mrs. Clinton's political career. Among these was the sensational claim that in 1974, during an argument with an aide to her husband, Bill, Hillary had called the aide "a fucking Jew bastard." The *New York Post* trumpeted the story on its tabloid cover; within hours, CNN was reporting it.

The next day, this "news" was trumpeted on all three network morning shows; on two of the three evening newscasts (NBC and CBS); on the cable talk shows, including *Hardball* with Chris Matthews; and on Murdoch's FOX News Channel. The Right went to town with an op-ed by Dennis Prager in the *Wall Street Journal* and columns in *National Review* and the *Washington Times* ("First Anti-Semite?"). The right-wing Web site NewsMax reported that an Arkansas state trooper recalled Hillary saying "Jew bastard" and "Jewish motherfucker" all the time, though this "revelation" was not disclosed in the trooper's extensive prior interviews with reporters.

The "story," pushed along in Mickey Kaus's *Slate* column, did not withstand scrutiny. Oppenheimer was a former reporter for the *National Enquirer*. His source, a former Clinton campaign aide named Paul Fray, had lost his law license for taking a bribe. The story of the campaign argument had been told by Fray to many reporters over the years—with no mention of the "Jew bastard" remark. In addition, Fray had written to Mrs. Clinton in 1997, apologizing for calling her names and spreading false stories about her. Oppenheimer misstated basic facts about Mrs. Clinton's family tree in an attempt to tar her entire family as anti-Semitic. Nor was it evident that Fray, a Baptist, was even Jewish.

•　　•　　•

A second right-wing media mogul is the Korean evangelist Sun Myung Moon of the Unification Church. Moon believes that he is the new Messiah and has said that he seeks to lead an "automatic theocracy to rule the world."[6] At an anniversary party for the *Washington Times* in the mid-1990s, Moon said, "Fifteen years ago, when the world was adrift on the stormy waves of the Cold War, I established the *Washington Times* to fulfill God's desperate desire to save this world."

Moon believes that "the separation of religion and politics is what Satan likes most" and that once they are joined he can establish a one-world government. He has made racist remarks about blacks, saying their contributions to society are limited to the "physical aspect," and this employer of Andrew Sullivan has labeled gays as "dung-eating dogs."[7] Moon has endorsed a staple of anti-Semitism: "By killing one man, Jesus, the Jewish people had to suffer for 2,000 years," Moon has said. "Countless numbers of people have been slaughtered. During the second World War, six million people were slaughtered to cleanse all of the sins of the Jewish people from the time of Jesus."[8] Right-wing Christians and neoconservative Jews embrace Moon and feed off his largesse, despite his highly offensive teachings.

Moon, who opposes constitutional democracy and calls the United States "the kingdom of Satan"—plainly anti-American beliefs—has had ties to a long line of GOP politicians. He staged a fast for Nixon. Reagan called Moon's *Times* his favorite newspaper. George H. W. Bush traveled with Moon to South America, where Moon founded a seminary, and took $100,000 for a speaking engagement where he praised the *Washington Times* as "a paper that in my view brings sanity to Washington, D.C." He attested to Moon's "respect for editorial independence" and described Moon as "the man with the vision."[9]

George W. Bush has promoted his "Faith-Based Initiative" to Moon front groups, which have received government funds from the program. Bush appointed one Moonie operative to head the government's VISTA national community service program and another, a former *Times* editor, as a top official in the Office of the U.S. Trade Representative. Moon himself appeared at one of the Bush faith-based rallies, declaring, "God's purpose is to establish a restored Adam and Eve, or True Parents, centering on true love."[10]

Moon believes he and his wife are the True Parents. After the GOP gains in the November 2002 elections, Moon declared, "Key Congressional committee posts were regained by people who respect the Father's vision and understand America's responsibility."

Seeking to win credibility and legitimacy for his overseas religious and business enterprises, Moon has pumped hundreds of millions into the *Washington Times* since it was founded in 1982—$100 million per year— to offer the *Washington Post* ideological competition, just as the *Post* was tracking right under Meg Greenfield. The *Times's* role was to "expand the spectrum" further right, taking up a crusading role against Communism in the 1980s and emphasizing sexual abstinence and "family values" in the 1990s. American women, Moon has said, are a "line of prostitutes." Moon seeks the "annihilation" of the United Nations, and his paper strongly supported the Iraq war.

The *Washington Times* provides a forum for thinly veiled racism. The *Times* "editor in chief," Wesley Pruden, has waxed nostalgic for the Confederacy in his opinion column, which is adorned by a small photograph of him wearing a cornpone straw fedora and a twisted smile. No other newspaper editor in chief in the United States regularly boosts one party and attacks the other in a dual role as a columnist. As Michelangelo Signorile has reported in the *New York Press*, *Washington Times* "assistant managing editor" Robert Stacy McCain has written commentaries for the paper and elsewhere sympathetic to the cause of white separatism. *Times* columnist Paul Craig Roberts, formerly a booster of supply-side economics at the *Wall Street Journal*, has written that *Brown v. Board of Education* has "no legal basis." He also wrote: "Today in the United States white people have no political representation. . . . What is the future for whites in a political system where both political parties pander to third world immigrants and support racial privileges for minorities? Having lost equal protection of law, what will whites lose next?"

The editorial page is run by Tony Blankley, a former flack for Newt Gingrich who also writes a syndicated column. Blankley said of George W. Bush, "There are only three newspapers that the President reads over breakfast—his local paper in Texas, and then the *Washington Post* and the *Washington Times.* So we are one of three newspapers that the president personally reads, not necessarily cover to cover every morning, but we get it at the presidential breakfast table. That's an impact." (Bush later said he does not read newspapers but rather receives briefings on them from senior staff.) Blankley predecessors Tod Lindberg and Helle Dale, now housed at the Hoover Institution and the Heritage Foundation respectively, appear as weekly columnists. The paper features an in-house column by Frank Gaffney, the former Reagan Defense official who heads the Center for Security Policy, on whose board Dick Cheney and William Bennett have served. Gaffney was so anxious to go to war with Saddam Hussein that he tried to link him to the Oklahoma City bombing.

More so than Murdoch's *Post*, the *Washington Times* set out to bust what it considered the liberal monopoly on news reporting, becoming the unlikely base camp for the conservative campaign to subvert journalism from within. Top *Times* editors, some of whom had little if any journalistic training, devised a product that was a mirror image of what they believed the "liberal" *Post* to be: a dishonest, intentionally slanted, and often inaccurate take on the news in the service of a predetermined political ideology. The *Times* set out on a propagandistic mission in its news columns to misinform rather than inform, while simultaneously denying it.

According to an investigator for a congressional committee that examined Moon's operations, Moon preaches a doctrine he called Heavenly Deception. Religious recruits are told that "the non-Moon world is evil. It must be lied to so it can help Moon take over. Then it can become good under Moon's control."[11]

Washington Times founding editor James Whelan, editorial page editor William Cheshire, and several of his staff all resigned, charging that Moon operatives had violated their editorial independence. In the 1980s, Wesley Pruden, then "managing editor," regularly rewrote headlines and story leads to reflect GOP spin. Within the newsroom, these forays became known as "Prudenizing," and a number of reporters quit after having their copy mangled for political ends. In one infamous incident during the 1988 presidential campaign, a *Times* story falsely suggested that Democratic nominee Michael Dukakis had sought psychiatric treatment in the late 1970s. Editors doctored a quote from Dukakis's relative, changing it from "It is possible, but I doubt it" to "It is possible."[12] Meanwhile, the newspaper ran front-page editorials soliciting money for the Nicaraguan Freedom Fund for the contras, a cause backed by various Moon political committees. The private-money fund, which led to the Iran-contra scandal, was chaired by William Simon.

Like Murdoch's *Post* in New York, publishing in Washington gives the

Times a buzz factor it wouldn't otherwise enjoy, considering that its circulation is less than that of the *Colorado Springs Gazette*. By the 1990s, both
papers were benefiting enormously from synergistic relations with right-
wing radio and cable talk television and from a compliant mainstream media
that accepted fraudulent journalism as an unavoidable part of the overall
media mix.

The *Washington Times* has two high-profile news reporters, Bill Gertz
and Bill Sammon, both of whom appear frequently on television and publish slanted right-wing books through Regnery Publishing with campy titles
like Gertz's *Betrayal, The China Threat,* and *Breakdown* and Sammon's
improbable *At Any Cost: How Al Gore Tried to Steal the Election.* Gertz has
had the distinction of appearing on the radio show of Rush Limbaugh, who
rarely has guests. Deranged right-wingers such as Reagan-era anti-
Communist agitator Jack Wheeler, who advocated torture "the old-
fashioned way, right out of the movies, with putting cigarettes on his
testicles, breaking his ribs, the whole brutal nine yards" for a captured al-
Qaeda leader, leap off the *Times* op-ed pages onto FOX and MSNBC.

And despite the *Times*'s own lack of ethics, it leads the charge in
impugning the journalism of well-respected professionals. A 2003 interview
with Saddam Hussein by Dan Rather of CBS News was dismissed by the
Times as "purveying Iraqi propaganda"—a charge repeated throughout the
right-wing echo chamber.

Like the *New York Post,* the *Washington Times* frequently perpetrates
political hits on its enemies that subsequently make their way through the
rest of the right-wing media and beyond, misinforming millions. For example, on November 8, 2001, two months after terrorist attacks on the World
Trade Center and the Pentagon had traumatized the nation, a *Times*
reporter, Joseph Curl, grossly misrepresented remarks that Bill Clinton had
made at a speech at Georgetown University. CLINTON CALLS TERROR A U.S.
DEBT TO PAST; CITES SLAVERY IN GEORGETOWN SPEECH, the *Times* headlined the story. In his speech, Clinton had observed that the United States
is still "paying a price" for slavery today; that comment was in no way linked
to his remarks about why the United States was targeted by terrorists on
September 11. The *Times* linked the remarks to falsely suggest that Clinton
had said that the United States had invited an attack because of its own past.
With the exception of right-wing outlets, no news reports on the speech
made this connection.

Curl's "story" prompted Andrew Sullivan, who had not read the text of the speech, to excoriate Clinton on his Web site for making "truly shocking" remarks. James Taranto did the same on *National Review*'s Web site. One day later, after checking Clinton's text, Sullivan wrote, "It's not equivalent to saying that America asked for the 9/11 massacre, as I implied from what I now see was an appallingly slanted piece in the *Washington Times*." Taranto retracted, too.

As detailed by the Daily Howler Web site, the "appallingly slanted" article had already done harm. On the day the piece appeared, it was highlighted on the Drudge Report and bounced around right-wing talk radio all afternoon. That evening, on Brit Hume's FOX News Channel broadcast, his regular panel of "All Star" commentators weighed in. "I don't understand why [Clinton] wants to join the 'we don't come to this with clean hands' school. It's ridiculous," said Fred Barnes. NPR's Mara Liasson, another Hume "All Star," said, "You know, I would have liked to have known where he was going with that, and what does it have to do with terrorism, and is he equating the two? . . . I'm just wondering if he is trying to make some kind of moral equivalence." Barnes then said, "He's implying a moral equivalence between us and Osama bin Laden and his terrorists." Ceci Connolly of the *Washington Post*, who doubles as a FOX News contributor, said: "It's hard to say. I mean, it appeared from the clip that he had some point and some thought-out sequence there, but it's not clear to me, sort of, what either the larger message was, or how he is trying to apply it to this circumstance. . . . Maybe he just wants back in the spotlight." Later that night, *Washington Times* "assistant national editor" Jeffrey Kuhner appeared on *The O'Reilly Factor* to denounce Clinton as "morally reprehensible. . . . Look, the people that committed these atrocious acts on September 11 weren't attacking us because of slavery," he said.

Even after the retractions by right-wing writers, the "story" was recycled in a column by Ann Coulter and in books by David Horowitz and FOX's Sean Hannity. The *Washington Times*, meanwhile, republished Sullivan's original smear in his column "The Dish," but not his retraction. And several days later, the false story was still the subject of nationally syndicated right-wing radio shows. Mark Williams said "it turns out" that Clinton is "in philosophical agreement with those who hate America." Clinton, he said, "appeared to be either very tired or very drunk" during the speech.[13]

A year later, the *Times* again made a gross misrepresentation designed to exploit the September 11 tragedy for political ends. The *Times* reported that the National Education Association (NEA) was suggesting that teachers tell students not to hold any one group responsible for the terrorist attacks. As Brendan Nyhan reported in *Salon*, the "story" was based on a passage found by a *Times* reporter on an incomplete Web site set up by the NEA to solicit ideas from teachers that the reporter misattributed as official NEA advice. According to an NEA official, the *Times* description was "absolutely the opposite of our position." Yet the erroneous *Times* account was discussed on MSNBC's *Hardball,* on which substitute host Mike Barnicle denounced the NEA as "nuts"; on FOX's *Hannity & Colmes* and *FOX & Friends;* and on CNN's *Crossfire,* where Tucker Carlson asked, "Why does the NEA hate America?" On CNN's *Lou Dobbs Moneyline, U.S. News & World Report* columnist John Leo "spread the smear that the NEA believes America deserved to be attacked, using extremely vague language to make this grave charge with no evidence," according to Nyhan.

The *Times* is a means for right-wing political groups to gain disproportionate national publicity for their misinformation. In August 2003, the *Times* carried a front-page article, "'How to Be Gay' Course Draws Fire at Michigan." The University of Michigan course, which examined the evolution of social, literary, and media views of homosexuality, was more than three years old. It had drawn "fire" for years from the Michigan branch of the Far Right group the American Family Association, which falsely claimed the course was designed to "initiate" students into homosexuality. Though there was no apparent news hook, the *Times* reported that the controversy had been "reignited," which became a self-fulfilling claim when CNN, Brit Hume's show on FOX News, MSNBC's *Scarborough Country,* and several right-wing editorial pages and columnists around the country took their cues from the *Washington Times* and ran with the concoction.

Moon now controls the once-venerable United Press International (UPI) news wire service, which employs retreaded right-wingers like John O'Sullivan, formerly of *National Review;* Arnaud de Borchgrave, former editor of the *Washington Times;* and Peter Roff, formerly of Newt Gingrich's political action committee. UPI is led by chief executive Dr. Chung Hwan Kwak, who is also chairman of the Unification Party in Korea. Dr. Kwak's "chief foreign correspondent," Martin Sieff, appears on shows like Greta van Susteren's on FOX.

•   •   •

Canadian media mogul Lord Conrad Black owns the third-largest newspaper chain in the Western world, with a combined circulation of more than ten million. Through his company Hollinger International, Lord Black of Crossharbour, now a member of the British House of Lords, until recently controlled more than half of daily newspapers in Canada alone, including the right-wing *National Post*, where David Frum of AEI and *The Weekly Standard* is a columnist. Black's wife, the antifeminist British writer Barbara Amiel, sometimes called Lady Black, is a top company executive; and Richard Perle, former secretary of state under Henry Kissinger, and former Reagan official Richard Burt sit on the board.

Black shares with Murdoch and Moon an utter disregard for journalism. When Hollinger acquires a newspaper, "they fire half the staff, they get rid of the environmental reporters and the social affairs and the education and health reporters, and they replace them with businesspeople—or they don't replace them at all. . . . Anyone not singing that very right-wing Newt Gingrich type of . . . line is soon let go," according to Maude Barlow of the Council of Canadians, a nonpartisan citizens' watchdog agency. Black has described journalists as "ignorant, lazy, opinionated, intellectually dishonest and inadequately supervised hacks."[14]

Hollinger is among the top twelve newspaper chains in the United States, with a combined circulation of about one million. The *Chicago Sun-Times*, syndicator of Robert Novak, is Hollinger's flagship American paper. Black also influences U.S. politics through publications like the (London) *Daily Telegraph* and the *Jerusalem Post*, "a leading conservative outlet for opponents of the peace process throughout the world," according to *The Forward* (a Jewish-oriented weekly). During the Clinton administration, the *Telegraph's* Washington bureau chief was Ambrose Evans-Pritchard, an infamous conspiracy theorist whose false stories, repeated widely on U.S. talk radio and repackaged in book form by Regnery, did much to propagate the fallacy that Vincent Foster was murdered. Anne Applebaum of the *Washington Post* was schooled at the *Telegraph*, and Lord Black now underwrites Irving Kristol's hawkish *National Interest* magazine.

Black recently purchased a newspaper widely circulated on Capitol Hill, *The Hill*, which had been apolitical under prior ownership. Through *The Hill*, he injects his ideology into the Washington debate and propels it

onto cable and talk radio. According to a report in *The American Prospect,*
The Hill's publisher, longtime journalist Martin Tolchin, resigned and was
replaced by Hugo Gurdon, a former editor at Black's *National Post* in
Canada. Gurdon had served as the "Warren Brookes Journalism Fellow" at
the Cato Institute, named after a deceased right-wing *Washington Times*
columnist. Under Gurdon, *American Spectator* alum Sam Dealey was
assigned to report on the 2004 Democratic presidential candidates, while
another former *Spectator* muckraker, Byron York, now the "White House
correspondent" for *National Review,* was given a weekly column. Among his
other journalistic sins, York was caught by *The American Prospect* misquot-
ing Democratic Senator Joe Biden, "egregiously misrepresenting what he
said at a crucial point in the [John] Ashcroft [nomination] hearings."

In 2002, Black became a major investor in the *New York Sun,* a new
daily newspaper designed to circulate even more right-wing opinion in the
Big Apple. He was joined in the $15 million investment by, among others,
Roger Hertog, a very wealthy Wall Street money manager, chairman of the
Manhattan Institute, and co-owner of *The New Republic.* Hired to edit the
paper was Seth Lipsky, a Robert Bartley protégé at the *Journal* and a former editor of *The Forward.* "I don't believe in journalists having 'responsibility,'" Lipsky has said. Of journalistic objectivity, he said, "If it's objective,
then you would fall asleep reading it—if you could still read it after throw-
ing up on it."[15]

The subsidized *Sun* is yet another employment agency for conserva-
tive polemicists, including Peggy Noonan, R. Emmett Tyrrell, *National*
Review's Richard Brookhiser, and Ellen Bork, daughter of the rejected
Supreme Court nominee and a deputy director of William Kristol's Project
for the New American Century. The paper runs columns by Lady Black
(who almost titled her memoir of ideological conversion from the Left
Fascist Bitch before settling on *Confessions)* and by Lipsky's wife, Amity
Shlaes, another longtime *Journal* editorial page hand and author of the book
The Greedy Hand: How Taxes Drive Americans Crazy and What to Do
About It.

The *Sun* has received universally bad reviews for sloppy and biased
journalism. It publishes front-page op-eds talking up Manhattan Institute
symposia, allows former Manhattan Institute president William Hammett
to write "news" stories on the state budget, and has referred to China as

"red."[16] Following an antiwar demonstration in Manhattan in February 2003, the newspaper published an editorial asserting that the protesters were providing "aid and comfort" to Saddam Hussein and therefore had committed treason in violation of the U.S. Constitution.

The *Sun's* circulation is only in the tens of thousands, suggesting there may be a saturation point in a media market now brimming with right-wing misinformation and opinion; but because of the way information travels and is magnified by the right wing, the *Sun's* treason editorial was quoted approvingly on talk radio nationally; it ricocheted around the Internet; and by pushing the edge of right-wing argument toward Fascism, it made hard Right voices like the *Journal's* seem almost reasonable.[17]

In fall 2003, Lord Black resigned his post as Hollinger's chief executive, and his media empire appeared to combust. Black and F. David Radler, publisher of the *Chicago Sun-Times*, "stand accused of pocketing millions of dollars in unauthorized payments that might have been due the company in deals related to the sale of numerous Hollinger newspapers," according to *Chicago* magazine, which noted that under Hollinger's ownership, the *Sun-Times's* "politics have grown considerably more conservative—and not just on the commentary pages . . . the news pages have been impacted as well." As the Securities and Exchange Commission initiated an investigation that drew in Hollinger director Richard Perle, observers predicted a massive sell-off of the Hollinger properties, which remain under Black's control. Black stood to lose his seat in the British House of Lords if found criminally culpable. Lord and Lady Black remained in seclusion in Toronto as press reports revealed they had taken as much as $30 million from the company in lavish perquisites.

In the heat of the scandal, the *New York Times* revealed that two prominent "Fifth Columnists," William Buckley and George Will, had been on Black's payroll for years as "advisers" to Hollinger. Earlier in the year, Will had used his syndicated column to heap praise on his patron, with no disclosure of his financial interest. In the world of right-wing media, clearly something other than the normal rules of journalism applied. "My business is my business," Will told the *Times.* "Got it?"

CHAPTER SEVEN

MINISTERS OF
PROPAGANDA

A FTER FOUNDING THE HERITAGE FOUNDATION, Paul Weyrich and his initial financial backer Joe Coors did not rest on their laurels. After leaving Heritage and chartering the Free Congress Foundation with Coors money in the mid-1970s, Weyrich masterminded the right wing's expansion into television. As a former broadcaster, he recognized the potency of the medium and how it could be used to further the conservative cause.

With Weyrich's prodding, Coors ventured directly into spreading the conservative word through the TV media. Coors provided initial funding for Television News Inc., a twenty-four-hour news service based in New York City in the days before cable.[1] As "news director," Coors hired Roger Ailes, the former Nixon aide and conservative publicist. That effort was short-lived. More than twenty years would pass before Ailes was tapped by Rupert Murdoch to head the FOX News Channel.

Weyrich, meanwhile, had secret blueprints drawn up outlining a multi-million-dollar plan to convert the politically dormant Evangelical Christian constituency to conservative policy positions through new media channels.[2] The effort was underwritten by Richard DeVos, the conservative president of the Amway Corporation, and by Dallas billionaire Nelson Bunker Hunt, a supporter of the John Birch Society, of George Wallace, of the National Conservative Political Action Committee, and of the Media Research Center.[2]

As Edith Efron had predicted in 1971, conservatives could take advantage of the so-called narrowcasting trend in the TV industry, which made it profitable to reach smaller audiences with special interests. The loyalty of the audience was more important than its size. A network of religious Right broadcasters, organized in a trade association called the National Religious Broadcasters, moved quickly to buy local TV stations, package programming for syndication, begin networks through newly available cable and satellite systems, and commandeer previously neglected UHF channels.[3]

Religious broadcasting, especially on radio, was not new, though in the past it focused more on cultural than political matters. The ABC television network, then run by conservative Republican executives, had given the Reverend Billy Graham a half-hour program in the 1950s, which he used to promote fundamentalist Christianity and bash Communism.[4] In the 1950s and 1960s, fundamentalist ministries stretching from New Jersey to Arkansas, attracting financial support from local businesspeople, reached large radio audiences; exposed listeners to Christian Fundamentalism; and railed against the teachings of Charles Darwin.

A few of these ministers were ferociously ideological and had a distinct political bias; for example, the Reverend Billy James Hargis used his Christian Crusade to denounce Communists, liberals, homosexuals, and the media. Hargis was aided by *Conservative Digest* publisher Richard Viguerie and his valuable direct-mail lists. Heard on 270 radio stations nationwide, Hargis said "the biggest traitors" were "liberals, welfare staters, do-gooders and one-worlders." "Don't talk to me of liberalism! It is a double-standard, Satanic hypocrisy," he proclaimed. The Christian Crusade published a magazine of the same name and several books, such as *The Facts About Communism & Our Churches, Communism: The Total Lie*, and *The Real Extremists: The Far Left*.[5] (A sex scandal caused Hargis to lose his ministry in 1976.)

The Reverend Carl McIntire of *The 20th Century Reformation Hour* reached some twenty million radio listeners through six hundred outlets, supplemented by mass mailings of "radio letters" and sponsored by McIntire's newspaper, the *Christian Beacon*. "His program runs a pattern," as George Thayer elucidated in *The Farther Shores of Politics.* "He opens with a folksy greeting that is offset by strains of some patriotic music such as 'The Battle Hymn of the Republic' . . . then comes the political pitch . . . 'these communists and these liberals are using the fear of the bomb to frighten us so we won't stand up for our principles of morality and we will retreat from freedom . . . and our political leaders—some of them—are being intimidated by this propaganda. . . .'"[6] Dr. Frederick Charles Schwarz of the Christian Anti-Communism Crusade convened "meet and scream" groups in which participants were "ready to condemn, attack, harass or intimidate at the first slip of a liberal phrase."[7]

Dallas oilman H. L. Hunt, Nelson Bunker Hunt's father, subsidized the Campus Crusade for Christ and broadcast *The Facts Forum,* later called *Life Line,* with a nominally religious bent. These radio programs, aired on 387 radio stations nationwide, reached as many as five million listeners per day. Underwritten by advertising from Hunt-owned companies, the programs campaigned against "teachers, psychologists, sociologists, psychiatrists, economists, and politicians," all of whom Hunt considered "practiced brain-twisters turned loose on our defenseless children." Hunt believed that the U.S. government was Communist-controlled. *Life Line* lost its tax exemption as a public charity in 1963 because its programming was so "one-sided."[8]

What was new in the 1970s was the fusion of religion and partisan politics coupled with technological capacity to reach a wider audience. Weyrich showed fundamentalist evangelical ministers such as Pat Robertson and Jerry Falwell how to politicize religion to the GOP's benefit while making boatloads of cash. Politics was projected onto the TV screen and cast as a morality play, a Manichaean struggle between the forces of light and darkness. Bad intentions, illegitimacy, and even Satanic powers were assigned to the "enemy."[9] "Rhetoric that equates the political work of the religious right with warfare is commonplace among the movement's leaders," analyst Dan Junas has written. "It reflects in part an apocalyptic vision of politics, and in part a conviction that their agenda reflects divine will." The "central, unifying ideology" of the various strains of evangelical belief, according to Junas, was that "Christians are mandated by the Bible to take control of all secular institutions and build the Kingdom of God on earth."[10]

"We are going to single out those people in government who are against what we consider to be the Bible, moralist position, and we're going to inform the public," Falwell announced. "Jesus was not a pacifist. He was not a sissy." Robertson said, "We have enough votes to run the country. And when people say, 'We've had enough,' we are going to take over." According to Robertson, "It's going to be a spiritual battle. There will be Satanic forces. . . . We are not going to be coming up just against human beings, to beat them in elections. We're going to be coming up against spiritual warfare."

"If you read Scripture, Jesus was not some sort of milquetoast person with supreme charity," Weyrich declared. "He cut people in two."

The new religious broadcasts echoed many of the racial and sexual themes of the direct-mail hit pieces and of new conservative magazines like *Conservative Digest*, which called for a national day "of fasting and prayer" to "devote completely to prayer, meditation, thanks and repentance for our sins." Robertson told his listeners: "There will never be world peace until God's house and God's people are given their rightful place of leadership at the top of the world. How can there be peace when drunkards, drug dealers, communists, atheists, New Age worshippers of Satan, secular humanists, oppressive dictators, greedy money changers, revolutionary assassins, adulterers, and homosexuals are on top?"[11]

Demonization of the "liberal media" was a rhetorical staple of the religious broadcasters; Hargis's ministry had put out a pamphlet called *The Ugly Truth About Drew Pearson*, attacking the integrity of the prominent columnist. On the Trinity Broadcasting Network's *Praise the Lord* show, Doug Clark compared critical press reports on Ronald Reagan to a "satanic attack on America" adding, "I think we're carrying [press] freedom a little too far."[12] Later, the Christian broadcasters played a key role in propagating the fiction that the Iran-contra scandal was an invention of a liberal media conspiracy as a way of deflecting aggressive media coverage.

On a deeper level, when many Christian activists criticized the "liberal" media, they were expressing concern that the media was a secular institution, rather than a fundamentalist Christian one. Their theology put them in conflict with the fact-based approach of objective journalism. In his book *Prodigal Press*, Marvin Olasky—the close adviser to both Newt Gingrich and George W. Bush, whom the latter called "compassionate conservatism's leading thinker"—identified the problem as "the almost total dominance of newspapers by non-Christians." Olasky described the *New York Times* as a once "great Christian newspaper." Of the newspaper's subsequent (and current) Jewish owners, the Ochs/Sulzberger family, Olasky wrote, "One generation died or departed. Owners and editors who knew not Joseph emerged." An example of "liberal bias" cited by Olasky was "materialist reporters [who] could not take seriously the belief that AIDS is a God-sent warning to homosexuals and adulterous heterosexuals and to anyone who scorns Him."

The ministers endeavored to present their theology in a journalistic style, with Pat Robertson acting as the unlikely assigning editor. The Virginia-based Robertson was the son of a U.S. senator, was a Yale Law School grad, and had attended seminary, where he came to believe that God had instructed him to purchase a TV station, which he did in 1959. Robertson hired Jim and Tammy Faye Bakker; together the three launched *The 700 Club* TV show in 1963. Funds were raised for the broadcast through telethons.[13]

In 1977, Robertson founded the Christian Broadcasting Network. CBN formed a "news department" and hired "correspondents," and *The 700 Club* moved beyond religious proselytizing to booking right-wing politicians and activists as talking heads.[14] On CBN, which was carried in thirty-six million homes by the mid-1980s, the conservative movement had just the kind of biased, crusading, counterfactual electronic powerhouse that they claimed to fear liberal partisans had established at CBS, NBC, and ABC.

Before FOX, before CNN, MSNBC, and CNBC, there was CBN. The head of the National Religious Broadcasters, the Reverend Ben Armstrong, observed that the televangelists had "done what Ted Turner tried to do and Rupert Murdoch wants to do—create a fourth alternative network."[15]

The broadcasts were a means for conservative spokespeople to politicize their base with their own brand of conservative "news." Christian reconstructionist activist Gary North, the son-in-law of Rousas Rushdoony, said that Robertson's CBN was a tool to create political "brushfires," rallying local ministers and their audiences around the country to adopt a proscribed point of view. "Without a means of publicizing a crisis, few pastors would take a stand," said North, who advocated stoning women who had abortions.[16]

In 1980, *Forbes* reported that three religious TV networks— Robertson's CBN, the PTL Television Network, and the Trinity Broadcasting Network—were grossing $140 million, compared with close to nothing in 1975. Religiously oriented TV stations numbered more than thirty nationwide. Christian preachers soon had sixty-two nationally syndicated shows. "One evangelical TV show, the Christian Broadcasting Network's '700 Club,' reaches cable TV systems with 8 million subscribers—more cabled homes than Home Box Office reaches," *Forbes* reported. "The '700 Club' is also carried on 150 television stations, almost as many as are affiliated with ABC. The '700 Club's' major religious rival, the PTL Television Network's 'PTL Club,' reaches 4 million cabled homes and is aired on 235 TV stations, more than are affiliated with CBS. Even Trinity's 'Praise The Lord' program, a distant number three in religious show biz, reaches 2.5 million cabled homes—more than Showtime, HBO's biggest rival."

Forbes also noted that "many evangelists are using their shows, financed with tax-deductible contributions, not only to preach the gospel but to promote politicians and political causes."

"The television evangelists, who each week explicate the moral issues and lament the state of the American nation and spirit, give the movement its appearance of a massive and single-minded constituency," the *New York Times* reported in 1980. The *Times* found reliable audience numbers difficult to come by, in part because cable was not then rated. Viewership estimates for the newly politicized TV preachers, once heard only in the Bible Belt but now appearing in major TV markets around the country, ranged as high as 115 million per week, although the actual figure may have been closer to 30 million. An unrepeated radio audience, tuning in to 1,300 religious radio stations, might have been about 15 million. The audience for Jerry Falwell's *Old-Time Gospel Hour*, aired on 325 TV stations and 300 radio stations each week, was anywhere from 6 million to 15 million per week.

At biweekly meetings in Washington of his secretive Library Court group, where he gathered the leadership of twenty-five right-wing think tank and advocacy organizations that had been chartered in just a two-year period (between 1978 and 1980), Paul Weyrich worked to reshape the messaging of the religious broadcasters—many of whom had supported the Southern Baptist Jimmy Carter in 1976—and he coordinated lines of communication. In 1979, Weyrich coined the term "moral majority" for the newly active Christian Right. "We are talking about Christianizing America," he said. "We are talking simply about spreading the Bible in a political context."

A frequent guest on Robertson's *700 Club* and on the Reverend Jim and Tammy Faye Bakker's *Praise the Lord,* Weyrich told the *Times* that before the 1980 election, he had met with "upwards of 10,000 pastors" nationwide, giving technical talks on how to frame issues and anti-Carter sermons in a way that would favor Reagan and other conservative candidates while trying to avoid running afoul of Federal Communications Commission rules that said hosts on broadcast television could not endorse political candidates.

Weyrich estimated that these efforts had resulted in the registration of millions of new fundamentalist Christian voters. Though they fell far short of constituting a "moral majority," they were zealous and highly dedicated viewers and participants who compensated for their minority status through intense activism. Given Reagan's popular vote margin of just over 50 percent—with just over half of eligible voters casting ballots—it was apparent that among other factors, this harnessing of new media power by highly emotive and manipulative right-winger leaders, who mobilized the social discontent prevalent in the country during the Carter years, had made a critical difference in the outcome of the 1980 election.

Though several of the high-profile televangelists were eventually ruined in a series of sex and financial fraud scandals, fundamentalist ministers continue today to reach deeply into the base of the GOP with right-wing messaging and "news." Thirty years after its founding, the Trinity Broadcasting Network is "not only the world's largest Christian television ministry, it is also the 10th largest television broadcaster in the U.S.," according to the Washington, D.C.–based Center for Public Integrity. Its programming includes *The 700 Club* and *Praise the Lord,* now hosted by the network's founders, Paul and Jan Crouch. According to the center, "While Trinity's dedication to spreading the word of the Lord seems admirable enough, some of the views expressed by regular contributors to the network, like John Hagee of John Hagee Ministries & Global Evangelism Television,

Inc., trouble some observers. Hagee's views on a coming Armaggedon might be considered quirky were it not for his huge audience and close ties to House Majority Leader Tom DeLay, who has spoken at Hagee events in support of the minister."

The ministers effectively parlay their prominence in the Christian media into prominence across every broadcast and cable news network in the country. Falwell and Robertson are generally interviewed respectfully, and even indulgently, by secular hosts, no matter how hate filled or fallacious their messages. Falwell, a cable regular, is rarely called to account for his role in selling copies of *The Clinton Chronicles*, a lurid videotape suggesting the Clintons were complicit in murder.

Despite his history of extremist speech, Robertson has appeared as an unexceptionable guest on virtually every mainstream TV news and talk show in the country. In 1985, Robertson remarked, "Whenever evangelization efforts meet with chronic resistance, extermination should follow." He told *New York* magazine, "The people who have come into institutions today are primarily termites. They are destroying institutions that have been built by Christians, whether it is the universities, government, our traditions that we have. The termites are in charge now, and that is not the way it ought to be, and the time has come for a godly fumigation."[17]

In his 1991 book, *The New World Order,* Robertson claimed that an international conspiracy of Jewish bankers controlled the financial system. "You're supposed to be nice to Episcopalians, Presbyterians, and Methodists," Robertson told the *London Observer.* "Nonsense. I don't have to be nice to the spirit of the anti-Christ." In a 1992 fund-raising letter, Robertson wrote, "The feminist agenda is not about equal rights for women. It is about a socialist, anti-family political movement that encourages women to leave their husbands, kill their children, practice witchcraft, destroy capitalism, and become lesbians."

In 2003, Robertson launched a twenty-one-day "prayer offensive" that he called Operation Supreme Court Freedom. Claiming that the court "has opened the door to homosexual marriage, bigamy, legalized prostitution and even incest," Robertson seemed to wish for the deaths of three justices. "One justice is 83 years old, another has cancer, and another has a heart condition," he said on *The 700 Club* Web site.[18]

Interviewing *National Review's* Joel Mowbray on *The 700 Club* about his Regnery book *Dangerous Diplomacy: How the State Department Threatens America's Security*, Robertson said, "I read your book. When you get through, you say, 'If I could just get a nuclear device inside Foggy Bottom, I think that's the answer.' I mean, you get through this, and you say, 'We've got to blow that thing up.' I mean, is it as bad as you say?" Mowbray replied, "It is." Six months prior, Robertson had said on the same broadcast, "Maybe we need a very small nuke thrown off on Foggy Bottom to shake things up."

Even after Falwell and Robertson blamed "abortionists, feminists and gays and lesbians" for the terrorist attack on September 11, they were welcomed back into the ranks of TV punditry as if they had never uttered those words. Falwell subsequently appeared—alone—on Bill O'Reilly's FOX show to discuss "Gays & the GOP."

Eclipsing Falwell and perhaps even Robertson is Dr. James Dobson, a right-wing psychologist who chairs a national network of more than eighty Christian fundamentalist ministries called Focus on the Family. Dobson's "internationally syndicated radio programs [are] heard daily on more than 3,000 radio facilities in North America and in 15 languages on approximately 3,300 facilities in over 116 countries," according to his Web site. "His commentaries are heard by more than 200 million people every day, including a program translation carried on all state-owned radio stations in the People's Republic of China. He is seen on 80 television stations daily in the U.S."

According to the site, Dobson reaches a combined radio and TV audience of twenty-nine million Americans, more than Rush Limbaugh. In addition to his own daily thirty-minute radio show, *Family News in Focus*, *The James Dobson Family Minute* ("nuggets of truth" culled from the thirty-minute broadcast), and *Focus on the Family Commentary* are syndicated to several major-market radio stations. Another nationally syndicated radio spot is *Washington Watch*, a ninety-second report hosted by right-wing Family Research Council spokesperson Genevieve Wood (a member of Heritage's "Media Advisory Board"), which "alerts each of us to current developments in public policy that promise—or threaten—to have a direct impact on the family values we hold dear."

Dobson's biography on his Web site says that he has been an adviser on "family matters" to Ronald Reagan, George H. W. Bush, and Bob Dole. He is the author of the best-selling book *Dare to Discipline*, with chapters titled "Love Must Be Tough," "Parenting Isn't for Cowards," and "Emotions: Can You Trust Them?" In 2002, he published *Bringing Up Boys*, in which he asked (and answered) "What Causes Homosexuality?" and "How Can It Be Prevented?" *Library Journal* cautioned librarians about the latter book, calling it "peculiarly mean-spirited." In it, Dobson dispenses "biblically-based" advice and defames feminists as women who "never married, didn't like children, and deeply resented men. . . ." The book was for sale on Sean Hannity's Web site, among other outlets.

Dobson uses his media platforms for political ends. In 1994, he achieved his first major victory by helping to defeat congressional legislation that would have required homeschool teachers to be certified. In summer 2003, Dobson's radio and TV commentaries focused on such topics as "Dobson Supports War Effort in Iraq"; support for the "Federal Marriage Amendment" banning gay unions; and thwarting "Judicial Tyranny" by confirming right-wing Bush judicial nominees. Supreme Court Justice Anthony Kennedy, a Reagan appointee who wrote a decision striking down anti-sodomy laws in Texas, was called "the most dangerous man in America." Dobson featured the book *A Parent's Guide to Preventing Homosexuality*, which claimed that homosexuality is "preventable and treatable" and resulted from "damaged relations with a father or an overbearing mother." (The book was featured on the FOX News shows *Hannity & Colmes* and *The O'Reilly Factor*.)

Dobson is a frequent guest on CNN's *Larry King Live*, where he appears for cordial, solo, hour-length interviews during which the kindly King does his best to humanize him, even when Dobson told King on the air that King—as a Jew—could not go to heaven. According to the Focus on the Family Web site, Dr. Walt Larimore, "vice president of medical outreach," has appeared on NBC's *Today* show, CNN Headline News, MSNBC, and several FOX News shows and has given dozens of print interviews to mainstream newspapers. Carrie Gordon Earll, "bioethics analyst," has been interviewed on CNN's *Wolf Blitzer Reports* and on National Public Radio.

Through this steady and mostly uncritical mainstream media exposure, these Christian rightists, with their polemical biblical interpretations and pseudosocial science, have come to stand for what it meant to be a politically committed Christian in the United States. Representatives of mainstream Christianity are far less frequently featured in the TV debate about politics and policy.

In 1993, what *Newsweek* called America's "first unabashedly ideological, political TV channel" was launched: National Empowerment Television (NET). Behind the operation was none other than Paul Weyrich. Ever since his experiences with Christian broadcasting in the late 1970s, Weyrich had been aiming to bring conservative ideology to the TV airwaves in a secular format. With NET, he got the chance.

By this time, Joe Coors's son Jeffrey had become chairman of Weyrich's Free Congress Foundation. The Coors family, Richard Mellon Scaife, and Christian Right activist Howard F. Ahmanson Jr. underwrote the new network, eventually to the tune of $17 million per year filtered through Weyrich's network of nonprofits. Ahmanson, an Orange County, California, multimillionaire, has backed a magazine called the *Chalcedon Report,* which "carried an article calling for gays to be stoned; a think tank called the Claremont Institute which promoted a video in which Charlton Heston praises the 'God-fearing Caucasian middle class'; and a scientific body which rejects the theory of evolution," according to a report about Ahmanson's activities in *The Guardian* of London.[19]

The chief operating officer of NET was Burton Yale Pines, a former Heritage official; the general manager was Brian Jones, a Bush operative in the 1992 campaign and future FOX News Channel executive. NET reached into about fourteen million subscriber households nationwide, with the largest markets in the South and West, and captured a predominantly male audience. Its approach was heavily interactive, giving conservatives an opportunity to phone in and receive direct political instruction on lobbying for or against legislation to "talk back to Washington," as Weyrich put it.

To promote the career of Newt Gingrich, whom Weyrich had trained in one of his seminars in the 1970s prior to his first race for Congress, NET broadcast a program hosted by Gingrich called *Progress Report* as well as a course Gingrich taught on "American civilization," both of which were underwritten by nonprofit foundations Gingrich sustained as adjuncts to GOPAC, his political action committee. Through NET, Gingrich received crucial exposure in the run-up to the 1994 congressional elections, a year of very low voter turnout when the GOP won control of Congress.

Among other personalities featured on the network were Bush aide Mary Matalin, Representative Susan Molinari, Robert Novak, Armstrong Williams, Grover Norquist, and Ronald Reagan's son Michael. Reed Irvine produced a series for NET called *The Other Side,* which promoted the theory that former White House counsel Vincent Foster had been lured into a "sex trap" at Fort Marcy Park, where his dead body was found. The National Rifle Association, the Cato Institute, and the Christian Coalition were featured prominently (some of the groups paid for the TV time). A "news and policy program" titled *Rising Tide* was produced by the Republican National Committee. Another show, *The Next Revolution,* focused on "America's abandonment of its traditional Judeo-Christian culture for the cultural Marxism of political correctness." Weyrich insisted that the network ban the words "gay," "African American," and "Native American" and replace them with "homosexual," "black," and "Indian."

A weekly NET show was hosted by conservative theorist William Lind, who advocated burning adulterers at the stake and branding women who held careers outside the home with the letter *C.* According to Lind:

> Hatred of certain things is a family value, and a very important one. In fact, if we are going to rescue our culture, we need a lot more hate. We need hate of the very things cultural Marxism most strongly promotes, including loose sexual morals, feminism and bad behavior by certain racial and ethnic groups.

In an article published by the Free Congress Foundation, Eric Heubeck explained why Weyrich sought a TV presence. He wrote:

> There is no medium more conducive to propagandistic purposes than the moving image, and our movement must learn to make use of this medium. A skillfully produced motion picture or television documentary has tremendous persuasive power. It has the power to bypass not only the old prejudices that have been assiduously cultivated by the Left over the past few decades, but also the innate skepticism of the viewer, the resistance to new ideas and all arguments made in print [that] tend to appeal to the rational, critical faculties of the mind to a greater or lesser degree.[20]

In 1995, after Republicans won control of Congress, Weyrich was able to convince Tele-Communications Inc. (TCI) cable systems to carry his fledgling network, clearing a very difficult hurdle for any new cable channel. TCI, the nation's largest cable operator at the time, was run by John C. Malone, who owned effective controlling interest in the company and was a prominent industry spokesman for deregulatory plans that the new Gingrich-led Congress would act on. Malone served on the board of the Cato Institute, and he praised Rush Limbaugh for being willing to "say politically incorrect things."[21]

The conservative mogul emerged in the mid-1990s as a key behind-the-scenes player in the political composition of the media. "Malone was the man who decided what went into the television sets of one in every four U.S. cable households—and what didn't," wrote Murdoch biographer Neil Chenoweth. When Rupert Murdoch launched the FOX News Channel in 1996, Malone made him a crucial deal, giving Murdoch access to TCI systems in return for the right to buy a 20 percent interest in the channel. Malone purchased two-thirds of MacNeil/Lehrer Productions, the producer of PBS's *NewsHour with Jim Lehrer,* and TCI owned significant interests in the Discovery Channel, Court TV, and Time Warner, which owned CNN and *Time* among other media properties. When Malone created his own news chat show, he hired future FOX anchor David Asman from the *Wall Street Journal* as host and called it *Damn Right!* He also brought to TCI Pat Robertson's Family Channel, formerly the Christian Broadcasting Network.[22]

Malone killed the '90s Channel, a liberal cable channel, by raising entry rates to his cable system and excluding it from a political package that included the heavily subsidized NET.[23] Democrats in Washington discussed plans to create a liberal NET, but nothing moved beyond the talking phase.

Political liberals did not have a media honcho like John Malone in their corner, nor did they have the deep pockets of a Rupert Murdoch or a Paul Weyrich. Weyrich was displaced as NET chairman due to erratic behavior in 1997; he was succeeded by former NBC executive Bob Sutton. By then, NET had lost its steam, but Murdoch was well on his way to filling the TV niche that Weyrich had identified and nurtured for more than twenty years.

CHAPTER EIGHT
TALKING HEADS

N JUNE 1980, SHORTLY BEFORE RONALD REAGAN'S nomination and as the Christian broadcasters were going full tilt, the Atlanta entrepreneur Ted Turner launched a twenty-four-hour-a-day pay-TV Cable News Network. First and foremost Turner was a businessman; after working out the technical snafus, CNN quickly won high marks for hiring experienced journalistic professionals and delivering a highly reliable news product. Its on-air political commentary was another matter, as a procession of secular right-wing ministers of propaganda suddenly graced the mainstream airwaves.

By this time, the major TV broadcast networks—under political and commercial pressure in the post-Watergate, post-Vietnam period—had all but dropped clearly labeled commentaries on the newscasts by rational and dispassionate anchors such as Eric Sevareid, Chet Huntley, and Howard K. Smith. The commentaries spanned the range from liberal to moderate conservative but leaned to the liberal side (a fact that undoubtedly contributed to suspicions by conservatives that the news itself was slanted). With commentary disappearing from the networks as they adopted a scrupulously neutral posture, movement conservatives were busily making inroads on the airwaves. William Buckley was hosting a PBS series, *Firing Line,* and through his *Washington Post* connection, George Will had won a spot on *Agronsky & Company,* a syndicated Washington-based political chat show. James J. Kilpatrick faced off against liberal journalist Shana Alexander on CBS's *60 Minutes.*

Because CNN broadcast around the clock, network executives found themselves in a position akin to that of the editors of the expanding op-ed pages. Partly to program all that time, and partly to incite controversy and brand itself as distinct from the opinion-free and increasingly bland network newscasts, CNN popularized the TV talking head, bringing a steady diet of strong partisan views to the airwaves for the first time—and in a news format to boot.

With few exceptions, print journalists previously had functioned on television as interviewers, not pundits. In the 1940s and 1950s, however, ABC had featured columnists Walter Winchell, Louella Parsons, and George Sokolsky, "virulent anti-Communist conservatives, who used their ABC air time and newspaper columns to encourage the blacklisting of actors, directors, producers, and other performing artists during the Joseph McCarthy–led witch hunts of the House Un-American Activities Committee."[1] Conversely, the liberal commentator William Shirer had been forced off CBS in 1947 after conservative sponsors falsely alleged that he was a Communist sympathizer.

Just before launching, CNN announced the hiring of a slate of commentators to opine on the air. The list included five conservatives: Senator Barry Goldwater, Phyllis Schlafly, Robert Novak, Rowland Evans, and William "the Terrible" Simon. Two liberals came aboard: consumer activist Ralph Nader and Democratic Representative Bella Abzug. Also on the roster were historian and political columnist Richard Reeves, a mildly liberal but nonpartisan analyst; Dr. Joyce Brothers, a pop psychologist; and the astrologer Jeane Dixon. CNN ran short commentaries from this stable throughout the day, "slipping them in like two-minute commercials," as Turner himself put it.[2]

In this original CNN lineup, the future of cable talk had taken shape. Conservative advantage on the nation's op-ed pages was being translated to a more powerful opinion sector on television. The ideological conservatives outnumbered the ideological liberals 5–2. Among the five conservatives, there were no representatives of traditional Republicanism, then still a significant force in the GOP. All five conservatives came from the Reaganite right wing, a rather sudden and dramatic expansion of the spectrum of opinion that had been seen regularly on network television and a bonanza for the right-wing media infiltration scheme.

The network commentaries had been delivered by seasoned and fair-minded newscasters; but on CNN, journalist and nonjournalist commentators commingled. Distinctions were blurred between the carefully hedged viewpoints offered by Richard Reeves, based on factual reporting and research, and the straightforward ideological advocacy of Phyllis Schlafly or the highly partisan attacks of a former Republican Cabinet official like William Simon. A similar pairing of journalism and advocacy already had been sanctioned on the op-ed pages, with the uneven equation of longtime *Times* newsman James Reston and Nixon henchman William Safire. The Right's political edge in pitting Safire against an unaligned, discriminating centrist liberal like Reston would be magnified many times over on television.

CNN threw open the mainstream media floodgates that had previously functioned as a kind of filtering coefficient for merit and the logical expression of ideas. As Edith Efron understood, if the regular media devoted so much space for the expression of right-wing ideas, the implication was that they had value. Reasonable people would think there must be something to them. Once legitimized, the conservatives would turn the media impulse to present both sides into an exercise in twisting the news through intolerance, misinformation, and ideological intimidation.

Ignorance and bigotry had never before been given a permanent place in the TV news lineup. Yet now a new outlet of the mainstream media—a mainstream media that, according to the conservatives, was trying to force a liberal social agenda on a conservative country—would give a platform to voices of the cultural right wing, who, like televangelists, based their arguments on perceived morality and theology rather than on facts and logic.

The sexist gay basher Phyllis Schlafly is sometimes called the mother of the conservative movement. Schlafly is also the mother of a gay son; she's a lawyer, a Harvard graduate, and a prolific writer and organizer who nevertheless spearheaded an anti-intellectual, antifeminist, antigay agenda. "The claim that American women are downtrodden and unfairly treated is the fraud of the century," Schlafly maintained. While supported by her Eagle Forum organization, Schlafly ran a nationwide campaign against sex education, calling the classes "like in-home sales parties for abortions."[3] "It's very healthy for a young girl to be deterred from promiscuity by fear of contracting a painful, incurable disease, or cervical cancer, or sterility, or the likelihood of giving birth to a dead, blind, or brain-damaged baby even ten years later when she may be happily married," she said.[4]

Condemning cultural diversity, Schlafly asserted, "Many years ago Christian pioneers had to fight savage Indians. Today missionaries of these former cultures are being sent via the public schools to heathenize our children."[5] Schlafly was a book banner, later becoming embroiled in a controversy in which she condemned a social studies curriculum for failing to include the views of Nazis and the Ku Klux Klan.[6] As late as 1997, Schlafly produced a video titled *Global Governance: The Quiet War Against American Independence,* which claimed that a "small elite" of "cosmopolitan" and "international" financiers were secretly working through the feminist, gay rights, and environmental movements for the formation of a Socialist one-world government.[7] GOP Senator and future Bush Attorney General John Ashcroft made a cameo appearance.

Since the Goldwater days, when she self-published her work for a wide audience, Schlafly had become a syndicated columnist, appearing in dozens of papers; she continued to do a radio commentary that was carried on hundreds of stations nationwide. When she joined CNN, Schlafly was perhaps best known for having led the fight against the Equal Rights Amendment (ERA) for women by spreading a phony scare story that it would outlaw separate bathrooms for the sexes. Schlafly's catchphrase "unisex bathrooms" was a perfect illustration of the kind of rhetorical trope the conservatives would bring to television—a crude and deceptive but highly evocative phrase. It gave ERA opponents a two-word club with which to beat back the arguments of its proponents. And it was a red herring that nonetheless put ERA backers on the defensive, forcing them to argue on Schlafly's terms.

The very presence in the TV media of misinformers like Schlafly and those who followed in her wake greatly advantaged the Right and greatly disadvantaged its opponents. Some people will believe anything. Once something is broadcast on TV, as on radio—no matter how irresponsible or illogical—it exists; it is "out there"; and it is not subject to the strictures of reason and accountability as it would be in print. It is also very difficult to rebut. Rather than engaging in legitimate debate, nonconservatives were forced to spend precious airtime answering right-wing lies.

Turning someone like Schlafly into a TV personality was a genius p.r. ploy, since she did represent the views of an extremist constituency in the Republican Party who were seldom heard on mainstream television. Like the new Christian-oriented networks that were attracting significant audiences, an upstart cable network needed only a fraction of the broadcast network audience to succeed. After decades of conservative books, newsletters, and magazines, the proliferation of op-ed columns of the late 1970s, and the takeover of the *New York Post* by Rupert Murdoch, the Right had created and cultivated an audience that didn't want to read journalism; rather, this audience wanted to see its opinions and prejudices reinforced in print. Now it was television's turn.

Through commentary on CNN, the right wing had a vehicle to reach impressionable viewers with its propaganda at a time when, primarily for commercial reasons in an age of the media conglomerate, the broadcast news divisions began retrenching in their coverage of policy and governmental matters in favor of softer subjects, doing fewer investigative reports, and ceding the political discussion to cable. Network affiliate news, meanwhile, devolved mostly into reports on local crime, weather, and sports. By 2003, *Broadcasting & Cable* magazine found that on a critical issue like the Iraq war, the conservative-dominated cable networks had become the primary source of news for 45 percent of Americans, while only 22 percent chose the broadcast networks' straightforward evening news as their first news source.

Though Ted Turner is best known now for his concerns about the environment and the proliferation of nuclear weapons, his financial support of the United Nations, and his marriage to Jane Fonda, all of that had yet to come. In 1980, when he started CNN and had more control over programming than he would years later, the press described Turner as a staunch free marketeer and an active supporter of the 1964 Goldwater presidential campaign. *Newsweek* called him a "sort of right-wing Ralph Nader" who accused a "bunch of pinkos" at the networks of "precipitating everything from a decline in the work ethic to a rise in the crime rate."

Turner appeared to do nothing to slant the news reporting, and CNN's brand was built on quality news, not politics or ideology. Yet whether he saw only a potential marketing opportunity or was speaking out of conviction, in the early years of CNN, Turner parroted the language of the right wing in describing CNN's mission as providing more "balance" than could be found on the networks—an implicit charge of liberal bias. CNN, he said, would give both sides "equal and fair treatment." CNN's decision that people like Phyllis Schlafly represented the "other side" of liberalism shifted the whole debate radically rightward.

A few years hence, Turner had a brief but telling liaison with the Republican Right in which he engaged in further media baiting. His desire to expand his holdings put him into contact with the political organization of Senator Jesse Helms, a college dropout who had made his name in North Carolina first as a fear-mongering radio commentator on the Tobacco Radio Network and later as one of America's first TV editorial commentators at a Raleigh-based station that billed him as "the Voice of Free Enterprise in Raleigh-Durham." Like Ronald Reagan, Jerry Falwell, and Pat Robertson, Helms was another right-winger who understood instinctively the persuasive powers of television and radio in a way that liberals either couldn't, or wouldn't, or were denied the opportunity.

Helms's broadcasts, which were created to "balance" the "prointegrationist bias" of David Brinkley of NBC News, made him the leading segregationist voice in his state. He denounced the "immorality" of blacks and spoke of "restless Negroes." "The question grows more ominous by the day. The hour approaches when we must decide whether we will be ruled by sanity or savagery," he said of integration. According to a profile in Raleigh's *News & Observer*, "From 1960 to 1972, Helms criticized the civil rights movement, hippies, the anti-war movement, Martin Luther King Jr., labor unions, welfare, the *News & Observer*, taxes, the war on poverty, foreign aid, Red China, and the United Nations." A syndicated column Helms wrote appeared in two hundred newspapers across the country; he also wrote one in *The Citizen*, the magazine of the white supremacist Citizens Councils of America, based in Mississippi.

With help from direct-mail wizard Richard Viguerie's mailing lists from the Goldwater campaign, Helms was able to raise money nationwide for his 1972 Senate bid, winning the seat with an ad denigrating his Greek American opponent: "Jesse Helms—He's One of Us." His future races, in which he did little campaigning or debating, all relied on lavishly expensive TV ads containing ethnic slurs and racial and homophobic undertones that were designed by Helms advisers Thomas F. Ellis and E. Carter Wrenn.

In 1984, Ellis and Wrenn formed a new organization, Fairness in Media (FIM), with the stated goal of conservative takeover of the CBS network (a plan originally pursued by H. L. Hunt in the 1950s). On behalf of this new pressure group, Helms mailed one million letters to conservatives urging them to win influence or control over news content by buying enough stock in CBS to install a new board of directors at the company. "For years, good Americans like you have asked President Reagan and me what can be done to combat the flagrant bias in the liberal news media. At last there's an answer to that question," Helms wrote. If each recipient of the letter bought twenty shares of stock, Helms calculated, that would be enough to "take control" of the network. "FIM is counting on you to become Dan Rather's boss," he wrote.

As part of the attack on CBS, conservatives funded a libel suit against the network inspired by a report in *TV Guide:* "Anatomy of a Smear: How CBS News Broke the Rules and 'Got' General Westmoreland." The piece was written by Don Kowet, who was to become "media critic" for the *Washington Times.* At issue was a CBS documentary by Mike Wallace titled *The Uncounted Enemy: A Vietnam Deception,* in which General William Westmoreland stood accused of inflating the strength of North Vietnamese troops to quiet criticism of the war. Westmoreland charged the piece was "a star-chamber procedure with distorted, false and specious information, plain lies, derived by sinister deception."

The $120 million Westmoreland lawsuit was secretly bankrolled by Richard Mellon Scaife and the Smith Richardson and the John M. Olin foundations as part of a broader assault on journalism and, specifically, on the libel standards set forth in the landmark Supreme Court decision *New York Times v. Sullivan.* In its 1963 decision, the High Court had given the press wide protection to engage in vigorous, even harsh, criticism of public officials provided they did not publish with reckless disregard for the truth and actual malice. This expanded constitutional protection permitted the media to aggressively cover the civil rights struggle, the Vietnam War, and Watergate.

The right wing, including people like Scaife, who was a publisher, had disdain for press freedoms. New organizations such as the American Legal Foundation and the Capital Legal Foundation were chartered by Scaife, the Coors family, and Mobil Oil to circumscribe the media's First Amendment rights by legal attack; meanwhile, Irvine's Accuracy in Media and the John Birch Society publication *Review of the News* were dispatched to publicize the lawsuits. Asked by a reporter for *Columbia Journalism Review* to explain his role in funding these activities, Scaife responded, "You fucking Communist cunt, get out of here."

The Westmoreland case made the cover of *Newsweek,* and the chief lawyer for the plaintiff declared, "We are about to see the dismantling of a major news network." Ultimately, CBS was able to prove the veracity of its report in court and Westmoreland lost the case; but in the process, the network was weakened for the attack by Fairness in Media, founded by the Helms political gurus Ellis and Wrenn. FIM was represented by lawyer Harry F. Weyher, who was president of the Pioneer Fund, a nonprofit foundation that supported research attempting to prove that blacks are genetically less intelligent than whites. Ellis, an officer of the fund, had withdrawn his nomination by President Reagan to the U.S. Board for International Broadcasting after his ties to the group were uncovered.[8]

At this juncture, Ted Turner entered the picture. When he founded CNN, Turner provided a point of entry for the right wing; now, he pandered to it to win political and financial backing for a grand design in which his Turner Broadcasting System would take over one of the major broadcast networks.

In 1984, Turner spoke to the National Conservative Foundation, the Reagan-era group, later activated by Terry Dolan of NCPAC, to campaign against the "liberal media." Turner said:

> Those networks need to be gotten in the hands of people who care about this country, and I'm going to keep trying to figure out a way to do it. They know what they're doing, and I've criticized them time and again. In my opinion, the greatest enemy that America has ever had, posing the greatest threat to our way of life, are the three television networks and the people who run them. . . .
>
> If we are going to survive, those networks have got to change hands. They've got to be intimidated and scared into straightening

up their act and putting on programming that is not against all the things that make this society strong.[9]

The conservative foundation soon released a TV commercial in which a still photo of Turner was paired with a crawl in which he said that the three networks were "the greatest enemies that America ever had" because "they are constantly tearing down everything that has made this country great."[10]

Within a few months, Turner launched a hostile bid for CBS, promising to bring "pro-family, pro-America type" programming to the network. In pursuing CBS, Turner contacted the Helms group, Fairness in Media, for assistance.[11] "I believe Ted Turner would be fairer in his dealings with CBS and would present the news fairer than the present management," Carter Wrenn said. "The present management has refused even to recognize the fact that there's an anti-Reagan bias at CBS." William Simon, the wealthy junk bond king and an architect of the right-wing message machine, was said to have agreed to back Turner with $50 million.

The takeover battle turned nasty on both sides. In rejecting Turner's bid, mostly on financial grounds, the CBS board noted, "In light of a number of pejorative statements by Mr. Turner about various minority, religious, and ethnic groups, we believe that TBS's acquisition of CBS would undermine the CBS network's present broad acceptance by the public." According to a report in the New York Times, the "pejorative" comments included a statement by Turner that he disliked a particular sports agent because "he wears a full-length fur coat and is a Jew"; a suggestion that the unrelated issues of black unemployment and how to deploy the MX missile could be solved by having "blacks carry missiles from silo to silo just as the Egyptians carried rocks during the building of the pyramids"; and a proposal to "build an iron curtain" along the borders of Texas, California, New Mexico, and Arizona to separate them from Mexico, lest Mexicans residing in those states try to "take them back."[12]

Following the failed attempt to buy a broadcast network, Ted Turner settled down, and, in time, he came to be seen as more visionary than vigilante. His by-then legendary outbursts were considered eccentric, not evidence of bigotry. Nonetheless, it was on Turner's watch that CNN developed

Crossfire, one of two signature political talk shows of the decade that redefined American politics by creating a vast opinion industry that, as Edith
Efron had predicted a decade before, was the key to the radical Right's infiltration of the airwaves. *Crossfire* was a forerunner of a pugilistic style widely
adopted by cable talk shows; it featured views that would have been considered beyond the pale a decade previously, before the right wing got
organized and cleaned itself up.

Extremism, it seemed, made for good television. Yet in practice, Edith
Efron's "proportional representation" scheme was applied only to one side,
leaving left-wing and even strong liberal voices out of the equation. The
result was that if you were a conservative with a voice in print, no matter
how extreme or dim, you could now get on television, where many more
will see you than ever read you. If you were a liberal, the springboard had
no bounce. Top conservative columnists like Will and Novak became familiar faces thanks to television, while Ellen Goodman and Molly Ivins were
widely read but rarely seen. Scores of B-list right-wing columnists and talk
radio show hosts clog the cable airwaves, which builds the market for their
columns and shows and books in an iron circle of conservative domination
of the opinion industry.

Everything about the format of *Crossfire* and the political chat shows
established thereafter was tailored to right-wing demagoguery. The demagogues were elevated, given a platform equal to that of their opponents,
who were often nonpartisan journalists sullied by the association. Every
issue, observation, point, and fact suddenly had "another side": the right-
wing side. That side was held up not by solid reportage, scholarship, and
analysis but by bald ideological assertion, pseudoresearch, and raw partisanship. Under the *Crossfire* formula, if 99 percent of scientists agreed the
earth was round, while 1 percent said it was flat, the two views were given
equal time and, thus, equal validity in the minds of viewers.

The shows were very fast paced to keep the viewers from flipping to
another channel, leaving no time for real argument. In the place of argument were sound bites: drive-by attacks, simplistic sloganeering, and caricature. The set was like a battlefield or a hockey rink. It was hot, primal,
rough—too much thinking was a handicap, as were manners. Hosts and
guests were encouraged to interrupt and shout. The goal was not to inform
the public but to trample the enemy. Right-wing bullies were at a premium,
and liberals suddenly looked like ten-pound weaklings.

Orlando Sentinel TV critic Hal Boedeker described *Crossfire* as "name-calling, condescension and theatrics by blow-hards. . . . Issues are black and white. Whoever yells the loudest—or delivers the swiftest punches—wins . . . the issues don't matter. Clarity and insight don't matter." In the ensuing squall, conservatism thrived. The center shifted right. And liberals and liberalism either moved right or were marginalized and demonized as antifamily, anti-American, and even anti-God.

This was the world not of William Buckley, nor even of George Will, but of Pat Buchanan—a dominant figure on the sets of both *Crossfire* and *The McLaughlin Group*, a nationally syndicated political roundtable carried on NBC and PBS. Buckley's *Firing Line* on PBS was a civil forum for reasoned and rigorous debate. The topics addressed were framed by Buckley in a conservative way; but Buckley, who had a kind of liberality about him, was not afraid to engage strong liberal and left-wing points of view without lapsing into shouting or caricature. For example, one frequent guest was Ira Glasser of the American Civil Liberties Union. *Firing Line* allowed for the airing of a genuinely full range on the ideological spectrum, and the conservatism it presented was by and large serious and respectable.

By contrast, the father of the attack on the "liberal media," former Nixon aide Pat Buchanan, brought the ideological extremism, boiling anger, slashing style, and cultural resentments of McCarthy, Goldwater, and Nixon into the nation's living rooms from his new media perches. Though he assailed Communism and "Big Government," these were not Buchanan's foremost themes. Buckley, Kilpatrick, and Will amply represented those views. What Buchanan brought to television was a strong dose of the GOP Southern Strategy—racism, chauvinism, gay bashing, and xenophobia—that appealed to what Buchanan had once called the "booboisie in the hinterlands."

According to Fairness & Accuracy in Reporting's 1996 compendium of Buchanan's stated views, Buchanan has claimed that Hitler was "an individual of great courage"; he endorsed the platform of ex-Klansman David Duke; and he argued that AIDS was divine retribution against the "pederast proletariat." Of women, he wrote: "The real liberators of American women were not the feminist noise-makers, they were the automobile, the supermarket, the shopping center, the dishwasher, the washer-dryer, the freezer."[13] These views—the racial, sexual, and religious flash points advanced in the right-wing alternative media netherworld by populist right-wing publications and the televangelists—had few if any spokespeople in the mainstream media because they were so far outside the mainstream of American life.

In Buchananism, a cable trend was born; in time, Buchanan would come to be seen as a thoroughly acceptable, even benign, spokesman and cable TV fixture.

By design, *Crossfire* was conceived to be balanced, though it never was. Originally paired against Buchanan, then forty, was Tom Braden, an elderly former columnist for the *Los Angeles Times* and executive director of the Museum of Modern Art in New York City. The two had a popular debating show on the NBC Radio Network. "Not much of a liberal himself, Braden generally clung to the center position like someone hanging on to a log in the middle of the Pacific, often not opposing Buchanan's attempts to sink guests who were left of center," wrote *Los Angeles Times* media critic Howard Rosenberg. Among the guests on *Crossfire* in these years were Jimmy Swaggart and a Ku Klux Klansman who appeared on the set in his robes.[14] The spectrum was expanding: By 2003, a representative of the Paw Creek Ministries would appear on *Crossfire* to denounce the *Harry Potter* books as "witchcraft."

In 1989, Braden was replaced by *New Republic* editor Michael Kinsley, considered among the most talented editors and writers of his generation. By virtue of his visibility in print and on television, Kinsley, whose columns were carried on the op-ed page of the *Washington Post,* became the personification of post-Reagan liberalism; his skepticism, ironic detachment, and highly nuanced style were widely imitated by a younger generation of aspiring liberal writers and pundits.

In print, where persuasive powers are based on reason, Kinsley was unparalleled in his ability to expose the fraudulence of the conservative movement. His cerebral approach and self-described "wishy-washy moderate" aesthetic were not nearly as effective on television.[15] Wearing large-framed spectacles, he came across as a vaguely effete smarty-pants. He was never comfortable in a partisan cable food fight; sometimes flustered, and occasionally snippy, he conceded ground and was willing to train his guns on his own side—marks of his intellectual dexterity but handicaps in the game Buchanan was playing. Kinsley could not have been less like the hardline, unflinching, fire-breathing Buchanan, who was conducting a nightly political campaign in the guise of a talk show. "There is no way I'm as far left as Pat Buchanan is right," Kinsley said. "Buchanan is clearly part of a movement—really, leader of a movement—in a way that I'm certainly not."

Though the cross-talk format had some inherent advantages for the right-wing pundits, who seemed by their training and nature to favor audaciousness over complexity, the advantages were not insurmountable if TV executives had presented even matches. The committed liberal advocate and blunt-speaking New York politician Mark Green was passed over for the slot that went to Kinsley. Rosenberg of the *Los Angeles Times* called the decision a "missed shot at political balance." He continued, "The hiring of Kinsley is a blow to liberal activists who had counted on a post-Braden 'Crossfire' giving them a regular voice—their only one—on national TV." One published report said Buchanan had vetoed Green, who proved a forceful opponent against Buchanan in auditions; CNN denied the report's claim.

Several years later, when Kinsley stepped down, he was replaced first by former California Democratic Party chairman Bill Press and then by Clinton political consultants James Carville and Paul Begala, all of whom more than held their own in the ring against Buchanan, Robert Novak, and Tucker Carlson. Liberals from politics—not journalists like Kinsley—seemed better opponents for the right wing. Yet by presenting themselves as journalists and independent commentators, the right-wingers still had an apparent advantage over the Democrats, who were dismissed by the Right as partisan political hacks, despite the facts that Press had both a syndicated column and a radio show, and Carville and Begala had published several books each. Attacking Carville and Begala, Rush Limbaugh said, "So you have two conservative journalists at CNN opposed to strategists from the Clinton White House on the Left." No matter the lineup, the conservatives seemed to maintain an edge.

Since *Crossfire* is essentially talk radio on cable, perhaps the most even matches on cable occur when liberal radio show hosts battle right-wing talking heads. In his appearances as a *Crossfire* guest, liberal San Francisco radio personality Bernie Ward, who looks and acts like a barroom brawler, has wiped the floor with all comers. Liberal radio talkers, however, are few and far between, and they don't seem to be sought out by TV producers in the habit of booking "wishy-washy moderates" to play the liberal role.

Another blunt-speaking liberal radio show host with a substantial following in Chicago, the telegenic Nancy Skinner, auditioned but was passed over to co-host a show on MSNBC, a cable network on which conservative hosts and commentators are ubiquitous. Liberal writers from the alternative left-liberal media, such as Richard Goldstein of the *Village Voice* and Eric Alterman of *The Nation,* among others, are quite effective in skewering the Right; but they, too, are seen infrequently on television.

Crossfire of the 1980s and the early 1990s had defined the cable spectrum: Pat Buchanan versus Michael Kinsley.

While Ted Turner originally booked strong liberal advocates like Ralph Nader, a critic of corporate excess, such liberals soon disappeared from cable. Though its news division remained highly professional and largely uncompromised by the right wing, CNN's opinion panels and chat segments retained the original conservative tilt begun by Turner in 1980.

Of the first group of CNN commentators, only Robert Novak was given an interview show on CNN with his partner, Evans. Novak's disdain for labor unions—"the damn left-wing unions"—workers, and the unemployed was palpable. The network later created *The Capital Gang* for Novak to compete head-on with *The McLaughlin Group.* On *The Capital Gang's* first Thanksgiving show, Novak's "Outrage of the Week" was TV coverage of, as he put it, "the homeless, poor people, and drug addicts slobbering over their Thanksgiving turkeys and ruining my Thanksgiving." He charged that the public grief over Princess Diana's death was a result of cultural "feminization" and that her mourners "must be missing something in their lives."[16]

On cable, Novak could be looser with the facts than he was in print, mischaracterizing and lying routinely. Arguing against extended unemployment benefits, Novak said people are unemployed because they don't want to work. According to Novak, "ordinary people" regard global warming as a myth, despite polls showing that three-quarters of the public view it as a serious environmental problem. Seeking to defend the pro-segregationist comment of former GOP Senate Majority Leader Trent Lott, Novak wrongly claimed that members of the audience had cheered when Lott made the comment.

Yet despite his on-air and obviously false insistence that "everyone who works at CNN is a liberal," Robert Novak became the network's most visible talking head, appearing on *Crossfire, The Capital Gang,* and, until it was canceled, the roundtable program *Novak, Hunt, and Shields.* Upon that show's demise, liberal columnists Al Hunt and Mark Shields got no new platforms, but Novak was given his own interview show, aptly titled *The Novak Zone.* Novak proffers unrebutted reports on Judy Woodruff's afternoon newscast, *Inside Politics,* that are presented as fact rather than spin, even though they are frequently off the mark and almost always derogatory toward Democrats.

The Capital Gang, begun in the late 1980s, is a seemingly well-balanced show, though it suffers from the same right-wing tilt as virtually every other cable political chat show on the air. Novak is executive producer of the show. The majority of "newsmaker" guests appear to be Republican. If it must be aired at all, the appropriate antidote to the propaganda of Novak or panelist Kate O'Beirne, the "Washington bureau chief" of *National Review,* might come from a left-wing opinion writer for *Mother Jones,* a talk radio gabber, or the partisan political operatives Carville, Begala, and CNN regular Donna Brazile (Al Gore's former campaign manager).

The two regular opposing panelists on *The Capital Gang—Time's* Margaret Carlson and the *Wall Street Journal's* Al Hunt—are longtime journalistic pros and members of the cautious, conventional Washington media establishment. Carlson and Hunt are both moderate liberals, but they don't see it as their job to defend their side or bash the other side with the dishonest histrionics of Novak or the Stalinoid steeliness of O'Beirne. Novak, at least, is loyal to ideology above party; but O'Beirne, who is married to the Pentagon's Bush White House liaison, may as well work at the Republican National Committee. Margaret Carlson, by contrast, does not wish to play a partisan role or even be identified ideologically. While Novak and Buchanan sign off as "from the right," as a substitute host of *Crossfire,* Carlson declined to say "from the left." She was "from Washington."[17]

The lineup on CNN's Sunday morning show, hosted by Wolf Blitzer, is similarly weighted to the right. The typical panel is Jonah Goldberg of *National Review;* Robert George of the *New York Post;* Peter Beinart of *The New Republic;* and Donna Brazile. That is, two movement conservatives subsidized by right-wing moneybags; Beinart, a hawkish Democrat who often takes aim at his own party and edits a magazine in which the chairman of the Manhattan Institute is a significant investor; and one liberal.

The discussion is bizarrely skewed on CNN's *Reliable Sources,* hosted by *Washington Post* media critic Howard Kurtz. The show is a critical review of the week's journalism. According to CNN's Web site, it offers "scrutiny of the media's fairness and objectivity by questioning print and broadcast journalists." Kurtz books a steady stream of journalistic practitioners, such as the *Wall Street Journal*'s John Harwood, *Time*'s Karen Tumulty, and the *Washington Post*'s Dana Milbank, who offer firsthand, nonpartisan analysis of the news business. Yet they are forced to share the set with such nonjournalists as radio show host Laura Ingraham and Jonah Goldberg, who came by his *National Review* job because he is the son of anti-Clinton provocateur Lucianne Goldberg. As the editor of *National Review*'s Web site, Goldberg, who is married to Attorney General John Ashcroft's chief speechwriter, has defended Joe McCarthy, and he openly hoped that the black Muslim sniper who terrorized Washington, D.C., would turn out to be gay as well—a "three-fer," as he put it.

Aside from Robert Novak, conservatism's greatest influence on the air at CNN comes in one hour at six p.m. every evening, in the personage of Lou Dobbs, "the nation's preeminent business journalist." His show, *Lou Dobbs Tonight,* which focuses on economic news but covers politics and culture as well, has a relatively small but very desirable upscale audience, so it is a major source of advertising revenue. Though he anchors a major news program, CNN gives Dobbs the title "commentator and analyst" so that he is free to editorialize. No other CNN anchor carries this designation.

Dobbs makes clear his support of conservative economic and foreign policies on his broadcast and in other appearances on CNN as well. Coanchoring CNN's coverage of Bush's 2002 State of the Union address, a cheerleading Dobbs proclaimed that Bush had "returned to his compassionate conservative roots!" In the name of "straight talk," Dobbs replaced the phrase "war on terror" with "war against radical Islamists" and has featured a long line of right-wing Middle East "experts," such as the Richard Mellon Scaife–funded Daniel Pipes—a *New York Post* columnist who has written on "Why the Left Loves Osama (and Saddam)"—to underline the point. During the war in Iraq, Pipes started Campus Watch, an organization that "reviews and critiques Middle East studies in North America" and compiles "dossiers" on faculty members at several universities who were insufficiently supportive of U.S. war aims.

Dobbs uses contrived conservative jargon like "political correctness." Interviewing Bernard Goldberg about *Bias,* Dobbs boomed, "There is a liberal bias on the part of this craft!" To discuss a landmark Supreme Court case that found school vouchers to be legal, he interviewed only William Bennett, a longtime voucher proponent. One *Lou Dobbs Tonight* regular is Philip Howard, who slams tort lawsuits and plaintiffs' attorneys, advocates a Bush plan to cap damages in medical malpractice cases, and appears solo and undebated. Critics have noted that the litigation explosion of which Howard speaks does not exist and that by day he defends corporate clients in product liability cases while appearing as a disinterested observer on *Lou Dobbs Tonight.*[18]

Other guests are not treated so kindly. When Dobbs interviewed Paul Krugman of the *New York Times,* the segment was titled "Liberal Bush Bashing?" In spring 2003, Dobbs banned CNN military analyst General Wesley Clark—at the time a mild critic of the Iraq war and a political independent—from his broadcast, according to *U.S. News & World Report.* At the height of the war, Dobbs made his own bias explicit. Reading viewer e-mail on air, he said: "And Willy Clarkson of Colorado writes, 'Your obvious bias for Republicans in this war are very disgusting. You're not acting as an unbiased journalist. Your lack of listening to the United Nations and its role was proof of that.'" Dobbs paused, looked into the camera, and declared, "You're right, Willy, I'm not unbiased!"

Dobbs is not only ideologically biased; he can be a wickedly partisan Republican and, indeed, was a financial supporter of George W. Bush's 2000 presidential campaign. Following the right-wing media line, when Democratic Senate leader Tom Daschle criticized the Bush administration for failed diplomacy in the run-up to the Iraq war, Dobbs blustered, "Senator Daschle has every reason to be saddened, but by his own words and deeds."

Alone among CNN anchors, Dobbs moonlights as an opinion columnist for *U.S. News & World Report.* In March 2003, as war with Iraq loomed, he wrote, "The critics of the war against terror and the absolute disarmament of Saddam Hussein must overcome their partisan myopia and do their best to understand that there's nothing at stake here less than the very survival of our nation and democratic civilization. In my opinion, the president has set us upon exactly the right course in the Middle East." Two months before, he issued a blunt endorsement of Bush's economic plans, writing,

"In our times, bold is the only policy option. But instead of recognizing and responding to the fundamental changes facing our economy and the nation, the Democrats have offered up a 'stimulus light' plan that would maintain the status quo. And they've offered up the same old tired arguments in support of their tired ideas." Invoking a familiar GOP talking point, he continued, "Now, the Democrats are using their 'class warfare' tactic, blasting President Bush for favoring the rich and reverting to the days of 'voodoo economics.'" He then referred derisively to Republican Senator John McCain for "making a career out of being a malcontent [and] rumbling about more middle-class tax relief."

Through the "Dobbs List" segment, Dobbs recommends favorite books to the CNN audience, promoting, for example, a tome by G. Gordon Liddy. On his radio show, Liddy, referring to agents of the federal Bureau of Alchohol, Tobacco, and Firearms, has counseled his audience to "kill the sons of bitches," revealed that he had had a "secret plan to kill columnist Jack Anderson," and announced, "I accept no responsibility for somebody shooting up the [Clinton] White House," after describing how he used photos of the Clintons for target practice on a shooting range.[19]

Liddy's book *When I Was a Kid, This Was a Free Country,* a clichéd attack on "enviroradicals," "fulminating feminists," "devotees of diversity," "politically correct nitwits," and "killer air-bags," made the Dobbs List. Dobbs described the book as "a celebration of sorts of a time when boys could go hunting with a pal, make their own fireworks, and just burn leaves on an autumn afternoon." With odd understatement, Dobbs introduced the Watergate felon as having served "several functions during the Nixon administration." When Liddy's crimes inevitably came up in the interview, Dobbs lauded Liddy for refusing to implicate others, saying, "You never said a word, held your own counsel, and took responsibility for your actions." To Dobbs, this was evidence of Liddy's "remarkable" character. Cutting to a commercial break, Dobbs said, "Next: Why the Democrats failed to scare voters on Social Security!"

Despite the presence of such open conservative bias on CNN, conservatives still call it the "Communist News Network," perhaps because, of the three cable networks, it is the least in thrall to the right wing. CNN is predominantly a news network, not an opinion channel. When news is not shot through with right-wing opinion, many conservatives have been conditioned to see "liberal bias" at work. Aaron Brown's CNN newscast, for instance, has been wrongly castigated by conservatives as "liberal" because it resembles the professionalism and calm of the network news. Brown regularly features conservatives, though rarely of the hyperthyroid or transparently fraudulent variety.

To move the press in their direction, Republican political leaders use a strategy once described by former Republican National Committee chairman Rich Bond as "working the refs."[20] With Republicans taking the White House and both houses of Congress in the 2000 elections, House Republican leader Tom DeLay tried to win Republican support for a boycott of CNN to drive it further to the right.

DeLay is the sort of conservative who labels as "liberal bias" anything that does not follow his rigid orthodoxy. He is a most unlikely judge of fairness or balance in the press, having once described Democratic voters as a combination of "Greenpeace, Queer Nation, and the National Education Association." DeLay does not believe in evolution, and he has compared the Environmental Protection Agency to the Nazi gestapo.

With DeLay's threats in the offing, in August 2001, then–CNN chairman Walter Isaacson, a former editor of *Time,* "met with top Republican brass in the House and Senate in an effort to burnish the network's image with conservative leaders and seek their advice on how to attract more right-leaning viewers," according to a report in *Roll Call.* New to the job, Isaacson apparently saw the move as a way to relieve competitive pressures emanating from the highly rated FOX News Channel. While the FOX audience is predominantly conservative, so is CNN's. Forty-six percent of FOX viewers are self-identified conservatives, 32 percent are moderates, and 18 percent are liberals; the CNN breakdown is 40 percent conservative, 38 percent moderate, and 16 percent liberal, according to a 2002 survey by the Pew Research Center for the People and the Press.

One Capitol Hill staffer told *Roll Call,* "Isaacson is panicked that he's losing conservative viewers. He said, 'Give us some guidance on how to attract conservatives.'" He also reportedly said he wanted to "change the culture" of the network. (Isaacson has said he was misconstrued.)

Shortly after the meeting, Isaacson tried without success to recruit Rush

Limbaugh to the network. William Bennett was hired by CNN as an on-air commentator. Bennett, who positioned himself as the Republicans' "morality czar," was exposed in news reports in spring 2003 as having a chronic gambling habit. Having left CNN of his own volition, Bennett is now seen much less frequently on television, though he has been resuscitated as a regular on FOX's *Hannity & Colmes.*

Several months after the Isaacson pilgrimage, a study by the Democratic National Committee reported that under Isaacson's leadership, from January 1 through March 21, 2002, CNN carried 157 Bush administration live events (96 percent), but only 7 Democratic leadership events (4 percent). Meanwhile, the producers of Wolf Blitzer's evening newscast were framing Democratic criticisms of the Bush administration as questions of whether the Democrats had "gone too far" or were engaging in a "blame game," rather than more neutral phrasing.

Media critic Eric Boehlert reported in *Salon* that when President Bush unveiled his proposal on federal funding for stem cell research in a major speech in August 2001, CNN booked many Republican officials to comment but no Democrats. In a 2001 year-end salute to "profiles in leadership," not one Democrat made CNN's honor roll.[21] In December 2002, anchor Paula Zahn, hired away from FOX News, emceed a Washington event at which President George H. W. Bush was given the "American Patriot Award." CNN highlighted the event on the air as "a *Who's Who* of Republican politics, not to mention CNN's morning line-up."

Like its cable competitors, CNN now books Far Right guests from talk radio to comment on the news. Appearing on Wolf Blitzer's program during the Iraq war, radio show host Mike Gallagher berated his liberal counterpart: "You're un-American. You're un-American . . . you hate America. . . . You're un-American. You're either with us or with the terrorists."

In June 2002, Richard Parsons, chairman and CEO of Time Warner Inc., which owns CNN, followed Isaacson's path to Capitol Hill. Parsons was cochair of George W. Bush's Commission to Strengthen Social Security, which recommended partial privatization; he is also a Bush-Cheney '04 donor. Other top company executives with Republican pedigrees include Robert Kimmitt (a State Department official in the first Bush administration) and Paul T. Cappuccio (a protégé of former independent counsel Kenneth Starr). AOL itself has deep Republican roots: Its founder, Jim

Kimsey, is a major Republican fund-raiser; and the former chairman and CEO of America Online, Inc., Steve Case, has donated millions in personal funds to a Christian Right school in Florida founded by the head of a notoriously antigay ministry.[22] AOL Time Warner, moreover, has contributed money to Grover Norquist's group, Americans for Tax Reform—the linchpin of his vast political operations—through which he pushes right-wing candidates and policies and touts GOP tax-slashing plans.

In the meeting with Parsons, "DeLay expressed appreciation that CNN has been willing to listen and improve its ideological balance," according to *Roll Call.* "They definitely have been reaching out in an effort to improve and listen to both sides," a GOP aide told the newspaper. A few weeks before Parsons's visit, DeLay had redoubled his boycott efforts after CNN hired the crack team of Carville and Begala for *Crossfire.* Though the boycott never took hold, the sentiment underscored that conservatives don't want a fair fight; they want a fixed fight.

In fall 2003, CNN revamped its schedule, creating a new prime-time vehicle for Paula Zahn and downgrading *Crossfire* to the late afternoon. Zahn's show continued the CNN tradition established long ago by Turner. Hired as "contributors" were *Time* columnist Joe Klein and former Defense Department spokesperson Victoria Clarke—that is, a well-respected journalist who has worked at *New York* magazine, *Newsweek,* and *The New Yorker,* among other publications, and has proven his ability to look skeptically at all ideological issues and political figures, and a nonjournalist GOP p.r. woman who spun the news for Defense Secretary Donald Rumsfeld during the Iraq war and whose new role at CNN appeared to be no different from her prior assignment. Upon her appointment at CNN, Clarke told the *Washington Post* that she agreed with the Bush administration "99.9 percent of the time."

CHAPTER NINE

MORT THE MOUTH

O N THE HEELS OF *CROSSFIRE* AND *The McLaughlin Group*, in the late 1980s a new TV niche opened, not further to the right, but bigger and considerably down-market. Like *Crossfire* and *The McLaughlin Group*, the new shows pretended to contribute to political debate, but they were little more than a new form of entertainment. To Tom Shales of the *Washington Post*, they were "Talk Rot"; the *New York Times* dubbed it "shock television." "News punks," *Newsweek* decried.

While talk radio had not yet become a national phenomenon, several so-called host/advocate TV programs were developed in the late 1980s for a handful of right-wing talk show hosts popular in local markets, including G. Gordon Liddy in Washington, Bob Grant in New York City, and Morton Downey Jr. in Sacramento.[1] Aired on a patchwork of local network affiliates, independent stations, and pay cable, the shows were copies of a right-wing talk show hosted by Los Angeles–based Joe Pyne in the mid-1960s. Pyne had told his critics to "gargle with razor blades" and placed audience members in a "Beef Box" on the set before humiliating them.

The most volatile and confrontational of the lot, Downey's nationally syndicated show immediately soared in the ratings. "I am not a talk show host. I am an advocate," said Downey. The show was the brainchild of media entrepreneur Bob Pittman, a political liberal who had founded MTV and would go on to co-found AOL. Pittman described the innovation of the show as pitting "extreme versus extreme." This was not really an innovation, since Ted Turner had discovered it years before; what was new was that the extremes were more extreme.

The show was filmed before a live, handpicked audience of raucous fans in Secaucus, New Jersey, who cheered on Downey as he became more and more angrily outrageous, with chants of "Mort! Mort! Mort!" Downey's subjects ranged widely from homelessness to civil liberties but often had a racial or sexual subtext; his shtick was to berate and abuse his noncelebrity guests, many of whom were booked to fight with him. A procession of strippers, prostitutes, and pornographers were booked to represent "the other side"—i.e., liberals. Downey always "won" the exchanges because he held the mike.

"Shut up, you old hag!" Downey berated one elderly woman. He told a candidate for office, "If I had a slime like you in the White House, I'd puke on you." He called liberals "pablum-puking" and "liberal slime." Another pair of guests were "two of the greatest sleazebags of our time." "Let's kick ass," he would tell the excited audience. To wild cheering, he once slapped a gay activist, prompting a lawsuit. "If you're not going to answer my question, and you don't like what I'm saying, get the hell out of here," he told another guest.

Misogyny was on unvarnished display. Downey told a female victim of child abuse, "Tooooo damn bad. . . . I've known women who are absolute, total bitches. If I were married to you, honey, I'd drop-kick you out the door." A professional stripper was denounced as a "pig," "tramp," "slut," and "fat, man-hating bitch."[2]

Downey was promoted as "one street-tough American." The Ayatollah Khomeini of Iran was the "Ayatollah Cockamamie." Government diplomats were "wimpy bastards" and "gutless bastards." He described the show as "not demagoguery, but a dictatorship." His motto: "Destroy! Destroy whatever you've gotta destroy!" In one show that never aired, he literally tried to strangle a guest with a telephone cord.

•　　•　　•

The son of a successful singer and songwriter, Downey had a privileged upbringing, shuttled around Manhattan by chauffeur. He later became estranged from his father and "spit out the silver spoon," as he put it.[3] Yet according to the *Washington Post's* Tom Shales, "He is anxious for you to know that he grew up amongst the Kennedys in Hyannis Port, that his Irish tenor daddy and Papa Joe Kennedy were the best of friends."

Downey "had a Ph.D. from a boiler-room university in Fresno and a law degree from a mail-order house," a profile in *Regardie's* magazine reported. He was fired from a string of jobs in local radio, where he was never terribly successful, once for striking an abortion rights supporter and once for launching a racial tirade against a Chinese American politician who received death threats afterward. According to the *New York Times,* Downey "routinely broadcast a segment of his program called the 'Executive Intelligence Report' in which he read from a magazine published by Lyndon H. LaRouche Jr., the right-wing political figure who in the past has associated with anti-Semitic and neo-Nazi groups."[4]

Downey was not a card-carrying Republican. In 1979, he was the "right to life" candidate for president of George Wallace's American Independent Party before withdrawing because the party was "too liberal."

Though Downey took familiar elements of tabloid television and placed them in a political context, his appeal was more emotional than partisan. In contrast with what has been described as the distancing effect of the formal network newscasters, with their stentorian manner and blow-dried hair, Downey offered the intimacy of a Phil Donahue or an Oprah Winfrey; although he lacked the manners and affability of these hosts, Downey was a familiar face with whom the viewer was on a first-name basis. To the lonely and disaffected, he offered participation and involvement.[5]

Downey's posturing was intended to convey the impression that he was penetrating the false veneer of double-talk, public relations, and complexities of regular public affairs programming. Downey said he represented the "little man" against the "social betters" and commanding figures in the "media elite." After eight years of Reaganism, he insisted that conservatives were powerless against the liberal leviathan. Yet he was independent enough from the GOP to capture an audience disconnected from politics, and his expressions of solidarity with blue-collar workers and the socially downtrodden gave him some crossover appeal; his was an unpredictable voice with quivers of humanity. A kind of base humor was also part of the package. "It's character assassination for the sake of entertainment," wrote one critic, ". . . [and] the destruction of character is a fundamental tactic of the totalitarian state."

"Hey, here's Downey, he's exactly like I am, he's as frustrated as I am, only this sonuvabitch is doing something about it! So I'll let him say it for me, because I get my jollies that way, and by God he's saying the same thing I'd like to say," Downey said, in explaining his appeal, to the *Washington Post*.[6] In another interview, he said, "My audience is just as smart as the roaches on 'Nightline.' There are no cosmetics on my show. The hatred beating in people's hearts goes out on the air. I don't want my audience to look like elitists. This show ain't no pressure pot, as all those liberal intellectuals are screaming. This show is a release valve from all their bullshit."[7]

Who were the people getting their "jollies" from seeing Downey bully and degrade his guests? The majority of the audience, more than two million viewers on a given night (in the same range as the top-rated FOX News Channel opinion shows today), comprised eighteen-to-thirty-four-year-old men living outside the major cities, although younger women watched, too. *Regardie's* described the attraction this way: "He champions the raw pent-up anger, aggression, and frustration that adults are supposed to vent in a mature, intelligent way. He's a product of the ignorance and prejudice that crawl along the bottom of the national soul; he's a demagogue from the heart of the American darkness. . . . His viewers make up one of America's lost tribes: people who are constantly at war with a social machinery that has little use for them, a lower-middle underclass that's been told to roll up its sleeves, to put up or shut up, and to button its lip."[8] At the same time, the show was such a spectacle that it attracted some segment of viewers who must have found it both repulsive and addictive, like watching a car wreck.

Many observers noted that Downey was "a symptom, not a cause," as one put it. "In their extreme way, talk shows like Morton Downey Jr.'s tend to satisfy the same viewer craving. They validate—however grossly—the emotional component missing from the cool cross talk of most TV discussions," according to the *Christian Science Monitor*. "Viewers say they like to watch people who represent not only their social and political views but also their feelings. They want guests and audience to yell—just the way they would in the same situation." One of Downey's producers told the newspaper that the format "has given people who are historically spoken to or at an opportunity to speak themselves. It's somewhere between rage and jubilation."

Yet after only a year and a half on television, Downey's ratings began to sag, and they plummeted after he reported to police a false story that he had been badly beaten and cut by a gang of skinheads in San Francisco. Apparently, Downey had mussed himself up as a publicity stunt and, when caught in the lie, lost credibility with his fans.

After Downey died in 2001, Rebecca Johnson, one of his former producers, published a piece in the *New York Times* in which she referred to her old boss as "a pathological liar." "I was a segment producer on the show, and it was my job to gather the facts and figures that would support Downey's viewpoint for each show . . . every night I would dutifully type up numbers from the Heritage Foundation or the Cato Institute on a blue card and hand them to Downey at the pre-show briefing," Johnson wrote. "When my statistics weren't persuasive enough, he would embellish them—or simply invent facts that better fit that day's rant. I'd been at the show only a few days when I heard Downey make something up. . . . Once you worked for him long enough, you eventually stopped hearing fabrications, in much the way you eventually get used to someone's lisp or accent."[9]

When Downey self-destructed, his market niche did not disappear with him. He went a few steps too far, but he was onto something big. Sensation, emotion, and raw right-wing populism sold in the emerging media market of the late 1980s. The traditional network anchors were fading out, losing their authority, edge, and audience share, especially among the young. Newspaper circulation was falling off dramatically. The "news punks" of talk television were on the way in. Syndication and cable were hot, bringing with them an itch to lower standards in the pursuit of new markets. And media ownership was consolidating and becoming more profit-driven. Politics was being fought out not only on the op-ed pages of the *New York Times* but also in nightly televised food fights.

Conservatism, too, was changing. More than anyone before him, Downey brought the anticonservative, antiestablishment tenor of the conservative movement to mainstream television. He was a pseudoconservative, catering to an appetite in the right-wing base unsated by the coat-and-tie conservatism of *Crossfire* or *The McLaughlin Group*. Within a decade, across talk radio, cable television, the book industry, and even the formerly intellectual right-wing journals, Downey's brand of conservatism was not the jarring exception but the rule.

CHAPTER TEN

GENERAL ELECTRIC THEATRE

NLIKE CNN'S *CROSSFIRE, THE McLAUGHLIN GROUP*— highly rated and closely watched during the 1980s—did not try to create the appearance of balance. The media spectrum was expanded to include the Far Right in the 1970s; yet now, a combination of the conservative biases of media executives, commercial market forces, and a ready stock of warm bodies from the subsidized right-wing message machinery was conspiring to narrow the spectrum of opinion again, only this time in reverse. Suddenly, conservatives had not only won an even berth, as on *Crossfire;* with the advent of *The McLaughlin Group,* they ruled.

At its high point, the syndicated *McLaughlin Group,* which airs on NBC and PBS affiliates nationally, had 3.5 million viewers, far more than the top-rated FOX News Channel opinion shows today. Host John McLaughlin, a former Jesuit priest, aide to Richard Nixon, and *National Review* alum, chose the topics, the sequencing, and his four fellow panelists. The show always pitted three or four conservatives against two or even only one liberal. Over the years, one of the liberal slots typically went to a nonideological reporter, such as the *Baltimore Sun's* dyspeptic Jack Germond. Often, the "liberal" guest, usually the bumbling Morton Kondracke, then of *The New Republic* and now with the FOX News Channel, was booked to endorse and bestow legitimacy on conservative views.

This arrangement left *Newsweek's* Eleanor Clift, the sole woman panelist, who was typecast as a screechy feminist, to fend off two or even three angry, white, conservative men. Among the regular panelists, only the liberals—not the conservatives—were trained reporters. Putting Clift and Germond—rather than liberal opinion writers—up against conservative ideologues bolstered the conservative caricature of all reporters as closet liberals; at the same time, it ensured that liberals would be more restrained and nuanced in their advocacy than their opponents.

This imbalanced and exaggerated TV picture was projected, to Washington and the nation, as if it were somehow a representative microcosm of political dialogue in the country during Ronald Reagan's presidency, leaving the indelible misimpression that conservatism was the dominant view in the country. Meanwhile, McLaughlin's buffoonery—his exaggerated manner, his nicknames for panelists, his reduction of politics into a game show—made conservatism seem unthreatening, and even funny. From the composition and tone of *The McLaughlin Group* panels sprang the stereotype that conservatives are entertaining, while liberals are whiny and boring—another seeming advantage engineered by the Right as the values of entertainment, rather than those of journalism, were prevailing on television.

The McLaughlin Group also was instrumental in establishing the now-widespread practice of "buckraking," whereby TV pundits take their show on the paid lecture circuit and for substantial fees reenact their TV roles, playing themselves before industry and trade associations looking for the Washington "inside scoop" or after-dinner levity. Buckraking added a powerful financial incentive for pundits to "stay in character" on television and for aspiring pundits to adopt a marketable style. Belligerent, cocksure conservatives, with liberals as their compliant whipping boys, seemed the meal ticket for both sides. Often, entire panels from shows like *McLaughlin* and CNN's *Capital Gang* go on the road, raking in tens of thousands of dollars apiece. Conservative TV pundits like George Will have taken huge fees speaking before industry groups about which they opine; the corporate market for left-wing pundits is not lucrative.

The McLaughlin Group plucked John McLaughlin from his relatively obscure post as *National Review* "Washington editor"—where, according to *The New Republic*, he employed ghostwriters to write under his byline— and made him one of the most influential media voices in the 1980s. When it began, the show was underwritten by the Edison Electric Institute, a front for the electric power industry with close ties to the GOP. The institute has been a client of Grover Norquist, who, in addition to his leadership of the conservative movement, has dabbled in lobbying on the side. McLaughlin had hoped to launch a conservative-slanted talk show since the mid-1970s, after raising his profile in TV appearances defending the Nixon administration and hosting a local Washington talk show with Robert Novak. He took money from a former Nixon aide to explore the idea.[1]

In 1986, when General Electric bought NBC's parent company, RCA, GE announced that it would become the show's exclusive sponsor and pumped cash into promoting it nationally. The deal was struck following a meeting between McLaughlin and GE chairman Jack Welch, convened at McLaughlin's request by President Ronald Reagan. McLaughlin already had been promoted by NBC with appearances on *Meet the Press* in the early 1980s; McLaughlin's then-wife, Ann, was a high-level Reagan official; and Reagan himself was a fan of *The McLaughlin Group*. Reagan also had a relationship with GE, dating back to his stint as host of television's *General Electric Theatre* in the 1950s. According to media critic Ben Bagdikian, GE had "launched Ronald Reagan as a national political spokesman by paying him to make nationwide public speeches against Communism, labor unions, Social Security, public housing, the income tax, and to augment the corporation's support of right-wing political movements."[2]

Thirty years later, GE's agenda hadn't much changed. Known as "Neutron Jack" for his hard-charging management style, Welch, who headed GE until his retirement in 2002, was a conservative Republican; like Ted Turner's early influence at CNN, Welch's role in promoting McLaughlin was an example of how the Right was able to steer the political debate with the approval of top-ranked media executives. McLaughlin expanded his visibility with the GE-sponsored *One on One* syndicated interview show, and he was given a third show on CNBC when that cable network was established by GE in the 1990s. Welch used his influence over *The McLaughlin Group* to promote commentators whom he saw as up-and-coming talent, such as

Reagan economics adviser Lawrence Kudlow, "economics editor" of *National Review*, member of the right-wing Club for Growth, and "fellow" of Newt Gingrich's Progress and Freedom Foundation. Kudlow now has his own CNBC show, on which he was forced to apologize on air for insulting a government witness in the Martha Stewart case as "limp-wristed."

GE funneled financial support directly into the right-wing message machinery. The company gave money to William Simon and Irving Kristol's Institute for Educational Affairs, which funded the racist, sexist, homophobic right-wing campus newspapers; to C. Boyden Gray's Citizens for a Sound Economy; and to the Hudson Institute, the American Enterprise Institute, and the Center for Strategic and International Studies.

In a 2002 interview on MSNBC's *Hardball* with Chris Matthews (who got his start on television with guest appearances on *The McLaughlin Group*), Welch spoke openly about his political views. "And this guy came in named Ronald Reagan that they all thought was stupid and he had a pretty simple thesis and you can disagree with some of his policies or other things, but this guy got American back on track. And the country thrived. . . ." Welch endorsed George W. Bush's proposals for "tort reform" and for ending taxation on stock dividends, an idea heavily promoted by Kudlow on CNBC's *Kudlow and Cramer* before the Bush administration adopted it. Welch has conceded that on Election Night 2000—when a critical call had to be made by network officials about who had won—he was in the NBC News Control Room, one of "two or three of us cheering for George Bush." He labeled as "crazy" unconfirmed stories that he had said, "What would I have to give you to call the race for Bush?"[3] NBC subsequently refused to release to congressional investigators a videotape of what went on in the room. NBC followed the FOX News Channel in calling the race, wrongly, for Bush.

In the Reagan years, *The McLaughlin Group* was the new normal. Twenty years later, it would be normal up and down the cable dial. The right wing was on call 24/7, while bona fide liberals were an endangered species. Syndicated columnist and former Moral Majority official Cal Thomas got his own show on FOX, while AEI's Ben Wattenberg got a PBS series. Until recently, the *Wall Street Journal* editorial board had its own hour-long weekly show on CNBC. The *Journal*'s Peggy Noonan and John Fund are regulars on the GE-owned MSNBC cable network. Alone among the nation's editorial page editors, Tony Blankley of the *Washington Times* is a highly visible TV pundit, with a permanent berth on *The McLaughlin Group*. *Time's* right-wing columnist Charles Krauthammer, who has not published a book, is a fixture on FOX News and *Inside Washington,* the D.C.-based political affairs show. *Time's* left-liberal columnist Barbara Ehrenreich, a runaway best-selling author, is invisible.

GE launched CNBC in 1989. In 1991, GE made a fateful hire that shifted the entire cable news industry dramatically to the right: Republican operative Roger Ailes became president of CNBC.

Ailes entered politics working for Richard Nixon, showing the campaign how to present paid political events so that they would appear to be news, in order to manipulate public opinion about the candidate. A false warm-and-fuzzy Nixon was sold by Ailes like a "car or a can of peas," as Joe McGinniss put it in *The Selling of the President, 1968.* Ailes's father was an Ohio factory foreman who complained of being talked down to by corporate executives at the plant. Ailes shared with Nixon contempt for "elites" and a knack for speaking to the racial prejudices of certain lower-class white men. Discussing the addition of a panelist to a staged Nixon "Man in the Arena" forum, Ailes said: "You know what I'd like? As long as we've got this extra spot open. A good, mean Wallaceite cab driver. Wouldn't that be great? Some guy to sit there and say, 'Awright, mac, what about these niggers?'"[4]

Ailes, who met Nixon while working as the producer of *The Mike Douglas Show,* went to work at the Nixon White House; but his relationship with the president's inner circle soon cooled, and Watergate dealt his career a further setback. Over the next few years, Ailes, a fine arts major who worked his way through Ohio University as a radio disc jockey, toiled in the political wilderness as a speech coach for business executives and moonlighted as an off-Broadway producer. He ran a few political races in the late 1970s before returning to television in 1981 as executive producer of Tom Snyder's hugely successful *Tomorrow: Coast to Coast.* When Ailes took the show down-market, ratings plummeted. In 1982, the show was replaced by *Late Night with David Letterman;* once one of NBC's biggest stars, Snyder never fully recovered. Ailes was more resilient.[5]

By 1981, the Reagan revolution had dawned, and Ailes's ability to craft appeals to Nixon's disaffected cultural conservatives was to prove invaluable. Working with his second wife, Norma, a TV producer, Ailes rose to become the country's preeminent GOP political consultant. He spoke the language of the so-called Reagan Democrats: the construction workers and housewives featured in his widely imitated ads.

Still, he was never truly a Reagan insider, and it was not until George H. W. Bush came along that Ailes finally found his horse. His relationship with Bush was cemented after he helped the vice president turn the tables in an interview about the Iran-contra affair with CBS anchor Dan Rather. Ailes prepped Bush to equate his misdoings in the scandal with a temper tantrum that the voluble Rather had once thrown on the CBS set. "Dan Rather is the most biased reporter in the history of broadcasting," Ailes exclaimed after the interview.

Under the direction of Ailes and the late Lee Atwater, the Bush campaign questioned Democratic nominee Michael Dukakis's patriotism, tarred him as an unfit commander in chief, and portrayed him as soft on crime. Though he claimed he had nothing to do with it, Ailes was burned in a controversy over an advertisement produced by an independent pro-Bush group that featured convicted African American murderer Willie Horton, who had committed rape after escaping from a weekend furlough program while Dukakis was governor of Massachusetts. According to *Time* magazine, Ailes said at the time, "The only question is whether we depict Willie Horton with a knife or without one." Atwater said that Ailes had "two settings: attack and destroy," yet Ailes had the temerity to call Dukakis "the dirtiest campaigner in America."

As a result of the ugly race-baiting campaign, Ailes himself became an infamous figure; his future clients, notably Rudy Giuliani in New York City, suffered a string of defeats. Frozen out of the 1992 Bush campaign, Ailes renounced his political career and announced a return to television.

One evening a few months previous, Ailes had run into Rush Limbaugh at the posh Manhattan restaurant 21. Limbaugh's radio show had established him as a political powerhouse, and Ailes convinced Limbaugh that a syndicated TV show was the obvious progression. Ailes became executive producer of Limbaugh's late-night syndicated talk show. Yet once he left the segmented medium of radio, Limbaugh failed to attract a large broadcast TV audience. Something about Limbaugh did not easily translate to mainstream

TV viewers or advertisers, and he eventually quit the show. In the meantime, Ailes—who had nursed resentments against the press in twenty years of dishonest political warfare—became a cable network news executive.

In the early 1990s, NBC president Bob Wright was looking for someone to take over CNBC. A friend recommended Ailes, who promptly flew to Nantucket and convinced Jack Welch that he was just the programmer NBC was looking for. Even as NBC executives offered assurances that Ailes had left politics for good, Ailes's NBC deal allowed him to remain affiliated with the floundering Limbaugh broadcast. While serving as both CNBC's president and Limbaugh's producer, Ailes went on Don Imus's radio show to promote Limbaugh's reports of a "suicide cover-up, possibly murder," in the death of White House counsel Vincent Foster. "The guy who's been doing an excellent job for the *New York Post* [Christopher Ruddy] . . . for the first time on the Rush Limbaugh show said that . . . he did not believe it was suicide. . . . Now, I don't have any evidence. . . . These people are very good at hiding or destroying evidence."

Politics aside, Ailes was a talented marketer and had a keen sense of production values. In just two years at CNBC, he helped transform it from a ragtag network into the number one financial news network in the United States. During his tenure, ad sales doubled, ratings tripled, and the asset value of the channel soared from about $400 million to more than $1 billion.

While the core of CNBC was business news, NBC's cable outlets fueled the proliferation of political talk television. Working within the confines of a mainstream cable network, Ailes seemed to resist his blunt right-wing instincts in favor of a broad political mix. Added to the roster of cable hosts that included Tom Snyder, Dick Cavett, and John McLaughlin were former Bush campaign aide Mary Matalin, former Clinton aide Dee Dee Myers, Cal Thomas, tabloid showman Geraldo Rivera, liberal actor Charles Grodin, and Ailes himself.

Yet Ailes's attraction to entertainment and partisan opinion—often uninformed and irresponsible opinion—over hard news and information had a subtly subversive political impact. In the late 1970s, the only Washington chat shows on the air were the traditional network Sunday morning shows and PBS's sober pair of journalism roundtables, *Agronsky & Company* and *Washington Week in Review*. In the 1980s came *The*

McLaughlin Group, *Crossfire*, and *The Capital Gang*. Now came a second generation of McLaughlin knockoffs as more cable channels sprung up. As Edith Efron predicted in *The News Twisters*, if the spectrum could be expanded to equate professional journalists and Far Right ideological polemicists, if standards of discourse could be altered, if objectivity was no longer prized, if consensus could be destroyed as everything in politics was made into a "he said/she said" standoff, then the right wing would win critical political inroads.

"Confining myself to *McLaughlin*-like shows and *Capital Gang*–like shows, every single one of them, if it disappeared tomorrow, journalism would be better off," the writer and editor James Fallows told the *American Journalism Review* in 1995. Fallows bemoaned the substitution of news for opinion and of solid analysis for pithy sound bites and prognostications: "The world would be better off. Government would be better off. The only people who would be worse off are the actual members of the shows."[6]

While turning CNBC around, Ailes's real interest was creating a new cable channel that he vowed would become the next MTV or ESPN. The new channel was christened America's Talking, and it was designed to reflect Ailes's "homespun woman-by-the-hearth, man-baling-hay Midwestern rugged individualism," according to one former producer. The shows, which Ailes created, included *Bugged!*, in which a film crew conducted man-on-the-street interviews to uncover what was "bugging" Americans; *Pork*, a call-in show about government waste and fraud; and *Am I Nuts?*, on which therapists dispensed advice. None of these corny entries succeeded. The only legacy bequeathed by America's Talking was Chris Matthews, a former Democratic political aide whom Ailes had chosen to coanchor a prime-time political gabfest.

Within NBC, it was not Ailes's politics but, rather, his temperament that rankled. Ailes's bond with Nixon had been instant and deep. As his colleagues described him, Ailes was paranoid and quick to abuse his power to punish perceived enemies, whom he belittled mercilessly. In late 1995, when GE was close to a deal with Microsoft to launch MSNBC, using the subscriber base of the defunct America's Talking channel, a power struggle broke out within the senior ranks of the company. "Let's kill the SOB!" Ailes exhorted his loyalists in discussing their approach toward a corporate competitor.

In a management reshuffling, Ailes in effect lost operational control of CNBC; when MSNBC was unveiled one month later, Ailes was given no role. Within a few weeks, he resigned. A few days after that, Ailes was appointed by Rupert Murdoch to head a new cable channel to compete with both CNN and MSNBC. It would be called the FOX News Channel.

Well before the FOX News Channel became a ratings powerhouse under Ailes's direction, MSNBC—although it bore the imprimatur of NBC News and its journalistic standards and professional practices, featuring top NBC correspondents in its lineup—moved the cable spectrum to the right. Until he died in January 2004, MSNBC's "editor-in-chief" was Jerry Nachman, a former editor of Rupert Murdoch's right-wing tabloid *New York Post.* According to an anonymous MSNBC source, a daily memorandum, which summarizes the news, suggests lines of questioning, and is circulated internally to producers and interviewers, "reads like Rush Limbaugh writes it."

Current MSNBC "analysts" include former GOP Representative Dick Armey, who called Hillary Clinton a "Marxist," referred to openly gay Representative Barney Frank as "Barney Fag," and compared bipartisanship to "date rape"; Peggy Noonan, billed as a "Capitol Hill insider," though she lives in New York; Steven Emerson, whose controversial research on terrorism has been supported by Richard Mellon Scaife; and Jed Babbin, a former Pentagon official who is a columnist for the right-wing American Prowler Web site, for *National Review Online,* and for the Moonie *Washington Times.*

The cable channel was originally marketed to a younger niche, as a foil to the older audience of CNN. Two early hires were the youthful right-wing blond lawyers Ann Coulter and Laura Ingraham, neither of whom had journalistic, media, or authorial credentials. Coulter was soon fired for telling a disabled Vietnam veteran on the air, "People like you caused us to lose the war." Ingraham was given her own short-lived solo show called *Watch It!,* though few did.

Thanks to MSNBC, right-wing commentators were now featured not only in *Crossfire* formats but as the sole anchors and arbiters of entire broadcasts. John McLaughlin, Oliver North, and Alan Keyes—the Far Right former Reagan aide and presidential candidate who believed that the "unbridled passions" of homosexuality were responsible for "totalitarianism, Nazism, and Communism"—came and went. Keyes had hosted an hour-long prime-time broadcast called, without apparent irony, *Alan Keyes Is Making Sense.* He was followed by former GOP Representative Joe Scarborough, radio show host Michael Savage, and Republican pollster Frank Luntz. After ceding his *Crossfire* chair to run twice for the presidency, Pat Buchanan found a home at MSNBC.

No liberals were given their own shows, though network officials have suggested that Chris Matthews is their in-house liberal Democrat. Matthews, who got his start in television thanks to John McLaughlin and Roger Ailes, is a registered Democrat who worked for years as an aide to President Jimmy Carter and House Speaker Tip O'Neill before breaking into the media.

Matthews is a Democrat only the conservative Republican upper eche-lons of NBC could love. Of Hillary Clinton, the most popular Democratic political figure in the country, Matthews has said, "I hate her. I hate her. All that she stands for," according to a 2001 profile of Matthews in the *Philadelphia Inquirer.* Interviewing then–Republican Senate leader Trent Lott, Matthews said, "You represent the working people who watch this show." According to the *Inquirer,* Matthews has contemplated running for the Senate from his native Pennsylvania but declines to say under which party banner he would run. Matthews has accepted speaking invitations from Richard Mellon Scaife–subsidized forums run to promote conser-vatism by neocon propagandist David Horowitz.

As he wrote in his book *Now Let Me Tell You What I Really Think,* Matthews believes American politics is governed by "attitude," by which he appears to mean that an inchoate set of instincts and atmospherics trumps substance and policy platforms. In a 2001 interview in *Playboy,* Matthews described his own political temperament, alluding to the now-infamous blue states/red states map of the 2000 presidential election: "Mentally I clearly am blue, but my gut is red. I can understand the resentment toward elitism of any kind, and domination by the media." Thus Matthews appears to accept and reinforce the right-wing critique of contemporary liberalism, and of the media, as culturally alienated from the values of most Americans. For him, the elitism of the Republican Party does not register. His program proceeds from these points.

Matthews grew up in a middle-class northeast Philadelphia household dominated by 1950s Catholicism. His father, a court reporter, was a "practical conservative," and his mother was a convert to Republicanism during the Joe McCarthy period, according to Matthews's book. Both parents were Irish Americans. "Dad was intensely self-reliant. Mom was just as intensely suspicious of the country's cultural elite," Matthews wrote. "In Catholic school there was a very strong identification between religion and the enemy. . . . It was very Manichean, good and evil," Matthews told *Playboy.* "It was the Bishop Sheen era: anti-Communist, pro-American, Kate Smith and God Bless America, fight for your faith, this is the Blessed Country. Mary is the patron saint of America. But I'm not a tribal Mick."

Indeed, during the Kennedy administration, Matthews became a "Goldwaterite" and a regular reader of William Buckley's *National Review.* After attending Holy Cross College a few years subsequent to NBC president Robert Wright and then graduate school at the University of North Carolina, Matthews found inspiration in the presidential candidacy of Democrat Eugene McCarthy, an antiwar, pro–civil rights liberal. Matthews became a Democrat. He joined the Peace Corps rather than be drafted into the Vietnam War. When he returned home, Matthews ran unsuccessfully for Congress from his neighborhood district in the post-Watergate 1974 cycle, when most Democrats won. He then embarked on a career as a Democratic aide in Washington. "If I could be president, I'd be president," he told John McLaughlin.

When he left Tip O'Neill's office at the end of the Reagan era, Matthews transitioned into journalism, taking a post with the *San Francisco Examiner.* He wrote a syndicated column, ran the paper's Washington bureau, and appeared regularly on television before being hired by Ailes at CNBC. Former congressional aide George Will was Matthews's "paradigm," Matthews has said, while his "hero" was William Safire. He paid "lifelong homage" to the "crusty Dixiecrat" James Kilpatrick.

In 2002, Matthews resigned from the column, writing, "I can't kid myself. I never made their world. They were the best writers in the business. . . . Even after a decade and a half of trying, I don't know how they do it: the endless flow of new ideas, the ever-surprising settings, the out-of-the-blue insights, the fine and faultless language."[7]

Though Matthews is far more knowledgeable about history and politics (he is the author of a serious book on the relationship between John F. Kennedy and Richard Nixon), in an article comparing Matthews to FOX News personality Bill O'Reilly, *The New Republic's* Noam Scheiber noted that the men share a "class-based populism" that is "the reigning ideological stance on the political talk-show circuit. . . . It is largely a white-ethnic Catholic tradition . . . the tradition of [former New York mayor] Fiorello La Guardia and Tip O'Neill; it is also the tradition of Richard Nixon's silent majority, the Reagan Democrats, and, to some degree, Pat Buchanan."[8]

It is also the inverted populism of Roger Ailes. Ailes's father had railed against corporate economic elites, but Ailes has forged a career exploiting cultural divisions in support of those same elite economic interests. "For them," Scheiber wrote of Matthews and O'Reilly, "the term 'working class'—the group both men consider their primary constituency—is defined not by income but by cultural values such as hard work, devotion to family, and respect for authority and tradition. . . . If working-class Americans have distinct cultural preferences that lean to the right, they also have distinct economic preferences that lean to the left. And it's these working-class economic interests that Matthews and O'Reilly—despite their in-your-face populism—generally ignore."

Like O'Reilly, Matthews mocks the intellectual class in a way that Spiro Agnew or even George Wallace might have found appealing. O'Reilly refers to "pinheads," while Matthews prefers "propellerheads." According to Scheiber, both hosts misrepresented the Bush tax cut plans, which skewed to the wealthy, as helping "the working stiff," in Matthews's words. Matthews has bristled at the comparison to O'Reilly, noting that FOX shows engage in race-baiting for ratings, which Matthews says he refuses to do.

Matthews, who has described his audience as "center right or centrist" and "angrier than I am," launched his CNBC (now MSNBC) show *Hardball* in 1997, shortly before the Monica Lewinsky sex scandal broke. Though Matthews did not quite favor removing Clinton from office, he did strike an obsessively anti-Clinton pose and sided with the right wing in the culture wars inflamed by the scandal. His ratings soared. The Clintons, he has declared, "are the Menendez brothers of American politics."

Salon called *Hardball* the "official cable club house for Clinton-haters." "Think of Matthews as a new kind of machine politician—and the machine is television," *New York* magazine reported in a 2001 profile. "Like a candidate tuned to the polls, he analyzes ratings, segment by segment, to see which topics keep viewers transfixed. His conclusion: Anytime you go hard right, your numbers go skyward."

According to *New York*, Matthews "defined a new form of news" driven by personality and opinion. While he draws far fewer viewers than does O'Reilly, his demographics are enviably younger. "In the scheme of people who watch TV, those who are devotees of news shows are a small percentage of overall viewers but are a huge slice of influential people in the business world and the political world," an NBC executive told *New York*. "Shows like Chris's can define agendas, shape the perception of public policy."[9]

Matthews has suggested that his Catholic upbringing, not cable ratings, informed his view of the Lewinsky story, which involved a sexual affair between the president and a young intern in the Oval Office. "I have a tremendous aversion to those who desecrate those institutions and those offices—e.g., Bill Clinton," Matthews explained to *Playboy*. "The critics don't like that, because their blue-part-of-the-map is based on a kind of 'we of the upper West Side' or 'we among the liberal aesthetic community' sense that their liberalism is waging a battle against the Philistines in the red part of the map." He continued, "Men don't like Clinton because he's not a stand-up guy. He's not a grown-up. Most men are basically loyal to their wives. Guys don't like guys who screw around."[10]

Shortly before he began hosting *Hardball*, Matthews quit drinking, which had contributed to his own boorish behavior with women. According to *New York*, Matthews, who is married to a local ABC Washington, D.C., news personality, recounted an afternoon of drinking at a party thrown by ABC's Sam Donaldson. "And I am *gone* at about six or seven at night," he said. "I've got my hand on somebody's leg. Where's this going? Who am I kidding?"

Matthews insisted that the sexual aspects of the Lewinsky scandal were not what sparked his interest in it. But in a 2003 appearance at Harvard University, Matthews was still preoccupied with Monica. "How many of you would support Bill Clinton?" he asked the assembled crowd, according to a report published by AlterNet.org. When students erupted in wild applause, Matthews snapped, "Oh yeah? Well, how old is the next Monica Lewinsky?" The crowd hissed.

To Matthews, Clinton represented "narcissism unlimited . . . [he has] no record of any interest in life." Matthews, however, is no stranger to empty self-absorption. He told *Playboy*, "*Washingtonian* magazine just did a list of the top 50 journalists in Washington, D.C. I'm like 36th, and Tim Russert is number one. I would argue for a higher position for myself, but after all the niceness, I just want recognition that I belong here. I'm 55 and I want to feel that I'm part of the first team. You can be on the second team at 25 or 36. But at some point you say, No, this is my opportunity, my life. I want to be on the first team." In an off-air exchange on the *Hardball* set with *Time's* Jay Carney, Matthews leaned across the desk and asked his guest, "What are people saying about me?"[11]

During his nightly coverage of the Lewinsky scandal, in addition to a regular lineup of vituperative Clinton critics and comically outlandish bit players (one Barbara Battalino, who had been placed under house arrest for lying about sex in a civil suit, made a *Hardball* star turn), Matthews gave a platform to two erstwhile liberals who shared his anti-Clinton biases: the British writer-provocateur Christopher Hitchens and the former Democratic pollster turned *West Wing* consultant Patrick Caddell.

These "*Hardball* Democrats" did not represent the views of the Democrats. Hitchens, who was once on the political Left but achieved second-tier cable fame as a Clinton hater, has referred to Clinton as "a real serious crook, a rapist, a war criminal, a perjurer, a thief . . . not just sleazy or cheap or shifty, but a monster."

Caddell, too, frequently asserted his Democratic credentials in order to attack the party, as he did not only during the Lewinsky scandal but also during the 2000 postelection standoff in Florida. "I'm a liberal Democrat. I started in Florida politics. I worked for George McGovern. I worked for Jimmy Carter. I've worked for Ted Kennedy, Mario Cuomo. Nobody can question, I think, my credentials and my convictions," Caddell sputtered. "But I have to tell you, at this point it's hard to believe that my party, the party that I've belonged to since my great-great-grandfather of my family, has become no longer a party of principles, but has been hijacked by a confederacy of gangsters who need to take power by whatever means and whatever canards they can say."

In *Warp Speed: America in the Age of Mixed Media*, media critics Bill Kovach and Tom Rosenstiel wrote, "'Hardball' has no grounding in reporting, no basic news function, is not designed to elicit facts or explore issues with policy-makers."[12] Indeed, Matthews got worked up into such a frenzy on the broadcast that he misrepresented important facts surrounding the impeachment case, as the Daily Howler Web site has documented. Matthews misstated the facts surrounding Clinton accuser Kathleen Willey's polygraph test, and he denied that the testimony of Linda Tripp contradicted Willey's, when, in fact, it had.[13]

"Clinton turned over health care to his wife, as a payoff: 'Here, you do this. I'm embarrassed by Paula Jones right now,'" Matthews said in a typical outburst. The claim was obviously wrong, as Clinton had "turned over" health care to the First Lady one year before Jones made sexual harassment claims that were later thrown out of court.

Matthews did not care much for Al Gore, either. Perpetuating the Republican spin that Gore is a liar and a hypocrite who suffers from multiple-personality disorder, Matthews compared the Democratic candidate to "Zelig" and insisted that Gore was "getting to be delusionary." According to a study of political media coverage in the year 2000 by the nonpartisan Project for Excellence in Journalism, Matthews's show accounted for fully 12 percent of all media reports that discussed Gore's alleged "tendency to exaggerate." Matthews seemed so unfair in his treatment of Gore that *Today* show host Matt Lauer upbraided him on the air, saying, "Let's be honest here. Al Gore *irritates* you." "The public has been saying that, too," a defensive Matthews replied.

After the election, Matthews, who declined to say how he voted, told *New York*, "Bush goes home at night to his wife. He's a good guy. He reads the Bible. He doesn't drink. He doesn't mess around. He works nine to five."

During the George W. Bush era, Matthews distinguished himself as the lone host of a cable talk show who opposed the Iraq war, joining hands with both the liberal Left and some members of the Far Right, such as Pat Buchanan. Matthews reserved his ire for a coterie of neoconservative intellectuals and strategists who had been promoting war with Saddam since the late 1990s. "They own the op-ed pages," Matthews told *Salon*. "I keep wondering: Is there such a thing as a neoconservative who doesn't have a column?"

Despite his skepticism about the war, Matthews followed the neocon line in questioning the patriotism of Democrats. "Did any Democrat cheer for our country today?" he asked when Iraq was liberated by American forces. He also lavishly praised Bush's personal qualities. "He's a helluva of a president, everybody likes him," Matthews said in July 2003. In an unfathomable *Hardball* segment dealing with Bush's landing on USS *Abraham Lincoln* in a flight suit, Matthews and radio show host G. Gordon Liddy marveled at Bush's purported physical attributes. "You know, he's in his flight suit, he's striding across the deck, and he's wearing his parachute harness, you know—and I've worn those because I parachute—and it makes the best of his manly characteristic," Liddy said. "You go run those, run that stuff again of him walking across there with the parachute. He has just won every woman's vote in the United States of America. You know, all those women who say size doesn't count—they're all liars. Check that out." Matthews giggled and said, "You know, it's funny. I shouldn't talk about ratings, but last night was a riot because . . . these pictures were showing last night, and everybody's tuning in to see these pictures again."

Hardball panels are consistently skewed to the hard right; pairings such as Bob Dornan, Pat Buchanan, and Armstrong Williams; Bob Dornan, Pat Buchanan, and G. Gordon Liddy; John Fund, Gary Bauer, and David Gergen offer little ideological diversity. Other panels give an appearance of balance—for example, two antiabortion commentators, Ken Connor and John Fund, against one abortion rights activist, Kate Michelman. Right-wing commentators such as Terry Jeffrey of *Human Events* square off against impartial journalists, like Howard Fineman of *Newsweek,* with no liberal representation. When liberal pundits do appear, they are paired with right-wingers who shout them down.

Conservative authors—such as Richard Miniter, who relied on false reports from a discredited Sudanese intelligence agent in his Regnery book blaming Clinton for the September 11 tragedy—are treated to respectful one-on-one interviews, while liberal authors have their time divided by conservative opponents as Matthews takes his turn at roughing them up, too. In a clash with Joe Conason, author of *Big Lies: The Right-Wing Propaganda Machine and How It Distorts the Truth,* Matthews denied Conason's contention that Ann Coulter had appeared on *Hardball* eight times after publishing her book *Slander.* Though Conason was correct, Matthews insisted that she had not appeared even once.

Hardball "expands the spectrum" to include disreputable "scholars" from the right-wing message machine and the most extreme right-wing talk radio hosts. For instance, *Hardball* has featured John R. Lott Jr. of the American Enterprise Institute, whose thesis that gun ownership reduces crime has been debunked by scholarly reviewers. "It is abundantly clear that there is no support for [Lott's] thesis," according to Stanford law professor John Donohue, who described it as "border[ing] on fraud." When controversy erupted over inaccuracies in his book *The Bias Against Guns*, Lott defended himself by taking to the Internet and posing as a woman, "Mary Rosh," who claimed to be a former student of his. Matthews did not challenge Lott about the controversy.

Also appearing on *Hardball* was radio host Michael Graham, author of two books: *Clinton & Me: How Eight Years of a Pants-Free Presidency Changed My Nation, My Family and My Life* and *Redneck Nation: How the South Really Won the War*. "Anyone listening to Hillary Clinton in her speech last week about patriotism, that screaming, screeching fingernail, I wanted to bludgeon her with a tire iron. That's what I wanted to do," Graham said on *Hardball*. According to Graham's Web site, Matthews has endorsed him as "the funniest political observer in the country. The guy turns the truth into a punch."

With Bush in office, Matthews's ratings plummeted from a high of almost one million during the Clinton presidency to often less than one third of that. While FOX News Channel ratings soared, Matthews appeared to copy some of the FOX network's signature promotional gimmicks and right-wing rhetorical flourishes, and he hired a producer with right-wing credentials. "Nobody Stops the Spin Like Chris Matthews," one ad blared. "Is the Left Writing God Out of American Life?" a network trailer for *Hardball* asked. Another plugged Matthews's cohort: "Liddy Takes on Lefties Who Criticize Bush and the War." In 2002, *Hardball* hired Howard Mortman as a producer. Known to friends as "Extreme Mortman," he came from *The Hotline*, a Washington insider newsletter, and MSNBC.com. Mortman had served previously as a "media fellow" at the Hoover Institution; before that, he was a flack for Empower America, the vanity think tank headed by Jack Kemp, William Bennett, and Jeane Kirkpatrick. None of the moves, alas, seemed to restore *Hardball* to its Clinton-era popularity.

MSNBC's sole prime-time political show is hosted by former Republican Representative Joe Scarborough. A former insurance defense lawyer,

Scarborough made his name in local politics by leading an antitax crusade and representing the civil legal interests of Michael Griffin, the convicted murderer of a Florida abortion provider. Scarborough hosted a call-in show on a local public access channel called BLAB-TV, and he came to Congress as part of the 1994 Gingrich "revolution."

Scarborough is also the founder and publisher of an independent weekly newspaper, the *Independent Florida Sun,* based in his Pensacola-area congressional district, which is known as the "Redneck Riviera." In rejecting Scarborough's newspaper for admission into the Association of Alternative Newsweeklies, the selection committee noted, "There's some honest journalism here, mixed in with a lot of pandering to the military, the religious right, and the Bushes. . . . It's not a typical alt-weekly. More like a vanity press for a smart, ambitious, potentially dangerous cabal." One AAN committee member wrote, "This paper scares me. From the patriotic publisher's note praising the Super Bowl—signed Joe—I had a bad feeling. Not only is it weirdly right-wing, it's almost impossible to figure out who wrote what—[Bush spokesman] Ari Fleisher?"

The motto of the freebie newspaper, funded by Scarborough's parents, is "Never Bound by the Truth." Scarborough writes under his own name and under the pseudonym "Izzy Walser," billed alternatively as "national correspondent," "religion writer," and "olfactory correspondent." The fictional "Izzy" was a Nixon spy in the George McGovern camp during the 1972 campaign and is serving a term in a Turkish prison for supplying arms to the Nicaraguan contras. Scarborough is suspected of also writing under the drag name "Esther Bankhead," identified as the proprietor of "Esther's Beauty Salon and Carburetor Repair."[14]

Amid rumors of marital infidelity, Scarborough divorced in 1999 and unexpectedly announced in May 2001 that he would resign his congressional seat. Two months later, a twenty-eight-year-old female staffer, Lori Klausutis, was found dead in Scarborough's Florida district office. Ruled by authorities to be the result of an injury from a fall, the death was barely mentioned in the media, even though the medical examiner in the case had his medical license revoked in Missouri in 1996 for falsifying an autopsy report. Two months previous, Chandra Levy, a federal intern with whom Democratic Representative Gary Condit admitted having an extramarital affair, disappeared. That story garnered sensational wall-to-wall cable coverage for months.[15]

Scarborough has joked about the young woman's death. "Have you seen

I'm a murderer? Do a Yahoo search, and . . . the second and third sites will say that I got a staff member pregnant and killed her, that I was cheating on my first wife. . . . Comparing me to Gary Condit."[16]

As his political career ended abruptly, MSNBC offered Scarborough the chance for a comeback. His show is called *Scarborough Country*, a pun on the Marlboro Country cigarette advertisements. The network calls it "the conservative experiment in prime-time." At the top of each broadcast, Scarborough identifies groups that do not belong in his country. "No French foreign ministers allowed," he announced one night. Another time he barked, "No Mexican ID cards allowed!"

Scarborough Country is the closest thing on cable to talk radio: one full hour every weeknight devoted to unchallenged GOP messaging on NBC's cable channel. Scarborough chooses the subjects and guests. When he loses control of interviews, usually when a liberal or a Democrat is parrying effectively, he cuts off the guest and goes to a break—or turns off his or her microphone midsentence.

The show opens with "Joe's Real Deal," a rip-off of Bill O'Reilly's "Talking Points Memo," during which the hosts freely editorialize. "The 'Real Deal' on the Democrats attacks: tasteless, and also untrue," is a typical entry. Many of the "Real Deal" bullet points are attacks on the "elitist" "liberal" media (especially the *New York Times*), which echo the "anti-cosmopolitan" rhetoric of the Far Right from the 1960s. "The president with an I.Q. of a pot of clay has made New York City elitists look like a bunch of bumbling idiots," according to Scarborough. On another occasion he yelled, "Maybe the rest of us are just plain stupid!"

Subjects on Scarborough's show have been labeled "the Left's Latest Lies," "Liberal Media Prophecies," "Disgraceful Democrats," "Liberals Against Prayer," "Liberal Elitism Gone Too Far," "Is the U.N. Worthless?," "Hollywood's Peaceniks," "The Left's WMD Hype," "Hard Left Nannies Want to Control Your Life," and "Creationists Want Equal Time." A segment called "Capitol Offense" focuses on "ridiculous ways Uncle Sam is spending your money." The Web site of the conservative group Citizens Against Government Waste is promoted. Another segment, "There They Go Again," appropriating Ronald Reagan's well-known rejoinder, is a nightly forum to bash Democrats and liberals, as are "Joe's Got Issues" and "The Buzz." "Barbra Streisand bugs the hell out of me!" was one of Joe's "issues."

Scarborough has attacked Democrats for misstating "basic facts," but he does this frequently himself. When retired senator Strom Thurmond died, Scarborough launched into an embarrassing on-air discussion about who would replace him in the Senate.[17] In a "Capitol Offense" segment, Scarborough blasted a congressional grant to the national peanut festival in Alabama, illustrated with a photo of former president Jimmy Carter; Scarborough failed to mention that the grant request was made by an Alabama Republican. An overheated piece faulting a "politically correct" homeowners association for engaging an ex-marine in a legal dispute over his desire to fly an American flag downplayed the fact that the dispute involved *how* the flag could be hung—either on a bracket or a pole—not *whether* it could be hung.

Just before the California recall election in October 2003, as allegations of sexual harassment were swirling around Republican challenger Arnold Schwarzenegger, right-wing radio show host and MSNBC "analyst" Kim Serafin appeared on *Scarborough Country*, accusing one of Schwarzenegger's alleged victims of being convicted of multiple drug and prostitution charges. Serafin's charges, broadcast to the MSNBC audience with no rebuttal, were false.[18] Only after the recall election did MSNBC correct the record.

Unlike *Hardball*, but like many of the FOX shows, *Scarborough Country* uses a formula that involves stirring up sexual, racial, and ethnic animosities through the stories Scarborough chooses to cover. Some are cited on-air to the unreliable DrudgeReport.com. The stories have included "gay scout masters," "English only" controversies, tuition discounts for students who are illegal aliens, the rights of transsexuals, and protests against campus affirmative action programs. On one show, Scarborough compared lesbians to "barnyard animals." He has called Democratic Senator John Kerry a "sissy" and a "sissyboy." When Disney announced it would make a movie by liberal filmmaker and author Michael Moore, MSNBC headlined the story "Disney's New Rat"; Scarborough asked, ". . . Mickey Mouse, M-I-C—C as in Communist?—K-E-Y M-O-O-R-E."

Like Bill O'Reilly and many talk radio hosts, Scarborough has used his show to target free speech rights and the livelihoods of those whose views he doesn't share. During the Iraq war, he supported the boycott of Dixie Chicks concerts after they criticized President Bush. He applauded when the Baseball Hall of Fame canceled an event featuring the antiwar actors Tim Robbins and Susan Sarandon. He instigated a "revoke the Oscar" campaign against Michael Moore. "I wonder," he demanded, "will [actor] Martin Sheen apologize now for providing aid and comfort to the Baghdad beast by working day and night against his immediate removal?"

Scarborough led an on-air "investigation" of the "extreme" views of actor Danny Glover, organizing a protest against Glover's role as a spokesman for telecommunications giant MCI. On his show, Scarborough gloated, "After two weeks of claiming that Glover's ads were some of the most popular ever aired by MCI, we received an e-mail today announcing that MCI would no longer be using Danny Glover as its spokesman. Because of your calls, Danny Glover is being held accountable for his comments."

In a concluding segment during which he reads viewer e-mail, Scarborough, aka "Esther Bankhead," sometimes chooses messages that compliment him as "tough, manly and attractive." Other messages suggest the opposite. "I love your poofy hair," an e-mail said. "My husband has gone to three different barbers to reproduce your poofy hair!"

One of Scarborough's favored guests was "Dr. Michael Savage, [who] tells it like it is like nobody else on television." When Savage was invited to "tell it like it is" on his own MSNBC show, he lasted only a few weeks.

When he joined MSNBC, Michael Savage ranked as the number four talk show host in the country, originating from San Francisco and reaching some six million listeners on three hundred stations per night. He also was the author of a *New York Times* best-selling book, *Savage Nation*, published through a partnership between the right-wing Web site WorldNetDaily and Thomas Nelson Publishers, a Dallas-based "Christian" book company. Though presented as original material, a review in *Salon* by Ben Fritz exposed the book as a collection of columns that appeared first on the Richard Mellon Scaife–backed NewsMax.com. Fritz listed numerous factual errors in *Savage Nation*, which sold hundreds of thousands of copies.

"The al-Qaida network is not America's most dangerous enemy," Savage contended in the book. "To fight only the al-Qaida enemy is to miss the terrorist network operating within our own borders. Who are these traitors?

Every rotten, radical left-winger in this country, that's who. . . . If you're tired of being attacked in school whenever you celebrate the achievements of America; if you're weary of being trampled on whenever you speak in favor of morality; if, as a Boy Scout, you've become a pariah while the perverts have become victims, you've come to the right place."

Savage vehemently opposes immigration, a cause historically associated with nativism and anti-Semitism. "America is well on her way from being the melting pot to becoming the chamber pot," he wrote. "When you alter the people, you alter the country. Does America want to be like Mexico, Central America, or China? Our most important and consequential inventions have come almost exclusively from white males."

Savage is executive director of the Paul Revere Society, an anti-immigration group that has called for "loyalty oaths" for immigrants. "You helped push the Republicans over the top. Now help the Paul Revere Society push the conservative agenda," Savage wrote in a donor solicitation after the 2002 elections. His Web site promotes "stories" from WorldNetDaily, NewsMax, and the *Human Life Review*. Viewers can "help Justice Moore," the Alabama Supreme Court judge removed from the bench for defying a judicial order to remove a display of the Ten Commandments from the courthouse.

Savage is everything he professes to hate: a Jew, the child of immigrants, a resident of San Francisco, and a man inordinately preoccupied with homosexuality. According to a profile in July 2003 in the *San Francisco Chronicle*, Savage, born Michael Alan Weiner in New York City to Russian immigrant parents, is "a mystery wrapped in the armor of a 'Savage' who blames America's ills on women, gays and lesbians, nonwhite people, 'liberals,' and immigrants. The bullying 'Savage' persona is rampaging id personified. In his winsome radio universe, this city is 'San Fran Freako,' its homeless people 'living rats.' Single career women over 40 are 'human wreckage in high heels.' Asians are 'little soy eaters,' Chinese people 'little devils,' and Koreans 'dog-grillers.' He once suggested that female students at a high school in Marin [County] participated in a volunteer feed-the-homeless program in San Francisco because of the titillating thought that they might be raped. 'Savage' once celebrated Yom Kippur a day early by playing tapes of Hitler's speeches to the accompaniment of German military music."

Savage has a long history of making vicious remarks about gays and lesbians. According to Fairness & Accuracy in Reporting, in 1999 "Savage . . . apologized to gay activists after saying he wished they would get AIDS"; he called the Million Mom March "the Million Dyke March"; he referred to "the grand plan to push homosexuality to cut down the white race"; and he has dubbed Supreme Court Justices Sandra Day O'Connor and Ruth Bader Ginsburg, along with Senator Hillary Rodham Clinton, a "sheocracy" who have "feminized and homosexualized much of America, to the point where the nation has become passive, receptive and masochistic." As *Boston Phoenix* media critic Dan Kennedy noted, one Savage column warned, "Your children's future is what we're talking about, a matter of life and death for their future. The gay and lesbian mafia wants our children. If it can win their souls and minds, it knows their bodies will follow. Of course, it wants to homosexualize the whole country, not just the children. This is all part of the war that is going on." After the 2000 election, Savage asked, "Were the ballot machines homophobic because some weak-wristed types had insufficient strength to press hard enough to register a vote?"

Before he became Savage, Michael Weiner worked as a teacher and social worker until entering graduate school, where he earned two master's degrees—in ethnobotany and anthropology—from the University of Hawaii and then a PhD from the University of California, Berkeley. A profile in the *Washington Times* reported that Savage failed to achieve his "life's ambition" when he was rejected for a faculty position. "He blames affirmative action, which he says translates to a policy of 'white males need not apply' at American universities." Savage told the paper, "They denied me my birthright. They wouldn't hire me as a professor, which is what I did want back in '78 when I got my Ph.D. I spent years after that, five or six years, trying to get a job teaching. . . ."[19]

In those years, Savage wrote several books (as Michael Weiner), mostly on health and nutrition, as well as a 1983 fiction collection titled *Vital Signs*. As *Salon* reported, the book's protagonist, Samuel Trueblood, is taunted by his father with antigay attacks such as "You're not a fag, are you, Sam?" Trueblood concedes he is attracted to "masculine beauty," but he says, "I choose to override my desires for men when they swell in me, waiting out the passions like a storm, below decks." Savage has written of being psychologically tortured by his father.[20]

On MSNBC, Savage did not temper his monologues. In his book chapter titled "Biased Liberal News Media Undermines America," Savage referred to MSNBC as "More Snotty Nonsense by Creeps." Upon his hiring to host a Saturday afternoon show, MSNBC hailed Savage as "brash, passionate, and smart." The MSNBC statement referred to Savage's show as "a legitimate attempt to expand the marketplace of ideas."

On MSNBC, Savage called the American Civil Liberties Union "the American Communist Liberal Union." The ACLU is "public enemy number one—they're out to destroy you." The homeless were called "bums," and Amnesty International was called "AmNASTY." When a caller said Savage's reference to third world nations as "turd world" bordered on racism, Savage screamed, "Moron! Moron! Moron! You're a racist . . . go gargle with Rogaine." Savage told another caller, "You can disagree, but if you say anything offensive, you will be disconnected." He compared Islam to the "religion" of San Francisco: "sadomasochism." Viewers were told that there is no global warming and that the United Nations is a "gigantic homeless shelter." And Savage declared, "Liberals will kill you because they're mentally deranged!"

When another caller challenged Savage, he asked the caller, apropos of nothing, if he was a "sodomite." When the caller answered in the affirmative, Savage replied, "Oh, you're one of the sodomites! You should only get AIDS and die, you pig! How's that? Why don't you see if you can sue me, you pig? You got nothing better than to put me down, you piece of garbage? You got nothing to do today? Go eat a sausage and choke on it. Get trichinosis. Okay, got another nice caller here who's busy because he didn't have a nice night in the bathhouse and is angry at me today?"

Savage was swiftly fired by MSNBC, which had been warned by the Gay & Lesbian Alliance Against Defamation about Savage's antigay history previous to his hiring. Savage called his critics "stinking rats who hide in sewers" and attempted to portray his firing as a violation of free speech rights. The day after his firing, Savage referred on the radio to Supreme Court Justice Ruth Bader Ginsburg as a "radical left-wing buck-toothed hag." His radio and book-writing career continues to flourish.

Shortly after Savage's firing, MSNBC announced that Republican pollster Frank Luntz would be given a weekly show in the Savage slot on Saturday afternoons. No Democratic pollsters host MSNBC shows.

Luntz did polling for Pat Buchanan's and Ross Perot's presidential bids in 1992, then went to work for Newt Gingrich, announcing, "I want the Republican Party to represent the hopes and concerns of the Perot constituency." Luntz was a principal strategist behind the Contract with America, the 1994 Gingrich campaign document written to appeal to Perot voters by omitting the right wing's social agenda. When Gingrich became House Speaker, Luntz became a favored adviser to the new class of Republican members of Congress, coaching them on how to sell their right-wing agenda to nonconservative voters through artful selection of language and deliberate, consistent phrasing. In Luntz's neolexicon, the estate tax is a "death tax," and school vouchers are "opportunity scholarships."

On television, Luntz tries to present himself as a moderate, although in a 1996 interview with the University of Pennsylvania's alumni magazine, the *Pennsylvania Gazette*, he ripped into the Clinton administration: "When people chanted *FOUR MORE YEARS!* at his inauguration, I think they were talking about his prison sentence, not his term of office. . . . [T]he problem with Bill Clinton's bridge to the 21st century is that it is a toll bridge, an expensive toll bridge, and Ted Kennedy is our driver, and I don't want to end up in the river. . . . The Clinton administration has hurt more people personally, has used character assassination to destroy more opponents, than even Nixon dreamed of, and yet he gets away with it because he's got this higher moral tone about it. It disgusts me, it really does."

According to his Web site, "Dr. Frank Luntz is one of the most honored communication professionals in America. *Time* magazine named him one of '50 of America's most promising leaders aged 40 and under' and he is the 'hottest pollster' in America, according to the *Boston Globe*. Frank was named one of four 'Top Research Minds' by *Business Week* and was the winner of the coveted *Washington Post* 'Crystal Ball' award for being the most accurate pundit in 1992. . . . He was a guest on 'Meet the Press,' 'This Week with David Brinkley,' 'Crossfire,' 'Capital Gang,' 'the Jim Lehrer News Hour,' 'The Montel Williams Show,' 'The Today Show,' 'Good Morning America,' 'The Charlie Rose Show,' 'Politically Incorrect,' and 'Hardball with Chris Matthews.'"

Luntz has conducted focus group research and "instant response" sessions not only for Republicans but for a wide range of corporate clients, including Merrill Lynch, Federal Express, Enron, AT&T—and NBC. He has done opinion surveys for the right-wing message machine, including Frank Gaffney's Center for Security Policy and David Horowitz's Center for the Study of Popular Culture. He is an "adjunct fellow" at the Hudson Institute.

Luntz distinguishes himself from other Republican pundits by virtue of his status as a professional pollster. Yet his research methods have been found unethical by independent polling professionals. While working for Newt Gingrich, he conducted a poll that "counted people as favoring 'tort reform' if they accepted the statement that 'we should stop excessive legal claims, frivolous lawsuits and overzealous lawyers,'" according to Luntz. "You can't measure public opinion with leading questions like these," said Diane Colasanto, former president of the American Association for Public Opinion Research. Donald Ferret of the University of Connecticut's Roper Center agreed that such leading questions "sharply overstate support for the measures in question."[21]

A Luntz poll on tort reform performed for an association of Nevada doctors suggested that "200 doctors have left Nevada"; but in the period between 1999 and 2002, the number of Nevada physicians actually grew by 450. When challenged by a Nevada TV reporter on his survey's wording, Luntz exploded, "That's bullshit! I can't believe you even asked that question."[22]

In 1997, Luntz was reprimanded by the American Association for Public Opinion Research for violating the association's ethics code for his work on the Contract with America, which he reported was supported by 60 percent of the public. During a fourteen-month inquiry, Luntz refused to share his research questions, his verification methods, or his data with the professional association. Confronted by *Salon,* Luntz replied, "Say you poll on an environmental issue, and on eight of the 10 questions the numbers are in your favor. Why release the other two? It's like being a lawyer. . . . This is my case, and these are the strong arguments and these are the weak ones. You go with your strongest case." Yet as *Salon* noted, the media regards Luntz as a professional researcher, not a partisan advocate.[23] David W. Moore, author of the book *The Superpollsters,* calls Luntz's work "propaganda masked as research."

In the 2000 election, Luntz signed a contract with NBC. "Frank conducted almost two dozen focus groups for MSNBC and CNBC, including live sessions following each night of both party conventions and presidential debates," according to Luntz's Web site. "He was a primary night and election night commentator for *The News with Brian Williams* on MSNBC."

Luntz selects the members of his focus groups, frames the questions, and interprets the responses. "The rub is that focus groups are more art than science," a profile of Luntz in *Washingtonian* magazine explained. "Unlike polls, they are messy affairs, dependent on the acumen of the moderator and subject to interpretation. Focus groups make no claim to scientific validity. They involve too few people to reflect the opinions of the public at large." *Washingtonian* followed Luntz as he conducted a focus group on a Bush speech that aired on Brian Williams's show. "As people start conversing, many realize they are friends of friends of friends. The supposedly random and representative sample is not that at all," the magazine found. "Several people are loosely connected to someone on Luntz's staff."[24]

Luntz's work for NBC in 2000 earned him another reprimand, this time from the National Council on Public Polls for "mischaracterizing on MSNBC the results of focus groups he conducted during the Republican Convention," according to an online report by the *Washington Post*. And while he was appearing across all of the NBC-owned news channels throughout 2000 as an "expert," Luntz was being paid by the Republican National Committee "to write a briefing tome on the words candidates should use," according to *Washingtonian*. "In it he implores Republicans to use phrases like 'tax relief' and not 'tax cuts.' Since [it] came out, Senate Republican leader Trent Lott always says 'tax relief' to describe cutting income taxes."

Luntz has written several memoranda to GOP leaders on how to spin their environmental policies. In a memo titled "The Environment: A Cleaner, Safer, Healthier America," he wrote, "Indeed, it can be helpful to think of environmental (and other) issues in terms of 'story.' A compelling story, even if factually inaccurate, can be more emotionally compelling than a dry recitation of the truth."[25]

Addressing George W. Bush's administration in a memo on global warming, Luntz conceded that "the scientific debate is closing [against us] but not yet closed. There is still a window of opportunity to challenge the science." Yet rather than "challenge the science," Luntz urged the administration to alter its rhetoric, suggesting use of the term "climate change" rather than "global warming," because "climate change sounds like a more controllable and less emotional challenge."

When the Senate changed hands in 2001, Luntz, still appearing frequently on the NBC cable channels as an "analyst," was the architect of a secret GOP strategy to demonize the new Senate majority leader, Tom Daschle. In a memorandum to the Senate Republican Caucus that was leaked to the *New York Times*, Luntz wrote:

> It's time for someone, everyone, to start using the phrase "Daschle Democrats" and the word "obstructionist" in the same sentence. . . . It's time for Congressional Republicans to personalize the individual that is standing directly in the way of economic security, and even national security. Remember what the Democrats did to Gingrich? We need to do exactly the same thing to Daschle.

As Luntz advised, a few weeks later George Will wrote a *Washington Post* column bearing the title "The Daschle Democrats" and used the word "Daschleized" nine times.[26] Rush Limbaugh called Daschle "El Diablo" (in Spanish, "the Devil"). Speaking to his "Devil analogy," Limbaugh said, "How many different versions of Satan, the devil, have you seen in your life? . . . We've seen the comic devil of TV shows. We've even seen the smooth, tempting devil in Hollywood movies. Is Tom Daschle simply another way to portray a devil?" During the Iraq war, Limbaugh called Daschle, a veteran of the U.S. Air Force, "Hanoi Tom" and "Tokyo Tom," booming, "You, sir, are a disgrace to patriotism, you are a disgrace to this country, you are a disgrace to the Senate." The right-wing Family Research Council took out print ads in Daschle's home state of South Dakota pairing the senator's photo with Saddam Hussein's. Vice President Dick Cheney followed Luntz's directive, referring repeatedly to Daschle as an "obstructionist."

According to a former Daschle staffer, his office—which had been targeted by a still unsolved anthrax attack in the wake of September 11—was deluged with hate mail addressed to "Tom 'The Devil' Daschle," "Tom 'Saddam' Daschle," and "Tom 'Osama' Daschle." The letters made "the FBI sit up and take notice."[27] A Wyoming man was charged with threatening

Daschle after he made an anonymous 911 call to police in which he said, "We're going to kill Senator Daschle today."[28] (When Daschle criticized the negative political tone set by Limbaugh, *Washington Post* media critic Howard Kurtz accused *Daschle* and the Democrats of demonizing Limbaugh. As evidence that Limbaugh was a "mainstream" commentator, Kurtz cited Limbaugh's role as an Election Night commentator—on NBC.)

Though he has consulted with telecommunications companies, Luntz appeared on *Scarborough Country* to say that the "American people" did not care about media regulation. He also convened a focus group for the show purporting to measure attitudes toward the United Nations. Embedded in the focus group was former New York mayor Rudy Giuliani, whom Luntz introduced as the "mayor of America—and some people call him the mayor of the world." Luntz concluded that Giuliani "represents the attitudes and opinions of most Americans." However, he did not disclose that Giuliani is a former client who paid him so much money that Luntz has said that half of his luxurious house in the Washington suburb of McLean, Virginia, was paid for by the former mayor, according to Capitol Hill newspaper *The Hill*.

In 2003, Luntz was retained by the Rescue California campaign committee, the anti–Gray Davis recall effort funded by Republican Representative Darrell Issa. In a strategy memorandum, Luntz recommended to the group seventeen ways to "kill Davis softly." "It is important to trash the governor," Luntz wrote, adding, "Issues are less important than attributes and character traits in your recall effort." Most Californians, Luntz wrote, "are unfamiliar with the recall process—and this uncertainty means voters can be easily swayed in either direction."[29]

Despite his role as a paid consultant for the recall forces, Luntz himself "trashed the governor" as MSNBC's pollster during the California recall election. Appearing on *Hardball*, Luntz told Chris Matthews that Davis would be recalled "because look, Stanford, the economics, the Hoover Institut[ion] has won the economic battle for California. Most Californians are conservative and they're ticked off at Gray Davis because he spends too much and taxes too much." Before Election Day, Luntz's own show, titled *America's Voices*, debuted. His subject: the California recall. His first guest: Darrell Issa.

In fall 2003, Republican senators were adopting yet another Luntz memo, this one titled "The Language of Judicial Nominations." Luntz advised that "the silver bullet in this effort—the one argument that consistently turns voters against the Democratic strategy and tactics—is timing. More precisely, virtually no one believes a nominee should have to wait more than six months for a vote—a year-long wait is simply unconscionable." Luntz also spoke at a session on "How to Communicate Medicare Back Home," hosted by the House Republican Conference.[30] All the while, Luntz was hosting his new MSNBC show.

Liberals have not fared so well on the NBC cable channels. On CNBC, Geraldo Rivera garnered very high ratings covering the O. J. Simpson murder trial. Rivera sustained and even grew the audience during the Monica Lewinsky scandal, when he emerged as an unabashed Clinton defender— hitting back hard, night after night, against what he saw as an unconstitutional impeachment instigated by partisan Republicans. His show, *Rivera Live*, consistently broke news throughout 1998 and gave the lie to the notion that a cable show appealing to liberal Democrats cannot find an audience. Yet Rivera's efforts to advance at NBC's cable network were spurned; enticed by his old boss Roger Ailes, Rivera left CNBC for FOX, where he is now consigned to a Sunday evening tabloid show called *At Large*.

Liberal actor Charles Grodin, also a Clinton defender during the impeachment drama, drew high ratings for four years on CNBC. Grodin had been hired by Ailes, who then proceeded to "attack" him behind his back, according to Grodin's memoir, *I Like It Better When You're Funny*. As Grodin told the story, when Ailes left for FOX, he was succeeded by William Bolster, who soon asked, "How did that Communist [Grodin] ever get his own talk show in the first place?" Jack Welch had promised to promote Grodin's show by securing a guest spot for him on *The McLaughlin Group*, but he never did, Grodin wrote.

Grodin covered the politics of the day, but he ventured into issues that are seldom addressed on cable, including homelessness, prison reform, poverty, and drug laws. Even these shows drew high ratings, although if his numbers were off even by one-tenth of 1 percent, Grodin claimed that CNBC executives would come down hard on him. The reaction "screamed out to me, content is irrelevant," Grodin wrote. "This business is no different from selling lamps."

Grodin clashed openly with Don Imus, whose daily radio show is simulcast on MSNBC, refusing to promote himself on the Imus show because "too often, I see Imus and his cohorts as unintentionally (I suppose) racist, homophobic, and just plain hateful." Grodin noted that the liberal online public interest journal *TomPaine.com* "published an Imus watch that listed some of the ways the Imus program refers to different minorities. In addition to referring to the Chinese as Chinks and Gooks, blacks were referred to as 'gorillas,' 'pimps,' and 'knuckle-dragging morons.' Gays were called 'homo,' 'lesbo,' 'load swallowers,' and 'carpet munchers.' That's only a tiny example of what is presented as humor." (During an appearance on Tim Russert's CNBC cable show to promote his book, Grodin was asked why people listen to Imus. "There are millions of people who are so unhappy that it makes them feel better when something wrong happens to someone else, when someone else fails or does poorly," Grodin replied.)

Grodin's popular show was moved from the prime-time lineup to eleven P.M., after a very low-rated rerun of Conan O'Brien's variety show. "I had, then, and now, gotten the highest ratings in the network's history, and I would be moved to 11," Grodin wrote. The show was canceled after Grodin booked Robert F. Kennedy Jr. to discuss allegations that GE plants were polluting the Hudson River. "When you're that high rated and you keep getting diminished, and then removed, it does make you wonder," Grodin concluded with evident understatement. (Grodin moved to CBS's *60 Minutes II* and does commentaries on the CBS Radio Network.)

When Grodin was canceled, then-Representative Dick Armey, now with MSNBC, said, "Thank the Lord. Thank the Lord twice."

In mid-2002, MSNBC announced the return of Phil Donahue, the father of daytime talk television, to appear in a prime-time slot. An unapologetic ideological liberal, Donahue experimented with various formats, from sitting behind a desk to the familiar format from his daytime years: on his feet, before a live studio audience. Donahue's shows were duly "balanced" by pundits from the extreme Right, such as the talk radio show host Steve Malzberg of NewsMax, though they also featured strong liberals of a type rarely seen on cable, such as antinuclear activist Dr. Helen Caldicott, and representatives of left-wing advocacy organizations and magazines. Yet unlike *Hardball* or *Scarborough Country,* which cover only the day's political developments, the impact of Donahue's shows was diminished because Donahue often interviewed celebrities and covered human-interest and tabloid fare with no political content.

After six months on the air, the show was abruptly canceled. At the time, Donahue was on a ratings upswing, averaging close to a half-million viewers per night; he already had the highest ratings of any MSNBC evening show, consistently beating *Hardball,* among others. As of August 2003, the show that replaced Donahue's, an evening newscast anchored by the apolitical Keith Olbermann, attracted 39 percent fewer viewers in the time slot. MSNBC was still running a distant third in the ratings race and had yet to find a profitable format.

MSNBC blamed Donahue's ratings for his cancellation. But an internal memo reporting an outside focus group's opinions soon surfaced; the memo called Donahue "a tired left-liberal out of touch with the current marketplace"; he was "a difficult public face for NBC in a time of war. . . . He seems to delight in presenting guests who are anti-war, anti-Bush and skeptical of the administration's motives." Though Donahue featured many pro-war voices, the memo warned that MSNBC's flagship show could become "a home for the liberal anti-war agenda at the same time that our competitors are waving the flag at every opportunity."[31]

Donahue was supposed to be free to do a liberal version of the right-wing shows on FOX. Yet in a column written by his close friend Ralph Nader, the consumer advocate whose 2000 presidential candidacy Donahue supported, Nader charged that "the corporate managers micromanaged, mismanaged, and refused to let Phil Donahue be Phil Donahue. About the only freedom Donahue had was the freedom to say what he thinks. Beyond that, he was often told what kinds of subjects to showcase and what kind of guests to have. And he was often chided for being too tough on some guests. . . . In the past few months corporate 'suits' even told Donahue that he had to have more conservative or right-wing guests than liberals on the same hour."[32]

"GE is a large corporation. . . . They were frightened of dissent. . . . They felt more comfortable without me," Donahue said on Sean Hannity's radio show after the cancellation. "They took surveys, it was determined by a focus group, not the kind of thing you would expect in news. I could have a conservative guest on alone, but not a liberal. . . . There is a terrible fear among the suits in all of broadcasting with being called liberal . . . the red states' reaction. . . . The fear was [of] being seen as unpatriotic. The accusation was I did not support the troops and was un-American."

Over at CNBC, *Meet the Press* host Tim Russert's weekly interview show, *Tim Russert,* has given the right wing valuable exposure and credence. On his cable show, Russert is far less adversarial than he is on *Meet.* He is respectful, even friendly. The Right exploits the forum to its maximum p.r. advantage.

The days when journalists like Edward R. Murrow could be counted on to expose demagoguery and fraudulence were long gone. Russert has seemed especially solicitous of Rush Limbaugh, instituting a tradition of booking him, for an hour by himself, to discuss the results of each national election. As Howard Kurtz noted in his 1996 book, *Hot Air: All Talk All the Time,* owing to Limbaugh's market success and his status as a leader of the conservative movement, he is treated as a credible person with normal views by the mainstream media. Standards collapsed under Limbaugh's weight.

Limbaugh has been featured as a serious commentator on the Persian Gulf War and environmental policy on ABC's *Nightline,* and he joined the roundtable on David Brinkley's *This Week,* ABC's influential Sunday morning show. Brinkley asked Limbaugh not about his history of racist and sexist speech or his record of lying but about "what he would do as president," Kurtz reported. Ted Koppel of *Nightline* told Kurtz, "I was one of the first people here to say you've got to pay attention to this guy."

"Tim Russert also became a fan," according to Kurtz. Russert, who hosted Limbaugh on NBC's *Meet the Press,* told Kurtz, "He is obviously very smart and has an astute understanding of trends."[33] On Russert's cable show, Limbaugh has attacked Democrats, called names, and questioned the accuracy of *Washington Post* news columns and of top reporters like Bob Woodward. And he has lied, unchallenged. In a November 2002 interview with Russert, Limbaugh said, "My—my—my whole diatribe here is policy oriented."

Russert has been quick to appease right-wing criticism. After questions were raised by callers to Limbaugh's radio show about Russert's handling of a 2003 interview with Secretary of Defense Donald Rumsfeld, Limbaugh e-mailed Russert seeking clarification. As if Limbaugh or his audience were appropriate judges of journalistic fairness, Russert promptly replied, and Limbaugh proudly posted Russert's response on his Web site. "Rush, thanks for the note. . . . Believe me, Rush, I know what our troops have done for the people of Iraq. They liberated them. I hope your listeners noted my cross-examination of the Syrian deputy ambassador. Really appreciate your note. Best always, Tim."

Russert has forthrightly stated that he believes Limbaugh's views deserve to be aired in the mainstream media. In an interview with Bernard Goldberg for his book *Arrogance: Rescuing America from the Media Elite,* a follow-up to Goldberg's *Bias,* Russert said of Limbaugh, "I don't sanction his political views by having him on. But to suggest that he does not deserve the opportunity to present his views—I mean, 'Meet the Press' is a forum for ideas! And to have censorship for his ideas . . . [Laughs] You may disagree with him philosophically, but his demeanor, his presentation was perfectly appropriate for 'Meet the Press.' And to suggest otherwise is absurd." (Russert devoted an entire episode of his hour-long cable show to a one-on-one discussion of *Arrogance,* a book convincingly exposed in a seven-part series at the Daily Howler Web site as a tissue of lies. By contrast, Eric Alterman's critically acclaimed *What Liberal Media?* was not featured on *The Tim Russert Show.*)

Russert also views FOX's Bill O'Reilly as an appropriate guest. In a May 2003 interview on *Tim Russert,* O'Reilly attacked Hillary Clinton as "a dangerous woman." He then attempted to put his own thoughts into Russert's head. "I don't think she's a particularly honest woman. I think she's ruthless. I think you know that she's ruthless. I think you, Russert, know she's ruthless, because all within the press have to deal with her machine. She's unaccountable, she doesn't answer questions, she's an elitist. Did I leave anything out?" When Russert stuck by his unargumentative style, moving to the next question, whether he meant to or not, he left the impression of his assent.

In a peculiar role reversal, O'Reilly established Russert's bona fides. A fellow Irish-Catholic who identifies what he calls his "hardscrabble, working-class upbringing" as the root of his supposed candor, O'Reilly complimented

Russert as, like himself, a "no-spin guy." "Buffalo did you a lot of good, Russert, because the one thing about you that you've maintained is you maintained a link to the people who live in Buffalo, even though you, yourself live in Washington, which isn't the real world. It's a theme park for pinheads, OK? Now most people like you live in the theme park and become one of the pinheads, all right? You're on the line, but the Buffalo saves you, and I think you know that." Russert changed the subject without comment.

In fall 2003, CNBC announced it was bringing conservative comedian Dennis Miller to its prime-time lineup. Formerly the "Weekend Update" correspondent on *Saturday Night Live* and the host of his own (since canceled) HBO show, Miller betrayed conservative instincts through the 1990s but also seemed to consider all ideologies and political parties as fair game for criticism. In an interview with *USA Today* in 1995, Miller said, "I might be profane and opinionated, but underneath are some pretty conservative feelings. On most issues, between Clinton and Newt [Gingrich], I'd choose Newt in a second, even though he is a bit too exclusionary." On the other hand, he called the 1994 Gingrich Congress "a band of fascist elves."[34]

As he veered further to the right, an approving article in *National Review* reported that Miller considers himself a "conservative libertarian," "never wavered in his support for the death penalty and his opposition to affirmative action," and "always contained a streak of right-wing populism." During the George W. Bush administration, the magazine said, Miller "consistently us[es] his distinctive brand of humor to endorse the Bush administration's policies in fighting terrorism. During appearances on *The Tonight Show,* he has also advocated profiling at airports and oil-drilling in the Arctic National Wildlife Refuge." He called Senator Robert C. Byrd, a critic of the Iraq war, a "moron."

To burnish his right-wing credentials, Miller began writing for the *Wall Street Journal* op-ed page and was rewarded with a weekly commentary slot on FOX's *Hannity & Colmes.* Hannity told Miller: "You have become the hero of conservative America."

Miller's CNBC show, *Dennis Miller Live,* debuted in January 2004. In an interview on the eve of the show's debut, Miller announced that his show would be a "mock-free zone" for President Bush, as the Associated Press put it. "I'm going to give him a pass," Miller told the AP. "I like my friends."

CHAPTER ELEVEN

HATE RADIO

THOUGH MORTON DOWNEY JR.'S STYLE is now identified exclusively with the right wing, it wasn't always so. In the early 1980s, one of the most well-known practitioners of bombastic talk was a political liberal named Alan Berg. His highly rated, Denver-based show, which at its peak reached thirty-eight states, was featured in a *60 Minutes* segment in early 1984 on the new and growing popularity of argumentative radio call-in shows. The career of Berg—the self-described "Last Angry Man" and "Wild Man of the Airwaves" who liked to "stick it to the audience"—became the inspiration for *Talk Radio,* a play by Eric Bogosian and later a movie directed by Oliver Stone.

Berg interrupted and sometimes cut off his callers while vehemently denouncing the American right wing, including neo-Nazis, whose tracts Berg read aloud. For his fiery condemnation of racial and sexual bigotry, Berg was targeted for years by extremist right-wing groups who wanted to silence him. In 1979, a Ku Klux Klan organizer burst into Berg's studio, pointed a gun at him, and said, "You will die." Five years later, shortly after the *60 Minutes* piece greatly increased his national profile, Berg was gunned down outside his Denver condominium by members of a neo-Nazi splinter

group of the Aryan Nations, called the Order; the group considered prominent Jews and liberals in the media to be enemies of the white race and
aimed to assassinate them.[1]

With Berg's assassination, the most aggressive liberal voice with a wide
following on talk radio was eliminated. Within a few months of his murder
that same year—1984—there was a second development that also would
change the face of radio and, with it, American politics. Radio executives in
Northern California were looking for a replacement for Morton Downey,
who had been fired by Sacramento radio station KFBK for making racist
remarks. They found Rush Limbaugh, who launched a radio show in a
"news talk" format at KFBK in October 1984 that was the prototype for the
nationally syndicated show that today reaches about fifteen million listeners per week and is widely copied in every radio market in the country.

Rush Hudson Limbaugh III was born in 1951 to a family of locally prominent Republican lawyers in Cape Girardeau, Missouri, a small city bisected
by the Mississippi River about one hundred miles south of St. Louis. His
uncle had been appointed to the federal bench by President Reagan, and
his first cousin sat on the Missouri Supreme Court. His father, Rush Jr., was
a conservative corporate lawyer and head of the Cape Girardeau County
Republican organization. Rush Jr. was a popular local speaker, denouncing
the evils of Communism and liberalism, as he did in political monologues
delivered to his wife and children at home. The elder Limbaugh issued daily
rants against CBS anchor Walter Cronkite.[2]

According to biographers, Rush III, known as Rusty, was a shy introvert
who battled a weight problem. He preferred the company of adults to that
of his peers, had trouble dating, and did not attend his senior prom. To his
schoolmates, he was "a dryball, a deadbeat," Limbaugh told the *Sacramento
Bee.*

Limbaugh sought refuge in radio as a way of relating to people and
becoming accepted and popular. His father's partial ownership in a local
radio station enabled Limbaugh to get on the air while still in high school,
becoming a disc jockey under the name Rusty Sharpe. To his parents' dismay, academic and social difficulties led him to drop out of Southeast
Missouri College. "I was a dumb ass," he told *Playboy* in a 1993 interview.

No longer eligible for a student deferment from service in the Vietnam War, Limbaugh was granted a medical deferment after giving his draft board a doctor's report that he had an open cyst at the base of his spine. He left Missouri to pursue a radio career at a small station in McKeesport, Pennsylvania, outside Pittsburgh. Rusty Sharpe became Jeff Christie.

Though his job was to play rock and roll, Christie slipped in humorous one-liners and played telephone pranks on the air. Christie claimed to be "often imitated, often mimicked, often copied, but never equaled," though according to Paul D. Colford, in *The Rush Limbaugh Story*, Christie lifted "actual lines and audible mannerisms" from Chicago disc jockey Larry Lujack, whom Limbaugh had idolized in his youth.[3] Christie was fired twice in the Pittsburgh market before returning closer to home in Kansas City, where he would be fired two more times for alienating listeners and advertisers.

In Kansas City, Christie manned a local "gripe line," verbally abusing and rudely dismissing his callers. At this time, his brief marriage, to a woman he had met at the radio station, collapsed, in part because he "wasn't the fathering type"; he told friends he was "through with women" and planned to become "asexual."[4] Out of work again, collecting unemployment compensation, disillusioned, and depressed, he left radio for a job as a salesman and special events coordinator for the Kansas City Royals. He worked in sales for five years, unfulfilled, before remarrying and returning to radio, this time under his given name: Rush Limbaugh.

With his new Kansas City show, under the coaching of a San Francisco–based radio consultant named Norm Woodruff, a closeted homosexual who was described as "cruel and vindictive," Limbaugh offered biting conservative commentary while "making [the audience] mad," as Limbaugh put it.[5] When the switchboards failed to light up, he was fired yet again but soon found his niche in Sacramento, where the local market had already been primed by Morton Downey. When Downey was fired, Norm Woodruff was consulting with the Sacramento station; he brought in Limbaugh, fussing with his appearance to make him more physically presentable.

In Sacramento, where Downey drew high ratings, Limbaugh and his closeted stage manager Woodruff molded the show into what it is today. For the first time, Limbaugh was able to deliver his broadcast uninhibited by nervous management. Believing that his skills as an interviewer were lacking and that guests were boring anyway, Limbaugh decided to incite listeners to tune in to him with no guests and a minimum of calls, a virtually unheard-of format that left little room for competing points of view. Limbaugh understood that radio was show business, and he wanted to be the sole reason to listen. He would be a "star" for the "ego thrills," he said.

Limbaugh said he was more interested in entertainment than in political commentary; and, with his sharp comedic timing, he had talent as a showman. The talent, which he described as "on loan from God," was of a certain level. He was not Robin Williams or Steve Martin or even Jay Leno. Much to his consternation, his later efforts to cross over into television failed. Limbaugh was bound not for Broadway but for vaudeville. On radio, a medium that had been friendly terrain for right-wing demagogues since Father Coughlin in the 1930s, Limbaugh would become king.

With the 1984 presidential race one month away, Limbaugh went against the dominant trend in radio by primarily discussing national rather than local political issues. "Antiliberalism" is how Limbaugh described his philosophy: "I think liberalism is a scourge. It destroys the human spirit. It destroys economies. It destroys prosperity. It assigns sameness to everybody." Limbaugh was no less crude or vicious than Downey, but he seemed more in control of his emotions; he tempered his invective with mockery, and he initially benefited by the comparison. Next to Downey, he appeared sane and, to many, persuasive.

Like Downey, Limbaugh had a new twist on the right-wing populism that had found a radio audience in years past. In a formula that would not vary in the years to come, rather than criticizing the powerful, he targeted those who had less power. In an extension of the GOP's Southern Strategy, this approach allowed his audience of lower-middle-class white men—who might support the Democratic Party on economic issues—to transfer their antipathy toward economic elites onto liberal cultural forces that were presented as threatening to their status, thereby switching their allegiance to the GOP.

"You can't trust women," Limbaugh announced. The National Organization for Women was "a terrorist organization." Feminists—"feminazis"—were "unattractive and hadn't found decent guys to marry." Referring to the campaign of Geraldine Ferraro for vice president, he said women should not become president or vice president for fear of what would happen to the country every twenty-eight days. He ran regular "Gerbil Updates," based on a bizarre claim that the use of gerbils for sexual gratification was a widespread gay practice, and he referred to AIDS as "Rock Hudson's disease." (Woodruff, the man who revived Limbaugh's career, died of AIDS.)

Limbaugh attacked the Reverend Jesse Jackson and the NAACP and called Mexicans "stupid and unskilled"; Jewish groups said he trivialized anti-Semitism. The prominent liberal Senator Edward M. Kennedy would make a good leader for the Soviet Union, he suggested. Advocates for the homeless and the environment were frequent objects of ridicule, and he celebrated their deaths on the air. His "Peace Update"—with sound effects simulating a bombing raid—were aired to "tweak any long-haired, maggot-infested, dope-smoking peace pansies who might hear it."[6] Though complaints from listeners poured in, management stuck with the show because ratings were up.

Limbaugh's audience had been steeped in the GOP's antimedia politics for years. In Sacramento and beyond, Limbaugh would position himself against the "flaming libs" in the media, tapping into right-wing hostility toward the media that had been simmering since the days of Goldwater, Nixon and Agnew. The heavily subsidized right-wing media critics like Reed Irvine, operating for fifteen years before Limbaugh came along, had built a foundation for him. Though his goals, techniques, and tactics were different, Limbaugh billed his show as "equal time" against the "liberal" media.

Limbaugh discovered that there was a sizable audience on the right for a media that articulated their views for them, a fact that would later help explain the popularity not only of right-wing radio but of a conservative cable channel and of right-wing books. Explaining his appeal in a 1994 article in Heritage's *Policy Review*, Limbaugh wrote, "The fact is that I am merely enunciating opinions and analysis that support what they already know. . . . Finally, they say, somebody in the media is saying out loud what they have believed all along."[7]

Limbaugh's broadcast was a daily demonstration of what his listeners wanted to hear—or, to put it another way, what they found missing in the regular media: right-wing propaganda, relentless attacks on liberals and liberalism, sexism bordering on misogyny, overt or subtle racism, and gay bashing.

To some extent, this content was already reflected in the widely circulated right-wing op-ed columns, in the *Washington Times* and the *New York Post*, in publications like *Human Events* and *National Review*, in the punditry of Pat Buchanan and Robert Novak on CNN, on *The McLaughlin Group*, and on so-called Christian television and radio. Still, Limbaugh was giving his audience the kind of media experience it could not get anywhere else in the mid-1980s. Through the unique intimacy of radio, which relies only on sound to establish a private bond with the listener, he provided a pseudocommunity for the conservative cultural minority—a powerful sense of participation, validation, and belonging that could not be achieved in print, through balanced news programming, or even through the new televised "crossfire" formats, which at least made the pretense of presenting both sides.

Limbaugh has described his effect as almost a form of self-medication. "Let's admit it," he told his audience. "Doesn't my voice coming out of your radio sound great? Doesn't it sound calm and soothing? Doesn't it sound like normalcy? Doesn't it sound like, 'Okay, things are now as they should be?' Admit, my friends. It does."

Unlike the mainstream media, Limbaugh provided the conservatives with a media that reinforced, rather than challenged, their social reality. "I don't . . . cause people to ponder," he told *Playboy*. In his world, the right wing was not only legitimate and respectable; it was always right, and it was the predominant political force in the country. On the radio in 1992, Limbaugh explained, "Every day we are inundated by what is supposedly natural in this country, what is supposedly normal, what is supposedly in the majority, by virtue of what the dominant media culture shows us, and most often it's not us. . . . We want to feel as much a part of the mainstream as anybody else." Because Limbaugh refused to have guests, and he manipulated carefully screened calls "to make me look good," as he has admitted, no one pierced this pseudoreality.[8]

In a 2003 *Newsday* article on the Limbaugh phenomenon, psychologist Paul Ginnetty offered this description of the core Limbaugh audience:

> Their certitude consigns them to what psychoanalyst Erik Erikson called the state of psychic foreclosure. Foreclosed persons are easily attracted to the beguilingly simple, one-size-fits-all belief systems of powerful others that they adopt as their own so as to avoid

the sometimes lonely rigors of personal searching. The foreclosed are the ready disciples of demagogues in every age. Social psychologists also point to the normal, near-universal need for "social comparison," the tendency to check out our impressions—say of a movie or, better yet, an ambiguous scene such as a bar fight or car accident—by instinctively comparing notes with other observers. Our hope is to confirm our own impressions and opinions in an effort to make the world feel more stable, less random. It's reassuring to be reading from the same page as others. Limbaugh's brand of talk radio provides a pathologically intense version of this wish to be singing from the same hymnal. Crucial to this phenomenon is the absence of any real controversy during the broadcast. There are constant sparks of apparent conflict that make for engaging entertainment as he shadowboxes (with one hand tied behind his back, of course) with select bites of Hillary Rodham Clinton or Ted Kennedy. . . .

Note that there are never any actual guests on the program; guests, even the conservative ones, risk obscuring simple truths with inconvenient facts or alternative hypotheses.

Sadly, the tradeoff seems to be worth it for them. What they sacrifice in terms of individuality and intellectual integrity is seemingly more than offset by the potent narcotic of reassuring simplicity. Many of them probably also derive a sense of inclusion and pseudo-intimacy via this electronic fraternity of kindred spirits. Consider the somewhat pathetic character, Marty, who checks in daily with his radio "buddy," Sean Hannity, a Limbaugh clone. There are plenty of other Martys out there who regularly light up the call boards of right-wing talk jocks—among them, G. Gordon Liddy, Matt Drudge, and Laura Ingraham—who unabashedly mimic the Limbaugh formula of ideological simplicity.

What's more, callers may get a sense of derivative celebrity and charisma from seeming to hang out—if only for a minute or two—with a mega-rich and politically powerful figure like Limbaugh. They get a chance to feel real smart when the master seems to agree with them, failing to see that it is actually they who are agreeing with him.

The right wing has long been able to attract sizable national audiences on radio. In the 1950s and 1960s, *The Dan Smoot Report* could be heard on eighty-nine radio stations and fifty-two TV stations in thirty-one states. Backed by a Dallas pet food mogul, Smoot pushed for the impeachment of the Supreme Court that desegregated the nation's schools, and he tarred the civil rights movement as Communist-inspired. The "fruits of liberalism" are street crimes, he claimed, and all crime was traceable to blacks. Smoot, who had trained in the FBI, referred to his "unimpeachable sources," which consisted of recycled right-wing books and newsletters. "Smoot believes that it is more American to decide in advance what is to be proved and then prove it rather than letting the facts speak for themselves," George Thayer wrote in *The Farther Shores of Politics*.[9]

The Manion Forum was carried on 265 radio and 15 TV stations in forty-two states. Run by Clarence E. Manion, a key organizer of the Barry Goldwater presidential campaign and adviser to the John Birch Society and the Christian Crusade, the *Forum* was antiunion, anti–income tax, and anti–Social Security. It promoted God in the classroom and "states' rights." Manion believed "traitors" were everywhere. Though the *Forum* "claimed to cover a wide spectrum of opinion . . . of 218 Forum speakers from 1955 to 1965, not one was noted for his liberal or left-wing views," Thayer wrote.[10]

Perhaps the largest audience, more than twenty million listeners on 483 stations, watched a program called *Behind the News,* hosted by Rudolph K. Scott and produced by a right-wing educational foundation, America's Future, Inc. Scott was a veteran of the segregationist Tobacco Network, based in North Carolina.[11]

As technology gave rise to new media, as the wall between various media became permeable in the age of cable and the Internet, and as the established press ceased to challenge the radical Right and even began to accommodate it, Rush Limbaugh would come to dominate the wider public discourse in a way that no other radio broadcaster ever had. He also proved that right-wing media could be immensely profitable.

In 1988, Ed McLaughlin, a former head of the ABC Radio Networks who had gone into the syndication business, approached Limbaugh about taking his show national, a possibility owing to advances in satellite technology. Among other successes, McLaughlin had nourished the career of the folksy conservative commentator Paul Harvey over the decades at ABC;

as Limbaugh would, Harvey had taken many liberties with the truth over his long career.[12] Since the 1960s, ABC also had provided a home in New York to right-wing radio commentator Barry Farber, who told his listeners that the John Birch Society was "quite noble."[13]

The time for a national political talk show seemed right. Throughout the 1970s, AM radio struggled against the clearer signals of FM. In the lucrative daytime slots, some AM programmers stayed with music, while others switched to all-news formats; neither seemed to work. In the less profitable evening hours, a handful of popular national shows hosted by apolitical or liberal-leaning personalities like Larry King, Tom Snyder, and Sally Jessy Raphaël began to attract sizable audiences. In local markets, hosts offering advice on everything from personal finances to relationships were catching on.

At the dawn of the Reagan administration, several hosts around the country revived the Joe Pyne style of angry political talk that enjoyed brief popularity in the mid-1960s. In a 1984 feature on these new hosts, an article sparked by Alan Berg's murder, *Time's* headline was AMERICAN AUDIENCES LOVE TO HATE THEM. The featured talkers were of every political stripe, though most were right-leaning; a common element seemed to be locker-room talk and bathroom humor, by male hosts, playing to predominantly male audiences. Howard Stern in New York City was the most renowned of the bunch. Still in Sacramento, Limbaugh did not warrant a mention.

AM radio programmers were beginning to see that the talk format might save them. With his connections at ABC, Ed McLaughlin was able to win for Limbaugh a slot on WABC in New York City, the top radio market in the country, in the relatively undesirable early afternoon. The New York station had already moved to capture the new niche market for bully-boy hosts by replacing the Los Angeles–based gentlemanly liberal host Michael Jackson with Bob Grant, a local right-wing hothead who would later be fired for making racist comments on the air—an occupational hazard for the conservatives but also an opportunity. Sean Hannity of the FOX News Channel—who had been fired from an earlier radio job for attacking gays and lesbians—took Grant's slot on WABC; Grant quickly found a new home at rival station WOR. Grant, in turn, had first made his name in Los Angeles, when Pyne was taken off the air for a few days after the assassination of President John F. Kennedy, due to Pyne's rabid on-air hatred of Kennedy.[14]

Before his firing, Grant had drawn large audiences in afternoon drive time. He was doing so well that WABC would not allow him out of his contract, foreclosing national syndication. Grant prepared the market for Limbaugh, as Downey had done in Sacramento. And just as Limbaugh used Downey as a foil in Sacramento, he positioned himself in New York as a more rational alternative to Grant, who referred to blacks as "subhumanoid savages."

Limbaugh had the decisive advantage and good luck of being the first to market with a national political talk show. For WABC, Limbaugh in midday was a lark. For Limbaugh, WABC—owned by the American Broadcasting Company, which had recently been purchased by Capital Cities—was a stamp of legitimacy. McLaughlin used the New York deal to market the Limbaugh show, originally for free, to desperate AM affiliates around the country. In two years, Limbaugh was on 244 stations, bringing high ratings and a flood of advertising revenue, while knocking off local programming—including a number of well-established liberal talk show hosts. Two years later, he had 529 stations and, by 1995, 660.

Despite his success, biographers reported that Limbaugh remained emotionally volatile, insecure, and a compulsive overeater. To interviewers, he conceded that popular radio personalities were "a little weird," "head cases," and living "a lie in that little room."[15] When his second marriage broke up, Limbaugh got married a third time to an aerobics instructor he met on the Internet, with Supreme Court Justice Clarence Thomas officiating. An advocate of the "traditional" family and "the sanctity of marriage," Limbaugh remained childless, did not attend religious services, and in his off-hours devoted himself to smoking the best cigars, drinking the finest wines that money could buy—and secretly nursing a severe addiction to illegally acquired drugs likened to heroin, an addiction that would not be publicly revealed until 2003. During the Reagan years, he never bothered to register to vote.

Limbaugh, who calls himself "the most dangerous man in America," established himself as arguably the most important political commentator in

America as well, with a contract reportedly worth more than one-quarter of a billion dollars. "He is more influential than Larry King or John McLaughlin or Dan Rather or Tom Brokaw or Peter Jennings," *Washington Post* media critic Howard Kurtz wrote in his book *Hot Air*.[16] Legions of Limbaugh fans—calling themselves "ditto-heads"—gathered in "Rush Rooms," restaurants and bars across the country that played his midday broadcast. Though a column Limbaugh claimed to be writing for the *Sacramento Union* proved short-lived when it was revealed that it was ghostwritten, Limbaugh demonstrated the immense cross-marketing potential of radio when he published *The Way Things Ought to Be*, which sold more than 4.5 million copies.[17] The 1993 book was also ghosted, this time by *Wall Street Journal* editorial writer John Fund.

The Limbaugh model was so profitable that stations began to plan whole formats around his show, programming wall-to-wall right-wing talk at the expense of nonconservative programming. Following in Limbaugh's footsteps were President Ronald Reagan's eldest son, Michael; convicted Watergate burglar G. Gordon Liddy; Iran-contra felon Oliver North; Dr. Laura Schlessinger, the family advice maven who was notoriously estranged from her own family; FOX News Channel personalities Sean Hannity and Bill O'Reilly; right-wing African Americans Ken Hamblin ("the black avenger"), Larry Elder, Alan Keyes, and Armstrong Williams; Mike Gallagher, who called for a "March on Washington" against Al Gore during the Florida recount controversy; former right-wing Representative Bob Dornan; Mark Levin of the Scaife-backed Landmark Legal Foundation; the Atlanta-based Neal Boortz, who calls liberals "bedwetters"; former Scaife operative Joseph Farah of the right-wing Web site WorldNetDaily; Internet gossip Matt Drudge; gay basher Michael Savage, broadcasting from "Sicko Frisco"; Wayne LaPierre of the National Rifle Association; right-wing cultural critic Michael Medved; right-wing women Janet Parshall (Family Research Council), Sandy Rios (Concerned Women for America), former Bush administration official Blanquita Cullum, and Laura Ingraham; Roger Hedgecock, convicted of conspiracy and perjury and forced to step down as mayor of San Diego; Tom Marr in Baltimore, Mike Rosen in Denver, Kirby Wilber in Seattle, Bill Cunningham in Cincinnati, Glenn Beck in Philadelphia, Howie Carr in Boston, and Chuck Baker, broadcasting from a gun shop in Colorado Springs—and literally hundreds more.

Emerging from the pack as the second most highly rated talk show host after Limbaugh—and reaching some ten million listeners per week—was another college dropout, the New York–born Sean Patrick Hannity. Hannity had been fired from his first job in radio, in Santa Barbara, California, after featuring a gay-bashing interview with Gene Antonio, the author of the book *The AIDS Cover-Up?*, which falsely claimed the disease could be transmitted through coughs and sneezes. Hannity moved from California to Huntsville, Alabama, and then to Atlanta, Georgia, where his approach was better received by management. A promotional blurb by the Georgia radio station boasted that Hannity was "making a proud name for himself by insulting lesbians."[18]

In Georgia, Hannity, who embraces the agenda of the Christian Right more fervently than does Limbaugh, came to the attention of Newt Gingrich. When the FOX News Channel was established in 1996, Ailes brought Hannity from Georgia to New York and gave him his own prime-time show. Before long, he was on the radio in New York, following Limbaugh, claiming to offer "stories that you can't find in the liberal media." The show attracted notice during a court case in which Haitian immigrant Abner Louima charged city police officers with beating him and sodomizing him with a wooden bat. Louima's claims were verified in trial testimony and confessions; Hannity had taken the other side, referring to the victim as "Lying Louima" and offering a false "story" that his injuries resulted from a self-inflicted "gay sex act."[19]

The show went national in 2001—"the Hannitization of America," according to the host—true to form, a good deal of it reflects Hannity's pre-occupation with sex, especially gay sex. "People choose homelessness," he said one day. The poor and the homeless need to stop smoking, drinking, and "oversexing themselves." Other subjects covered in detail have included gay men who supposedly seek out the AIDS virus; same-sex schools; "pro-homosexual" plays in schools; sex education (Hannity wanted to know if "ingesting semen" and "fisting" were taught); and "eleven-year-olds being taught to masturbate." Explaining his own stilted sex life before meeting his wife, Hannity, who had studied to become a Catholic priest, said, "I didn't have it from either side. My wife was the only one who would marry me." (Hannity has used his celebrity to raise money for political initiatives, such as the drive to amend the U.S. Constitution to prohibit gay marriage.)

Altogether, there were some four hundred significant right-wing shows by the end of the 1990s and perhaps a handful of liberal ones. By 2003, conservative leader Paul Weyrich estimated the number of right-wing radio hosts to be 1,700. Limbaugh could be heard in virtually every corner of the United States, multiple times a day, and drew about twelve million listeners per day, "as big as any top-rated TV show on a broadcast network and dwarf[ing] any show delivered on cable," according to *Mediaweek*.[20]

A vivid snapshot of what goes on during such broadcasts was provided by a 1996 content analysis conducted by the Annenberg Public Policy Center of the University of Pennsylvania, directed by Kathleen Hall Jamieson, of 150 hours of political talk from fifty programs. Unlike the regular media, in which an attempt is made to counterbalance ideological messaging and partisan viewpoints, the radio talk shows are openly biased and one-sided. According to the study, G. Gordon Liddy said that 1996 GOP presidential candidate Bob Dole was going to "run for president against a yellow coward who turned and ran, someone who's got a thumb up his ass instead of a bullet in his heart." Rush Limbaugh said that if feminists founded their own country, it might be called "Ovaria," "Hysteria," "Estronia," or "Lesbanon." The study also noted his monologue involving a news report on prosthetic testicles for dogs, and his comment that feminists and their male companions might want to see a veterinarian to get some for themselves. The Annenberg content analysis also revealed that Bob Grant had called New Jersey Democratic Senator Frank Lautenberg "vicious," referred to African American comedian and civil rights activist Dick Gregory as a "slimeball," and failed to challenge a caller to his show who referred on the air to controversial Harvard Law professor Alan Dershowitz as a "scumbag" and used the phrase "those black douchebags."

"We did hear parodies suggesting that Bill Clinton is a philanderer and a 'liar,' suggestions about Hillary Clinton's sexual preferences, and assertions that Ross Perot is 'crazy,' as well as statements that were plainly inaccurate (e.g., Rush Limbaugh's claim that Willie Horton was a 'mass murderer'). And typical of partisan political discourse, we heard a great deal of one-sided argument that ignored the evidence on the other side. . . . We heard Chuck Harder discuss the 'Arkancides' (Arkansas plus suicide) of the Clinton presidency. On Michael Reagan's show a guest suggests that Hillary Clinton had an affair with Vincent Foster. . . . On April 16, [Ken] Hamblin told a caller who identified himself as a drug dealer and insisted that no one would take care of his children without welfare and affirmative action, 'Bring your woman to me so that I can gut out her reproductive organs [and] . . . if your son shows signs of being like you, I want to castrate him so that he cannot reproduce and be a burden to society.'"[21] (Hamblin, also a *Denver Post* columnist who is nationally syndicated by the *New York Times,* was suspended for two months for directly plagiarizing several paragraphs from a rival newspaper, according to *Columbia Journalism Review.* He is rated one of the top ten hosts in the nation, featured on more than 120 stations.)

The Limbaugh broadcasts are especially hate-filled. According to the writer Edward Olshaker, when a twenty-two-year-old environmentalist died, Limbaugh posted on his Web page, "If a Wacko Falls Out of a Tree— Some tree sitters on the left coast were just days away from ending a three-year perch when one of them slipped and fell. Can you believe the trees around her just stood and watched? They could've at least reached out and saved her, right? . . . So it looks like we've had our first tree suicide bomber, or suicide dropper, as the case may be." When another environmentalist died of breast cancer in 1997, Limbaugh played the sound of a buzzsaw and said the woman had "finally been cut down to size! . . . She'll never be able to bark up the wrong tree again." Olshaker detailed Limbaugh's racism— he said that Bush had actually won the 2000 election by a landslide if you discounted the black vote—as well as his "sick comedy on the HIV infection suffered by Magic Johnson."[22]

On various broadcasts throughout 2002 and 2003, Limbaugh made the following comments. Citing a commendation in the press of former president Jimmy Carter for having "made a difference" through the Habitat for Humanity project of building low-income housing, Limbaugh said, "Hitler made a difference." Limbaugh addressed "you sick liberals out there." When a caller told Limbaugh she listens to his show in awe, with her mouth open, he said, "I hope Bill Clinton isn't in your neighborhood." A GOP talking point on Senator John Kerry—that he "looks French"—was picked up by Limbaugh and repeated in subsequent references to the senator. He regularly referred to Kerry, a decorated Vietnam veteran, as a "reputed veteran" and often gratuitously reminded the audience that Kerry had a Jewish grandfather. When a *New York Times* reporter was found dead, a suicide by leaping from a building, Limbaugh played the song "It's Raining Men."

Howard Dean was "Nikita Dean." "There is a cold wind blowing in Hillary Clinton's bedroom," Limbaugh told his audience. Attendees of a National Abortion Rights Action League were "perverts" drinking "Bloody Marys" and eating "clam dip." According to Limbaugh "the baby-sitter for every Democratic candidate for president" was Scott Ritter, the former UN weapons inspector who had previously been accused of attempting to lure an underage girl to a meeting over the Internet. (The accusations were later dropped.) Searching for a name "worse than Communist" during the Iraq war, Limbaugh settled on "Francokrauts." He wondered how "interracial marriage" will affect the future of affirmative action. The Supreme Court "expelled gas" in striking down antisodomy laws in Texas. Supreme Court Justice Sandra Day O'Connor is a "racist" for upholding affirmative action programs. Liberals are "depressed, suicidal, on the brink of a nervous breakdown." They base their arguments on "emotion, not thought." Foreign aid recipients constitute an "excrement list—you piddly little worthless countries." He purposely stumbled over the pronunciation of Jewish surnames and mocked Hispanic ones. New Mexico is "New-meh-hee-co," and the Bush White House counsel is "Alberrrto Gonthalez." He said he didn't endorse the sentiments of a gay-bashing article on the right-wing American Prowler Web site but read it anyway, "because you gotta' know what's out there."

Democratic National Committee chairman Terry McAuliffe is a "punk," and Clinton has "Teflon testicles." When one caller said that condoms help stop the spread of AIDS, Limbaugh said, "You're wrong. There is no other side. There is no disagreement." When the caller persisted, Limbaugh said, "Take him off the air . . . we don't filibuster here." In a discussion of "how women have changed," he said they've become "too liberal" and "tramps." John Kerry's wife, Teresa Heinz, was called "one of the nation's leading wackos . . . in love with a dead man." (Her first husband, Senator John Heinz, died in an airplane crash.) Women would not look to "Big Government" to solve problems if "they could find men" to marry them, he said, offering to open a dating service. "White liberals," he said, "keep slavery alive." Of African Americans, he said, "These people have been complaining for fifty years." Liberal columnists Michael Kinsley and Al Hunt are not "real men." Reviving a right-wing conspiracy theory that had been promoted in places like the *Wall Street Journal* editorial page in the 1990s, Limbaugh said that the Arkansan Wesley Clark might suffer the same fate as Vincent Foster. "If Wesley Clark doesn't look out, I mean, his family is going to go looking for him in Fort Marcy Park [where Foster's body was found] before it's too long."

While regularly equating liberalism and Fascism—"Mussolini was a liberal," according to Limbaugh—he called for a crackdown on political dissent. Referring to actor Tim Robbins's criticisms of Bush, Limbaugh said, "Tim Robbins, who thinks he can say anything at any time . . . I have a question: How is it that Tim Robbins is still walking free?"[23] Limbaugh attacked antiwar protesters as "anti-American, anti-capitalist Marxists and Communists."

"Hell," "damn," and "ass" peppered Limbaugh's remarks. "Pussy-whipping" was mentioned. Limbaugh called a sex change operation an "add-a-dick-to-me," speculating "if the womb is transferred back, you can screw yourself." He referred to "gang-bangin' liberals" and to Democrats as the "two-inch crowd." Representative Richard Gephardt is called "little Dick." (LITTLE DICK PROMISES FASCISM IF ELECTED was a headline on Limbaugh's Web site in April 2003.) Limbaugh appeared to refer to his own penis in claiming he has a big "part," then paused for effect and said he was referring to "the part on my head."

George W. Bush, Limbaugh announced, "is the closest Americans will have come to someone like me in the White House."

Limbaugh and his fans are quite right when they say that the racist, sexist, and homophobic messaging of his broadcast cannot be found in the mainstream media, although they don't seem to understand why that is. When the ESPN cable channel hired Limbaugh to give commentary on the "Sunday NFL Countdown," he tested his views with a mainstream audience. Limbaugh called it "the fulfillment of a dream." He was dropped from the broadcast in four weeks.

Before he was hired by ESPN in 2003, Limbaugh had a long history of racist speech. He told one black caller, "Take that bone out of your nose and call me back." "Have you ever noticed how all composite pictures of wanted criminals resemble Jesse Jackson?" he asked. "The NAACP should have riot rehearsal. They should get a liquor store and practice robberies." When discussing former Illinois senator Carol Moseley Braun's presidential run, an announcer on the show said, "I don't know nothin' about runnin' for no president."[24]

On ESPN, Limbaugh claimed that Philadelphia Eagles quarterback Donovan McNabb is overrated because he is African American. "I think what we've had here is a little social concern in the NFL. The media has been very desirous that a black quarterback do well. There is a little hope invested in McNabb, and he got credit for the performance of this team that he didn't deserve. The defense carried this team," Limbaugh said.

"Limbaugh's remarks brought down the house, and not in a good way," Bill Berkowitz wrote in the online publication *WorkingForChange*. "On its merits, his comments showed what skeptics had charged all along, that he really knows little about football. He wrongly criticized the skills of McNabb, an all-pro quarterback who has helped carry his team to playoff games over the past few seasons. And Limbaugh's larger point that the so-called liberal media was trying to shine an uncritical light on black quarterbacks was also patently ridiculous: All you have to do is go into the archives and check out the negative coverage that African American quarterbacks Tony Banks and Kordell Stewart have received over the past few years."

ESPN defended Limbaugh initially, but he was forced to resign a few days later. He and his defenders blamed the controversy on "political correctness"; said his free speech rights had been abridged; and rolled out the old chestnut that "an opinion is an opinion"—all arguments used by the Right to expand the spectrum of discourse ever rightward. In pressing Limbaugh's case, the right-wing think tank network succeeded in placing a mild defense of Limbaugh in the *New York Times* by a "senior fellow" of the Manhattan Institute. Writing in the *Washington Times* under the headline POLITICAL CORRECTNESS INVADES SPORTS COVERAGE, John R. Lott Jr., a "resident scholar" at AEI, charged that "no one has tried to compare the news coverage of any two black quarterbacks, let alone generally between black and white quarterbacks in the NFL." In fact, a professor at Florida Atlantic University had done just that. According to a report on the professor's findings in the *Palm Beach Post*, an analysis of more than ten thousand stories from twenty-five major papers showed "no significant statistical difference" in coverage of black and white quarterbacks. "The performance of black quarterbacks was panned in 12.2 percent of stories, while white quarterbacks were criticized in 11.7 percent of articles. Black quarterbacks were praised in 9.2 percent of stories, compared with 9.1 percent for their white colleagues," the paper reported.[25]

While Limbaugh's rhetoric proved unacceptable once he left the right-wing media universe, it does set the parameters for hundreds of talk radio show hosts across the country who routinely make racist remarks. Commenting on a newspaper photograph of a gorilla standing at a bus stop, John Dennis, a Boston-based host, said the animal was "probably a Metco gorilla waiting for a bus." (Metco is a voluntary busing program in Boston that allows inner-city youth to attend suburban schools.) Dennis was suspended for a few days. Radio show personality Steve Lonsberry was fired from a Rochester station for referring to the city's African American mayor as an "orangutan." While Limbaugh lost his job at ESPN, there appeared to be no repercussions for Pat Robertson, who, on his *700 Club* broadcast, defended Limbaugh by questioning whether the African American actor Morgan Freeman was also overrated. Conversely, liberal Harvard law professor Alan Dershowitz was fired by ABC radio for telling the truth about his ABC colleague, Bob Grant—namely, that he is a racist.

In his book *Hot Air,* Howard Kurtz compiled examples of talk radio fare from the Limbaugh wannabes around the country, many of whom seek out a market niche that is further right than Limbaugh's. Mike Siegel in Seattle spread the falsehood that the city's mayor was shot by his wife after engaging in homosexual conduct; Emiliano Limon of KFI in Los Angeles suggested homeless people be put to death; Bob Mohan of KYFI in Phoenix said gun control advocate Sarah Brady "ought to be put down"; J. Paul Emerson of San Francisco said every taxpayer ought to be able to shoot illegal immigrants crossing the border; Chuck Baker called for "armed revolution"; Bob Grant suggested that police officers "mow down" gay activists with machine guns; a self-proclaimed Nazi was on the air in New Orleans, while a white supremacist held forth in Nashville.[26] The callers are no less brazen on Sean Hannity's show: With respect to Clinton, one asked, "Lee Harvey Oswald, where are you?"

The focus on the extremism and outlandishness of talk radio obscures the reality that the hosts talk about issues of interest to a broad spectrum of listeners, at times make legitimate points, and can be amusing. Thus the audience for political talk is significant and extends far beyond the extreme Right.

The Annenberg study found that in 1996, 24 percent of the public listened to political talk at least once per week and 18 percent twice per week. In 2002, a survey by the Pew Research Center for the People and the Press found that 37 percent of the public said they "regularly" or "sometimes" listened to political talk radio shows, while 17 percent rely on call-in talk radio as part of their "regular news consumption."[27] An American National Election Study pilot survey in 1995 found that 27 percent of voters listen to Rush Limbaugh.[28] In a January 2003 Gallup Poll, 31 percent of those surveyed said that they got their news every day or several times per week from talk radio, up from 17 percent in 1995. Twenty-two percent of those who listen to talk radio every day consider themselves political independents, according to Gallup. The American National Election Study found that up to 42 percent of the talk radio audience is comprised of moderates and independents.

Early scholarship on the demographic profile of talk radio audiences in the 1980s suggested that the audience for such programming skewed toward older, less affluent, and less educated listeners, socially and politically alienated from the mainstream of society—the prototypical inarticulate "angry white male." In *Talk Radio and the American Dream*, Murray Levin described talk radio in those years as "the province of proletariat discontent, the only mass medium easily available to the underclass."[29] Over time, however, the audience broadened. Today, listeners are likely more affluent, better educated, and more politically interested than nonlisteners.[30] The audience continues to skew to the elderly, with one-third over the age of sixty-five, according to the Arbitron ratings service.

An unscientific study by the Talk Radio Research Project, run by *Talkers* magazine, described the audience for talk radio as predominantly white and male. Sixty-one percent had a high school education or some college, while 33 percent had college degrees. Seventy-seven percent made $70,000 a year or less. A whopping 70 percent said they voted. Fifty-two percent described themselves as independent, 23 percent as Republican, 12 percent as Democrat, and 8 percent as libertarian. Thirty-seven percent said they were conservative, 23 percent moderate, and 11 percent liberal. They chose the FOX News Channel and the Internet as their biggest sources of nonradio "news."

As compared with conservative talk radio overall, Rush Limbaugh's listeners are older, whiter, more male, less well-off, less likely to have a college degree, and more likely to call themselves "born again" Christians, according to the book *Rushed to Judgment,* by David C. Barker. They are also quite a bit more conservative and Republican.[31] Andrew Kohut, the respected pollster, has described the typical Limbaugh listener as a "white male, suburbanite, conservative [with a] better-than-average job but not really a great job. Frustrated with the system, with the way the world of Washington works. Frustrated by cultural change. Maybe threatened by women."[32]

Another insight into the Limbaugh audience is provided by the advertisers who support it. Limbaugh runs ads for hair loss treatments; golf instruction; stress tabs; the anti-inflammatory emu oil; and Enzyte, which promises insecure men "an increase in erection size."

Though companionship and entertainment are part of the draw, talk radio listeners tell pollsters that the main reason they tune in is for information.[33] Limbaugh assures his audience that he is a "truth detector," refers to his network as "Excellence in Broadcasting," calls himself "Professor Limbaugh," says "Whatever we say here is right," and compares his show favorably to the *New York Times,* telling his audience that, unlike the *Times,* he has no "credibility" problems. In the *Playboy* interview he said, "I am a profound success because I relentlessly pursue the truth, and I do so with the epitome of accuracy. That sets me apart from mainstream journalists."

A number of books and articles published over the years have documented Limbaugh's falsehoods and lies. Among the books are Al Franken's *Rush Limbaugh Is a Big Fat Idiot* and *Lies and the Lying Liars Who Tell Them; Logic and Mr. Limbaugh* by philosophy professor Ray Perkins Jr.; *The Great Limbaugh Con* by Charles M. Kelly; and *The Way Things Aren't: Rush Limbaugh's Reign of Error,* compiled by the staff of Fairness & Accuracy in Reporting. Separately, FAIR has published several reports on Limbaugh's misstatements that are available through the organization's Web site. The Environmental Defense Fund issued a sixteen-page white paper illustrating how Limbaugh's "information" flies "in the face of scientific evidence with misleading, distorted, and factually incorrect statements."

Perhaps the most extensive study of the Limbaugh phenomenon is University of Pittsburgh political scientist David Barker's *Rushed to Judgment.* Through a battery of tests and analyses, Barker and his team of social scientists examined Limbaugh's techniques and ability to persuade. Barker concluded that Limbaugh has substantial skill in this area. He is not simply "preaching to the choir," as is commonly thought. "When Limbaugh levels criticism toward particular ideas, groups, or individuals on at least half of his broadcasts, regular listeners show a marked tendency to 'buy' the Limbaugh message—displaying hostility toward those items beyond what can be accounted for by ideology, party identification, exposure to other conservative messages, affect for Limbaugh, or a host of other factors. Moreover, regular listening not only correlates with attitudes that reflect Limbaugh's message; listening also leads to opinion change toward greater conservatism and antipathy toward Limbaugh's favorite targets."[34]

According to Barker's study, conservatives favorably disposed to Ross Perot turned against him after listening to Limbaugh's attacks. Those who listened every day were 7.78 times as likely to vote for Bob Dole over Bill Clinton in 1996. In 2000, Republican views of Republican Senator John McCain—a frequent Limbaugh target who ran against Bush for the party presidential nomination—were similarly affected. "Thus voters who listen five days a week are 3.35 times as likely to prefer Bush [over McCain] than Republican voters who never listen to Limbaugh," Barker wrote.

Barker discovered that Limbaugh is more skilled at generating opposition than support. And he found that Limbaugh was less effective when he used traditional rhetorical argument than when he used heresthetics, which is the framing of issues by appealing to core values. As Barker defined it, rhetoric involves convincing an audience member to adopt a view by presenting new information; heresthetics persuades by calling one value to the attention of the listener at the expense of a competing one. Limbaugh persuades by repetitively "priming" one value over others, rather than by providing information. With rhetorical argument, the listener's response is often counterargument; with the heresthetic approach, even the sophisticated listener is taken in, because the core value being primed is a preexisting belief. Barker reported that Limbaugh's propaganda works even on those presumably most resistant to it:

By priming the values of economic freedom and self-reliance, as opposed to other equally cherished values such as humanitarianism and equality of opportunity, Rush Limbaugh was able to

increase the likelihood that subjects would oppose federal spending to assist the disadvantaged more than fivefold. This apparent
persuasion occurred even though those who were exposed to the
Limbaugh value heresthetic stimulus reported, on average, strong
and disproportionate hostility toward the talk show host, considerable negativity toward conservatives, displayed liberal tendencies
in terms of general attitudes toward the role of government, and
endured distractions throughout the experiment.[35]

Limbaugh doesn't simply persuade; he gives people the wrong ideas.
According to Barker's data, even though listeners of right-wing talk are
more interested in politics than are nonlisteners, there was a significant cor-
relation between listening to Limbaugh and to four other prominent right-
wing hosts and being both less informed—and misinformed—about
rudimentary political facts. Moreover, these incorrect beliefs become
strongly held and inspire political action. The effects of listening to two nonconservative talk show hosts showed the opposite result: These listeners
were more informed, and better informed, than nonlisteners.[36]

Listeners to right-wing talk had more difficulty than nonlisteners in
answering questions about the American political system, such as the length
of terms for members of Congress. And they more frequently gave wrong
answers on a battery of political questions, ranging from whether the
budget deficit had grown during the Clinton presidency to whether the
United States spends more money on welfare or defense. Thus, aside from
the lies and false information spread by the right-wing hosts, Barker showed
that a more insidious effect is achieved through the "inferential reasoning
of the audience itself" and the connotations the audience picks up from
the broadcasts (for instance, Clinton is bad, so the deficit *must* have gone
up on his watch, when it fact it was wiped away). Through repeated exposure to right-wing talk, the right-wing audience constructs its own "political
reality . . . structured around a particular ideological worldview" that bears
little relation to facts, evidence, or truth, Barker found. In this way, he concluded, talk radio of the Limbaugh variety may diminish rather than
enhance democracy.[37]

•   •   •

As a defensive maneuver, Limbaugh presents himself as an entertainer—he introduces himself as "El Rushbo" and the "Maha Rushdee"—but he has admitted his ideological and partisan intentions. "Not only am I a performer, I am also effectively communicating a body of beliefs that strikes terror into the heart of even the most well-entrenched liberals, shaking them to their core," he has said. In *Policy Review,* he wrote, "The battle is not simply for political control, it is for re-establishing control of America's institutions."

According to David Barker, Limbaugh's broadcast involves a "fundamental call to action."[38] Because both the host and the callers encourage the idea that "conservatism dominates the mind-sets of average Americans," Limbaugh listeners come to feel "vindicated and confident"—and "ready to spread the conservative gospel to others." Through consistent and repetitive messaging, the radio broadcasts tell audience members what to say and teach them how to say it, politicizing every church social, every pool hall, and every workplace across the country. This "nontraditional social network" produces both great conformity within the conservative movement and "emboldened" political participation, Barker wrote. Conversely, when liberals are exposed to right-wing media, they turn cynical and confused and tend to withdraw from politics, according to Barker's tests.[39]

In the early 1990s, the Republican Party and the conservative movement began to make use of the widening talk radio network, which became a means of running a free, daily political advertising campaign. As with many political ads, the talk radio campaign was characterized by distortions, exaggerations, and outright untruths; illogic; hypocrisy; projection, by which the targets of the right wing were accused of doing precisely what the right wing was doing; and utter shamelessness.

With the flick of a switch, these hosts were able to blow every event, every statement, every small gesture or voice inflection, into a raging "controversy" that invariably redounded to the benefit of the GOP and to the detriment of the Democratic Party. In the world constructed by talk radio, Republican initiatives were lavishly praised, while Democratic ones were trashed. Republican criticism of Democrats was underlined and reinforced, while Democratic criticism of Republicans was called partisan, illegitimate, and even unpatriotic, as in host Mike Gallagher's references to "Senator Dianne anti-American Feinstein." Major Republican scandals were deflected, while even minor Democratic scandals were accentuated. Blacks were assailed for their loyalty to the Democratic Party, which stood accused of playing racial politics by hosts playing racial politics. Hosts like Sean Hannity denounced the "vitriolic, demagogic, mean-spirited propaganda" of the Democrats. Even after leaving office, Bill Clinton remained the root of all evil.

The Limbaugh show was intimately tied to the GOP. His "eyes and ears" in the capital in the 1990s were those of Joel C. Rosenberg, who had worked at the Heritage Foundation and at William Bennett's Empower America organization before becoming the "director of research" for *The Limbaugh Letter*, a monthly publication with a circulation of five hundred thousand. "Everyone who can't get to Rush on the phone calls up Joel and pleads with him to get Rush to mention their pet cause," William Kristol told the *New York Times*. "That's his role in our nation's capital."[40]

After leaving Limbaugh's employ, Rosenberg became "political columnist" for Marvin Olasky's *WORLD* magazine, which interprets the news through a literal biblical lens, and joined the faculty of the World Journalism Institute, a "rigorous theological boot camp" whose goal is to "place aspiring evangelical journalists into the mainstream newsrooms of this country" so that the "cosmic struggle between truth and falsehood" can be advanced, according to its Web site. Rosenberg published the novel *The Last Jihad*, in which the "war on terror" goes nuclear. The *Washington Post* called it "an act of terrorism on the reader's brain." Sold on Limbaugh's show, it became a *New York Times* best-seller.

Rosenberg was a familiar figure in the halls of Congress and a player in Republican Party strategy sessions. Working through Rosenberg, the Republican leadership and conservative activists got Limbaugh to approve or condemn various legislative proposals as a way of keeping GOP members in line. With the exception of NAFTA, the free trade agreement that was approved by Congress in 1993, every aspect of the early Clinton legislative agenda was targeted for defeat, including bills on gun control, crime, and health care. "According to a Kaiser Foundation survey of members of Congress and their staffs, 46 percent found talk radio the most influential media source during the health care debate, with many naming Limbaugh in particular," Howard Kurtz reported. "By contrast, only 15 percent cited the *New York Times*, 11 percent said the *Wall Street Journal*, 9 percent said television, and 4 percent each said the *Washington Post*, the *Los Angeles Times*, or the *Washington Times*. On health care, at least, talk radio had eclipsed the establishment press."[41]

"More important, Limbaugh stays in private contact with key Republican operatives and, as a result, his on-air comments regularly promote party policy and strategy," *U.S. News & World Report* reported in 1993. "Rep. Newt Gingrich, the deputy Republican leader, calls the arrangement a 'very loose alliance,' but concedes there is a 'very close symbiotic relationship' between party leaders and Limbaugh." Gingrich faxed Limbaugh memos on his legislative strategies.[42] According to the *Los Angeles Times*, "Keith Appell, a veteran publicist for conservative causes, says his firm stays in close contact with as many as 400 talk-show hosts around the country. 'For conservatives, talk radio is still the most reliable and quickest way to mobilize support,' he says."

According to Rich Lowry in *National Review*, "These are the conduits through which Beltway conservatives seek to send out their message. The House Republican Conference, for instance, faxes out daily updates to hosts. Once Limbaugh and other conservative hosts begin hammering on an issue, they can help turn the national debate." Tom DeLay told Lowry, "We [are] able to energize the nation in two hours. . . ."[43]

Talk radio is an efficient delivery vehicle for the $1 billion right-wing message machinery. "Fax networks are another way conservatives communicate," columnist Deroy Murdock explained in 1995. "Washington's National Center for Public Policy Research, for example, uses its industrial strength fax machine to distribute Scoop, a thrice-weekly newsletter on conservative activities and strategies. Scoop reaches 700 radio stations, 400 business groups, 250 Capitol Hill offices and 150 activists." William Bennett's Empower America fax machines "spin out weekly reports for a network of 500 radio talk-show hosts across the country." The conservative National Forum Foundation "regularly sends out suggested guest lists and talking points on major issues to some 200 talk show hosts."[44] When *Talkers* magazine, an industry publication, sought a venue for a forum on the 2004 elections, it chose the Heritage Foundation.

Limbaugh's entry into partisan politics began with the 1992 presidential election, when he endorsed Pat Buchanan over the incumbent president Bush in the GOP primaries. When Bush won the nomination, he curried favor with Limbaugh to placate the party's disaffected right-wing base. Howard Kurtz reported that Roger Ailes, the architect of Bush's 1988 presidential campaign and the future executive producer of Limbaugh's ill-fated TV show, brokered the deal. Limbaugh was invited to spend the night in the Lincoln Bedroom at the White House; Bush said he had "a lot of respect" for Limbaugh; and Limbaugh went on NBC's *Today* to say that Bush was a "genuinely nice guy."[45]

The 1992 Republican National Convention in Houston featured the culture war declarations of Pat Buchanan and Pat Robertson from the rostrum. Overlooking the proceedings in prime time was the Maha Rushdee, invited to sit in the vice president's box one night and in the Bush family box the next. Limbaugh was introduced at a huge rally by Phyllis Schlafly. "By fall, Limbaugh, who had already appeared at several Republican fundraisers, seemed a full-fledged member of the Bush team," Kurtz wrote.[46] Limbaugh broke his no-guest rule, hosting both the first President Bush and his vice president, Dan Quayle, for one-sided interviews. Limbaugh told *Playboy* that he could control the votes of his listeners "if I choose to."

When his prediction of a Bush victory by four to six points proved wrong, Limbaugh declared that President-elect Clinton had "no mandate," and he set out on a mission to derail Clinton's presidency. Kurtz's *Hot Air,* published in 1996, contained five pages documenting Limbaugh's lies, half-truths, and distortions in the first few years of the Clinton administration, a period in which Limbaugh forged close relations with Republican leaders Bob Dole, Newt Gingrich, William Bennett, and William Kristol. Limbaugh's monologues included such falsehoods as "Clinton took cocaine while in office"; that the *New York Times* had never run a story on the Whitewater scandal; and that Chelsea Clinton had been given an assignment at school to write an essay titled "Why I Feel Guilty Being White." Most infamously, Limbaugh told his listeners, "Brace yourselves. This fax contains information that I have just been told will appear in a newsletter to Morgan Stanley sales personnel this afternoon . . . that claims Vince Foster was murdered in an apartment owned by Hillary Clinton, and the body was taken to Fort Marcy Park."[47] That lie caused the stock market to tumble.

On Capitol Hill in 1993, Democrats discussed strategies for curbing Limbaugh's influence, though none were implemented.[48] One activist began publishing a *Flush Rush* newsletter that sought to expose Limbaugh's lies, although the publication was short-lived. Emissaries of the Clinton White House held discussions with radio executives about opening the airwaves to non-right-wingers but were rebuffed. As the writer David Neiwert has noted, the complacency of nonconservatives in the face of the Republican propaganda blitz is interpreted by the Right, and by the mainstream media, as complicity. "The left's generally superior, dismissive attitude about right-wing extremists has only helped further [the Right's] ability to penetrate broader society," he wrote.[49]

The GOP was using radio the way the Christian Right began using its media in the late 1970s: to create "political brush fires," to energize the base to take political action, and to dupe the undecided to adopt the party-line spin. This happens 365 days a year on right-wing talk radio, which is not only able to invent a "controversy" where there otherwise might not be one but also ensures that its view of the "controversy" prevails in the public mind.

The awesome market power, and the sheer volume of noise, emanating from right-wing talk radio began to shape the entire media, which was increasingly seeking profits and ratings over quality journalism. Limbaugh said his program "redefined the media." And he bragged openly about the Limbaugh "echo chamber syndrome," through which themes enunciated by Limbaugh resonated throughout the media and "onto the floors of the U.S. House of Representatives." When Vice President Gore criticized the Bush administration's Iraq policy in September 2002, Brian Williams—the heir to Tom Brokaw's anchor chair at NBC—began his newscast on CNBC, "Today our friend Rush Limbaugh told his radio listeners he almost stayed home from work not due to any health reasons, but because he was so livid at the speech given yesterday by former Vice President Al Gore criticizing the Bush administration. . . ." Limbaugh's criticism of Gore had become national news on a mainstream cable channel.[50]

Limbaugh's "echo chamber syndrome" played a critical role in shaping public perceptions of a memorial service for Minnesota Senator Paul Wellstone, who died in an airplane accident while running a hotly contested reelection campaign in 2002. The Minnesota Republican Party and the Republican National Committee moved quickly to turn the tragedy into a weapon. Supposedly indignant Republicans claimed that the memorial demonstrated grossly excessive and crassly inappropriate Democratic partisanship—even though the Wellstone family, not the Democratic Party, organized it; and the event itself was a celebration of Wellstone's life, not a funeral. Republicans claimed that Wellstone's Republican colleagues were booed and shouted down by mourners while trying to deliver eulogies; that the interruptions were prompted by captions run on large TV sets behind the stage; and that Republican Senator Trent Lott walked out of the memorial feeling insulted. All three claims were false.

The smears against the Wellstone mourners entered the media bloodstream and the national consciousness thanks to a right-wing media wilding. A local Limbaugh wannabe in Minnesota, Thomas Barnard, spread those false claims, which were picked up nationally by Limbaugh and then repeated by pundits such as Tucker Carlson on CNN, Kellyanne Conway on C-SPAN, Peggy Noonan in the *Wall Street Journal,* George Will, and Christopher Caldwell in *The Weekly Standard.* Jerry Falwell declared: "While Ecclesiastes teaches us that there is a time for everything, including a time to mourn and to heal, for modern-day Democrats there is only time for one thing—and this is the raw and callous quest for power." The right-wing noise was so enveloping, it caused nonconservative pundits to internalize right-wing propaganda. On CNN's *Capital Gang,* Margaret Carlson, from Washington, chose the Wellstone memorial as her nominee for "political outrage of the year."

The event had been broadcast only on C-SPAN, so most Americans never saw it; they only heard the GOP spin about atrocious Democratic behavior and deeply offended Republicans. Exit polls found that 68 percent of voters in the midterm election, held one week after the memorial, had heard about the memorial controversy; 66 percent had a negative impression of it. Forty-nine percent of voters and 67 percent of independents said that what they heard made them less likely to vote for a Democrat. With control of the Senate hanging in precarious balance, 74 percent of those surveyed who made up their minds on how to vote in the last few days of the race voted Republican. The Republicans won control of the Senate in the election by a two-seat margin; the contest for control was so close that if just forty-one thousand votes in two states had gone the other way, Democrats would have kept their majority. The power of the right-wing media forced "the mainstream media to cover the story, which in turn created outrage that ultimately may have cost the Dems Wellstone's seat in the 2002 election," according to Brian C. Anderson, writing on the *Wall Street Journal's* Web site OpinionJournal.com.

Radio was a national weapon for the Republican Right and also a local one. Across the United States, Republican candidates for office took to the friendly radio airwaves, boosting their candidacies with free media and joining the right-wing hosts in slamming their Democratic opponents. As Howard Kurtz pointed out, Democrats were portrayed as loathsome, lying, Communist, Fascist, America-haters, abnormal, immoral, irreligious, cowards, sissies, and dykes. Opposition from local talk show hosts was credited in part with the 1994 defeats of House Speaker Tom Foley of Washington state (denounced as the "sphincter of the House") and Governor Mario Cuomo of New York, assailed by the racist Bob Grant.[51] And according to the *Los Angeles Times,* right-wing talk radio hosts drove the 2003 recall effort against California Governor Gray Davis. The first signatures on a petition to make the recall effort official were collected by a right-wing talk show host in Sacramento, the birthplace of *The Rush Limbaugh Show.* "Since recall efforts began in earnest, several hosts have dedicated time each day to the issue, often characterizing Davis along a narrow range that includes 'jerk,' 'incompetent,' 'dishonest' and 'corrupt.' . . . And more than two dozen hosts statewide have received regular talking points via email from organized recall backers," the *Times* reported. Republican officials quoted by the *Times* compared the hosts to modern-day "ward leaders." Said one, "In many ways talk radio is replacing the old political organizations that used to exist."[52]

Even in small markets, the Limbaugh wannabes are able to start "political brush fires" at whim, creating local "controversies" that inflame the Right and stigmatize its enemies. In spring 2003, Des Moines radio show host Jan Mickelson became enraged when he learned that a Straight and Gay Alliance at a local school had observed a "Day of Silence" to honor the memories of victims of social intolerance, such as Matthew Shephard, a gay Wyoming college student who was the victim of a gay-bashing hate crime in 1998. Mickelson blasted the extracurricular student-run club as "the sodomy club." He falsely claimed the group involved all students, used tax money, and conducted its activities during class time. "You've got activists now in control of the Des Moines school system and . . . they are defining the rules. They didn't ask your permission, they're just doing it. And then if you say no you don't like it, they call you a bigot," Mickelson railed. Only "perverts" care about the feelings of gays, he said. He also claimed there was no such thing as being gay: "It's junk science that says they are, and tells them to define themselves on the basis of their inclinations."

According to *Des Moines Register* columnist Rekha Basu, Mickelson "graphically described to one student caller how he envisioned a sex act between two men." The outburst provoked a torrent of angry and threatening calls to the school principal and to the school counselor who is the club sponsor. The callers repeated Mickelson's false assertions and accused school officials of advocating homosexuality. Student phone clerks were replaced at the school switchboards because the callers were so abusive and vulgar.[53]

Right-wing radio also has incited physical violence. In 2003, radio show hosts in Cleveland, Houston, and Raleigh "suggested motorists blast horns at cyclists, and speed past them and slam on their breaks in front of them," according to the Associated Press. The Raleigh host encouraged drivers to throw bottles at cyclists. Clear Channel Communications, which owns the three offending stations, insisted that on-air apologies be issued and paid $10,000 to plug bicycle safety on the radio.

In the 1994 election, in a low turnout even for a nonpresidential election, only 39 percent of registered voters went to the polls. They delivered control of the House to the Republicans for the first time in forty years and brought in two Bush governors, George in Texas and Jeb in Florida—both of whom received "a far higher level of support from talk radio listeners than they received from the electorate as a whole," according to network exit polls.[54] One in five voters that year was a regular Limbaugh listener. And 90 percent of Limbaugh listeners said they went to the polls.[55]

As in the late 1970s, the Republican Right, still a distinct political minority, was moving politics its way through the media. After the election, the new House Speaker, Newt Gingrich, described the voting as "the first talk radio election." Republican leader Vin Weber said, "Rush Limbaugh is really as responsible for what has happened as any individual in America. Talk radio, with you in the lead, is what turned the tide." Limbaugh was made an "honorary member" of the new Republican majority. And Limbaugh declared himself the Gingrich revolution's "conquering hero." The Republican Congress would soon return the favor, moving to change telecommunications policy to lock in Republican domination of the radio airwaves.

CHAPTER TWELVE

"INFORMATION WARS"

N O MATTER HOW MUCH he trashed the news media, Newt Gingrich had a keen understanding of how it could be used to forward the political agenda of the Republican Right. "We are engaged in reshaping the whole nation through the news media," he said.[1] In his 1995 book, *To Renew America,* Gingrich devoted an entire chapter to "Why Rush Limbaugh and His Friends Matter."

Unlike liberals, whose conception of the media was as a place for the airing of a wide range of diverse views through which the public could discern its opinions and make informed decisions, conservatives such as Gingrich saw the media as a propagandistic extension of their political campaigns. Gingrich was not the first Republican politician to hold this view, nor was he the first to use his political power to gain leverage over the media by promoting consolidation of media power in few corporate hands.

In 1972, Richard Nixon made a deal with the major conservative-oriented newspaper chains that changed the face of the industry and virtually sealed the Republican lock on newspaper editorial board endorsements nationwide. As Ben Bagdikian reported in *The Media Monopoly,* Nixon offered to drop his opposition to the 1972 Newspaper Preservation Act, which allowed newspaper chains to expand and concentrate their ownership (and, thus, cut down on competition while increasing profits) in return for editorial backing for his reelection.

In the past, chain-owned newspapers had generally favored Republicans in their endorsements, but not overwhelmingly so. In every presidential election since 1932, Republican candidates had won a majority of editorial board endorsements, with the exception of 1964, when President Lyndon Johnson bested Senator Barry Goldwater. In 1972, after the act passed, "every Hearst paper, every Cox, and every Scripps-Howard paper endorsed Nixon," who received "the highest percentage of newspaper endorsements of any candidate in modern times," according to Bagdikian, who also concluded that these three major chains suppressed Watergate revelations before the 1972 election. "Because of the high degree of concentrated control over the mass media," Bagdikian wrote, "the seven chains that benefited from Nixon's change of mind owned the papers read by most voters."

Eventually, most papers in the United States would become part of large chains, while most cities would become one-newspaper towns. The net effect of the new market dominance by the chains was to reduce "editorial vigor" and to encourage more uniformity in the endorsement process, according to Bagdikian. By 1975, a survey showed 85 percent of chain newspapers had a GOP-leaning endorsement policy.[2] Before the late 1980s brought a dramatic drop in daily newspaper readership, newspaper endorsements were found to have influenced up to 7 percent of the vote in national elections.[3] Since 1972, only one Democratic presidential candidate has been able to break the pattern and win a majority of newspaper endorsements: Bill Clinton in his 1992 race against incumbent George H. W. Bush.

Picking up where Nixon left off, Ronald Reagan took office determined to further deregulate the communications industry. The Reaganites viewed the broadcast media not as a public trust that was obligated to operate in the public interest by providing a free flow of ideas from a variety of sources, but as any other commercial business—a position at odds with fifty years of federal policy, court decisions, and journalistic traditions. The

Reagan era saw a number of media companies absorbed into larger conglomerates, increasing pressures for profits and relaxed standards.

As broadcast properties were swallowed up, by the late 1980s there was
a discernible impact on content, favoring, for example, the kind of profitable
right-wing trash talk offered by Morton Downey. "Deregulation has brought
in a new breed of broadcaster to whom public service matters less. They're
willing to close their eyes and say 'Go ahead and put it on.' This creates pressure for broadcasters who know better and say privately they hate this kind
of programming but have to do it to compete," Andrew Jay Schwartzman of
the Media Access Project told the *Washington Post* in 1988.

The Federal Communications Commission is a government agency
established in 1934 to regulate the public airwaves to maximize "the public
interest and to encourage a diversity of voices so as to promote a vibrant
democracy." To chair the agency, Reagan appointed Mark S. Fowler, a communications lawyer who had served on the Reagan campaign staffs in 1976
and 1980. "The perception of broadcasters as community trustees should be
replaced by a view of broadcasters as marketplace participants," Fowler
said. Fowler famously compared the TV broadcast media to a "toaster with
pictures." And he declared his contempt for public affairs journalism as
"Dudley Do-Good" programming.

Earlier, Fowler had been an announcer, disc jockey, and station manager in Florida and West Virginia, where he had been irritated by federal
regulations, known as the Fairness Doctrine, to provide balanced programming. The regulations, adopted by the FCC in 1949, were written to ensure
that licensed broadcasters provided ample opportunity for contrasting
points of view. Their premise was that scarce broadcast licenses—unlike
readily available printing presses—made it incumbent on broadcasters to
air all sides of controversial issues, a standard that they had to meet contin-
ually to win license renewals.

Father's Coughlin's right-wing tirades appear to have provided some
impetus for the fairness rules.[4] The Kennedy administration used the
Fairness Doctrine to challenge the imbalanced presentations of right-wing
radio broadcasters. And throughout the 1970s and 1980s, the Fairness
Doctrine was invoked by, among others, parties seeking time to respond to
biased broadcasters of the religious Right.

In 1969, the Supreme Court unanimously upheld the constitutionality of the Fairness Doctrine, ruling for an author, Frederick J. Cook, who had been attacked on a Christian Crusade broadcast aired on a radio station in Pennsylvania. When Cook requested time to reply under the Fairness Doctrine, the station refused. The court ruled that the station failed to meet its obligations under the FCC rules and wrote a sweeping opinion holding that under the First Amendment, citizens had the right to a full and free exchange of ideas, including opposing views, on the public airwaves:

> But the people as a whole retain their interest in free speech by radio and their collective right to have the medium function consistently with the ends and purposes of the First Amendment. It is the right of the viewers and listeners, not the right of broadcasters, which is paramount.[5]

Mark Fowler disagreed. On the air, he had been known as "Madman Mark." At the FCC, he would be called "the Mad Monk of de-regulation."[6] Assuming the reins of the commission, he set about "pruning, chopping, slashing, eliminating, burying and deep-sixing" fifty years of regulations that guarded against monopolistic practices and excessive commercialism and protected the public interest standard. Rupert Murdoch, who would win favorable regulatory rulings from the Reagan FCC allowing him to expand his media empire, called Fowler "one of the great pioneers of the communications revolution" and "perhaps the most successful of any Reagan appointee."[7] (A decade later, under new leadership, the FCC concluded that Murdoch had misled the Reagan-controlled agency when giving assurances that News Corp. was not foreign-owned and -controlled.)

Among other changes, Fowler aimed to gut the Fairness Doctrine, opening the public airwaves to "rigidly partisan" views, with no safeguards for balance. To act as general counsel of the FCC, Fowler appointed the right-wing lawyer Bruce E. Fein, a creature of the right-wing network's subsidized legal arm. Fein held research posts at the Heritage Foundation and the American Enterprise Institute and was "Supreme Court editor" of a publication called Benchmark, published by the Center for Judicial Studies, which was directed by a former aide to Senator Jesse Helms. As a midlevel official of the Reagan Justice Department, he had been tasked with judicial selection. Though in the Fairness Doctrine debate he would pose as one,

Fein was not a friend of the First Amendment or of independent journalism. He argued that the landmark Supreme Court case *New York Times v. Sullivan* was "wrong," and he called for congressional investigations into "media inaccuracy, bias, and misreporting."

As the architect of the Reagan assault on the Fairness Doctrine, Fein argued that the advent of cable, and the explosion in the number of radio stations licensed by the government to broadcast since the late 1940s, rendered moot the fear that a handful of broadcasters could dominate the airwaves with a few points of view or censor opinions they didn't favor. In fact, he said, the Fairness Doctrine was inhibiting a diversity of views in the media and thus might be unconstitutional. Fein claimed that the federal regulation had made the airing of "controversial programming" prohibitively expensive for broadcasters, because they had to spend money airing the other side of controversies. The result was an "undisputatious and unedifying" media landscape, as Fein described it.

For Fowler and Fein, revoking the Fairness Doctrine was another way of "expanding the spectrum" rightward, along the lines originally suggested by Edith Efron, who had argued that openly biased right-wing broadcasters should be allowed to compete with the slanted "liberal" TV networks without Fairness Doctrine constraints requiring them to air competing perspectives. Yet Efron's analysis of the networks was wrong. There were no partisan liberal broadcasters to compete with partisan right-wing broadcasters. Despite what he said, Rush Limbaugh was not "equal time" for Dan Rather; they were not in the same business. Only Limbaugh would benefit from the license to be unfair.

The right wing was split on the question of repealing the Fairness Doctrine; among others, Reed Irvine and Phyllis Schlafly, who had used the regulation as a way to insert their ideology into the media over the years, supported its retention. But the big guns on the Right backed repeal. NCPAC's Terry Dolan, who had launched and funded an attack on the "liberal media," was a key supporter, as was the Heritage Foundation. Richard Mellon Scaife's Landmark Legal Foundation challenged the constitutionality of the doctrine in the courts.

A new front group was established specifically to attack the Fairness Doctrine. The misnamed Freedom of Expression Foundation, which received money from the communications, tobacco, and beer industries, and from the Olin Foundation and Rupert Murdoch, was headed by Craig Smith, a former official of the National Republican Senatorial Committee who would serve on the Bush transition team in 1988. The foundation's purpose, Smith said, was to "coordinate the repeal effort using non-public funds . . . which could provide lobbyists, editorialists, and other opinion leaders with needed arguments and evidence."[8]

In 1986, the Court of Appeals for the District of Columbia Circuit, which had been packed by Reagan with right-wing ideologues, upheld a loose interpretation by the Reagan FCC of an aspect of the Fairness Doctrine ruling that Congress had never made the doctrine a binding requirement, despite statutory language suggesting that it had.[9] The vote was 2–1, with Judges Antonin Scalia and Robert Bork in the majority. In 1987, the Reagan FCC, under the chairmanship of Dennis Patrick (a young Reagan aide who took office upon Mark Fowler's departure), used that decision, and a subsequent one from the same court, as an invitation to repeal the doctrine entirely.

The move also was supported by some professional journalists' associations and many political liberals who viewed the Fairness Doctrine as an infringement of the First Amendment rights of broadcasters. They failed to see that the right wing was invoking the First Amendment while seeking to undo it.

"Madman Mark" killed the Fairness Doctrine. Congress promptly restored the doctrine by a wide bipartisan margin, but the legislation was vetoed by President Reagan. Subsequent efforts to revive it were thwarted by veto threats from the first President Bush; again it was kept down during the Clinton administration by an all-out right-wing media offensive. The Heritage Foundation warned against government bureaucrats interfering with "pugnacious talk show hosts" and Rush Limbaugh campaigned against what the *Wall Street Journal* editorial page called the "Hush Rush Rule."

Dominance of the radio airwaves by the political Right would not have been permissible under the Fairness Doctrine. With that protection removed in 1987—in an action engineered by right-wing activists, politicians, and judges—radio stations were free to program as many hours of one-sided right-wing talk as they wished and to eliminate competing views at will. The newly powerful right-wing hosts were able to say anything—to misrepresent, distort, and lie without challenge or rebuttal.

In 1988, former ABC executive Ed McLaughlin took Rush Limbaugh's show national. Unlike the subsidized right-wing media such as the *Washington Times* and *The American Spectator* that provided a good deal of his content, Limbaugh had emerged on his own, catching a wave of resentment against the gains of women, ethnic minorities, and gays. He was filling a void not only in an untapped market but also in the conservative movement, following the Reagan presidency. In some ways, he literally filled in for Reagan, who had been on the radio every day for five years in the 1970s reaching millions of listeners per week. "Now that I've retired from politics, I don't mind that you've become the number one voice for conservatism in the country," Reagan wrote Limbaugh.

The difference between Reagan in the mid-1970s and Limbaugh in the late 1980s was that Reagan was one voice among many competing ones, just as Joe Pyne had been in the 1960s. Pyne usually had a liberal on the air with him; with their one-sided messaging, Limbaugh and his progeny would corner the market in radio, which now had government permission to become a purely commercial enterprise like the entertainment or pornography industries.

Among other things, the end of the Fairness Doctrine meant that stations could reflect the political perspectives of their owners. Alongside efforts to eliminate the fairness requirements, the Republicans were working to make it easier for a handful of corporate owners to dictate content. Beginning in the Reagan administration and continuing through the administration of George W. Bush, waves of Republican-backed deregulation undid government protections against ownership consolidation and concentration. As fewer owners chased the same audiences, the right wing tightened its grip on the broadcast media, and other views were shut out.

The political effects of deregulation were felt most keenly in radio. For fifty years, government limits on radio ownership were designed to encourage local and diverse programming. Regulation made radio a very competitive industry and kept many small owners viable. Under long-standing rules, a company could own no more than twenty-four stations nationwide and only two in the same local market. In 1996, these ownership caps were lifted by the Gingrich-controlled Congress, creating in effect a government-sanctioned oligopoly that all but ended competition and diversity of views on the radio airwaves, that sabotaged First Amendment principles, and that threatened democracy.

Today, three companies own half of the radio stations in the United States. By remaining true to no higher principle than milking the highest profits possible from the right-wing market niche, station owners saw to it that virtually every talk show personality who gained a foothold in national syndication in Limbaugh's shadow was a Far Right conservative, while liberals were effectively shut out of what would become an ideologically uniform medium more like that of a totalitarian society than of a democracy.

Radio is ruled by niche markets, and Limbaugh was the first to develop a profitable niche just as talk was emerging as the fastest-growing format in the country—the savior of AM radio. In 1981, there were 82 all-talk stations. By 1995, there were 1,308. By and large, radio station programmers were opportunistic followers, not innovators. Programmers were loath to challenge what was buoying the ratings. Station profits are built on loyal audiences with particular tastes—be it country music or conservative talk—that advertisers want to reach. Just as country music fans do not want jazz interrupting the programming on their station, right-wing listeners expect wall-to-wall right-wing opinion whenever they tune in, and they balk when they don't get it.

The right wing and its financial backers had gotten to market first and locked up the entire day's programming on desirable high-powered stations around the country. Because radio's electromagnetic spectrum is finite, there was less room to establish powerful liberal talk stations or networks even if there had been the financing to do so. While conservatives like Sean Hannity could be "discovered" by doing practice runs while substituting for Limbaugh, liberals had no viable launching pads. The few brand-name liberals who were given an opportunity in radio (such as former New York governor Mario M. Cuomo) were not seasoned broadcasters; they were typically sandwiched between right-wing hosts on right-wing stations and, predictably, failed to find wide audiences. Then, too, fundamentally, talk radio is an antimedia medium, and liberal constituencies were not organized around charges of media bias in the way the right wing was.

Radio is also a populist medium. Right-wingers of the Limbaugh variety become faux populists with their cultural appeals, while remaining supportive of the agenda of economic elites. Former Texas railroad commissioner and best-selling author Jim Hightower is a left-wing economic populist who sees politics on an "up-down" rather than a "left-right" continuum. Hightower's well-rated ABC radio show was canceled after he criticized ABC's parent company, Disney, and station sponsors began to complain about his ideological slant. Hightower's experience suggested that while there may be a radio market for left-oriented populism that exposes the nexus of money and politics, highlights corporate abuses, and advocates economic equality, radio's corporate owners and advertisers may be reluctant to support it.[10]

Conservatives have claimed that the market for liberal talk is filled by National Public Radio. "[NPR] is all left, top to bottom," FOX's Bill O'Reilly told the *Washington Post*. "That's where the left goes . . . they listen to Diane Rehm." Rehm, who regularly features conservatives like Tony Blankley and David Brooks on her weekday program, told the *Post*, "If a liberal is a talk radio host who represents more than just one view, then I am indeed a liberal. . . . I've never felt there's just one way and one way only. [Some hosts] espouse one view over and over again, whereas our message is far more confusing because we're open to ideas and let you make up your own mind." Unlike commercial radio, NPR is subject to regulations requiring balanced programming. NPR could not do what Limbaugh does, even if it wished to do so.

While conservative voices are heard on NPR, liberal and left-wing voices are scarce on commercial radio. Though more Americans are registered Democrat than Republican, and hundreds of millions of Americans do not listen to Limbaugh or his wannabes, today the top five radio station owners in the country, controlling forty-five powerful radio stations, broadcast 310 hours of nationally syndicated right-wing talk every weekday. Only 5 hours of nonconservative talk are aired nationally on those stations, according to a study by the Senate Democratic Policy Committee. The liberal FOX News personality Alan Colmes fills 3 of these 5 hours on a new Murdoch-owned radio network.

As stations cater solely to the tastes of a dedicated minority of listeners, even predominantly liberal communities—from New York City to Eugene, Oregon—are saturated with more than 80 hours of right-wing talk per week, with virtually no liberal talk available. Edward T. Monks reported in the *Register-Guard* of Oregon:

> Eugene is fairly representative. There are two local commercial political talk and news stations: KUGN, owned by Cumulus Broadcasting, the country's second largest radio broadcasting company, and KPNW, owned by Clear Channel Communications, the largest such company.
>
> KUGN's line-up has three highly partisan conservative Republicans—Lars Larson (who is regionally syndicated), Michael Savage and Michael Medved (both of whom are nationally syndicated) covering a nine-hour block each weekday from 1 p.m. until 10 p.m. Each host is unambiguous in his commitment to advancing the interests and policies of the Republican party, and unrelenting in his highly personalized denunciation of Democrats and virtually all Democratic Party policy initiatives. That's 45 hours a week.
>
> For two hours each weekday morning, KUGN has just added nationally syndicated host Bill O'Reilly. Although he occasionally criticizes a Republican for something other than being insufficiently conservative, O'Reilly is clear in his basic conservative viewpoint. His columns are listed on the Townhall.com website, created by the strongly conservative Heritage Foundation. That's 55 hours of political talk on KUGN each week by conservatives and Republicans. No KUGN air time is programmed for a Democratic or liberal political talk show host.
>
> KPNW carries popular conservative Rush Limbaugh for three hours each weekday, and Michael Reagan, the conservative son of the former president, for two hours, for a total of 25 hours a week.
>
> Thus, between the two stations, there are 80 hours per week, more than 4,000 hours per year, programmed for Republican and conservative hosts of political talk radio, with not so much as a second programmed for a Democratic or liberal perspective.[11]

What happened in Eugene was not an accident. Many who participated in deregulating radio in the mid-1990s later claimed not to have foreseen its consequences. One who never expressed regrets was Newt Gingrich.

Gingrich was blunt in expressing his overriding goal with respect to the country's news media. "Here's the plain unvarnished truth: If the conservative movement is to survive, we must neutralize the national liberal media," Gingrich said in a speech to Brent Bozell's Media Research Center. "The national press has become the most powerful arm of the left. And they are bent on destroying our conservative movement through deceit, lies, and character assassination."

As part of their ideological program, the Gingrichites favored radical deregulation of the media. The theoretical underpinnings of the maneuvers were laid out in the works of Rupert Murdoch adviser Irwin Stelzer, of AEI and the Hudson Institute; George Gilder, a "senior fellow" of the Seattle-based Discovery Institute, author of the supply-side economics text *Wealth and Poverty,* and erstwhile *American Spectator* publisher; and Peter Huber, "senior fellow" of the Manhattan Institute.

Huber was especially influential. In his book *Law and Disorder in Cyberspace,* Huber, a close Gingrich adviser, called for the outright elimination of the FCC, which he contended had ushered in "the nightmare of totalitarian government . . . national socialism" in the United States. Huber had written an earlier book, *Orwell's Revenge: The 1984 Palimpsest,* in which he argued that George Orwell's warnings, of a frightening high-tech future in which "Big Brother" ruled through centralized information control, were misplaced. Huber argued that technical advances would free, rather than enslave, citizens.[12]

Gingrich, too, was fascinated by how political change would be shaped through advances in communications technology. He viewed government regulation of the media as an impediment to what he called the "Knowledge Age," in which information is the source of power. He saw the future as one of "information wars" in which new media, particularly the Internet, outside the "social order or credentialed spectrum," would be pitted against the traditional TV networks and prestigious national print press.[13] New media would succeed through "de-massification" and "differentiation"—that is, niche marketing to political partisans. Gingrich and his advisers believed the information revolution would undermine the authority of journalism. "We are all gaining, inch by inch, the power of a Dan Rather or a Peter Jennings," Peter Huber said.

These sentiments had been echoed in a rare 1993 political speech by Gingrich's patron, Rupert Murdoch, in London. The remarks were apparently drafted by Irwin Stelzer and recorded by Murdoch's biographer Neil Chenoweth: "I must add (with maybe a touch of regret) that this technology has also liberated people from the once powerful media barons. . . . The media mogul has been replaced by a bevy of harassed and sometimes confused media executives, trying to guess what the public wants." "Consumers," rather than trained news professionals, Murdoch said, were in control, and technology was "galloping over the old regulatory machinery," rendering it "obsolete."[14] Approvingly, Murdoch described the new media environment as "anarchistic."

Gingrich had come to power in part owing to his instinctive understanding of the "anarchistic" possibilities of new media. He was one of the first politicians to realize that he could reach vast numbers of politically engaged citizens through C-SPAN's congressional coverage, even when he was speaking to an empty House chamber. Paul Weyrich's propagandistic National Empowerment Television, on which Gingrich had his own show, provided an "alternative" to the "distortions" of the "media elite," Gingrich told the *New York Times* in 1995.[15] In *To Renew America*, he wrote glowingly of his experiences with talk radio in 1993, as he drove to a congressional majority.

One of his first acts as House Speaker was to find space in the Capitol from which the friendly talk radio show hosts could broadcast. The existing radio-TV gallery had been ruled by the broadcast networks as off-limits to the talk show hosts, because they were not considered journalists. Gingrich wrote:

> Roger Hedgecock, the top-rated host in San Diego, brought a planeload of listeners who spent three days walking the corridors promoting the Contract With America while Roger broadcast from the basement of the Capitol. By the end of the hundred days, the flood of radio hosts had become almost overwhelming. During the last week of the Contract, we had over forty talk shows broadcasting from the Capitol. Space was so short that we had shows broadcasting from the corridor outside my office and from the balcony outside my window.

The Speaker-elect moved swiftly to enact his deregulatory agenda. Unlike traditional GOP politicians, Gingrich understood the right-wing strategy of building momentum, credibility, and media exposure behind radical ideas through the think tank network. So in 1993 the prescient Gingrich had set up his own shop. His nonprofit Progress & Freedom Foundation was backed by right-wing foundations and top telecommunications firms, including the Turner Broadcasting System. Chaired by Dr. George A. Keyworth (the science adviser to President Reagan who had championed the Strategic Defense Initiative), and run by Jeffery A. Eisenach (the former head of Gingrich's PAC), the foundation issued the "Magna Carta for the Information Age," which called for control of "cyberspace" to be unregulated by the government. Listed as coauthors of the manifesto were Keyworth, Gilder, Internet expert Esther Dyson, and Dr. Alvin Toffler, author of *Future Shock* and *The Third Wave*.

Since the 1970s, Gingrich had been drawn to the ideas of Toffler, whom Gingrich called "the single smartest and most successful intellectual in American politics," and his wife and coauthor, Heidi. Toffler was an ex-Marxist whose specialty was "futurism"—the "study of, and interest in, forecasting or anticipating the future, or theorizing on how to impose controls on events." The core of the Contract with America, Gingrich said, could be found in the Tofflers' *The Third Wave*, which posited that the industrial or second wave era was giving way to a third wave era of technological breakthroughs in which bureaucracies would become obsolete. Gingrich called himself a "conservative futurist."

The Gingrichites couched their agenda in buzzwords like "individual empowerment," "freedom," "choice," and "decentralization." But their actions suggested something else. On the one hand, they argued that a "Big Brother" would never emerge; on the other hand, they seemed to want to play Big Brother. Of Murdoch, Neil Chenoweth wrote: "Whatever twist or turn the information revolution took going into the next century, he wanted to be the gatekeeper." Of Gingrich's Magna Carta, Richard K. Moore, writing in *Information Society*, observed, "Much of its rhetoric seems to imply a concern with individual liberties, but its substance would devolve power and privilege to the biggest corporate players in the telecommunications industry. . . . PFF's manifesto supports the power of communications monopolies—with each to have unregulated control over its own cyberspace fiefdom. Rather than being a charter of liberties, the manifesto promotes a regime of robber barons in cyberspace."

Gingrich appeared eager to do the bidding of these major communications companies, many of which were shifting their political money to the newly ascendant GOP as they sought to virtually eliminate limits on ownership. "When Newt Gingrich was running the House of Representatives, effective in the fall of 1994, he called all the media owners together in a room down on Capitol Hill, and according to what people who were there told me, he told them he'd give them relaxed rules allowing media concentration in exchange for favorable coverage. Now I wasn't there, but that's what they said they understood he meant," Reed Hundt, chairman of the FCC during the Clinton administration, told *Salon*.[16]

During this period of favor-trading, Gingrich also attempted to line his own pockets, striking a $4.5 million book deal for *To Renew America* with Murdoch's HarperCollins Publishers. Murdoch stood to gain directly from actions that Gingrich could take either legislatively or with respect to federal regulators. When the book deal came to light, Gingrich declined the advance and took only royalties earned from sales. Though the book was a *New York Times* best-seller, sales were not strong enough to have justified a multimillion-dollar advance.

Politically, the deregulation effort—which would strengthen the hands of a smaller group of top owners and advertisers and further accelerate commercial pressures on the quality and standards of journalism—was a continuation of the decades-long attack by the Republican Right on the autonomy of journalism. Gingrich believed that the values of the business class coincided more with the conservative agenda than did the values of journalism. In 1997, Gingrich told a meeting of the Georgia Chamber of Commerce that business and advertisers should flex their muscles in newsrooms for ideological ends.[17] Though he was not able to carry it off, Gingrich entertained privatizing the Public Broadcasting System and National Public Radio as a way of eliminating altogether the threat to the right wing of independent noncommercial journalism. He held meetings with Murdoch and John Malone of TCI, the Cato board member and Rush Limbaugh fan, to discuss "carving up" public television and radio.[18] In an interview with *Wired* magazine later in 1994, Malone joked about "shooting" Clinton's FCC chairman.[19]

The radio ownership limits were of special concern to the Gingrich Congress, whose members were on record as saying that they owed their seats to talk radio. The GOP Congress ordered the FCC to allow the radio industry to consolidate, paying back its political supporters with the opportunity to greatly increase profits and sealing ideological control of the medium for the right wing under far fewer owners. In negotiations with Congress over the 1996 Telecommunications Act, President Clinton was able to scale back the extent of the radio deregulation Gingrich favored and to protect print and television from the Gingrich scheme.

Under George W. Bush's administration, however, the FCC, with Secretary of State Colin Powell's son Michael serving as chairman, moved to complete the Gingrich trifecta, lifting limits on ownership in the print and TV media. Ownership rule changes approved by the FCC lifted prohibitions on broadcasters from owning daily newspapers in their markets and relaxed limits on the total number of stations broadcasters can own nationally. "It's the culmination of the attack by the right on the media since independent media challenged and helped topple Richard Nixon," Reed Hundt told *Salon*. In early 2004, the Bush FCC's plans faced significant challenges in Congress and in the courts.

A handful of companies is now responsible for the ideological uniformity of radio, where competition is limited to conservatives competing with one another for shares of the market. A 2003 study of ownership consolidation in the radio industry conducted by the Future of Music Coalition found that "ten parent companies now dominate the radio spectrum, radio listenership, and radio revenues, controlling two-thirds of both listeners and revenue nationwide. . . . Virtually every local market is dominated by four firms controlling 70 percent of market share or greater. In smaller markets, consolidation is more extreme. The largest four firms in most small markets control 90 percent of market share or more."[20] A 2003 survey by the Benchmark Company, a market research firm, found that 40 percent of talk radio listeners think the format "lacks balance." This view was held by moderates and liberals but not by conservatives, 85 percent of whom said they were happy with the political composition of radio as it is.

A company's ownership of both programs and distribution channels puts it in a uniquely powerful position that can be leveraged to force stations to air shows that they might not otherwise gamble on and to pressure advertisers to support shows even if the ratings don't justify it. Reaping huge profits, the big syndicators can afford to pay stations hundreds of thousands of dollars to carry shows as they try to establish them.

While the TV networks and major newspapers receive a good deal of public scrutiny—including baseless speculation from the right wing about perceived liberal political agendas—the powerful radio industry operates largely in the shadows. The largest radio station owner in the United States, and the chief beneficiary of the 1996 Telecommunications Act, is Clear Channel Communications, a Republican-controlled company with more than 1,200 stations nationwide. Before it was allowed to go on a buying spree, Clear Channel owned only forty stations. Through its syndication arm, Premiere Radio Networks, Clear Channel syndicates Rush Limbaugh, Dr. Laura Schlessinger, Matt Drudge, and other right-wing talkers to its own stations and others.

Clear Channel now owns more than 10 percent of all stations across the country; owns a much higher percentage of the major stations; rakes in 20 percent of all radio advertising revenue; and reaches about one-third of Americans—about 100 million people. In smaller cities, it might own half the stations. "No potential competitor owns even one-quarter the number of Clear Channel stations," according to the Future of Music Coalition. "If given another 10 years to spread unchecked, Clear Channel might cover the dial from end to end, not just in some cities but coast to coast," Walter Kirn wrote in the *New York Times*.

Clear Channel is an unusual media company. "The company is known for allowing animals to be killed live on the air, severing long-standing ties with the community and charity events, laying off thousands of workers, homogenizing playlists, and a corporate culture in which dirty tricks are a way of life," according to Eric Boehlert, who wrote a series of investigative articles on Clear Channel for *Salon* in 2001.

Among other nefarious practices, Boehlert's reporting uncovered an atmosphere of hostility toward women and minority employees at the company. The chief of the company's radio division is Randy Michaels, a former radio shock jock who was born Benjamin Homel. "Behind the mike he made a reputation for himself back in the 70s and 80s farting on the air, cracking jokes about gays, and tantalizing listeners with descriptions of 'incredibly horny, wet, and ready' naked in-studio guests. Along with getting hit with a sexual harassment suit, Michaels pulled in big ratings wherever he went," according to Boehlert. Further, "he once roamed the station halls with a flexible rubber penis around his neck, accosting female employees," Boehlert reported, adding that, in an interview with ABC, Michaels "rejected" the charge made by a former employee.

The company's top two executives are close political and financial supporters of George W. Bush. They have contributed tens of thousands of dollars to his campaigns for governor and for president; Clear Channel gave 85 percent of its donations to the GOP in 2002. Bush is particularly close with Clear Channel's vice chairman, Tom Hicks. Hicks bought the Texas Rangers for a hefty sum from a syndicate in which Bush was an investor, making Bush a multimillionaire and easing his way to the state house. When Bush became governor, he appointed both Hicks and Clear Channel chairman and CEO L. Lowry Mays to the board of a nonprofit corporation formed to manage the money of the University of Texas. The board funneled billions to private investment firms run by Republican cronies.[21]

Together with another top donor to Bush, Clear Channel also has a substantial ownership stake in the Hispanic Broadcasting Corp., which joined several companies in a merger to create a new media company that would control 80 percent of Spanish-language television and radio in major U.S. markets. According to the *Washington Post,* the deal, approved by George W. Bush's FCC, included the powerful Miami radio station Radio Mambi, which had urged its conservative Cuban American listeners to storm a vote-canvassing facility during the 2000 postelection Florida recount, forcing officials to stop manually counting ballots at a crucial juncture when Bush was only slightly ahead of Gore. Had the counting continued and Gore pulled ahead, the political-media dynamic would have shifted considerably in his favor.

Clear Channel chairman Mays shared the view of Mark Fowler and Rupert Murdoch: The media is nothing more than a commodity. "If anyone said we were in the radio business, it wouldn't be someone from our company. We're not in the business of providing news and information. . . . We're simply in the business of selling our customers products," Mays said.[22]

During the war with Iraq, Clear Channel drew unwelcome publicity when it was learned that a network of local radio stations, owned by the Texas-based conglomerate, was paying for pro-war rallies around the country and then covering them as "news." The idea for the "Rally for America" events had been proposed by the Philadelphia-based talk host Glenn Beck, syndicated by Clear Channel's radio network.

Meanwhile, Cumulus Broadcasting, a top Clear Channel competitor, banned the Dixie Chicks band from its country music stations during the war. The band members had been accused of treason by conservative leaders such as Paul Weyrich for saying they were embarrassed that President George W. Bush was from Texas, their home state. "The Dixie Chicks my rear end!" Rush Limbaugh exclaimed. MSNBC *Hardball* regular Christopher Hitchens, author of attack books on Mother Teresa and the Clintons, called the Chicks "fucking fat slags." Angry right-wingers burned and smashed Dixie Chicks CDs and tapes.

Columnist Ellen Goodman referred to talk radio as "the Bush National Radio Network—a support system for the pro-war movement." As the Dixie Chicks incident showed, right-wing radio was not only broadcasting right-wing propaganda; it was also attacking dissenters and narrowing their free speech rights. According to a report in the *Washington Post,* a number of "news consultants" hired by radio stations for advice on programming and staffing urged the promotion of pro-war views and discouraged coverage of antiwar sentiment. "Get the following production pieces in the studio *now.* . . . Patriotic music that makes you cry, salute, get cold chills! Go for the emotion," McVay Media of Cleveland told its clients in a "War Manual." "Air the National Anthem at a specified time each day as long as the USA is at war."[23]

In Chicago, liberal talker Nancy Skinner, who is broadcast on an ABC affiliate, faced harassment. "WLS officials have always offered tepid support at best to lefty hosts, and Anderson [Skinner's co-host] and Skinner were no exception," *Chicago Tribune* columnist Eric Zorn reported. "Management did not promote their show, ordered them off the Hyde story [about questionable dealing with a bank in which Henry Hyde, the veteran GOP representative, was implicated] and cut them back to one time slot a week from two, even though their ratings were respectable. In the ultimate exhibition of craven stewardship of the public airways, WLS pre-empted 'Ski and Skinner' the weekend after the bombing started in Iraq in order to replace them, temporarily, with yet another cheerleader for the war." When Skinner goes on the air, right-wingers flood the stations with demands that she be fired.

Clear Channel fired the community affairs director of a San Francisco radio station after he aired the antiwar views of Democratic Representative Barbara Lee. In Greenville, South Carolina, a host on a Clear Channel station who had been named South Carolina radio personality of the year in 2002 filed suit against the company, saying she was fired for opposing the U.S. invasion of Iraq. And Clear Channel sent a memo to its station managers telling them not to play songs advocating peace, such as John Lennon's "Imagine."[24]

When liberals run afoul of management, they are downgraded or fired; but when conservatives stray, the right-wing network comes to the rescue. A Michigan public radio station fired disc jockey Thayrone (Terry Hughes) for injecting biased politics into his broadcast. The story of his firing was picked up on Matt Drudge's Web site, and Thayrone was featured on Bill O'Reilly's FOX News show and was quickly signed by a Clear Channel station in Ann Arbor.

Clear Channel has yet to put a liberal talker into national syndication, despite the fact that some of its liberal hosts, such as Ed Schultz in Fargo, North Dakota, beat out Limbaugh with strong numbers regionally or locally. Schultz, who has higher ratings than Limbaugh on stations in a seven-state region in the Midwest, believes that Clear Channel has an ideological agenda, not just a business mission. In January 2004, the smaller Jones Radio Network put Schultz into national syndication.

Another popular host is Randi Rhodes, who has scored higher ratings than Limbaugh on the same station in Palm Beach County, Florida. Rhodes has claimed that Limbaugh told his Clear Channel bosses that he would take his show elsewhere if Rhodes were nationally syndicated.[25] As if he fears his franchise might be endangered, Limbaugh has spoken out frequently against liberals gaining a platform in radio. "Liberal talk radio isn't going to work," according to Limbaugh. "Who wants to listen to a bunch of people run down the country and run down the institutions and traditions that made this country great?"

Citadel Communications, described by the Washington-based Center for Public Integrity as "the next big radio conglomerate to challenge the likes of Clear Channel," is owned by the leveraged buyout firm Forstmann Little & Company, whose chairman, Theodore J. Forstmann, is a well-known right-wing financier and former member of the board of *The American Spectator.* Citadel owns more than two hundred radio stations in midsize markets.

Other major players in the radio industry are apolitical media companies such as ABC, which syndicates such talkers as Paul Harvey and Sean Hannity. Hannity's affiliation with ABC means that his broadcast is punctuated by news updates from Peter Jennings, lending Hannity a patina of credibility. Another big syndicator, Westwood One—whose founder and chairman is Norm Pattiz, a major supporter of Democratic causes—boasts Bill O'Reilly (underwritten in part by FOX) and G. Gordon Liddy in its stable.

Laura Ingraham, Lucianne Goldberg, Bob Dornan, and Michael Savage are syndicated by a more exotic and ideologically charged company, the Oregon-based Talk Radio Network, which Richard Mellon Scaife operative Joseph Farah of the Web site WorldNetDaily helped to start. The network was launched by cult leader Roy Masters of the Foundation of Human Understanding, a quasi-religious "human potential" sect. Masters views talk radio as "the best weapon against the disease of socialism and moral corruption infecting the United States." Masters has said he started the network because views like his could not receive a hearing in the "liberal media." According to a report in a local Oregon newspaper, these views include "that most AIDS victims deserve what they get; that starving Somalis also are getting their just desserts; that strong-willed women are corrupting men and the nation, and the media 'doesn't like decent people.'" Talk radio tells conservatives "that they're not strange, they're not stupid," Masters said.[26]

According to the Talk Radio Network's Web site, Masters, who hosts his own show, is "the flip side of Dr. Ruth": "eccentric" but for "traditional values." In the early 1950s, the British-born Masters had been a radio preacher and professional hypnotist. He left Southern California in the late 1970s for Oregon, where he runs the Foundation of Human Understanding, which has a following of several thousand "Roybots," as they are known. According to Masters: "Women are the cause of all misery and suffering on earth"; "All Democrats are Communists"; "The more educated you are, the more perverse you become"; "I am ashamed to be an American"; and "I could get people to die for me any day. I've got more power over people than Adolf Hitler and Jim Jones combined, because I'm smarter." He has called himself "the closest thing on earth to Jesus." Masters's ex–daughter-in-law has accused her ex–father-in-law of physically assaulting her and her two daughters.[27]

Another major radio consolidator that won big in the era of deregulation is Salem Communications, which calls itself "the undisputed leader in providing and distributing content to the religious and family themes audience." According to its Web site, Salem owns 92 stations in thirty-six markets nationwide, with 23 stations in the top ten markets and 58 stations in the top twenty-five markets. In addition, the Salem Radio Network syndicates its own talk programming to about 1,600 affiliated radio stations. Among Salem's talkers are conservatives Michael Medved, Hugh Hewitt, Mike Gallagher, Janet Parshall, Dennis Prager, and Cal Thomas. Medved, Hewitt, and Parshall sit on Salem's "editorial board." Salem's "Christian" stations air Michael Savage's racist, sexist, and homophobic broadcasts.

The latest entry into radio is Murdoch's News Corp., which inaugurated the FOX News Radio Service in 2003—a service offered to radio stations at a lower cost than established news services, with the assist of Murdoch's deep pockets. The Murdoch strategy appears to be to offer the "fair and balanced" FOX News Service as an alternative to professional news services like ABC's, in the belief that AM radio's conservative audiences will prefer it. Once again, the right wing's heavy investment in its "liberal media" campaign was redounding to its benefit. A Dallas-area programming director told the *Wall Street Journal*, "I would get voice mails and emails from people complaining about us carrying that 'slanted, liberal ABC News.'"

The Dallas station subscribed to FOX. With "FOXification" of the radio news airwaves just getting started, the "FOX effect" was being deeply felt across the cable news dial.

CHAPTER THIRTEEN

"FAIR AND BALANCED"

B Y 1996, THE ORGANIZED RIGHT had spent twenty-five years and tens of millions of dollars promoting the charge of "liberal media bias," through which it chilled, disciplined, and infiltrated the professional media while seeding the market for a vast alternative right-wing media. That year, the FOX News Channel became the first media outlet founded explicitly upon the foundation of this deliberate strategy. "The fact is that Rupert [Murdoch] and I and, by the way, the vast majority of the American people, believe that most of the news tilts to the left," Roger Ailes, hired by Murdoch to head the channel, told *Brill's Content* magazine in 1998. In papers filed by FOX in a 2003 copyright infringement lawsuit against Al Franken, author of *Lies and the Lying Liars Who Tell Them: A Fair and Balanced Look at the Right*, FOX maintained, "FOX News was created as a specific alternative to what its founders perceived as a liberal bias in the American media."

Though the Right had never produced any evidence that the news media was systematically biased to the left, Ailes used this widespread misperception both to cultivate his audience and to rationalize what his channel was really up to. Rather than create an unbiased news channel dedicated to journalistic objectivity, Ailes did precisely what he accused the established media of doing: He forged the first so-called news channel that was systematically biased, dedicated to filling the TV airwaves with conservative opinion and misinformation. No news broadcast advances liberal politics the way FOX advances right-wing politics.

When he decided to launch a conservative version of CNN to add news to his vast entertainment holdings, Rupert Murdoch risked hundreds of millions to set up a news operation and pay exorbitant fees to cable carriers. Where money alone was not enough, political pressure was brought to bear. After being turned down for carriage in New York City by Time Warner Cable, the city—then under the leadership of Mayor Rudy Giuliani, a former Ailes client—leaned on the cable company to carry FOX during talks on the city's renewal of its franchise. A judge later found that New York City "abused its power" to "reward a friend and further a particular viewpoint," while another judge declared that "FOX News is not persuasive in its claim that its dealings with the city do not constitute corruption."[1]

The sticking point in FOX's plan for "conservative news" was the potentially negative reaction among viewers, advertisers, and cable carriers to "news" with an announced ideological slant—an unprecedented development in television. In addition, FOX owned a broadcast network and local broadcast affiliate stations. Federal regulations prohibit "intentional and deliberate falsification (distorting, slanting, rigging, staging) of the news" on broadcast television.

Faced with this dilemma, the experience of Ailes, a veteran Republican adman, was invaluable. In an audaciously brilliant piece of rhetorical trickery, Ailes coined the slogans "Fair and Balanced" and "We report, you decide," not only to deny FOX's rightward tilt but to appropriate the very language of professional journalism as, of all things, a FOX branding initiative.

Once the channel was up and running, Ailes—who has a résumé in the field of politics unlike any other figure in a major American news network yet has been named for two years running by *Electronic Media* as the most powerful figure in TV news—clung to this fiction tenaciously, though always with a bit of a wink and a nod, as if letting everyone in on the joke. FOX News Channel is "not a conservative network!" Ailes protested to *Brill's Content* in 1998. "I absolutely, totally deny it. . . ."

Like Murdoch, throughout his professional life Ailes had evinced nothing but contempt for both journalists and for what he saw as the sanctimonious liberal elite of which they were said to be a part. He had contempt for the network anchors and for the *New York Times,* the high and mighty people and institutions trained and empowered to deliver the news to the public in accord with the Progressive Era ideal that journalism should aspire to objectivity, impartiality, and professional norms. He had contempt, too, for what he viewed as the weakness of these so-called liberal elites—their inability, as shown in innumerable political campaigns—to defend themselves. The soft and hypersensitive journalism profession, he knew, again from firsthand campaign experience, had been effectively neutralized by aggressive right-wing critics. Ailes was about to wage the final battle in the Right's war on journalism, and he knew he could win it.

The time for FOX was ripe. "Liberal media bias"—first branded into the national consciousness by Ailes's political mentor, Richard Nixon, decades before and deeply rooted to anti-Semitism and racism—had taken firm hold in the public mind. (One of Ailes's stock criticisms of the media is that it "beats up on Jesus.") The racist, sexist, and homophobic messaging of the Republican Right—not least by Ailes himself in the Nixon, Reagan, and George H. W. Bush presidential campaigns—had divided the country along a cultural fault line and had sparked a resurgent strain of right-wing populism. The $1 billion think tank network, and the billions in subsidies being poured into the *Washington Times/New York Post/ American Spectator/National Review*/NewsMax distribution channels, had harnessed this powerful backlash into a wildly successful political campaign against "Big Government," against "political correctness," against unions, against the United Nations, and against affirmative action. In the era of new media, this Republican Noise Machine resounded on talk radio, on the op-ed pages, on cable news, in the book market, on "Christian" radio and television, on the Internet, and, to a lesser but noticeable extent, even on broadcast television. Through the media, conservatism had been thoroughly mainstreamed; and Republicans had taken control of the U.S. House for the first time in forty years.

In the era of media deregulation, meanwhile, news values had succumbed to the ratings imperatives of entertainment and tabloid fare, a formula that Ailes, who had met Murdoch when he was a consultant to FOX's

A Current Affair, knew well. To FOX, he would bring all that and more—fast pacing, jazzy graphics, Kewpie-doll news readers, and plenty of attitude. That politics already had become an extended version of *Crossfire*—everything reduced to an irresolvable matter of opinion and spin, with hard-charging right-wingers outgunning opponents who were too thoughtful and evenhanded to carry partisan spears—made Ailes's job easier.

Through his experience with Rush Limbaugh, Ailes had learned that alternative media most easily gains a foothold as an oppositionist force; and despite GOP gains in 1994, 1996 saw the reelection of Bill Clinton, whose socially progressive, elite-educated, technocratic, and meritocratic administration perfectly represented all that Ailes—and his potential audience—despised. Ailes was still running a campaign, and he knew where to find his constituencies. In marketing terms, he executed a segmentation strategy perfectly suited to cable.

As Michael Wolff explained in *New York* magazine, "[FOX is] about having a chip on your shoulder; it's about us versus them, insiders versus outsiders, phonies versus non-phonies, and in a clever piece of post-modernism, established media versus insurgent media. . . . It's the tweak. This is really the Fox narrative device. The entire presentation is about tweaking Democrats and boomer culture."

Ailes invented the kind of opinion network first envisioned by Edith Efron in 1971. Efron had wanted to supplant news—facts and information—with a "full spectrum of opinion." Because facts and information threatened to undermine its ideology, the right wing long had been hostile to news and had never been able to produce it successfully, much less profitably. Thus, beginning in the 1970s, the opinion sector had been the Right's way into the media. "Opinion" was a way of winning equal billing for often false, offensive, and absurd viewpoints that had trouble gaining legitimacy in straight-news formats.

Ailes's project was on a grander scale: He sought to collapse and destroy the distinction between news and opinion. For years, the distinction had been under assault from polemicists like Robert Novak, who insisted he was a "reporter"; from "opinion journalists" at *The Wall Street Journal* editorial page; from "investigative reporting" in *The American Spectator;* from "stories" in the *Washington Times;* from the "correspondents" on *The 700 Club;* from "Internet journalist" Matt Drudge; and, above all, from the braying right-wing radio hosts, who insisted they were a reliable source of "news."

Ailes's contribution was to bring this approach to television, the most powerful and imitative medium of all. Around the clock, FOX News offered opinion, not news. FOX appeared to deny the possibility of "objectivity," which was necessary for news. Instead, it called itself "balanced," a term more aptly applied to commentary than to news. FOX was far from balanced—its opinion tilted to the right—but even if the opinion it offered was strictly balanced, opinion was still not news. People watched FOX not to hear the news but to know what to think about the news.

"The attentive viewer, over time, inevitably detects in the welter of talk, banter, chat, debate, repartee, raillery, and badinage an unmistakable conservative biosphere, and a tendency to launch dialogue from right-of-center assumptions that need sorting out before discourse can begin," noted *Columbia Journalism Review*.[2]

Yet the question of FOX's politics was almost a distraction from the more grave matter at stake: Ailes was not wiping out liberal opinion, which was heard on the channel. "Balance" was beside the point; Ailes was wiping out news itself. The process that the highly rated FOX set into motion within the entire TV news industry—observers began to call it "FOXification"—ultimately meant that news was being replaced by partisan opinion about the news. And should it ever come, the end of news—the end of true facts and good information absent spin—would mean the end of democracy.

The most visible on-air FOX News personalities were political and ideological partisans of a character rarely seen in professional news organizations. David Asman, a daytime anchor, had come from the *Wall Street Journal* editorial page and the Manhattan Institute. Brit Hume of ABC News, anchor of an evening newscast, moonlighted as a freelance writer for the Far Right *American Spectator* and the neoconservative *Weekly Standard*. Tony Snow, a sometime anchor and until recently host of FOX's Sunday morning show, was a former editorial page editor of the *Washington Times*, a White House speechwriter for George H. W. Bush, and a substitute host for Rush Limbaugh. While anchoring on FOX, Snow penned an article for the Republican National Committee's magazine, *Rising Tide*, endorsing Bob Dole in 1996. Catherine Crier, who has since left the network, had been an elected Republican judge in Texas.

Suspicious of network newspeople, Ailes assembled a senior management team that, with a few exceptions such as Brit Hume, had no national network news experience.[3] He surrounded himself with a tight clique of loyalists, one of them a former GOP investigator on Capitol Hill. Departing staff at FOX complained of a disdain for the culture of journalism among the network's top ranks. According to *Columbia Journalism Review*, "several" former FOX staffers "complained of 'management sticking their fingers' in the writing and editing of stories to cook the facts to make a story more palatable to right-of-center tastes." One ex-FOX worker said, "I've worked at a lot of news organizations and never found that kind of manipulation."

Veteran ABC newsman Jed Duvall, who worked at FOX for one year before leaving in 1997, told *New York* magazine, "I'll never forget the morning that one producer came up to me, and rubbing her hands like Uriah Heep, said, 'Let's have something on Whitewater today.' That sort of thing doesn't happen in professional news organizations."

In the early days, Ailes's most influential adviser was Chet Collier, who produced *Mike Douglas, Merv Griffin,* and *David Frost* before Ailes hired him for the failed America's Talking venture at CNBC. In hiring on-air anchors and reporters, Collier favored looks over experience, confiding to one ex-FOX executive, "I'm not hiring the talent for their brainpower." His theory of the news, according to several inside accounts, was that "people don't want to be informed; they only want the illusion of being informed."

In a blunt statement of opinion that would have brought opprobrium upon his professional competitors, John Moody, FOX's chief news executive and a veteran conservative *Time* correspondent, told *Columbia Journalism Review* in 2003, "We don't accept the liberal truisms. They have no doubt, for example, that Nelson Mandela is the best thing that ever happened to South Africa. I'm not so sure that's true. They insist that the most pressing health issue in the U.S. is AIDS. I think more people would rather cure cancer. They want homosexuals treated not just as equals, but given special treatment. On the street where I live, most people would say 'no thank you' to that idea."

Moody kindled a number of newsroom controversies. On the first anniversary of the Oklahoma City bombing, in April 1996, he assigned a story about "good works" done by some militia groups. FOX's criticism of

ABC's exposé of abuses at the Food Lion grocery store chain—without any response from ABC—was assailed on an internal FOX intranet bulletin board as an unfair and hypocritical slam on the competition. And former CBS producer Don Dahler quit FOX after being directed by Moody to play down statistics on the progress of African Americans.

Managing the Washington bureau is Brit Hume's wife, Kim, formerly of ABC. She glibly explained the network's philosophy this way: "In the D.C. bureau [at ABC] we always had to worry what the lead story would be [the next day] in the *New York Times,* and God forbid if we didn't have that story." Stories covered by such established journalistic enterprises, she said, are "all mushy, like AIDS, or all silly, like Head Start. They want to give publicity to people they think are doing good."

In fall 2003, former FOX producer and writer Charles Reina weighed in publicly on FOX's journalistic ethics, posting a long comment on the widely read insider media news Web log edited by the Poynter Institute's Jim Romenesko.

> Not once in the 20 plus years I had worked in broadcast journalism prior to Fox—including lengthy stays at the Associated Press, CBS Radio, and ABC/Good Morning America—did I feel any pressure to toe the management line. But at Fox, if my boss wasn't warning me to "be careful" how I handled the writing of a special about Ronald Reagan ("You know how Roger feels about him"), he was telling me how the environmental special I was to produce should lean ("You can give both sides, but make sure the pro-environmentalists don't get the last word").
>
> But the roots of FNC's [FOX News Channel's] day-to-day on-air bias are actual and direct. They come in the form of an executive memo distributed electronically each morning, addressing what stories will be covered and, often, suggesting how they should be covered. . . . The Memo was born with the Bush administration, early in 2001, and, intentionally or not, has ensured that the administration's point of view consistently comes across on FNC. This year, of course, the war in Iraq became a constant subject of The Memo . . . For instance, from the March 20th memo: "There is something utterly incomprehensible about Kofi Annan's remarks in

which he allows that his thoughts are 'with the Iraqi people.' One could ask where those thoughts were during the 23 years Saddam Hussein was brutalizing those same Iraqis. Food for thought." One day this past spring, The Memo warned us that anti-war protestors would be "whining" about U.S. bombs killing Iraqi civilians, and suggested they could tell that to the families of American soldiers dying there. Editing copy that morning, I was not surprised when an eager young producer killed a correspondent's report on the day's fighting—simply because it included a brief shot of children in an Iraqi hospital."

FOX dismissed Reina's account as that of a "disgruntled ex-employee." But Reina's take was soon corroborated by Matt Gross, now an assistant editor at *New York* magazine, who posted his own comments on Romenesko's site:

> As a former editor at Foxnews.com—and therefore clearly a disgruntled ex-employee—let me just say that the right-wing bias was there in the newsroom, up-front and obvious, from the day a certain executive editor was sent down from the channel to bring us in line with their coverage. His first directive to us: Seek out stories that cater to angry, middle-aged white men who listen to talk radio and yell at their televisions. . . . What followed was a dumbing-down of what had been an ambitious and talented news operation. . . . More and more effort was devoted to adapting FNC "scripts" into Web stories, which meant we were essentially correcting the errors of FNC "reporters" who couldn't be bothered to get the facts. . . . To me, FNC's reporters laziness was the worst part of bias. It wasn't that they were toeing some political line (though of course they were; see the embarrassing series on property rights from 2000), it was that the facts of a story just didn't matter at all. The idea was to get those viewers out of their seats, screaming at the TV, the politicians, the liberals—whomever—simply by running a provocative story.

Throughout the day on FOX, such bias and unprofessionalism is flagrant. One typical FOX poll asked: "Babs Babbling? Barbra Streisand has urged Dems to 'go on the offensive' against the Iraq war. What do you think? Options: 'She should shut up—what does she know?' Or 'She's exercising her freedom of speech.'"⁴ Disparaging a book deal made by Senate Democratic leader Tom Daschle on host John Gibson's program *The Big Story* was Al Regnery of the right-wing Regnery book-publishing company, appearing as the sole guest. On FOX's morning show, *FOX & Friends*, anchor Brian Kilmeade interrupted antiwar actress Janeane Garofalo with, "Okay. So you are—Saddam must love you." Eric Muller, a radio shock jock who calls himself "Mancow" on the air and frequently appears on *FOX & Friends*—where he is referred to as the broadcast's "naughty little brother"—has spoken of "lesbian nights" in the Clinton White House.

This is what "balance" means on FOX: Asked about FOX's coverage of Christopher Ruddy's conspiracy theories about the "murder" of Clinton Commerce Secretary Ron Brown, who died in an airplane accident, Brit Hume told *Columbia Journalism Review,* "We're not going to endorse the conclusion the way a lot of right-wing people want us to, but it's a story that's worth giving airtime to." Opposing voices have been presented on FOX "sharply criticizing Ruddy's work," according to Hume. Yet the *Review* asked, "But is it really worth airtime, since independent medical authorities who examined x-rays of Brown's skull say the theory is nonsense?"

And this is FOX's idea of "fair": In narrating a piece about the declining popularity of the name "Hillary," a smirking Hume mused about how the names Adolf, "as in Hitler," and Ebenezer, "as in Scrooge," had suffered a similar fate.

As Ailes might have foreseen, with the exception of the professional journalism reviews, a handful of media critics (notably the media watchdog group Fairness & Accuracy in Reporting), and the few genuinely liberal voices in the media such as Al Franken, the compliant institutions of mainstream journalism essentially accepted FOX's legitimacy; predictably, once it garnered high ratings, many of them began to imitate it. In an interview on FOX, GE's chairman and CEO Jeffrey Immelt said, "I think the standard right now is Fox. I want [MSNBC] to be as interesting and edgy as you guys are." Accepting a top job with FOX as Tony Snow's replacement on Sunday mornings, veteran ABC correspondent Chris Wallace called the channel "serious, thoughtful, and even-handed." *Washington Post* media critic Howard Kurtz has said FOX's news reporting "tends to be straightforward."

Yet a major report by Fairness & Accuracy in Reporting in August 2001 found that "an attentive viewer will notice that there are entire blocks of the network's programming schedule that are set aside for conservative stories. Fox's website offers a regular feature on 'political correctness' entitled 'Tongue-Tied: A Report from the Front Lines of the Culture Wars,' whose logo is a scowling 'PC Patrol' officer peering testily through a magnifying glass. It invites readers to write in and 'keep us up on examples of PC excess you come across.' "5

FAIR pointed to:

> a series of stories about one conservative cause after another: from white firefighters suing Boston's fire department for discrimination, to sawmill workers endangered by Clinton-Gore environmental regulations (without comment from a single supporter of the rules), to property owners who feel threatened by an environmental agreement "signed by President Clinton in 1992." (The agreement was actually signed by George Bush the elder, who was president in 1992—though that didn't stop Fox from using news footage of a smiling Bill Clinton proudly signing an official document that was supposed to be, but wasn't, the environmental pact in question.)
>
> Fox's news specials are equally slanted: "Dangerous Places" (3/25/01), a special about foreign policy hosted by Newt Gingrich; "Heroes," an irregular series hosted by former Republican Congressmember John Kasich; and "The Real Reagan," (11/25/99), a panel discussion on Ronald Reagan, hosted by Tony Snow, in which all six guests were Reagan friends and political aides. "Vanishing Freedoms 2: Who Owns America" (5/19/01) wandered off into militia-style paranoia, suggesting that the U.N. was "taking over" private property.
>
> There is a formula to Fox's news agenda. . . . An embarrassing story about Jesse Jackson's sex life. The latest political-correctness outrage on campus. A one-day mini-scandal about a Democratic Senator. Much like talk radio, Fox picks up these tidbits from right-wing outlets like the *Washington Times* or the Drudge Report and runs with them.

One of the most partisan features on Fox is a daily segment on "Special Report," called "The Political Grapevine." Billed as "the most scintillating two minutes in television," the Grapevine is a kind of right-wing hot sheet. It features Brit Hume at the anchor's desk reading off a series of gossipy items culled from other, often right-wing, news outlets.

The key to the Grapevine is its story selection, and there is nothing subtle about it. Almost every item carries an unmistakable partisan message: Democrats, environmentalists, and Hollywood liberals are perennial villains (or butts of the joke), while Republicans are shown either as targets of unfair attacks or heroes who can do no wrong. Political correctness run amok, the "liberal bias," of the mainstream media and the chicanery of civil rights groups all figure prominently. When Rep. Patrick Kennedy tussled with airport security (3/21/01), Democrat Pete Stark used intemperate language (4/18/01) and California Gov. Gray Davis uttered a string of curse words (4/18/01), it made it onto the Grapevine. When the *Sacramento Bee* ran a series on the shortcomings of the big environmental groups, its findings earned a mention on the Grapevine (4/21/01). When it emerged that Al Gore booster Ben Affleck didn't bother to vote in last year's election, you heard about it on the Grapevine (4/25/01).

Republicans are treated differently. "Since [New York's] Rudolph Giuliani became the mayor," one item cheered (4/24/01), "the streets are cleaner and safer, and tourism reigns supreme in Times Square." When George W. Bush ordered men to wear a coat and tie to enter the Oval Office, Grapevine (5/14/01) noted that "his father had a similar reverence for the office," while "President Clinton used to come into the Oval Office in running shorts . . . and sometimes he did not remain fully clothed while he was there."

FAIR noted that FOX claims it is covering stories that the liberal media won't touch, yet the claim turns out to be false:

According to Bill O'Reilly, Fox "gives voice to people who can't get on other networks. When was the last time you saw pro-life people [on other networks] unless they shot somebody?" (Philadelphia

Inquirer, 4/10/01). O'Reilly's question is easily answered; in the last three years, the National Right to Life Committee's spokespeople have appeared on CNN 21 times (compared with 16 appearances for their main counterpart, the National Abortion Rights Action League).

In a 1999 *Washington Post* profile (3/26/99), Ailes offered another example. He said he was particularly proud of a three-part series on education that Fox had recently aired, which reported that "many educators believe self-esteem teaching is harmful to" students. "The mainstream media will never cover that story," Ailes told the *Post*. "I've seen 10,000 stories on education and I've never seen one that didn't say the federal government needed to spend more money on education." But just weeks prior to Ailes' interview, CNN's weekly "Newsstand" series (2/28/99) aired a glowing profile of an upstate New York business executive who had turned around a troubled inner-city elementary school "by bringing the lessons of the boardroom into the classroom." CNN's report came complete with sound bites from a conservative education advocate ("the unions are a major impediment to education reform") and lines from host Jeff Greenfield like, "Critics have said that for decades, the public education system has behaved like an entrenched monopoly with little or no incentive to improve its performance."

Other FAIR surveys of FOX have shown systematic bias in its lineup of guests. "Fox News is anything but fair and balanced when it comes to political guests," FAIR concluded, based on a tally showing "fifty of 56 partisan guests interviewed on Brit Hume's daily news show over a five-month period were Republican, and only six were Democrats. . . . By contrast, during the same period, FAIR found that Wolf Blitzer's CNN program featured 67 partisan guests—38 Republicans and 29 Democrats."

In spring 2003, Ken Auletta, the media writer for *The New Yorker,* spent four months watching FOX News. "I saw a network that was not, as advertised, free of bias and 'fair and balanced,'" Auletta said in an interview on the magazine's Web site. "This is not to say that Fox doesn't do some things well. It is to say that the network, like many political candidates, is not always what it claims to be. The network proclaims, 'we report, you decide.'

But, too often, Fox both reports and decides. The anchors are opinionated throughout the day, not just in the evening hours with Bill O'Reilly or Sean Hannity. Too often, the commentators tilt to the right and don't present both sides—certainly not the non-conservative side—and many of the network's 'liberal' commentators are somewhat meek. Many Fox reporters do offer opinions. In its desire to right the excesses of what it sees as liberal press bias, Fox often goes overboard."

Liberal guests—political consultants, activists, academics, and writers—appear regularly on FOX shows. But FOX's choice of in-house "liberals"—those on the Murdoch payroll appearing most frequently—are far from reliably liberal. On the contrary, they often seem to be used by FOX to sabotage the liberal position from within.

NPR's Mara Liasson, for example, is a regular "All Star" panelist on Brit Hume's evening political roundtable, appearing opposite such conservatives as Fred Barnes and William Kristol of *The Weekly Standard* and Charles Krauthammer. NPR's ombudsman, Jeffrey Dworkin, has objected to the arrangement, writing, "Fox hosts often imply that NPR reporters are the embodiment of liberal journalism by placing them against openly conservative personalities. This may confirm in the minds of some viewers that NPR must be as ideologically committed in its own way as Fox is to the conservative cause."

Liasson, who assured Ailes that she was a Republican before being hired, has said she appears on the show as an "analyst," not a "liberal." She has referred on the air to right-wing activist Grover Norquist as "a friend of mine." According to FAIR, "Her liberalism consists of little more than being a woman who works for National Public Radio; she has proposed that 'one of the roots of the problem with education today is feminism'; . . . and she called George Bush's reversal on carbon dioxide emissions a 'small thing.'"

When two Democratic members of Congress visited Baghdad before the war, Liasson opined, "These guys are a disgrace. Look, everybody knows it's 101, it's politics 101, that you don't go to an adversary country, an enemy country, and badmouth the United States, its policies and the president of the United States. I mean, these guys ought to, I don't know, resign." NPR ombudsman Dworkin later chided Liasson for "appear[ing] to abandon her role as reporter." Liasson conceded, "I certainly shouldn't have said it."

NPR's Juan Williams is also cast by FOX as a "liberal" commentator.

While he was at the *Washington Post* during the Clarence Thomas Supreme Court confirmation hearings, Williams stepped out of his reportorial role to pen an op-ed column attacking Thomas's opponents. Williams maintained that "liberals have become monsters" and scalded the "so-called champions of fairness: liberal politicians, unions, civil rights groups and women's organizations."

In addition to his roles at NPR and FOX, Williams is the host of *America's Black Forum,* a nationally syndicated TV show founded in the late 1970s as a platform for African American journalists and their guests to discuss public policy issues in the manner of the network Sunday morning talk shows. The show was begun by the publishers of *Black Commentator* and had a successful run for many years with a professional approach and nonpartisan tone. In the mid-1990s, the show was taken over by Uniworld, a black-owned advertising agency, Williams was brought in, and the broadcast lurched to the right, regularly featuring such black right-wingers as Strom Thurmond protégé Armstrong Williams and Niger Innis, the right-wing son of Congress of Racial Equality founder Roy Innis. Like his father, Niger Innis is supported by white conservatives to attack civil rights leaders. He was the New York State chair of Alan Keyes's presidential campaign and sits on the board of Project 21, the right-wing foundation-funded black Republican front group.

"ABF has devolved into a menagerie of professional Black propagandists in service of the most vicious elements of the Republican Party," charged an article in *Black Commentator* in December 2002. "White ideologues of the Right regularly reinforce their darker partners on the set, providing their own peculiar analysis of the Black condition. For a time, Pat Buchanan, whose name is synonymous with 'Nazi' in many circles, seemed to be a regular on the show. Obscure clones of racist commentator Ann Coulter share insights on world and national politics for the benefit of a Black commercial television audience. It is a bizarre experience."

Two professional reporters are frequently booked to fill the "liberal" chair on Hume's roundtable. One is Jeff Birnbaum, the Washington bureau chief of *Fortune.* When Birnbaum suggested that price caps might be an answer to California's energy crunch, he was sharply upbraided and belittled by Hume, who asked him, "Did you ever have any economics in college?" The next day, Birnbaum came back on the broadcast, sheepishly recanting his point. "No apology required," Hume told him.[6]

Ceci Connolly of the *Washington Post* appears on FOX opposite conservative ideologues. In the 2000 campaign, she wrote a series of inaccurate and misleading pieces in the *Post* that portrayed Al Gore as having a problem telling the truth, after the Republican National Committee had crafted and marketed the theme. Eric Alterman's *What Liberal Media?* noted that her errors included her false claim that Gore said he "invented" the Internet. On FOX, Connolly has departed from her reportorial role; for instance, she scolded Gore for speaking up against Bush domestic policy, saying it "didn't seem quite appropriate" after September 11.[7]

Sitting in the "middle" of the Hume panels is Morton Kondracke, who resists ideological labeling (in the late 1980s, Kondracke announced that he was a Democrat who is "disgusted with the Democratic Party"). Commenting on Democratic questioning of Bush's foreign policy on the Hume show, Kondracke advised, "He's the daddy driving in a hail storm. Leave him alone for a while." Kondracke also appears alongside Fred Barnes on *The Beltway Boys,* a weekend FOX political chat show supposedly offering balance. Barnes, Kondracke, and Charles Krauthammer, another FOX contributor, were all consulted on the Showtime movie *DC 9/11: Time of Crisis,* produced by "naked out-of-the-closet Republican" Lionel Chetwynd. The film mixed fact and fiction to make Bush appear more assured in the wake of the attacks than he was.

Alan Colmes, the co-host of *Hannity & Colmes* and host of a FOX-syndicated daily radio show, is one of the few liberals with a regular highly rated platform anywhere in television. Colmes told *The American Prospect* that he defines a "true liberal" as "someone who sees both sides." Admirable though that sentiment may be, Colmes epitomizes why the liberals chosen by media owners to compete in cable and radio formats have had difficulty gaining ratings: he is so enamored with the idea of being fair-minded that he seems compelled to let his own side down just for the sake of it—and he is also dull as dishwater. His style is no match for that of his opponent, the fiery radio demagogue Sean Hannity, who helped choose Colmes for the slot over sharper potential sparring partners who auditioned, such as Joe Conason of the *New York Observer* and *Salon.* Tom DeLay, Orrin Hatch, Trent Lott, and James Dobson have all declared Colmes to be their favorite liberal.[8]

FOX broadcasts a bit of Hannity's radio show each afternoon but does not give Colmes equal treatment. Studies by FAIR have shown "conservatives out-number, out-talk and out-interrupt their liberal opponents" on the show. To his discredit, Colmes, whose presence is critical to FOX's "fair and balanced" charade, is an apologist for the Murdoch empire, claiming it does not have a right-wing bias.

Many other FOX programs fall short of the "fair and balanced" standard. The *Tyndall Report,* a nonpartisan newsletter that covers TV news, was commissioned in February 2002 by PBS's *NewsHour with Jim Lehrer* to study the content of the three cable news networks. Analyzing Brit Hume's newscast, Tyndall found that "of the six print journalists that we saw appearing in that [daily] panel during the week we looked at it, three were from explicitly right-wing publications and three were from mainstream publications. None was from an explicitly left-wing publication."

Following Hume in the evening is another highly rated newscast, anchored by Shepard Smith. Tyndall described it as "unlike anything I've seen on national television news anywhere":

> If you imagine what you see on a local news sportscast at 11 PM, where you have a whole slew of video clips, and someone with a very loud voice talking very fast, telling you in a somewhat flippant tone about the exciting things that happened in the world of sports, well, Shepard Smith takes that principle and applies it to the world of news.
>
> On the day when we saw it, which was the day when the Californian Taliban [John Walker Lindh] was being returned back to Virginia for, to stand trial for terrorist conspiracy, all other newscasts called him John Walker Lindh. As far as Shepard Smith was concerned he was "Johnny Jihad."

Asked about FOX's "fair and balanced" claim by PBS, Tyndall said, "There are multiple times during the night where they're unbalanced. However, none of those are the dominant mood of the programming. They're little inflections that come in once in a while. Maybe three times an hour you'll hear something that is clearly not balanced. As for 'fair,' they like fur flying, and if they can use innuendo or unfair tactics in order to get some excitement going, they're absolutely prepared to do that. . . . What I'm talking about is a 'hothouse atmosphere' of coverage, where there's very little that is not highly ideologically charged, where opinions aren't being thrown constantly, back and forth. . . . The reason why you'd watch Fox News wouldn't be to be persuaded of a certain political agenda. It would be to bathe in this hothouse of opinion, spin and analysis. . . .

"The thumbnail recommendation I would have to people," Tyndall concluded, "would be if you want a news-gathering channel, then go to CNN. If you want an opinion channel, got to Fox News. And MSNBC is confused between the two."

Though they are not really in the same business, CNN and FOX are locked in a tight ratings race. On any given night in prime time, FOX's top shows, such as *The O'Reilly Factor* and the *Crossfire* knockoff *Hannity & Colmes*, draw several hundred thousand more viewers than CNN's newscast *NewsNight with Aaron Brown* or the nonideological *Larry King Live* interview show. Throughout the day, though more viewers tune into CNN, FOX garners a higher average audience number because its viewers stay with its programming for much longer stretches of time. FOX's audience appears to be a bit more affluent than CNN's, though CNN still commands a higher advertising rate than FOX and makes far more revenue. FOX's audience is slightly younger than CNN's, though not by much (an average age of sixty-one versus fifty-seven). FOX's audience self-identifies as more conservative than CNN's, though again not by much (46 percent to 40 percent). Liberals appear to make up a relatively small portion of the overall cable news audience.

As a news source, CNN is more trusted than FOX. According to a Pew Research Center poll in August 2002, 37 percent of Americans who had an opinion said they believe "most or all" of what they see on CNN, while only 24 percent believe FOX. FOX does not fare nearly as well on its Web site, suggesting that viewers are likely seeking something other than news from FOX. Of the top twenty news Web sites, FOX ranks fifteenth, trailing CNN, MSNBC, the *New York Times*, the *Washington Post, USA Today,* and *Slate,* according to Nielsen/NetRatings in August 2003. The FOX News Web site attracts only 20 percent of MSNBC.com's audience.

The average audience for cable news has spiked significantly in recent years. After a slow start, FOX picked up heads of steam during the 1998

Clinton impeachment, the 2000 standoff in Florida, and in the aftermath of September 11. In early 2002, FOX overtook CNN in the ratings race for the first time. As the United States went to war in Iraq, FOX's dominant position solidified. Of FOX's war coverage, Mark Jurkowitz wrote in the *Boston Globe:*

No outlet taps into that [pro-American] tilt as effectively and overtly as the Fox News Channel, where the Stars and Stripes floats in the upper left-hand corner of the screen and the logo "War on Terror" morphs into the words "Operation Iraqi Freedom." (The juxtaposition of those phrases helps reinforce the White House case that Hussein is a legitimate target in the war on terror.) . . .

On the Fox News Channel, B-52 bombers make a "grand entrance . . . into battle" and host John Gibson introduces a report about U.N. Secretary General Kofi Annan's suggestion that there still may be a role for U.N. weapon inspectors by snorting: "I can only ask: Huh?"

. . . Talking about the antiwar protestors in Hollywood, business anchor Neil Cavuto impatiently asks one military analyst, "Would you tell them to shut up or what?"

The outlet's world view is deeply imbedded in the DNA of the people who show up in its stories and studios. Hannity and O'Reilly, two of its prime-time stars, moonlight as very successful conservative talk-radio hosts. So does Colonel Oliver North, an "embedded commentator" for the network. Bill Kristol, editor of the conservative *Weekly Standard*—and a driving intellectual force behind the policy of regime change in Iraq—is a Fox News contributor, as is former Republican House Speaker Newt Gingrich.

Sometimes, the parade of guests puts out a barrage of spin that is remarkably in synch with the administration view. Earlier this week, on an afternoon when viewers were getting the first sense that Iraqi forces might put up surprisingly stiff resistance, Hannity dismissed the naysayers by declaring, "We're gonna win this in short order." Kristol counseled that "any war has its ups and downs. . . . People just need to calm down." And pundit David Horowitz characterized anti-war protestors as "so-called commu-

nists [who] hate America and . . . want to lose the war on terror"
and who are engaged in a "sabotage campaign against our cities."

Media critic David Folkenflik of the *Baltimore Sun* described FOX's coverage as "patriotic" and "pugilistic." "As the invasion of Iraq unfolds, this visceral approach has become more the rule than the exception at Fox News," he wrote. "Always presented as an alternative to the rest of the establishment press, FOX has switched into even higher gear, encouraging a resolutely pro-American, sometimes explicitly pro-war stance. Almost every FOX News program includes a flag in the left-hand corner and the use of the Defense Department's name for the war—'Operation Iraqi Freedom'—as the network's own catchphrase for its coverage. The United States quickly becomes 'our' in reporters' parlance."[9]

Folkenflik pointed to Neil Cavuto, host of a nightly business show on FOX, as exemplifying the FOX style. Rebutting a complaint about his lack of objectivity from a journalism professor who had written to the network, Cavuto called the professor an "obnoxious, pontificating jerk," a "self-absorbed, condescending imbecile," and an "Ivy League intellectual Lilliputian." "So am I slanted and biased? You damn well bet I am, professor!" Of those who opposed the war in Iraq, Cavuto has said, "You were sickening then; you are sickening now." When *New York Times* op-ed columnist Paul Krugman criticized Cavuto for blatant partisanship, Cavuto responded with a piece titled "Potshots from a Hypocrite," calling Krugman "as phony as you are unprofessional . . . [a] sanctimonious twit . . . a pretentious charlatan . . . [and an] ass. . . . Now may I suggest you take your column and shove it?"

The FOX anchors betrayed their biases off the air as well. "Right now, the U.N. is irrelevant, except if you are a diplomat, you can park anywhere you want and they can't put you in jail. . . ." Tony Snow said in an October 2003 speech at a retirement community in Georgia. "Parts of Europe have lost their souls. The French don't believe in anything anymore. Not even a 35-hour work week." Switching topics to the California gubernatorial election, Snow said of Republican candidate Arnold Schwarzenegger, "He ran on values. He's a great story because he was unapologetic about loving his county. . . . We want a sense of America that is strong and unapologetic."[10]

Oliver North, a "military contributor" to FOX, reported on the air "rumors" that French officials in Iraq were trying to hide evidence of French complicity in Saddam's purported buildup of chemical and biological weapons. The "rumors" were bogus.[11] On FOX programs, North derisively refers to Bill Clinton as "William the Zipper."

Trying to minimize the political fallout from mounting American casualties, Brit Hume said:

> Two hundred and seventy-seven U.S. soldiers have now died in
> Iraq, which means that, statistically speaking, U.S. soldiers have
> less of a chance of dying from all causes in Iraq than citizens have
> of being murdered in California.

A few weeks before, Secretary of Defense Donald Rumsfeld had made a similar comparison, using Washington, D.C., rather than California in the analogy.[12]

The George W. Bush administration was the first in history to have a TV network rooting for it, a fusion of power that the White House used to its full propaganda potential. On the night of the 2000 election, FOX had been the first to declare Bush the victor. Within a few minutes, all the other networks followed suit. "That call—wrong, unnecessary, misguided, foolish— has helped to create a sense that this election went to Bush, was pulled back and he is waiting to be restored," said Tom Rosenstiel of the Project for Excellence in Journalism.[13] Working the FOX election desk and participating in the decision was John Ellis, a cousin of George W. Bush who had resigned a job at the *Boston Globe* because his "loyalty" to his cousin was interfering with his ability to do his job. Ellis later told *The New Yorker,* "It was just the three of us guys handing the phone back and forth—me with the numbers, one of them a governor, the other the president-elect. Now that was cool."

As U.S. troops advanced on the Iraqi capital, FOX apparently had superior access to images of Baghdad than did its competitors. According to the *Sydney Morning Herald,* a U.S. military spokesman said, "Fox may well have more access. They have good contacts and they asked the right questions in the preplanning." When President George W. Bush made a surprise visit to U.S. troops in Iraq on Thanksgiving 2003, CNN was rotated out of the press pool in favor of FOX. Other signs of favoritism included a June

2003 announcement by Bush Press Secretary Ari Fleischer that the FOX correspondent would be moved from the sixth to the second row in the White House pressroom. On "Radio Day" at the White House—when conservative hosts from around the country are invited to "interview" administration spokespeople en masse—Sean Hannity was pulled aside and ushered into the Oval Office for a private meeting with President Bush. White House offices, U.S. military installations, and Republican offices on Capitol Hill are tuned to FOX, as is the Heritage Foundation, which warned its employees that watching FOX on their computers was causing the system to crash.

FOX also aided the Republicans in an attack on the freedom, integrity, and patriotism of journalists. In response to a column by Helen Thomas naming President George W. Bush "the worst President in all of American history," the Republican National Committee instructed its supporters to "call her out," urging them to e-mail, phone, and fax complaints to Hearst, which syndicates Thomas.[14] Right-wing Web sites were filled with invective, calling Thomas "the dumbest bitch of them all." Brit Hume referred to Thomas—who had peppered the White House spokesman with skeptical questions about the war—as "the nutty aunt in the attic of the White House press corps . . . [asking questions] not of the kind that any professional journalist would ask."

When award-winning CNN foreign correspondent Christiane Amanpour criticized FOX, the network accused her of working in league with terrorists. Appearing on CNBC's *Topic A* with Tina Brown, Amanpour said, "I think the press was muzzled, and I think the press self-muzzled. I'm sorry to say, but certainly television and, perhaps, to a certain extent, my station was intimidated by the administration and its foot soldiers at Fox News. And it did, in fact, put a climate of fear and self-censorship, in my view, in terms of the kind of broadcast work we did." Brown then asked Amanpour if there was any story during the war that she couldn't report. "It's not a question of couldn't do it, it's a question of tone," Amanpour replied. "It's a question of being rigorous. It's really a question of really asking the questions. All of the entire body politic in my view, whether it's the administration, the intelligence, the journalists, whoever, did not ask enough questions, for instance, about weapons of mass destruction. I mean, it looks like this was disinformation at the highest levels." FOX retorted, "Given the choice, it's better to be viewed as a foot soldier for Bush than a spokeswoman for al-Qaeda."

The FOX "foot soldiers" repeatedly misinformed their audience about the war. According to an October 2003 study of news coverage during the war, conducted by the Program on International Policy Attitudes at the University of Maryland, those who depended on FOX News for information about the war were substantially more likely to have false perceptions than those who did not. In the survey, news sources were listed as FOX, CNN, NBC, ABC, CBS, and PBS-NPR. Respondents were asked if they agreed with three common misperceptions about the war: that evidence linked Iraq and al-Qaeda; that weapons of mass destruction had been found in Iraq; and that "world public opinion approved of the U.S. going to war with Iraq."

Results showed that FOX News Channel viewers were the worst informed, while the PBS-NPR audience was the best informed. "Fox News watchers were most likely to hold misperceptions—and were three times more likely than the nearest network to hold all three misperceptions. In the audience for NPR/PBS, however, there was an overwhelming majority who did not have any of the three misperceptions, and hardly any had all three." For example, 33 percent of FOX viewers believed wrongly that the United States had found weapons of mass destruction; 20 percent of CNN viewers believed this; and 11 percent of PBS-NPR users did.

Overall, Republicans and those with less education were more likely to hold false beliefs on the war, although even in these groups the FOX effect was demonstrable. Republican FOX viewers, for example, had a 54 percent misperception rate, while Republicans gleaning their news from PBS-NPR had only a 32 percent misperception rate. Misperception levels were measurably higher the more news a viewer received from FOX, and the closer attention they paid to it. "Among those who primarily watch Fox, those who pay more attention are more likely to have misperceptions. Only those who mostly get their news from print media, and to some extent those who primarily watch CNN, have fewer misperceptions as they pay more attention," the study found.

The study factored in the political bias of the viewer and still found that FOX significantly misinformed its audience: "For example, 78 percent of Bush supporters who watch Fox News thought the U.S. had found evidence of a direct link to al-Qaeda, but only 50 percent of Bush supporters in the PBS and NPR audience thought this. On the other side, 48 percent of Democratic supporters who watch Fox News thought the U.S. has found evidence of a direct link to al-Qaeda, but not one single respondent who is a Democratic supporter and relies on PBS and NPR for network news thought the U.S. had found such evidence."

The crucial audience numbers for FOX are garnered in prime time, during which FOX airs a highly rated schedule built around Bill O'Reilly. Before joining FOX, O'Reilly was an anchor for the tabloid show *Inside Edition,* and he now hosts what he calls a "No Spin Zone" on FOX, where for an hour each weekday night he poses as an independent, populist truth-teller in what is essentially a remake of the popular *Morton Downey Show* from the late 1980s.

Like FOX itself, O'Reilly is highly biased yet is at pains to deny it. The signature broadcast on the "fair and balanced" channel cannot be ideologically or politically aligned or else the whole fiction would crumble. "No one has been able to prove [that FOX is conservative]," O'Reilly has declared. Yet O'Reilly has admitted that "Fox News is right of center," according to the *Philadelphia Inquirer.*[15] On his show, which he describes as "without an agenda or any ideological prejudices," he has claimed to be a registered independent. But he was actually a registered Republican in Nassau County, Long Island, where he lives, when he made that false claim. Caught out by the *Daily News,* O'Reilly reregistered as an independent.

Throughout the 1970s and 1980s, O'Reilly had an undistinguished career in network and local news. At CBS Evening News, O'Reilly's idea of a hot story was his discovery that Provincetown, Massachusetts, had become a popular place for gays and lesbians to vacation. He was miffed when the network passed on the idea of profiling the town where "a thousand people [were] running around looking like Dolly Parton."

O'Reilly vented his frustrations with the TV industry in a little-noticed novel, *Those Who Trespass: A Novel of Murder and Television,* about a network anchor who bears an uncanny likeness to the author. The O'Reilly character, "Shannon Michaels," becomes a serial killer, murdering other characters, such as the news director, based loosely on O'Reilly's real-life coworkers. The murderous rampages, described in grotesque detail, are referred to as "righteous slaughter."

In the novel, a criminal psychologist explains the term: "If you completely humiliate a narcissist, you can ignite a bomb. If you take away his ability to get positive attention, and then compound the problem by bringing negative attention to him, chances are you've made a mortal enemy of him. The narcissistic personality can easily become enraged and feel that he's morally justified in retaliating against people who hurt him. He sees nothing wrong in demonizing those who bring him pain. And the bigger the humiliation, the more drastic the retaliation. Remember, the narcissist does not feel for other people. 'If they die,' he thinks, 'well, they definitely deserved it.'"

"There is one woman who I kill in *Those Who Trespass* who still is in a position of power at ABC News," O'Reilly told the *Boston Globe.* "She is the most despicable person on the face of the earth, a rank informer, somebody who is there with no journalistic skills, only to inform on other people in the company. And if she doesn't like you, she'll make stuff up." The novel was optioned by the actor Mel Gibson, whom O'Reilly has defended against charges of anti-Semitism.

O'Reilly has spoken of "nailing," "slapping around," and "murdering" various guests and subjects of his ire. When Al Franken exposed O'Reilly as a serial and perhaps pathological liar in his book *Lies and the Lying Liars Who Tell Them,* O'Reilly said he wished he could have "put a bullet" into Franken's head. On the dust jacket of one of his nonfiction books, O'Reilly is called "madder today than when he wrote his last book."

After leaving *Inside Edition* in the mid-1990s when his syndicators rejected his idea of hosting a "populist *Nightline,*" he went to Harvard's Kennedy School of Government, a frequent destination for those seeking to burnish their résumés and rethink their careers in midlife, to earn a master's degree in public policy. According to a *New York Times* article, O'Reilly, born William James O'Reilly in the Long Island suburbs, believed that if he had had a better familial and educational pedigree, he would have been more successful in television. He looked at Stone Phillips and Maria Shriver of NBC with class envy, the article suggested.

The first line of his book *The O'Reilly Factor* is, "The question for this age in America is: What class are you?" He continued:

Like most working-class kids, I first learned about the class system
and its rigidity when I left home in Levittown for the wider world. As
a freshman at Marist College in Poughkeepsie, New York, a fine
and affordable school, I was like most of my class: "ethnic" instead
of old-line WASP, smack dab in the middle of the middle class, and
a little rough around the edges in social situations. Vassar, at that
time still a tony women-only college that boasted Jane Fonda as an
alumna, was nearby, but Marist guys were not considered prizes at
Vassar dances. The Ivy Leaguers up from Princeton or down from
Cornell got the dates; we were treated like the help. Our clever
response to such snobbery? We overturned the punchbowl . . .
thus proving their point!

Rather than taking his Harvard degree and remaking himself as a serious newsman, O'Reilly had other ideas. One was to run for Congress as a
Republican. The other was to turn the Harvard credential, in effect, against
it. "I'm not sure where the business is going, but my gut says it's going in
the direction of Rush, and man, I'm going to be there," he confided to a
friend, according to the *Boston Globe.* Soon thereafter O'Reilly met Roger
Ailes, and the two forged a professional marriage made in hell.

O'Reilly, whose monologues seem self-consciously punctuated by "dis"
and "dat," rather than "this" and "that," presents himself as a spokesman for
"the folks," average Americans, railing against liberal elites, political elites,
and occasionally corporate elites. The perception that he is an average Joe
is central to O'Reilly's claim to be, as the title of his most recent book suggests, "looking out for you." Among other things, *Who's Looking Out for
You?* is a catalog of real or imagined social slights directed against O'Reilly.
"Now, I rarely go to parties, primarily because I'm not invited," he wrote.
Yet there are painful wannabe scenes where O'Reilly gets to meet Bill
Clinton, Tina Brown, and Queen Noor of Jordan.[16] When ABC's Barbara
Walters graces his show to promote her big interviews, O'Reilly beams with
awkward self-satisfaction, even as Walters corrects his facts on air.

To burnish his everyman credentials, O'Reilly fetishizes his working-
class upbringing, telling interviewers he grew up in Levittown on Long
Island, a quintessentially working-class suburb of the postwar period. Yet an
article in the December 2000 *Washington Post* quoted O'Reilly's mother as

saying he actually grew up in neighboring Westbury, a richer suburb, where he attended Catholic school. In that school, he wrote, "I was in with a bunch of Garden City rich kids, and the culture gap was huge. I had one sport jacket from Modell's; they had six sports jackets from Saks. And they made fun of my one sport jacket from Modell's, and I punched them in the mouth."[17]

Though he makes in the range of $10 million per year from his combined enterprises—the FOX show; a nationally syndicated radio show; a syndicated column; best-selling books; and speaking fees that are, he claims, second only to President Clinton's—he says he still lives simply. "What we [he and his wife] don't buy is a list that is almost un-American; since we don't fall for the $4 frappacinos or the $400 cashmere scarves: no designer coffee, tobacco products, furs, jewelry, trendy cars, shirts with polo ponies on them, souvenirs of any kind from anywhere, expensive barbecue grill or tools, first-class airline tickets, silk or linen clothing, or any product at all labeled 'gourmet' or 'fat-free,'" he wrote in *The O'Reilly Factor*. "And you won't catch either of us wearing clothing with a logo; for advertising the manufacturer, we expect the clothing gratis!" When caught by a reporter stepping into a limousine, O'Reilly claimed there had been a "mix-up" with the car. Another time, he caught himself lying: "I have a little Honda . . . well, not really. But I have a sedan, all right, just a small sedan."[18] (While Limbaugh lets his listeners know about his lavish Palm Beach estate, FOX's Sean Hannity—who makes in the neighborhood of $10 million per year—follows O'Reilly's poor-man shtick, mentioning Hamburger Helper suppers, his beat-up Jeep, and his two pairs of shoes.)

The *Factor* is now the top-rated show in cable news, reaching more than two million viewers per night; but because of the way the media climate has been altered by cable, radio, and Internet in the past fifteen years, its impact is much larger than *The Morton Downey Show*'s ever was. "O'Reilly is a big, big factor in politics today," Howard Fineman of *Newsweek* has said. According to the *Boston Globe*, "O'Reilly may just be the future of broadcast news." And O'Reilly says of his show: "It's the most powerful news program in the country as far as effecting change."

At least once, O'Reilly has admitted his core audience is "moderate conservatives," though to fuel the fantasy that he is an "equal opportunity provocateur," he also has maintained it is "47 percent Democrat," citing a survey by the Pew Research Center. The center found that 56 percent of O'Reilly viewers say they are conservative, and only 5 percent say they are liberal; it never asked party affiliation. Still, there is no question that O'Reilly reaches a large segment of moderate and independent viewers with his messaging.

On both economics and social policy, O'Reilly is a right-winger, and he has strongly defended the Bush administration against critics. "I'll submit to you that George W. Bush is the closest modern president to what the Founding Fathers had in mind," he said. Another time, O'Reilly opined: "I'm telling you that President Bush is doing just what Jesus would have done." O'Reilly was a major supporter of the Bush tax-cutting plans, which disproportionately benefited the well-off like himself. "It is your money that is being flushed down the john, and the process is never-ending," he declared. He routinely misinforms his audience about the tax burden on the middle class, sometimes claiming that it is twice what it actually is.[19]

The show is not as one-note ideological or as reliably partisan as Limbaugh's, which may be why it does not work nearly as well on radio as it does on television. Though he has assailed the environmental movement, O'Reilly has said he "believes in" global warming, and he opposes the death penalty—but only because it is "too lenient a punishment." O'Reilly advocates a "gulag" instead.

On other subjects, O'Reilly appears to be to the right of Limbaugh, who does not talk much about religion. "I am the only commentator on television at this point that routinely attacks the secularists," he said. O'Reilly campaigns for school prayer and features "stories" such as "anti-Catholic art at Princeton." One show asked, "Tonight: Is God on America's Side in the Iraq Situation?"

Unlike Limbaugh, O'Reilly builds the show on brash, quicksilver confrontations with guests, most of whom disagree with him. Each of these segments is an exercise in domination and humiliation. Without liberal punching-bag guests, who are hectored, interrupted, and insulted, O'Reilly would not have a show. Though he has said, "I've never attacked anybody personally on this program ever," guests have been called "insane," "idiot," "geek" "dopey," and "stupid."

Following in the Morton Downey tradition, O'Reilly stacks the show with convicted sex offenders, members of the North American Man-Boy

Love Association, purveyors of the "lesbian Barbie Doll," and defenders of terrorist tactics by environmental radicals as representing the "liberal" side of the debate. Interviewing the author of *Conversations with a Pedophile*, O'Reilly demanded, "Did he come off as a homosexual?"

In his book *The No Spin Zone: Confrontations with the Powerful and Famous in America*, O'Reilly reprints transcripts from his favorite interviews. The subjects range from "sexual deviants who prey on children" to "sex ed in your child's classroom," "violence and sleaze in our living rooms," "the legacy of Bill Clinton," "tough talk on moms, kids, and work," "taxes in America," "America's drug culture," and "not liking O'Reilly." Among the guests are Dr. Joycelyn Elders, the former surgeon general of the United States; former New York governor Mario Cuomo; actress Susan Sarandon; activist Al Sharpton; former Clinton strategist James Carville; and CBS anchor Dan Rather. O'Reilly includes a fake interview with Hillary Clinton, "America's most dangerous politician," under the header "It Would Take a Village to Drag Hillary into the No Spin Zone." O'Reilly proudly claims, "I have pounded this woman into pudding," though she was not there for the pounding.

O'Reilly adds to the conventional list of conservative bugaboos—"pointy-headed" professors, "political correctness," the "incredibly vicious" ACLU, Hollywood celebrities, and the civil rights movement—a virulent strain of anti-immigration sentiment, recalling the nativist history of the old Right that many modern-day conservatives eschew. On the air, he has referred to Mexicans who cross the U.S. border illegally as "wetbacks." Attacking "the demonizers, the witch hunters" who criticized him afterward, O'Reilly lied about the exchange, claiming that the guest, a Democratic member of Congress, had used the "wetback" remark.[20] According to the *Morning Call* newspaper in Allentown, Pennsylvania, O'Reilly had used the derisive term previously in a speech before a local political group.

Race and sex are at the core of O'Reilly's broadcasts. "We do more reporting on race on 'The Factor' than any other program in America," O'Reilly has said. Much of this "reporting" comprises attacks on the country's African American leaders, particularly Jesse Jackson. Playing Joe McCarthy, O'Reilly hinted darkly, "We have his tax returns . . . he won't discuss them." According to O'Reilly, "We have black leaders in this country who blame everything on Whitey, everything's the system's fault, and that gives a built-in excuse to fail and act irresponsible. 'Oh, I can't get a job. Whitey won't let me,' or 'I can't get educated. The teachers are bad, so I'm going to go out and get high and sell drugs. That's the only way we can make money here.'"

On one show, O'Reilly asked, "Will African Americans break away from the pack-thinking and reject immorality—because that's the reason the family's breaking apart: alcohol, drugs, infidelity. You have to reject that, and it doesn't seem—and I'm broadly speaking here, but a lot of African Americans won't reject it." He has observed, "I've been to Africa three times, all right? You can't bring Western reasoning into the culture, the same way you can't bring it to fundamentalist Islam."[21] He also has wondered when blacks "will start thinking for themselves."

The O'Reilly Factor contains a chapter called "The Sex Factor," in which the author describes the United States as a "sex madhouse." He lists a "back up stat" that does not back up him up: "For example, *American Demographics* magazine reports that the average American adult—man or woman, heterosexual or homosexual, foot fetishist or 'lipstick lesbian'— reports fifty-eight 'sexual episodes' a year. Using my calculator, this came out to slightly more than once a week."

As part of his effort to distinguish himself occasionally from the conservative line, O'Reilly has claimed to be tolerant of homosexuality and an advocate of "basic rights" for gays. Yet there are limits to O'Reilly's tolerance. He told one lesbian activist on the show, "I wouldn't let you anywhere near my seven-year-old, with all due respect." Of Gay Pride parades, he said, "People who see that have a right to not like homosexuals the way they're being portrayed in the parade. . . . They have an absolute right to condemn that behavior, to say it's corrupting to my children, I don't want to see it, and if this is what the gay pride thing is all about, then *blank* them."[22] "Guys should not walk down the street holding hands," he instructed one guest. "Don't flaunt it, don't dress up like Dolly Parton," he advised another.

Along with pedophilia, transsexuality—a rare occurrence in the population—is an O'Reilly fixation. "I'm not a gal until I move to San Francisco," he proclaimed one night. "If I'm out of work, I'll become a gal and move to San Francisco and sue!"

O'Reilly uses the show to promote right-wing political activism among his audience. GOP Representative Tom Feeney appeared on the show to launch Washington Waste Watchers, a group that "reminds bureaucrats that we're watching what they do with our tax dollars." In California, he tried to force authorities to release the amount of money paid to a public defender in a celebrated murder case. He featured the founder of a Web site called NoIndoctrination.org, a vehicle for harassing campus "left-wingers."

O'Reilly insists "The spin stops here!," rails against the "intellectual dishonesty" of the "liberal" media, and claims that his show is highly rated owing to "superior reporting." He denounces "despicable people," "selfish, manipulative people," and "untrustworthy people." "There is dignity in honesty," he has written.

Yet O'Reilly misinforms his viewers with astonishing regularity. A May/June 2002 report by FAIR documented more than eight false statements made by O'Reilly over several months, including wildly overstating how many single mothers receive welfare; overstating the percentage of blacks who attend college in Florida; overstating the amount of foreign aid given by the United States; misrepresenting the terms of the 2000 Camp David negotiations; falsely claiming that blacks make less money than whites because they don't stay in committed relationships; inflating the amount of money the government spends on antipoverty programs; and wrongly stating that conservatives do not appear on NPR. Most often, O'Reilly's falsehoods emerge in clashes with liberal guests, whom O'Reilly blasts as "wrong," "bogus," and "socialist."[23] When he is offered data that does not support his presumptions, he yells, "Dat's a socialist stat!"

The author of the FAIR report, Peter Hart, expanded it into a 151-page book, *The Oh Really? Factor,* which listed a truly staggering number of O'Reilly falsehoods. "What struck me most, and should bring pause to everyone who reads this book, is the cavalier manner in which O'Reilly routinely lies, exaggerates, and misstates the truth," media historian Robert W. McChesney wrote in the book's introduction. "It is one thing to make misstatements on a daily TV program; that is going to happen periodically under the best of circumstances. But O'Reilly does so repeatedly and shamelessly. O'Reilly's disinterest in truth, in principle, in interrogating his own assumptions and in intellectual consistency is little short of breathtaking."

O'Reilly seems especially incapable of telling the truth when it comes to his own career. For example, he claimed that the *Orange County Register* had dropped his syndicated column "because I was in favor of the war." Yet the paper stopped running the column months before the war began. The paper's editorial director wrote, "The columns were more and more about Bill O'Reilly and Bill O'Reilly's television show and what happened to Bill O'Reilly on Bill O'Reilly's television show. In short, all about Bill." O'Reilly has claimed that he cannot get booked on NPR. However, Peter Hart reproduced an e-mail to O'Reilly from a producer of the NPR show *On the Media*, who noted, "You've turned down requests to be on our show" and called his complaints "self-serving bull."[24]

When confronted on a C-SPAN call-in show about a comparison he had made on *The O'Reilly Factor* of the Koran to Adolf Hitler's *Mein Kampf*, O'Reilly denied making the comparison and interrupted, "No, ya can't finish! Because once ya lie, you're out of the box!" When the C-SPAN host asked if he wanted to respond substantively, O'Reilly barked, "To what? He's an idiot." But the caller was correct. On his show, O'Reilly had said, "I wouldn't read [the Koran]. And I'll tell you why, I wouldn't have read *Mein Kampf* either. If I were going to UNC in 1941 and you, professor, said, 'Read *Mein Kampf*,' I would have said, 'Hey, professor, with all due respect, shove it! I ain't readin' it.'"[25]

O'Reilly claims to "like a robust debate" and says "dissent is good." Yet he repeatedly squashes debate and ridicules dissenters. Antiwar demonstrators are "dishonest, disgusting, un-American," he charged, later amending that to "bad Americans." Protesters should be "condemned by Americans and shunned." Judges with whom he disagrees are denounced by name as "subversive." When losing a debate, he will interrupt with, "Look, you don't like the country, take a bus to Mexico!" or, "That's Fascism and it's wrong," or, "We're going to liberate Iraq no matter what propaganda you spew," or simply, "My butt!" and then will abruptly end the interview.

One evening, O'Reilly issued the following edict:

Once the war against Saddam begins, we expect every American to support our military, and if they can't do that, to shut up. Americans, and indeed, our allies who actively work against our military once the war is underway will be considered enemies of the state by me.

O'Reilly has used his power to attack and chill the expression of other commentators. During the war, for several nights running O'Reilly assailed antiwar columnist Robert Scheer of the *Los Angeles Times* as a "fanatical left-winger," a "traitor," someone who holds "anti-American motives," and whom "many perceive to be a hater of the USA." Scheer is "a hater of the U.S., he hates his country!" If the *Los Angeles Times* became any more left-wing, "they'll have to put a hammer and sickle on the news head," he said.

O'Reilly says he doesn't "bully" guests. Yet this was the exchange when O'Reilly booked Jeremy M. Glick, an opponent of the war on Iraq whose father was killed in the September 11 terrorist attacks:

GLICK: Well, actually my father thought that Bush's presidency was illegitimate. . . .

O'REILLY: All right, I don't want to—

GLICK: Maybe—

O'REILLY: I don't want to talk politics with you.

GLICK: Well, why not? This is about world politics.

O'REILLY: Because, number one, I don't really care what you think.

GLICK: Well, okay.

O'REILLY: You're, I want to—

GLICK: But you do care because you—

O'REILLY: No, no, look—

GLICK: The reason you care is because you evoke 9/11—

O'REILLY: Here's why I care—

GLICK: —to rationalize—

O'REILLY: Here's why I care—

GLICK: Let me finish. You evoke 9/11 to rationalize everything from domestic plunder to imperialistic aggression worldwide.

O'REILLY: Okay. That's a bunch—

GLICK: You evoke sympathy with the 9/11 families—

O'REILLY: That's a bunch of crap. I've done more for the 9/11 families by their own admission—I've done more for them than you will ever hope to do.

GLICK: Okay.

O'REILLY: So you keep your mouth shut when you sit here exploiting those people.

GLICK: Well, you're not representing me. You're not representing me.
O'REILLY: And I'd never represent you, you know why?
GLICK: Why?
O'REILLY: Because you have a warped view of this world and a warped view of this country— Cut his mike. I'm not going to dress you down anymore, out of respect for your father.

When the cameras turned off, O'Reilly screamed, "Get out, get out of my studio before I tear you to fucking pieces!" The next night, O'Reilly denounced Glick on the air as "out of control and spewing hatred." He then lied, saying Glick had "accused President Bush of knowing about 9/11 before it happened."[26]

Bruce Kluger was invited on *The Factor* to discuss a critical piece he had written about the show in *USA Today*. "In the nine minutes, 58 seconds we were on the air, O'Reilly resorted to playground pejoratives no fewer than 20 times, calling me, among other things, 'cheap,' 'sleazy,' 'foolish,' and 'a left-wing journalist out for blood.' At one point he even referred to me as a 'weasel'—the name he had reserved for actor George Clooney—but then took it back," Kluger reported in the *Los Angeles Times*.

O'Reilly presents himself as a champion of civil discourse. "It makes me sick to see intellectually dishonest individuals hide behind the First Amendment to spread propaganda, libel, and slander," he told the *Daily News*. "But this is a growing trend in America, where the exchange of ideas often degenerates into verbal mud wrestling with intent to injure." Yet one of O'Reilly's favored tactics is to tell his guests to "shut up." Responding to critics who have questioned this tactic, O'Reilly said on his show that "the 'shut up' line has happened only once in six years." Jack Shafer of *Slate* printed twenty-nine incidents where O'Reilly had directed the phrase on the air to "Al Franken, Tom Daschle, Jimmy Carter, Rosie O'Donnell, gay people who talk about their sexual orientation, atheist Scouts, peaceniks, both [political] parties. . . ."[27]

O'Reilly's belligerence appears to be a product of his upbringing. "My father didn't tell me anything. My father just said, 'Shut up,'" he has said. In a 2003 interview with Terry Gross on NPR's *Fresh Air*, O'Reilly offered a rare glimpse of his personal history. In Catholic school, he said, he grew tired of the authorities "putting me in a closet and putting me in the dumb row," though he also credits this mistreatment as a form of discipline. "I'd be in a penitentiary right now without [it]," he told Gross.

Before O'Reilly abruptly terminated the interview when Gross challenged him about his habit of using his TV show to personally attack book reviewers who haven't liked his work, O'Reilly revealed to Gross that as a child he had been subjected to excessively punitive and unnecessary corporal punishment from his father. "It was a very tough environment," he said, though he went on to deny that he was "abused." O'Reilly told Gross that when he was seventeen, he incited a physical brawl with his father, punching him and breaking lamps in the house. "The physical stuff had to stop," he told Gross.

In *The O'Reilly Factor*, O'Reilly wrote that his father's child-rearing practices "would have won praise from Mussolini." He described growing up under a "rigid, sometimes brutal regime." "In our house there were never any 'time-outs' but plenty of 'knockouts.'" Young Bill would "quake" in his room, awaiting "punishment" to be meted out, according to his account. "Next I heard my father's footsteps on the stairs. Decades later I can still hear my father's footsteps on the stairs," he wrote. One time, his father "shocked [him] nearly senseless." "I expected only one thing from my dad," he wrote. "Leave me alive to celebrate my next birthday."

"Forget all the bad stuff they did to you when you were a kid," O'Reilly advises readers in a chapter called "The Parents Factor." O'Reilly has not forgotten. Yet if such issues linger in his psyche, he appears unlikely to seek professional help. "Maybe my rough edges are a reaction to the way my father's generation had to live," O'Reilly concludes. "I'm not paying any shrink to find out."

CHAPTER FOURTEEN
DIRTY BOOKS

FOR MORE THAN FIFTY YEARS, conservative book publishing—books published by and for conservatives—has been a critical means of spreading the word while bypassing the editorial standards, tastes, and traditional market mechanisms of mainstream publishing. Until more recently, the vast majority of conservative books were not published by regular book publishers or sold in regular bookstores. In the 1950s and 1960s, conservatives set up their own publishing houses, mainly to service academics and writers connected with new periodicals, such as *National Review* and *Human Events*, who could not attract established publishers. Like followers of occultism, conservatives established their own bookstores and book clubs because existing stores did not stock their work. Many conservative activists like Phyllis Schlafly resorted to self-publishing their books and distributing them through right-wing political clubs.

Classic works published by Henry Regnery Sr., who founded a publishing company in 1947, formed the intellectual underpinnings of the nascent conservative movement. These included Russell Kirk's *The Conservative Mind*, William Buckley's *God and Man at Yale*, Whittaker Chambers's *Witness*, and Barry Goldwater's *The Conscience of a Conservative*.

Arlington House, a publishing company founded in New Rochelle, New York, by the Buckley family, brought out titles "with less mainstream appeal," as Alan Crawford put it in *Thunder on the Right*. Some of these were *Hippies, Drugs, and Promiscuity; How to Survive in Your Liberal School;* and *None Dare Call It Witchcraft*. Right-wing activists founded Green Hill Publications in Illinois to publish *The Gun Owners Political Action Manual; How to Start Your Own School;* and North Carolina Senator Jesse Helms's *When Free Men Shall Stand*.[1]

"If a person with right-wing sympathies . . . wanted more information or more verbal ammunition," George Thayer reported in *The Farther Shores of Politics*, "he might write away to Jab A Liberal Series (Arcadia, California), Tapes for Patriots (Houston), or Fight Communism Stickers (Minneapolis). Undoubtedly he would be in contact with Suppressed Books (Shreveport, Louisiana), the Joe McCarthy Bookstore (Boston), and the Patrick Henry Book Store (Los Angeles) as well as two of the largest publishers and distributors of right-wing material in the country: Omni Publications (Hawthorne, California) and The Bookmailer (Linden, New Jersey)." The John Birch Society opened American Opinion Bookstores around the country, while the Reverend Billy James Hargis's Christian Crusade published such works as *The Real Extremists: The Far Left* and *Communism, Hypnotism and the Beatles*, which argued that "Communists have a master music plan for American youth designed to make them mentally ill and emotionally unstable."

The 1964 presidential campaign of Barry Goldwater was the occasion for a flood of proselytizing books, many of them purchased in bulk and turned into best-sellers by wealthy conservatives and right-wing organizations that distributed them for free at Goldwater events. Phyllis Schlafly's self-published *A Choice, Not an Echo* was issued that year, selling six million copies, distributed primarily by the John Birch Society and pro-Goldwater groups. *LBJ: A Political Biography*, which compared LBJ to Hitler and Mussolini, was published by the racist Liberty Lobby, which distributed ten million copies before the election at every convention hall and motel lobby where conservatives gathered. Perhaps the most famous of these tomes was John Stormer's *None Dare Call It Treason*, which sold more than six million copies in eight months, also through John Birch Society channels.

Stormer, a Baptist pastor and the state chairman of the Missouri Young Republicans, wrote on the theme that ran through many of these books: The liberal-internationalist-Communist conspiracy was subverting the United States from within. Stormer claimed to offer the "carefully documented story of America's retreat from victory." He argued that the U.S. military had fought on the side of the "communist conspiracy" in World War II and identified the Council on Foreign Relations, an august body of American diplomats and foreign policy experts, as pro-Communist. In his book *The Paranoid Style in American Politics*, Richard Hofstadter pointed to Stormer's heavily "documented" work as a prime example of the style:

> [The paranoid style] is nothing if not scholarly in technique. McCarthy's 96-page pamphlet *McCarthyism* contains no less than 313 footnote references, and [Birch Society leader] Mr. Welch's fantastic assault on Eisenhower, *The Politician,* is weighed down by a hundred pages of bibliography and notes. The entire right-wing movement of our time is a parade of experts, study groups, monographs, footnotes, and bibliographies. . . . What distinguishes the paranoid style is not, then, the absence of verifiable facts (though it is occasionally true that in his extravagant passion for facts the paranoid occasionally manufactures them), but rather the curious leap in imagination that is always made at some critical point in the recital of events.

Today, Stormer's book, with a "25 Years Later" preface, is available for purchase on the John Birch Society Web site, as are *None Dare Call It Conspiracy* (published in 1990) and *The Shadows of Power* (published in 1998)—both of which echo Stormer's thesis of a conspiracy by a shadowy worldwide "establishment" to institute a global Socialist government. Pat Robertson's 1991 *New World Order,* with its anti-Semitic passages, followed in a similar vein.

Though these books appear to sell in some small number, primarily to homeschoolers, the John Birch Society is no longer a force in conservative publishing, much less in the conservative movement. The neoconservative influx into the conservative movement in the mid-1970s brought an understanding that if right-wing attacks on social spending, government regulation, racial and sexual equality, the separation of church and state, science, economic theory, the internationalist foreign policy consensus, the media, and liberal politicians were to be taken seriously, the Right would have to make inroads into the New York publishing industry.

As he did on so many fronts, Irving Kristol led the way. For most of the 1960s, Kristol had served as executive editor of Basic Books, a publisher of books on social policy that became something of an early laboratory for neoconservative thinking. Midge Decter would later serve as a senior editor at the house, while Kristol was replaced by his protégé Erwin A. Glikes, a former academic administrator who was drifting into the neocon orbit as he rose through the ranks of publishers row. Glikes would bring a long list of conservative writers into mainstream publishing and make a pile of money doing it.

It all began in 1982, when a then obscure professor at the University of Chicago, Allan Bloom, wrote an article in *National Review* bemoaning the state of higher education in the United States. At the time, Bloom, a philosophy professor and mentor to a younger generation of neocons who studied under him, was the co-director of the John M. Olin Center for Inquiry into the Theory and Practice of Democracy. His faculty friend, the novelist Saul Bellow, encouraged Bloom to turn the article into a book proposal. Bloom followed Bellow's advice and took the proposal to Glikes, who had published his translations of Greek philosophy at Basic Books. Glikes had moved on to become a senior executive at Simon & Schuster.

Bloom's 1987 book, *The Closing of the American Mind,* an attack on cultural relativism and the idea of equality, was a number one *New York Times* best-seller and made the author a millionaire. Passionate debate followed, with Bloom's credentials as a scholar coming in for heavy criticism, especially from his academic peers. Bloom's was a book "decent people would be ashamed of having written," wrote critic David Rieff. But because it was a moneymaker—as Limbaugh changed radio and as FOX News changed cable—*The Closing of the American Mind* changed the publishing industry.

By the time Bloom's book landed in stores, Glikes had acquired his own imprint, the Free Press, then part of Macmillan Publishing. Glikes had chafed for years at Simon & Schuster, where, he charged, the sales force had been hostile to marketing right-wing books, such as Norman Podhoretz's 1980 volume, *The Present Danger,* an alarmist accounting of the

Soviet military buildup, that provided grist for the Reagan campaign. Glikes wanted the authority to control his own sales force and promotional budgets; as the man who discovered Allan Bloom, he could command it. At the Free Press, with Saul Bellow's son Adam serving as his apprentice, Glikes identified a market for conservative books that had existed for decades but had never been served by mainstream publishing, bringing out books by Robert Bork, George Will, Dinesh D'Souza, William Bennett, Francis Fukuyama, Robert Bartley, and Charles Murray. All but Bartley's became best-sellers.

Glikes was interested in more than sales. Like Irving Kristol, who had arranged for the private financing and publication by Basic of Jude Wanniski's supply-side economics tract, *The Way the World Works*, in 1978, Glikes was engaged in political and cultural warfare; he saw books as vehicles to move public discourse to the right. Because he was oriented toward the established media institutions of the East Coast and was a learned man, he was attracted to books that advanced conservative ideas, and he carefully tailored them to be well received in publications that set intellectual trends, such as the *New York Times* and *The New Republic*. George Will, who had columns in the *Washington Post* and in *Newsweek*, became a reliable puffer of these books, as did the *Wall Street Journal* editorial page, which controlled the newspaper's books section.[2]

As a successful publisher, Glikes also was concerned with the bottom line. He acquired most of his books cheaply, which he was able to do because so many of his authors—including Bork, D'Souza, Murray, and Fukuyama—had subsidized sinecures within the right-wing think tank network. The think tanks paid the authors' salaries, awarded research grants, provided support staff, and established marketing and public relations funds to supplement the budgets of the commercial publishers. In 1978, Kristol funneled $40,000 in foundation money to Wanniski; by the late 1990s, as Eric Alterman reported, "Dinesh D'Souza enjoyed $483,023 at AEI; Irving Kristol $380,600 also at AEI; Robert Bork managed to scare up $459,777 for his office at [AEI]; and William Bennett, also at Heritage, garnered $275,000 in addition to his considerable book earnings."[3] Liberal foundations did not respond in kind.

Right-wing foundations stepped in to fill the role played during an earlier era by the freelancing right-wing millionaires who had bought up large quantities of books and distributed them through political clubs. The Bradley Foundation alone supported four hundred books in fourteen years. "We have the conviction that most of the other media are derivative from books," Bradley president Michael Joyce told Eric Alterman. "Books are the way that authors put forth more substantial, more coherent arguments. It follows that if you want to have an influence on the world of ideas, books are where you want to put your money."[4]

The Web site MediaTransparency.org lists an array of such promotional and distribution schemes for books that otherwise would have very limited—if any—appeal in the market. They included "a publicity campaign for the book *The Secret World of American Communism*," funded by Olin; "support for the [Bradley foundation's] purchase and distribution of *Creating Equal*"; $88,200 "to support the distribution of the book *Not Yet 'Free at Last'*" by Bradley; Bradley's "purchase and distribution of *The March of Freedom*" by Heritage president Ed Feulner; "marketing and distribution of *The Thirty Years War*" by GOP activist Tom Pauken; grants to the Foundation for Economic Education and the Institute for Contemporary Studies for "Promotion Distribution and Implementation of Policy Recommendations in Books" by the Scaife-controlled Carthage Foundation; "distribution of *Eco-Sanity*" by Bradley; Olin's "publication and distribution of *The Ratification of the Bill of Rights: 1789–91*"; $25,000 from Olin to support "the distribution of *How the Relentless Growth of Government Is Impoverishing America*" by the Club for Growth's Stephen Moore; "promotion of the book *Exhibitionism: Art in an Era of Intolerance*" by Bradley; Olin's $25,000 "promotion of *Ronald Reagan: How an Extraordinary Man Became an Extraordinary Leader*," a best-seller by Dinesh D'Souza; Olin's "promotion of two books, *The Diversity Myth* and *The Melting Pot*"; $180,000 for "two fellowships and the promotion of *America in Black and White*" by Stephan and Abigail Thernstrom; Olin's "promotion of the ideas in the book *Who Stole Feminism?*" by Christina Hoff Sommers"; "printing and distribution of book entitled *Memoirs of a Dissident Publisher*" by Henry Regnery"; and so on.

In 2002, *Philanthropy* magazine, published by the right-wing Philanthropy Roundtable, ran a cover story titled "Eight Books That Changed America," written by John J. Miller, a writer for *National Review* and "Bradley fellow" at the Heritage Foundation. Each of the eight books was substantially underwritten by the Four Sisters—the same four family foundations that supported the think tank network. According to *Philanthropy*, Myron Magnet's *The Dream and the Nightmare*, a repudiation of the 1960s, "would not have been written without the Sarah Scaife Foundation, a supporter of the Manhattan Institute's book program in the early 1990s." *Politics, Markets and America's Schools*, a book promoting school choice that was written by two scholars at the Brookings Institution, was supported by the Olin Foundation. "We were interested in getting these ideas ensconced at liberal places," said Olin's executive director, Jim Piereson. D'Souza's *Illiberal Education* "might not have been written but for the support of the Olin foundation, which agreed to fund D'Souza's position at AEI without knowing precisely what he would do there." *Free to Choose*, a free market economics tract by Milton and Rose D. Friedman, was compiled from the transcripts of a PBS series by the same name paid for by the Scaife and Olin foundations. Richard John Neuhaus, a Catholic priest and founder of the Olin and Bradley foundation–funded Center on Religion and Society, published *The Naked Public Square*, an attack on the separation of church and state. "We used the Center's facilities, coordinated efforts with the publisher, pushed the book and its argument in our newsletter—the usual promotional racket," Neuhaus said.

When Erwin Glikes died in 1994, Adam Bellow took the reins at the Free Press, but he had difficulty following in Glikes's footsteps and departed as the imprint returned to its nonpartisan traditions. Conservative publishing was changing: The phenomenal success of right-wing radio and the advent of opinion talk shows on cable created new media personalities and new cross-marketing opportunities that did not fit the comparatively gentlemanly Free Press style. Other publishers who had more money for advances, an intrinsic understanding of the down-market world of radio, and closer ties to the conservative movement moved in on the profitable Free Press turf and hit the jackpot.

One of these was HarperCollins Publishers, now owned by Rupert Murdoch, and in particular an imprint there under the direction of Judith Regan. Regan's background as a former reporter for the *National Enquirer* could not have been more different from that of Glikes and Bellow. Even as it moved to the right, the Free Press had tried to maintain editorial standards. When Dinesh D'Souza's second book, *The End of Racism,* was found to contain errors after it went to press, the flawed batch was junked, and the book was reprinted. The Free Press rejected a fallacious "biography" of Bill Clinton titled *Boy Clinton,* submitted by R. Emmett Tyrrell of *The American Spectator,* but Regan had no such inhibitions. Murdoch saw journalism as nothing but a commodity; Regan had the same view of books.

Though she attended Vassar College, Regan's upbringing was decidedly less tony, and she shared the class and status anxiety of everyone who succeeded in the Murdoch empire, from Murdoch himself to Roger Ailes and Bill O'Reilly on down. A notoriously foul-mouthed divorcée who saw politics and popular culture in terms of sexual domination and exploitation, Regan had the Murdoch knack for appealing to the vulgar tastes of the mass market. For instance, she was known for choosing author photos based on whether potential readers would want to "fuck" the writers.[5] When she moved to HarperCollins from Simon & Schuster, where she had published runaway best-sellers by Rush Limbaugh and Howard Stern, Murdoch gave Regan an imprint called ReganBooks and a weekend TV show on the FOX News Channel: *This Evening with Judith Regan.* Press accounts said her imprint was responsible for as much as 25 percent of HarperCollins's revenues.

In addition to *365 Glorious Nights of Love & Romance, Down & Dirty Sex Secrets, The Happy Hooker, Sex Tips for Straight Women from a Gay Man,* the "Zone" diet, and the novels of Jackie Collins, Regan brought to the bookstores Sean Hannity's *Let Freedom Ring,* Peggy Noonan's *The Case Against Hillary Clinton,* and Dick Morris's *Off with Their Heads.* Fact-checking Hannity's book in an investigation for *Salon,* Ben Fritz and Bryan Keefer demonstrated that it was "a poorly researched effort full of blatant falsehoods and highly distorted versions of the truth."[6] Noonan and Morris were no more reliable; all three authors were best-sellers, peddling their work on the FOX News Channel, where two of the three were employed. For books that did not sell well but did serve the right-wing cause, Regan applied Murdoch's *New York Post/Weekly Standard* loss-leader strategy. These included Midge Decter's *An Old Wife's Tale* and *Rumsfeld: A Personal Portrait; How Ronald Reagan Changed My Life* by Peter Schweizer of the Hoover Institution; and FOX News contributor Linda

Chavez's *An Unlikely Conservative*. The Regan books varied widely in quality: Decter is a masterful polemicist; Noonan is an interesting if weird stylist; and Hannity writes like the college dropout he is.

One of the least noticed but most influential books to come out of Regan's shop was *Bush vs. the Beltway: How the CIA and the State Department Tried to Stop the War on Terror*. It was written by Laurie Mylroie, a neoconservative Middle East specialist affiliated with the American Enterprise Institute and its band of Iraq war hawks, including Richard Perle and current Undersecretary of State John Bolton. An article in *The Washington Monthly* by Peter Bergen, a journalist and noted expert on Osama bin Laden who teaches at John Hopkins University, referred to Mylroie as the "neocons' favorite conspiracy theorist." Bergen contended persuasively that the idea that Saddam Hussein was responsible for anti-U.S. terrorism had come from an earlier Mylroie book, *The War Against America: Saddam Hussein and the World Trade Center Attacks: A Study of Revenge*, which posited Iraqi complicity in the 1993 bombing of the World Trade Center. "Virtually all evidence and expert opinion" contradicted Mylroie's thesis, which was nonetheless embraced by key neocon foreign policy figures, including top Pentagon official Paul Wolfowitz and the current chief of staff to Vice President Dick Cheney. As an extension of *The War Against America*, Mylroie pushed the theory that the mastermind behind the September 11, 2001, attacks was an Iraqi intelligence agent; when no evidence could be found to bear that out, she wrote *Bush vs. the Beltway*, confecting a conspiracy among U.S. officials to thwart a thorough investigation. "She is, in short, a crackpot, which would not be significant if she were merely advising, say Lyndon LaRouche," Bergen wrote.[7]

Meanwhile, the oldest conservative publisher in the country, Regnery, had been greatly diminished in the 1980s and early 1990s by the success of the Free Press. Adding to its troubles was that the business had been inherited by Henry Regnery's sons. One son, Alfred Regnery, was a Justice Department official in the Reagan administration who resigned his post when the press reported that a stash of hard-core pornography had been found in his home during a police investigation of a claim made by Regnery's wife that she had been sexually assaulted by an intruder. At the time, Regnery had been advising a Reagan antipornography campaign on behalf of Attorney General Edwin Meese.[8]

The second heir to the Regnery publishing fortune was Alfred's brother, William, who partly funds the Charles Martel Society, named for an eighth-century Frankish warrior whose successful battles are regarded as the reason Christians, rather than Muslims, rule Europe. The society was created to give American racists the trappings of a research institute and a "scholarly" journal, *Occidental Quarterly*. In an essay in that publication, William Regnery proposed chopping up the United States into separate ethnic and racial enclaves, creating a new, all-white sovereign state. The Southern Poverty Law Center has put the Charles Martel Society on its list of hate groups.[9]

After leaving the Reagan administration, Alfred Regnery, as Regnery's chief executive, turned to publishing political pornography. But he had little success until 1993, when the company was rescued by Tom Phillips—a major Republican Party donor who owned Eagle Publishing, which published *Human Events* and right-wing newsletters like the *Evans-Novak Political Report*. Phillips owned the Conservative Book Club, with 108,000 members, founded during the Goldwater campaign of 1964 as "America was walking down Lyndon Johnson's path to a socialist Great Society." The Christian Family Book Club was also an Eagle property. "But perhaps most significant—given the central role direct mail has played in the conservative resurgence of recent decades—is Eagle's list brokerage operation, which rents out Eagle's own customer lists and those of organizations like Newt Gingrich's GOPAC, Empower America, the Western Journalism Center, and the Ronald Reagan Presidential Foundation, not to mention Pat Buchanan's American Cause and the Steve Forbes for President campaign," reported Nicholas Confessore in *The American Prospect*.[10]

Unlike the old Regnery of the 1950s, the new Regnery published few if any books with intellectual or journalistic merit. Most of the books are facsimiles of the Bircher literature transported forty years to the present. They are so replete with falsehoods, gaps in rudimentary logic, and bizarre allegations—most of it in the "reported" or "documented" paranoid style described so well by Richard Hofstadter—that they were likely unpublishable anywhere else.

In the overheated media climate of the 1990s, as conservatives won dominance of sectors of the media that offered tremendous promotional opportunities, once a right-winger committed something to paper and two

covers were slapped on it—even if it made no sense to a minimally discriminating reader—it could be sold in huge volume. "In fact, nearly all the
conservative authors who made it onto the *New York Times* bestseller list
over the past 52 weeks are either the hosts of or regular guests on a radio
or TV chat show," the *Los Angeles Times* reported in 2003. "We know our
market," Alfred Regnery told the *New York Times*. "It's not uncommon for
a Regnery author to be interviewed on 200 to 300 radio shows." Liberal
authors—who have not been tapped to host TV chat shows, have no cable
channel devoted to propagating their views, and are all but shut out of talk
radio—did not enjoy the same competitive advantages.

"It's no exaggeration to describe this surge of conservative publishing as
a paradigm shift," Brian C. Anderson wrote in the *Wall Street Journal's*
OpinionJournal.com. ". . . This 'right-wing media circuit,' as *Publishers
Weekly* describes it, reaches millions of potential readers and thus makes
the traditional gatekeepers of ideas—above all, *The New York Times Book
Review,* and *The New York Review of Books,* publications that rarely deign
to review conservative titles—increasingly irrelevant in winning an audience for a book." Peter Collier, David Horowitz's writing partner who now
runs a small Bradley Foundation–funded publishing house called
Encounter, told Anderson, "A Q&A on National Review Online sells books
very, very well. It's comparable to a major newspaper review." "A bold
Drudge Report headline will move far more copies than even good newspaper reviewers, claims Regnery's Marji Ross," Anderson reported.

It is impossible to compile even a brief catalog of the false information
backloaded into the media by Regnery, whose books mirrored the 1990s
Republican Party strategy of smearing Democrats with phony scandals and
impugning their patriotism. Regnery's biggest seller of the decade, Gary
Aldrich's number one *New York Times* best-selling *Unlimited Access: An
FBI Agent Inside the Clinton White House*—publicized worldwide in both
right-wing and mainstream media—was later reduced to a laughingstock
when the author admitted to *The New Yorker* that his most sensational alle-
gation—that President Bill Clinton was leaving the White House hiding
under a blanket in an unmarked car on his way to sexual trysts in a
Washington hotel—was "hypothetical." In the ensuing controversy,
Regnery himself admitted to "problems" with the book.[11] Yet in 2003,
Aldrich, since embraced by the right wing and installed as the head of the

Patrick Henry Center for Individual Liberty while writing columns for NewsMax.com and Heritage's Townhall.com, was back with another Regnery title, *Thunder on the Left,* described as a "compelling case" that the Democratic Party "represents a clear and present danger to our national security." Aldrich sold the book on FOX's *Hannity & Colmes.*

The Regnery titles alone tell the story: *Partners in Power: The Clintons and Their America; Betrayal: How the Clinton Administration Undermined American Security; Year of the Rat: How Bill Clinton Compromised U.S. Security for Chinese Cash; The Secret Life of Bill Clinton: The Unreported Stories; The Impeachment of William Jefferson Clinton: A Political Docu-Drama; Power Grab: How the National Education Association Is Betraying Our Children; Disney: The Mouse Betrayed; Guns, Crime, and Freedom; Hell to Pay: The Unfolding Story of Hillary Rodham Clinton; Bias: A CBS Insider Exposes How the Media Distort the News; Shut Up and Sing: How Elites from Hollywood, Politics and the U.N. Are Subverting America; Persecution: How Liberals Are Waging a War Against Christianity; Losing Bin Laden: How Bill Clinton's Failures Unleashed Global Terror; Dereliction of Duty: The Eyewitness Account of How Bill Clinton Endangered Long-Term National Security; Invasion: How America Still Welcomes Criminals and Other Foreign Menaces to Our Shores; Icons of Evolution: Science or Myth; Leftism Revisited: From de Sade and Marx to Hitler and Pol Pot; More Guns, Less Crime; The Myth of Heterosexual AIDS; The New Color Line: How Quotas and Privilege Destroy Democracy; Useful Idiots: How Liberals Got It Wrong in the Cold War and Still Blame America First; Legacy: Paying the Price for the Clinton Years;* and *The Final Days: The Last Desperate Abuses of Power by the Clinton White House.*

Many of these books were best-sellers. Through Eagle, Regnery has special access to the Conservative Book Club, which duly features the titles in its solicitations. Like the Book of the Month Club, selection by the club bolsters print runs and sales. "Take 3 books for $1 Each, Plus a Fourth for $7.95," the club announced in a full-page ad in *The Weekly Standard* in July 2003. Over the next two years, club members must buy four more books at full price. Virtually every right-wing Web site, including the high-traffic Drudge Report, carries advertisements for the Conservative Book Club offering such discounted deals.

"If you want books that affirm your beliefs, your principles, your core values, you need look no further," the club's solicitation reads. "Imagine you clandestinely 'acquire' a secret list of the books Geraldo Rivera, Ted Kennedy, Spike Lee, Hillary Clinton, Barbra Streisand, Patricia Ireland, Dick Gephardt, Al Franken, Jesse Jackson, and David Bonior WOULD LIKE TO BURN MOST. All the books we select are guaranteed CONDEMNED by the Washington-Hollywood left-wing axis."

Conservative organizations also mastered the buying of books in bulk orders, which substantially increased the likelihood that right-wing books would make the best-seller list—a strategy first employed by the Nixon White House to push Edith Efron's *The News Twisters* up the charts. Bulk orders are purchases of more than five hundred copies of a book at one time. Because just a few thousand sales in a given week can affect whether or not a book makes the best-seller list, strategically placed bulk sales can make all the difference. The *New York Times* denotes that a book has been bought in bulk by placing a small dagger next to its listing on the best-seller charts. Most right-wing books that make the best-seller list bear the dagger.

Regnery offered for free many right-wing books, even those it did not publish, in massive direct-mail solicitations culled from Regnery's list brokerage operations for new subscriptions to *Human Events*. On its own Web site and across virtually all right-wing Web sites, the Scaife-subsidized NewsMax offered dozens of free books in exchange for a $42.95 subscription to *NewsMax* magazine. In August 2003, these free books included Ann Coulter's *Treason,* Dick Morris's *Off with Their Heads,* and Tammy Bruce's *The Death of Right and Wrong*—all of them best-sellers. In addition, leaders of right-wing organizations appear to buy their own books in bulk and give them away. For example, in December 2003, David Horowitz's Scaife-funded Center for the Study of Popular Culture was offering free copies of his book *Left Illusions* for those who contributed $50 to his FrontPageMag.com.

Liberals had no racket to help them conquer the book market. In fall 2003, several books by liberal authors, including Molly Ivins, Paul Krugman, and Joe Conason, made the best-seller list. None of these books bore the bulk-buying dagger. Nor is there a "liberal book club" to guarantee distribution and spur discounted sales. Because liberal books are generally more honest, more accurate, and of a much higher quality than are right-wing books, liberals apparently do not feel the need to build distribution networks to end-run bookstores.

Another major shift that benefited conservatives was in the retail part of the book business, which had for decades been dominated by discriminating independent owners who appreciated literary merit and original thought. These owners tended not to be right-wingers. By contrast, chain booksellers like Wal-Mart and Internet megastores like Amazon.com—that, combined, now account for a large percentage of total book sales—regard books as no different from any other product; they sell what sells. They also promote books by publishing nonprofessional reviews. "Amazon's Reader Reviews feature—where readers can post their opinions on books they've read and rate them—has helped diminish the authority of elite cultural guardians, too, by creating a truly democratic marketplace of ideas," according to OpinionJournal.com's Anderson. Yet in the realm of ideas, the marketplace has never been a guarantor of quality: In its day, *Mein Kampf* was a best-seller.

By forcing right-wing books up the best-seller charts, conservatives are able to ensure that their messaging—once confined only to the readers of such extremist tracts—was injected into the wider media conversation. And by creating best-selling authors—who march into the studios of such mainstream venues as the network morning shows—they create, brand, and legitimize new pundits.

The infamous pundit Ann Coulter is a case in point. Coulter had been a lawyer, Republican congressional aide, and employee of a Scaife-funded right-wing legal arm before writing *High Crimes and Misdemeanors: The Case Against Bill Clinton,* published by Regnery in 1998. The book was promoted by the Conservative Book Club and by *Human Events;* and it was a beneficiary of bulk buying. The question the country faced regarding Clinton, as Coulter put it, was "to impeach or to assassinate."

Now a best-selling author, throughout the impeachment saga Coulter became a familiar cable guest. In her TV appearances, Coulter labeled Clinton as "crazy," "like a serial killer," "creepier and slimier than Kennedy," "a horny hick," and "white trash." To Coulter, Hillary Clinton was a "prostitute." In a CNN segment about the dragging death of James Byrd, an African American Texan, Coulter fumed, "There is a constitutional right to hate." Such outbursts caused Coulter to lose her regular gig on MSNBC.

For her second book, Coulter moved from Regnery to Murdoch's HarperCollins. When her editor there died, the book was picked up by Crown Publishers, a Random House imprint. As MSNBC tried to out-FOX FOX, now mainstream publishing—theretofore an almost quaint outpost of civility in a media culture gone mad—would try to out-Regnery Regnery. For the right wing, there could not have been a greater imitation in reverse of the New Left's Rudi Dutschke's "long march through the institutions." *Slander: Liberal Lies About the American Right* was published in June 2002 and sold hundreds of thousands of copies.

Perhaps because it bore the imprimatur of a division of Random House, considered one of the highest-quality publishers in the business, *Slander* won some early more or less favorable reviews in the mainstream press, notably a review in the *Los Angeles Times* by Andrew H. Malcolm. "[H]er bright writing, sense of irony and outrage, and her relish at finally hitting back at political opponents (especially in the media) is what make *Slander* such refreshing and provocative reading," he wrote. Malcolm admired Coulter's thirty-six pages of footnotes—as did many other credulous reviewers—and pronounced the book a "clever, documented diatribe." A former *New York Times* writer who is now on the editorial board of the Los Angeles paper, Malcolm had served as "deputy communications director" for the 2000 George W. Bush presidential campaign between his media postings. Bolstered by such reviews, Coulter was hosted on dozens of TV shows across the cable and broadcast dial. Appearing on NBC's *Today* show—a coveted booking for authors—she compared "America's Sweetheart" Katie Couric to Hitler's mistress, Eva Braun.

In *Slander,* Coulter declared that "journalism is war by other means." Given time to scrutinize her ammunition, many reviewers concluded that Coulter was shooting blanks and that a more apt title for the book might have been *Slander: Right-Wing Lies About the American Left.* "The good folks at the *American Prospect*'s Web log 'Tapped' went to the trouble of compiling Coulter's errors chapter by chapter," Eric Alterman wrote in *What Liberal Media?* "The sheer weight of these [errors], coupled with their audacity, demonstrates the moral and intellectual bankruptcy of a journalistic culture that allows her near a microphone, much less a printing press."

The sales of *Slander* inspired Crown officials to charter a new imprint, Crown Forum, dedicated to publishing conservative books. Penguin

Putnam followed with its own conservative imprint. Both Crown and Penguin hired editors from Regnery to handle the books. Bookspan, owner of the Book of the Month Club, announced plans to start a conservative book club to compete with Eagle's operation and hired a former editor of *National Review* to run it. As Crown vice president Steve Ross observed, "The center of the culture has moved to the right."

Now, book publishing would catch up. The first book from Crown Forum was Coulter's third effort, *Treason: Liberal Treachery from the Cold War to the War on Terrorism.* With its attempt to rehabilitate McCarthyism and its attendant accusations of treason—a crime punishable by death—against Democratic Party leaders from Harry Truman to John F. Kennedy, Lyndon Johnson, Hubert Humphrey, Bill Clinton, and Tom Daschle (and by implication all those who supported them), Coulter's *Treason* was an eerie echo of John Stormer's *None Dare Call It Treason.*

Since the publication of Stormer's book in the 1960s, the suspicion that liberals betray and hate the United States had become a rhetorical staple of the right wing. Yet Coulter went a step too far even for her right-wing brethren. Her historical distortions were exposed by several right-wing writers—including David Horowitz, Andrew Sullivan, and a critic on the *Wall Street Journal* editorial page—who used the occasion to distance themselves from similar arguments that they repeatedly make. "Coulter's critics fear that her legions of fans—and lots of others, too—see no appreciable difference between her ill-informed comic diatribes and their high brow ultraserious ones, particularly since Coulter's previous performances were praised by some now on the attack," the historian Sam Tanenhaus wrote in *Slate*. ". . . [Coulter] has exposed the often empty semantic difference between the 'responsible' right and its supposed 'fringe.'"[12]

The conservative backlash did little to temper Coulter; in fact, it may have had the opposite effect. In an August 2003 column about former Vice President Al Gore and California Governor Gray Davis in Horowitz's *FrontPage* magazine, which continued to publish Coulter despite Horowitz's lengthy review exposing *Treason*'s manifest dishonesty, Coulter advocated the assassinations of Gore and Davis, writing, "Both were veterans, after a fashion, of Vietnam, which would make a Gore-Davis presidential ticket the only compelling argument in favor of friendly fire." Conservatives were mum about that column and about another one, an October 2003 anti-Semitic screed that was featured on Heritage's Townhall Web site:

> There's Joe Lieberman: Always Jewish. Wesley Clark: Found Out His Father Was Jewish in College. John Kerry: Jewish Since He Began Presidential Fund-Raising. Howard Dean: Married to a Jew. Al Sharpton: Circumcised. Even Hillary Clinton claimed to have unearthed some evidence that she was a Jew—along with the long lost evidence that she was a Yankees fan. And that, boys and girls, is how the Jews survived thousands of years of persecution: by being susceptible to pandering.

The sales of *Treason* must have convinced many of her fellow conservative writers that Coulter was so popular with the right-wing base that she was immune to further criticism. And the truth was that she didn't need her conservative colleagues anymore. Coulter promoted *Treason* on *Good Morning America* and later remarked "how polite" Diane Sawyer had been to her. When she encountered more challenging interviews, Coulter had a new defense: "Uh, I can assure you, I'm published by Random House."

A second Crown Forum book was titled *Hillary's Scheme: Inside the Next Clinton's Ruthless Agenda to Take the White House.* It was written by NewsMax.com "reporter" Carl Limbacher. The promotional materials promised:

> *Hillary's Scheme* lays out the shocking evidence and confirms the worst fears of millions of Americans: Hillary plans a grand political coup—one that will put her and her disgraced husband back into the Oval Office.
>
> *Hillary's Scheme* is more than the unmasking of Hillary's presidential ambitions. It's a book making seismic waves as it exposes the former First Lady's greedy ambition and shows her for the power crazed woman she is.
>
> If you love to hate Hillary, or are just curious about one of America's most powerful women, there's plenty in this book to make your blood boil.

Though there is a market for "hate," Crown Forum couldn't find it. As with MSNBC's desultory performance vis-à-vis FOX, the task of pandering to right-wing book buyers might be better left, after all, to professionals like Regnery, with its book clubs and direct-mail lists and bulk-buying ingenuity. Limbacher's book did not sell well and sank with barely a trace.

CHAPTER FIFTEEN
SUNDAY MORNING

ESPITE THE RIGHT'S INSISTENCE on seeing evidence of liberal opinion in the voice inflections, body language, and facial tics of the three network anchors, the broadcast networks air little opinion. When they do, the forum is more dignified than that of cable, and political balance is generally maintained by neutral moderators. This decorum and strict balance annoys conservatives, who, as Edith Efron once suggested, would prefer that the networks look more like cable and talk radio.

In reasoned political debate on the networks and PBS, conservatives have trouble steamrolling their opponents. When CBS News paired former New Jersey senator Bill Bradley with Laura Ingraham for a rotating commentary slot on the weekend, Ingraham was such an embarrassment the network junked the whole idea. On *The NewsHour with Jim Lehrer*, the scrappy Mark Shields often bests David Brooks (who offered a negative appraisal of Hillary Clinton's *Living History* before admitting to the host that he hadn't read the book),[1] as he did the *Wall Street Journal's* Paul Gigot before him. When right-wing columnist Michelle Malkin sat in for Brooks in August 2002, she seemed as if she had beamed in from another planet.

Liberals come off quite well in *Nightline* debates, while rabid neocons like David Horowitz appear unhinged. Democrat Bob Beckel fought conservative Fred Barnes point for point on CBS's *Morning Show* in the 1980s. When *60 Minutes* revived its "Point/Counterpoint" segment with Bill Clinton and Bob Dole, neither had a distinct advantage.

The networks' Sunday morning shows, beamed from studios in Washington, are the only hours on network television during which viewers get a steady dose of opinion; though the tone remains more elevated than that of cable or radio, here the conservatives enjoy a structural advantage. Like cable, these shows, while reaching a relatively small audience, have disproportionate influence on the ebb and flow of public debate, because the viewership is highly influential and politically attuned.

Alone among the three hosts of the Sunday morning shows, *Face the Nation's* Bob Schieffer reads a weekly commentary. A well-respected CBS newsman and Washington bureau chief, Schieffer has taken some staunchly conservative positions in his commentaries. Schieffer endorsed Bush's 2001 tax cut, candidly noting that it would benefit high-income earners like himself; he was also in favor of the war with Iraq. He opposed Bush's later tax proposals, though chiefly out of concern for the deficit—not because they were inequitable.

Schieffer's competitors, Tim Russert of NBC's *Meet the Press* and George Stephanopoulos of ABC's *This Week,* don't give their views. Both are former aides to Democratic politicians (Russert having worked for Daniel Patrick Moynihan and Mario Cuomo, and Stephanopoulos worked for Bill Clinton); now both Russert and Stephanopoulos host shows that subtly and consistently favor the right wing.

A typical *Meet the Press* journalist's roundtable might include longtime regulars William Safire, Robert Novak, David S. Broder of the *Washington Post,* and, say, Robin Wright of the *Los Angeles Times.* Safire and Novak are right-wing; Broder is a centrist reporter and columnist, miscast as a liberal; and Wright is an impartial news reporter, miscast as a liberal. Other times, historian Doris Kearns Goodwin or NBC's chief diplomatic correspondent Andrea Mitchell, neither of whom are ideological or partisan, face off against right-wing ideologues.

Very rarely does Russert feature journalists or advocates as liberal and partisan as Safire and Novak are right-wing and partisan. The only remotely comparable figures are the *Washington Post's* E. J. Dionne, a gentle, thoughtful liberal columnist, and the *Wall Street Journal's* Al Hunt, who appear with less frequency than either Novak or Safire. Where are *The Nation's* Katrina van den Heuvel, David Corn, and William Greider? What about Lewis Lapham of *Harper's* and Michael Tomasky of *The American Prospect*? Columnists Molly Ivins, Ellen Goodman, Tom Oliphant, Robert Scheer, Joe Conason, Richard Reeves, and Julianne Malveaux? Eric Alterman?

Yet booking more ideologically committed or partisan liberals would still not provide "balance" to Novak. In June 2003, Novak misrepresented the Bush tax cut proposals. Novak's take was so flagrantly false that both Al Hunt and Russert intervened to correct him.

Being caught red-handed on the air was not enough to bar Novak from *Meet*. In September 2003, Russert hosted another typical roundtable, featuring right-wingers Novak and Safire, as well as news reporters Robin Wright and Ronald Brownstein of the *Los Angeles Times*. The week before, General Wesley Clark had announced his candidacy for the Democratic nomination for president. While nonpartisans Wright and Brownstein handicapped the race, Novak and Safire opened fire on Clark, previewing partisan columns that each would publish the next morning.

With the imprimatur of Russert and *Meet*, the Republican Noise Machine was up and running. The Novak and Safire columns, both enthusiastically billboarded by Matt Drudge, were featured throughout the coming days on radio and cable, negatively shaping the public view of Clark's debut. As several Web sites subsequently pointed out, Novak's error-filled column slammed Clark for meeting with "indicted war criminal" Serbian general Ratko Mladic, though the meeting had occurred one year before he was charged with any crimes. Safire's column, positing that Hillary Clinton was the hidden power behind the Clark candidacy, was a product of his imagination.

Much the same pattern has been followed across town at *This Week*, which for more than a decade was produced by Dorrance Smith, a former communications director in George H. W. Bush's White House. For years, the show was moderated by the legendary David Brinkley, who occasionally revealed his conservative sympathies. For example, he referred to Bill Clinton's first tax package as a "sick, stupid joke."

Before Stephanopoulos took over as host, *This Week's* roundtable featured two right-wing ideologists, George Will and William Kristol (hired by Smith, who was his former White House colleague), with Stephanopoulos as the liberal counterbalance. In his role as liberal analyst, which he assumed while penning a memoir in which he expressed some regret for having served in the Clinton administration, Stephanopoulos sometimes echoed Republican talking points, such as when he referred to Al Gore's "Pinocchio problem" during the 2000 campaign. Newsman Sam Donaldson also appeared to be positioned as a liberal, though when he leaned that way (he once said defensively that he had voted for Barry Goldwater), it was not with the philosophical commitment or rhetorical tenaciousness of Will or Kristol. According to the *Washington Post's* Howard Kurtz, "[Donaldson] did not support Bill Clinton the way George Will ardently backed Ronald Reagan; in fact, he often joined Will in bashing the Democratic Party." When he did step up as a liberal advocate, Donaldson sent the misleading message that ABC's longtime White House correspondent was a closet liberal ideologue and that journalists were biased against conservatives. Like many other journalists on such TV panels, Donaldson was forced to straddle two roles, while the conservatives did only one job and therefore usually did it better.

When Stephanopoulos moved into the neutral role of host, ABC's weekly roundtable featured two regulars, George Will pitted against Michel Martin, who was on the one hand constrained by her dual role as an impartial ABC News reporter and on the other ill served in the latter assignment by being pushed into a partisan advocacy role on Sundays that didn't always fit. While Martin sometimes counterpunched effectively, she tended to analyze; Will simply spun like a top. The third seat rotated, with *Newsweek's* Fareed Zakaria, who appeared to be a centrist but is nonetheless a member of the board of the right-wing Manhattan Institute, turning up most frequently. When matched with an unfettered liberal who could take on Will on an equal footing, the conservative's traditional demeanor of command dissolved. In January 2003, *Mother Jones* columnist Todd Gitlin easily cut through Will's illogic. Typically, the pundits who are positioned against the right wing on the Sunday shows are not from the Left, like Gitlin but, rather, as Margaret Carlson once put it, "from Washington." Thus the entire Sunday morning debate is skewed to the right, because the pundits "from Washington" have their own interests, their own values, their own folkways—and the role they see themselves as playing is not to defend the Democratic Party or liberalism any more than it is to defend the Republican Party or conservatism.

For several years after Brinkley retired—and before George Stephanopoulos was elevated—ABC's Cokie Roberts, presiding over *This Week's* political roundtable, was perhaps the ultimate personification of the pundit "from Washington." The scion of a prominent Democratic political family and a National Public Radio fixture, Roberts might have been seen as a liberal counterweight to Will and Kristol. But Roberts's commentaries were not liberal; they represented not an ideology or even a consistent point of view but, rather, the reigning zeitgeist among Washington media insiders.

When the Republican Right took over the party in Reagan's election, wiping out GOP centrism, what it meant to be a mainstream Republican changed radically, and the center of political dialogue in the capital shifted right, helped along by such right-wing inventions as *The McLaughlin Group* and by neoconservative gains at the *Washington Post* and *The New Republic*. As the ground shifted under her, more often than not, Roberts and her fellow pundits "from Washington" seemed to reinforce the Right rather than challenge it.

To Roberts, hewing to the new center in Washington, the Democratic Party seemed too far left—out of the American mainstream—and this became her favorite theme over the years, as FAIR has documented. "Michael Dukakis was totally out of the mainstream of the American public," she said in explaining his loss to George H. W. Bush in 1988 despite the fact that Dukakis ran even with Bush in the Midwest and among middle-income voters. In 1997, she explained, "The Democratic caucus in the House of Representatives is way to the left of where the party is and where the public is." In the next election, the Democrats picked up enough House seats to sweep Newt Gingrich from the speakership.

After the Monica Lewinsky story broke in January 1998, Sam Donaldson, George Will, and William Kristol predicted breathlessly that Clinton could be out of office within days. The next Sunday, Donaldson read out poll numbers showing Clinton's approval ratings rising; he threw up his hands and said, "Go figure," as the panel went on to issue the same dire prognostications served up one week before. The media is "way ahead of the public on this," Roberts pronounced. "The public will understand soon enough."[2] Throughout the controversy, the public consistently opposed impeachment, and Clinton's approval ratings remained high.

As did many of her colleagues "from Washington," Roberts went along with the Republican Noise Machine's shaping of political stories. Asked to explain why the media failed to write about untruthful statements made by George W. Bush during the 2000 campaign, choosing instead to focus exclusively on the GOP caricature of Gore as a liar, Roberts said, "The story line is Bush isn't smart enough and Gore isn't straight enough. In Bush's case, you know he's just misstating as opposed to it playing into a story line about him being a serial exaggerator."[3]

In early 2003, Fareed Zakaria of *Newsweek* was singing from Roberts's song sheet on *This Week*, warning against the "Pelosi-ization" of the Democratic Party, a reference to the election of Nancy Pelosi as House minority leader by an overwhelming margin and an echo of a concerted right-wing attack on Pelosi as a dangerous leftist. (The *Washington Times* had compared Pelosi to the Manchurian candidate, implying that she had been brainwashed to become a Communist, as were the American soldiers depicted in that movie.) Zakaria said not a word about Tom DeLay's simultaneous ascension to the position of House majority leader; DeLay was at least as far outside the American mainstream as Zakaria believed Pelosi to be. In Washington, if not in the country, the middle had moved so far right that "DeLay-ization" was not worth addressing.

Whatever balance was achieved on *This Week*'s roundtable was undone when, alone among the panelists, George Will sometimes narrated a closing piece from his point of view. Will has used his ABC News pulpit to promote "products" from the right-wing message machine, as when he cited an AEI study conducted in conjunction with David Horowitz's Center for the Study of Popular Culture that purported to show that "the Left" dominated university faculties by a factor of eleven to one. Campuses, Will averred, "are intellectually akin to North Korea." The survey, however, examined only social science faculties, leaving out more conservative schools of medicine, law, business, and engineering.[4]

In May 2003, Laura Ingraham sat in on the roundtable for George Will, a sign that cable and talk radio values were bleeding into the networks. A trend that had begun in the 1980s, as nonjournalists from the Republican

Right were invited onto broadcast networks to interpret the news—the Republican operative Roger Ailes, before he was tapped to head CNBC, was featured regularly on NBC's *Today;* Pat Buchanan was on ABC's *Good Morning America;* and ABC News hired George Will as a convention commentator—had reached its nadir.

Shortly after Ingraham's debut, during which Michel Martin openly wondered if ABC had adopted a policy of affirmative action for right-wing pundettes in short skirts, the ABC roundtable was nixed entirely. A new show was unveiled, but it suffered from the same bias as the old one: The polemical Will, though not Martin, now joined the neutral Stephanopoulos at the front of the show, questioning newsmakers. Shortly after the new format launched, Stephanopoulos had to read a correction on the air of Will's distortion of Democratic Senator Russ Feingold's position on the Patriot Act.

The newest entrant into the Sunday morning sweepstakes is *The Chris Matthews Show,* syndicated by NBC. In its first year, Matthews's show averaged 2.36 million viewers, well behind *Meet,* just behind *This Week,* but ahead of Bob Schieffer's *Face the Nation* and Tony Snow's show on FOX. On the broadcast network, Matthews has a much larger audience than on MSNBC; and in keeping with the decorum of network television, the show is more serious and informative. He seems to ratchet down his own tone and temperament as well.

Matthews typically features four "political reporters" to discuss the news of the week in a half-hour format. Journalists such as Andrea Mitchell, Gloria Borger of *U.S. News & World Report,* Howard Fineman of *Newsweek,* and Claire Shipman of NBC share their insights. Yet most weeks, following the format of the other Sunday morning shows, conservative pundits such as Tucker Carlson, David Brooks, Paul Gigot, and *National Review's* Byron York invariably show up to skew and spoil the impartial proceedings.

CHAPTER SIXTEEN

20/20's VISION

HAVING SUCCESSFULLY INTRODUCED right-wing bias and misinformation onto the broadcast TV networks under the guise of opinion on the Sunday talk shows, the conservatives undertook their final goal of tilting professional news reporting at the major networks their way. Citing the success of FOX and of Bernard Goldberg's book *Bias*, Mark Tapscott, the "director of the Center for Media and Public Policy" at the Heritage Foundation, wrote in 2002: "The end of the Liberal Media Establishment could be right around the corner. . . . Sooner or later," Tapscott speculated, "falling ratings and economic necessity will force a network news executive to mandate the Fox formula, the 'we report, you decide' approach that stresses fairness and accuracy. When that network's ratings turn around, how long do you think it will take the other two broadcast giants to follow suit?" In his follow-up book to *Bias*, titled *Arrogance: Rescuing America from the Media Elite*, Goldberg proposed a kind of affirmative action program for conservatives, arguing for forced "ideological diversity" in newsrooms.

The case of the only high-profile conservative "newsman" in the business does not augur well for this approach. John Stossel first attracted attention as a well-respected consumer affairs reporter at a network affiliate in New York City in the late 1970s, specializing in factual reports on corporate abuse. He soon joined ABC News, where he worked this beat through most of the 1980s, picking up Emmys along the way. As the values of the TV news business were changing from public service to profit, and a niche was opening up in the media market for conservative views, Stossel began to track to the right—a path that led to greater fame and to much greater fortune.

Stossel now calls himself a free market libertarian. "Markets are magical and the best protectors of the consumer," Stossel told the *Oregonian* in an interview in 1994. "It is my job to explain the beauties of the free-market."

Advertisers and newly powerful right-wing interest groups were pleased by the new Stossel, who turned his old career on its head, taking up virtually every cause of the corporate Right in his reportage for ABC. "I think one John Stossel segment taking a skeptical look at government is worth a million dollars to the movement," Stephen Moore, "director of fiscal policy" at the Cato Institute and director of the Club for Growth, told *Brill's Content.*

Stossel has attacked government programs, government regulation, the consumer movement, trial lawyers, environmentalism, feminism, and affirmative action. Environmentalists are portrayed as technophobes who would have Americans "running around naked, hungry for food, maybe killing a rabbit with a rock, then dying young, probably before age 40."[1] He has defended corporate abuses, "robber barons," and "greed." "[Junk bond king] Michael Milken made a billion and went to jail," Stossel's announcer said on one show, according to a report in *Brill's Content.* "Mother Teresa died without a penny. Who did more for the world?"

In a speech to the right-wing Federalist Society—a chief actor behind the "tort reform" movement that he has championed on the air—Stossel, who makes several million dollars per year as ABC's in-house conservative, explained why he moved from consumer advocacy to favoring unregulated markets, tax cuts for the wealthy, and antigovernment bromides. "I got sick of it," Stossel told the Federalists. "I also now make so much money I just lost interest in saving a buck on a can of peas." Stossel also implored the group, "I certainly would encourage any of you who knows somebody who buys advertising on television to 'please buy an ad on those Stossel specials.'"[2] The speech was an apparent violation of ABC policy that prohibits reporters from giving paid speeches to groups that have an interest in the subjects on which the journalists report.[3]

Stossel appears to be the only network reporter free to deliberately color his news reports with his opinions. He has occasionally admitted to his right-wing biases in interviews and in speeches to right-wing groups. In an ABC News online chat, he said, "I clearly do have a point of view," and, "I also admit my report was one-sided."[4] In 1995, after Newt Gingrich became House Speaker, Stossel spoke on the "evils of regulation" before a congressional caucus on deregulation.

Yet on his broadcasts, Stossel poses as a skeptic and a contrarian, a commonsense reporter cutting through so much liberal cant to get to the truth. His crisp, clear, and highly watchable reports are a variation of the formula that has worked well on cable, whereby conservatives have been able to turn ordinary viewers against their own economic interests by bashing government and various so-called cultural elites. One of Stossel's first producers, Lowell Bergman (who left ABC for CBS's *60 Minutes* and later PBS), told *The Nation*, "The sad thing about Stossel and his ascendancy is that he is the future. He symbolizes the transformation of news into ideological entertainment."

ABC—where Stossel appears on the weekly newsmagazine *20/20* and on prime-time news specials—allows Stossel to wear two hats, presenting him not as an editorialist but as a reporter. The viewer is rarely clued in to the fact that Stossel's reports, which are still delivered in the breathless style of his investigative consumer reports, are laced with highly questionable right-wing suppositions. Mark Dowie reported in *The Nation:*

> In those specials and his regular "Give Me a Break" column on
> *20/20*, Stossel expressed his politics through story topics like
> Chilean Social Security (totally privatized, and for Stossel the way
> to go, despite the loss of benefits to millions of Chileans), govern-
> ment regulation (which Stossel regards as thuggish paternalism),
> tort lawyers (ambulance-chasing bloodsuckers), environmental edu-
> cation (green "scaremongers" terrifying innocent schoolchildren),
> chemical sensitivity (pushed by whiny hypochondriacs exploited by
> greedy doctors), greed (a good thing for the economy), risk (the dis-

torted creation of "junk science"), Erin Brockovich (all wet about PG&E), disabled Americans (a powerful lobby that's costing business billions), product liability (crackpot lawsuits), school-bus seatbelts (a waste of money) and an hourlong special, loaded with spurious statistical data, claiming that by any measure of social or economic strength America is "Number One."

ABC occasionally flashes the word "Commentator" under Stossel's image, apparently when his reports are especially opinionated. But opinion aside, the network has done nothing to deal with a more serious issue: Stossel's repeated misstatements, manipulations, and distortions of fact in the service of his ideology.

For many years, Fairness & Accuracy in Reporting has been chronicling instances of what it calls Stossel's "shoddy, one-sided propaganda." These have included a false assertion that Parkinson's disease kills more people than does AIDS, offered as part of an argument that the government spends too much on AIDS research; understating the number of graduates from public schools in making the case that private schools are more "efficient"; overstating wage increases for factory workers in defense of rising corporate compensation; overstating government welfare spending; and falsely claiming that Title IX mandates proportional participation by male and female student athletes.[5]

The Stossel reports are peppered with right-wing jargon such as "equality police," "bureaucrats," "junk science," "environmental police," "government schools," and "victimhood." While taking a view in opposition to established scientific opinion, Stossel doesn't simply disagree—he masks his opinion as fact by offering up his own "science" and a panoply of experts to back it up; meanwhile, he gives short shrift to experts with whom he disagrees. Many of his dubious claims, and his sources, appear to originate in the right-wing think tank network, with which Stossel has a web of close ties.

According to FAIR, a Stossel special called "Are We Scaring Ourselves to Death?," which tried to downplay various environmental concerns, was based on a Manhattan Institute book titled *Health, Lifestyle and Environment: Countering the Panic.* Two ABC producers resigned rather than participate in the program. Claiming that ten times as many scientists have signed petitions questioning the risk posed by global warming as have warned of its consequences, Stossel failed to note that while the smaller petition was circulated by the respected Union of Concerned Scientists, the larger petition was a project of the right-wing George C. Marshall Institute and the Oregon Institute of Science and Medicine and included signatories, such as dentists, who had no professional qualifications to judge the issue. He has relied heavily on sources such as Peter Huber of the Manhattan Institute; right-wing economist Walter Williams; and Michael Fumento, author of the discredited book *The Myth of Heterosexual AIDS.* "Mr. Stossel Goes to Washington"—a diatribe designed to show that Americans are "overtaxed"—featured "tax expert" Amity Shlaes of the *Wall Street Journal* editorial page and statistics from a tendentious study by the right-wing Tax Foundation. "Greed"—a program that extolled the virtues of the vice— repeatedly cited David Kelley, who was called a "philosopher," though his position as head of the Institute for Objectivist Studies, a think tank comprising followers of novelist Ayn Rand, was not mentioned.

A Stossel report for *20/20* titled "The Food You Eat," which charged that "buying organic could kill you," was deeply flawed and resulted in a Stossel on-air apology. According to a report in *The Nation*, a primary Stossel source was organic food critic Dennis Avery, introduced by Stossel as a "former researcher for the Agriculture Department." "[Yet] . . . it was Avery's most recent position with the Center for Global Food Issues, a project of the conservative Hudson Institute, that informed his ardent support of chemical agriculture," Mark Dowie wrote. "The Hudson Institute and Avery's project are both supported by generous contributions from Monsanto, DuPont, Novartis, ConAgra, DowElanco, the Olin Foundation, and the Ag-Chem Equipment Company, all of whom profit from the sale of products prohibited in organic production."

In the wake of the broadcast, the Environmental Working Group, a Washington advocacy organization, alleged that a study (showing that pesticide residues were present in neither conventional nor organic foods), which Stossel claimed was conducted by ABC, was, in fact, never performed. When the *New York Times* corroborated the Environmental Working Group's charges, reporting that the study cited by Stossel on the air was fabricated, the right-wing support network leapt to his defense. The right-wing Competitive Enterprise Institute launched a Web site called

SaveJohnStossel.com, and officials at the Cato Institute and at Brent Bozell's Media Research Center wrote letters to the editor. ABC reprimanded Stossel, who told viewers, "That was just wrong. . . . I apologize for the error [and] am deeply sorry I misled you." The producer of the show was also reprimanded and left ABC after signing a gag order never to discuss the matter.

Soon thereafter, another controversy erupted when a group of parents complained to ABC that Stossel had deceived them and manipulated interviews with their children for a 20/20 segment on environmental education titled "Tampering with Nature." Stossel's point appeared to be that educators were needlessly "scaring" children about threats to the environment and pumping them full of bad information, and he asked leading questions of the schoolchildren to get the responses that fit this script. Months before Stossel's producers went to work on the piece, Michael Sanera, "director of environmental education" at the antienvironment Competitive Enterprise Institute, circulated this e-mail: "I have been contacted by ABC News. A producer for John Stossel is working on a program on environmental education. He needs examples of kids who have been 'scared green' by schools teaching doomsday environmentalism in the classroom. (He needs kids and/or parents on camera.) I have some examples, but I need more. Would you send out a notice to your group and ask if they know of some examples."[6]

There have been no Emmys adorning Stossel's résumé of late. Instead, he travels the lucrative right-wing and corporate speakers' circuit. According to *Brill's Content,* he made twenty-seven such appearances in a two-year period, raking in close to $250,000. The American Legislative Exchange Council, founded by Paul Weyrich to coordinate the activities of state-based right-wing think tanks, awarded Stossel the "Warren Brookes Award for Excellence in Journalism." Other recipients have included a *Who's Who* of right-wing media, such as FOX's Tony Snow, Paul Craig Roberts of Cato, John Fund of the *Wall Street Journal,* Walter Williams, and *Washington Times* columnist Donald Lambro.

Stossel says he donates his speaking fees to charity. One of his favored charities is the Palmer R. Chitester Fund, a foundation dedicated to popularizing right-wing economic and social policies that appears to be underwritten by grants from the Olin, Bradley, and JM foundations, among others. According to Chitester's Web site, Bob Chitester (the group's founder, a former owner of public TV stations, and a content producer for John Malone's TCI cable network) is also "managing partner" with Milton and Rose Friedman of Free to Choose Enterprises, which manages the licensing and sales of the Olin- and Scaife-subsidized PBS series *Free to Choose*.

Chitester's main project is repackaging Stossel's network specials and selling them to public and private schools as instructional materials under the name "Stossel in the Classroom." The series "crosses the line between edgy journalism and pure propaganda," according to a report in *Salon*. "Many if not most of the 35 to 40 footnotes accompanying each guide cite predictably conservative sources like the Heritage Foundation, the Cato Institute, the Hoover Institution and Young America's Foundation and the *Wall Street Journal* editorial page." Walter Williams, a frequent on-air guest on Stossel's ABC specials, has been a Chitester board member. The selling of these reports is in turn subsidized by grants to Chitester from the Olin and Bradley foundations.

Stossel's biased and inaccurate journalism is a lesson in the concept of conflict of interest, but it doesn't seem to have hurt Stossel's ratings or ABC's bottom line. He is said to have among the highest "Q" numbers—which measure on-air likability—in TV news. In *The Nation*, Mark Dowie wrote that his presence on ABC is also a kind of insurance policy for the network against allegations of "liberal bias."

In mid-2003, ABC announced that Stossel was being promoted to co-anchor with Barbara Walters of *20/20*. In Rupert Murdoch's *TV Guide*, an ABC News source explained, "These are conservative times . . . the network wants somebody to match the times."

AFTERWORD

THE RIGHT-WING CAMPAIGN to mainstream conservatism and to discredit its opponents through domination of the media has been so successful because few have risen to oppose it. The good news is that by early 2004, several progressive initiatives were under way to reverse that dynamic, even up the media playing field, and restore a diversity of views in the public discourse.

The Center for American Progress, headed by former Clinton White House chief of staff John Podesta, has been founded as a progressive counterweight to right-wing institutions like the Heritage Foundation. In the manner of Heritage and hundreds of other right-wing think tanks, the center offers policy expertise across a broad range of issues to political leaders, opinion leaders, the media, and the general public.

Because existing progressive institutions have tended to be narrowly focused on single-issue concerns, until now no one has taken on the responsibility to do the intellectual work required to refine, brand, and market progressive ideas and issue a sustained, across-the-board critique of conservatism. In addition to providing space for long-range thinking, and a critically needed infrastructure for fellows, affiliated scholars, columnists, and book authors, the center is highly media focused, developing a network of progressive analysts and pundits and working hard to put them into the media every day. This should go a long way to remedying the current imbalance on the TV chat shows, where all too often right-wing pundits are pitted against professional journalists who do not argue from an ideological perspective. The center has raised a war chest in excess of $10 million, though this is only about one-third of Heritage's annual budget—not to mention the approximately $300 million per year the right wing spends on similar efforts to win the "war of ideas."

Democracy Radio—on whose advisory board I sit—is a new nonprofit working to support a progressive presence in talk radio. As I discussed in chapter 12, several progressive talkers currently perform extremely well in regional and local markets. Yet owing to a combination of consolidation in the industry, conservative ownership, conservative success in serving a substantial niche in the marketplace, limited shelf space, and the widespread misperception that progressive talk cannot be profitable, the challenge of putting progressivism on the air is daunting.

Democracy Radio's innovative answer is to raise funds to subsidize the move of established and highly rated progressive talkers into wider syndication. By seeking to promote hosts who are already proven broadcasters, the group hopes to avoid the pitfall of prior progressive radio efforts, which featured a range of personalities who were not accomplished radio broadcasters. By offering to produce, promote, and market these shows to get them off the ground, Democracy Radio reduces the financial risk to skeptical syndicators and stations. Their model is actually no different from that of the new FOX Radio Network, which has been offering to underwrite, to the tune of hundreds of thousands of dollars, the launch of a new show hosted by Tony Snow. The deep pockets of Rupert Murdoch continue to put progressive media voices at a competitive disadvantage, though it is not an insurmountable one, provided there is adequate funding for Democracy Radio. By late 2003, the organization had struck deals to bring the North Dakota–based Ed Schultz, who outperforms Rush Limbaugh in his regional market, into national syndication. If progressive talk show hosts are afforded the opportunity, and if they succeed nationally, they in turn may become sought-after guests for the cable shows, and publishing houses may publish their words—giving progressives the cross-marketing opportunities for their work currently enjoyed only by the right wing.

A for-profit venture headed by entrepreneur Mark Walsh, Progress Media, is also seeking to bring progressive talk to the airwaves. The strategy of this group is to buy radio stations and offer a full menu of progressive talk throughout the day, thereby circumventing the potential roadblock of placing progressive talkers at stations that already program much of their day around right-wing talk or that might be hostile to airing progressive talk.

Press reports indicated that best-selling author Al Franken was among those being courted by this group to host his own daily radio show. In 2003, Franken joined Hillary Clinton and Michael Moore in a trio of progressive authors who sold millions of copies of books.

As these book sales indicate, there is a substantial underserved market of Americans who want to read—and watch and listen to—news and opinion other than Republican noise. One study showed that in households voting for Al Gore in 2000, fifteen million people believe the media is too conservative. A liberal-leaning program like *The Daily Show with Jon Stewart* currently attracts an average audience of one million viewers, roughly the average audience size of CNN. FOX and CNN have shown that cable can be profitable with relatively small audiences.

Perhaps with these facts in mind, former Vice President Al Gore has pursued a $70 million plan to buy an existing cable network and relaunch it as a youth-oriented news channel that would not skew to the right. As the existing cable news channels serve an older, predominantly conservative demographic, this could be a promising cable niche. By serving a new audience, the network might avoid the challenge faced by Phil Donahue, a liberal who was introduced in isolation onto an existing network whose audience skewed to the right. One hitch for Gore may be carriage; Murdoch was willing to lose $400 million to pay cable companies to carry the FOX News Channel before FOX reached profitability in 2001.

The precise formulas for success in these new media ventures are not yet known. My view is that, given the overall conservative tone of so much of the media today, there is ample opportunity for new media initiatives that provide their audiences with the kind of solid information and straightforward liberal advocacy that can't be found in either right-wing or mainstream media channels. The sensibilities of the liberal market are likely different from those of the right-wing market; liberals will have to do more than simply package preexisting beliefs and regurgitate them back to the audience. Liberals as a rule don't carry on their shoulders a chip like conservatives do. Whatever their political difficulties, liberals do not feel alienated from American culture. They are more discerning as media consumers. And as a group, they may not be as angry—although that could be changing as they begin to contemplate years in the political wilderness thanks to the efforts of the Republican Noise Machine.

Yet as I have detailed throughout the book, the appeal of right-wing media is deeper than its ideological, psychological, and anti-intellectual roots: Right-wing programming provides a show business aesthetic that people seem to like; allows listeners and viewers a sense of participation in the broadcasts; and has a strong populist component, positioning itself against established political and cultural authorities (real or imagined). Liberals ought to keep those qualities in mind when fashioning their responses.

For the moment, progressives will have to find ways to compete within the existing ownership structure, and according to the corrosive commercialized values, of media institutions. But with an eye to the long run, progressives must undertake political and educational efforts now to begin restoring the media to its original mission: serving the public interest and providing the space for the airing of the full diversity of views on which American democracy depends.

This will involve reversing the damage done to the media by the waves of deregulation, and ownership concentration and consolidation, that were ushered in by the Reagan administration and continue today under George W. Bush. More government regulation is necessary to break up media monopolies and reintroduce legitimate competition. For example, Senator Russ Feingold, a Wisconsin Democrat, has introduced the Competition in Radio and Concert Industries Act of 2003 to curb consolidation and anti-competitive practices in radio. The strong progressive response to the Bush deregulatory proposals of 2003, organized by groups such as MoveOn.org, Common Cause, and a number of organizations devoted to media reform, is encouraging. I also think political leaders should examine the desirability of reinstituting the Fairness Doctrine, which had for years before its repeal protected the public airwaves from being overtaken by the propaganda of a single political faction.

In the meantime, existing progressive alternative media—magazines like *The American Prospect, The Nation, Mother Jones,* and *The Washington Monthly,* among others, and the Web magazine *Salon,* need more financial support from the progressive community so that they may more effectively compete with the massively subsidized right-wing media. We need to see more writers from these publications on television and radio.

Speaking of *Salon,* many view the Internet as a promising new media vehicle for progressives. While only about 20 percent of the public consider themselves liberal, close to 40 percent of those who say they get their news from the Internet are self-identified liberals. Ronald Brownstein of the *Los Angeles Times* has written that the Internet may, in the end, provide the powerful media presence for liberals that talk radio does for conservatives. Certainly if one wants to be fully informed about politics and policy, or seeks unvarnished liberal views, several progressive Internet sites and Web logs are now must-reading. Yet unlike right-wingers on the Internet—who have the brand-name recognition and the money that enable them to appear on television and radio—most of the progressive Web remains purely an online phenomenon.

In writing this book, I came to the conclusion that there is a need for another type of organization, whose specific mission is to restore accuracy and reliability to the public discourse. Such is the power of the partisans to distort every public issue in each news cycle that a book, no matter how widely circulated, is not equipped to push it back.

So I have created a nonprofit organization that is envisioned as the leading media watchdog group in the United States. Because a healthy democracy and sound public policy depend on public access to factual information and a wide range of informed opinion, this organization will run a research and educational campaign to ensure accuracy, fairness, and a legitimate accounting of diverse views in the media.

The situation I have described in *The Republican Noise Machine* is intolerable in a democracy. It is well past time that concerned citizens organize to redress it.

Washington, D.C.
February 2004

NOTES

Introduction. The Republican Noise Machine

1. Eric Alterman, *What Liberal Media?* (New York: Basic Books, 2003), 163–164.
2. Bob Somerby, "Extra! One Question Only for the *Washington Post:* When Will Charles Krauthammer Be Fired?" December 5, 2003, www.dailyhowler.com.

Chapter One. Nixon's Revenge

1. Edith Efron, "Black Man's Burden," *Reason,* February 1992.
2. Edith Efron, "Can the President Think?" *Reason,* November 1994.
3. William Bennett, "Cancer and Its Causes: A Grim Debate," *Washington Post Book World,* July 22, 1984, 5.
4. Virginia Postrel, "The Woman Who Saw Through Walls," www.dynamist.com/edith.html.
5. Edith Efron, *The News Twisters* (New York: Manor Books, 1972).
6. John M. Crewdson, *New York Times,* August 19, 1974, 16.
7. Elizabeth Mehren, "'Insanity' in Nixon's White House," *Los Angeles Times,* February 18, 2003.
8. Katharine Graham, *Personal History* (New York: Alfred A. Knopf, 1997), 476–477.
9. "Remembrances," *Newsweek,* May 2, 1994, 24.
10. Crewdson, op. cit.
11. Edith Efron, *How CBS Tried to Kill a Book* (Los Angeles: Nash Publishing, 1972).
12. Ben Bradlee Jr., "The Buchanan Role: GOP Protagonist," *Boston Globe,* March 3, 1996, 1.
13. Ibid.
14. "Pat Buchanan's Skeleton Closet," www.realchange.org/buchanan.htm.
15. William Safire, *Before the Fall: An Insider's View of the Pre-Watergate White House* (New York: Doubleday & Company, 1975), 364–365.
16. Wilson Carey McWilliams, "Pretty and Pink," *In These Times,* March 22, 1998, 24.
17. Richard Reeves, *President Nixon* (New York: Simon & Schuster, 2001), 471–472.
18. Ben H. Bagdikian, *The Media Monopoly* (Boston: Beacon Press, 2000), 42–43.
19. "Billy Graham's Bigotry," *Boston Globe,* March 15, 2002, 14.
20. Graham, op. cit., 476–477.
21. Safire, op. cit., 353.
22. "Spiro Theodore Agnew: Television News Coverage," www.americanrhetoric.com/speeches/spiroagnew.htm.

23. Marc Gunther, *The House That Roone Built* (New York: Little, Brown & Company, 1994), 73.

24. Lance Morrow, "Naysayer to the Nattering Nabobs; Spiro Agnew, 1918–1996," *Time*, September 30, 1996, 36.

25. Martin Schram, "GOP Campaign Tactic: 'Working the Refs,'" *Newsday*, September 10, 1992.

26. Alan Crawford, *Thunder on the Right* (New York: Pantheon Books, 1980).

27. Rick Perlstein, *Before the Storm: Barry Goldwater and the Unmaking of the American Consensus* (New York: Hill & Wang, 2001).

28. Ibid.

29. Richard Hofstadter, *The Paranoid Style in American Politics* (Cambridge: Harvard University Press, 1996), 140.

30. Ibid., 43.

31. Perlstein, op. cit.

32. Ibid.

33. Hofstadter, op. cit.

34. William Rentschler, "Barry Goldwater: Icon of Political Integrity," *USA Today* (magazine), March 2000.

35. Perlstein, op. cit.

36. David Gordon, "Up from Buckleyism," *Mises Review* (Spring 1995).

37. Crawford, op. cit., 229–231.

38. Richard Harwood, "Along the Cultural Divide," *Washington Post*, August 21, 1992, 25.

39. Ed Bark, "Chicago Will Be David Brinkley's Last Convention," *Buffalo News*, August 25, 1996, 2TV.

40. Perlstein, op. cit., 381.

41. Taylor Branch, "The Year the GOP Went South," *Washington Monthly*, March 1998, 34.

42. Robert W. McChesney, *Rich Media, Poor Democracy* (New York: New Press, 1999), 49.

43. Ben Bagdikian, op. cit., 68.

Chapter Two. "Guerrilla War"

1. "Confidential Memo: Attack on American Free Enterprise System," www.media transparency.org/stories/powellmanifesto.htm.

2. Jerry M. Landay, "The Powell Manifesto," August 20, 2002, www.mediatrans parency.org/stories/powell.htm.

3. William E. Simon, *A Time for Truth* (New York: Reader's Digest Press, 1978).

4. Crawford, op. cit., 10.

5. "Buying a Movement: Right-Wing Foundations and American Politics," People for the American Way, 21.

6. Landay, op. cit.

7. Crawford, op. cit., 269.

8. David Brock, *Blinded by the Right* (New York: Crown Publishers, 2003), 58.

9. Stuart Butler and Peter Germanis, "Achieving a 'Leninist' Strategy," *Cato Journal* (Fall 1983).

10. Peter Ross Range, "Thunder on the Right," *New York Times Magazine*, February 8, 1981.

11. Sidney Blumenthal, *The Rise of the Counterestablishment* (New York: Harper & Row, 1986), 126.

12. Michael Lind, "The Weird Men Behind George W. Bush's War," *New Statesman,* April 7, 2003.

13. Arthur Jones, "Michael Novak," *National Catholic Reporter,* January 13, 1995.

14. Eric Alterman, op. cit., 89–93.

15. Glenn C. Loury, "The Conservative Line on Race," *Atlantic Monthly* (November 1997).

16. Adam Shatz, "The Thernstroms in Black and White," *American Prospect,* March 12, 2001.

17. "Buying a Movement," 23.

18. John Maggs, "Grover at the Gate," *National Journal,* October 11, 2003.

19. "Buying a Movement, 5.

20. John B. Judis, *The Paradox of American Democracy* (New York: Routledge, 2001).

21. The surveys are conducted regularly by Michael Dolny of California State University, for Fairness & Accuracy in Reporting, www.fair.org.

22. Trudy Lieberman, *Slanting the Story: The Forces That Shape the News* (New York: New Press, 2000).

23. Bob Somerby, "Spin Search! A Pundit Was Fooled by Bush Spin, but Where Did the Slick-Spin-Point Come From?" Daily Howler, www.dailyhowler.com, January 20, 2003.

24. Curtis Moore, "Rethinking the Think Tanks," *Sierra* magazine (July/August 2002).

25. Michael Winerip, "What Some Much-Noted Data Really Showed About Vouchers," *New York Times,* May 7, 2003, B12.

26. "The Upper Brackets: The Right's Tax Cut Boosters," People for the American Way, March 27, 2003.

27. Karen Paget, "Lessons of Right-Wing Philanthropy," *American Prospect,* September 1998.

28. Michael Tomasky, "Breaking Kristol," *American Prospect,* April 2, 2003.

29. Jim Lobe, "Iraq Schemers Have Their Way," Inter Press Service, www.atimes.com.

30. Margie Burns, "The Pens of August," *Progressive Populist,* August 1–15, 2003.

31. Gene Weingarten, "Below the Beltway," *Washington Post Magazine,* February 2, 2003, W05.

32. Laura Flanders, "Why Read the Right?" *Extra!* (March–April 1995).

33. Adam B. Kushner, www.prospect.org, March 20, 2003.

34. Crawford, op. cit., 270.

35. Andrew Rich, "U.S. Think Tanks and the Intersection of Ideology, Advocacy, and Influence," *NIRA Review* (March 2001).

36. Sam Husseini, "Brookings: The Establishment's Think Tank," *Extra!* (November–December 1998).

37. McChesney, op. cit., 291.

38. Bagdikian, op. cit., 216.

39. "Buying a Movement," 5.

Chapter Three. The Big Lie

1. Landay, op. cit.

2. Michael Massing, "Who's Afraid of Reed Irvine?: The Rise and Decline of Accuracy in Media," *The Nation,* September 13, 1986.

3. See Accuracy in Media, Council for the Defense of Freedom, and World Anti-Communist League, www.namebase.org.

4. Walter and Miriam Schneir, "The Right's Attack on the Press," *The Nation,* March 30, 1985, 361.

5. See Accuracy in Media, www.namebase.org.

6. Massing, op. cit.

7. Peter Hart and Steve Rendall, "Meet the Mythmakers," Fairness & Accuracy in Reporting.

8. Massing, op. cit.

9. Crawford, op. cit., 184.

10. Kevin P. Phillips, *Mediacracy* (New York: Doubleday & Company, 1975).

11. Schneir, op. cit.

12. Crawford, op. cit., 216–217.

13. Schneir, op. cit.

14. Ibid.

15. Scott McConnell, "Among the Neocons," *American Conservative*, April 21, 2003.

16. Crawford, op. cit., 169.

17. Schneir, op. cit.

18. Crawford, op. cit., 207.

19. Mark Jurkowitz, "The Right's Daddy Morebucks," *Boston Globe*, February 26, 1998, E1.

20. Hart and Rendall, op. cit.

21. Don Bonafede, "One Man's Accuracy," *National Journal*, May 10, 1986.

22. Edward S. Herman, "The Illiberal Media," www.zmag.org, January 1997.

23. Michael Schudson, "The Media Elite," *Los Angeles Times*, October 12, 1986.

24. David Croteau, "Examining the 'Liberal Media' Claim," www.fair.org/reports/journalist-survey.html.

25. Kathleen Hall Jamieson, *Everything You Think You Know About Politics . . . And Why You're Wrong* (New York: Basic Books, 2000), 187.

26. Norman Solomon, "The Media Politics of Impeachment," AlterNet.org, June 20, 2003.

27. "Liberal Bias of Media Alleged by NCF Campaign; National Conservative Foundation," *Broadcasting*, July 8, 1985.

28. Richard A. Dunham, "A Whirlwind Tour of Inauguration Day," *Business Week Online*, January 22, 2001.

29. Howard Kurtz, "A Crusade to Right Left-Leaning News Media; Brent Bozell Hopes to Give the Electorate a New Slant," *Washington Post*, June 6, 1996.

30. Hart and Rendall, op. cit.

31. Glenn Garvin, "CNN Is Soft on Castro, Study Says," *Miami Herald*, May 14, 2002.

32. Mark Weber, "The MRC and Liberal Media Bias: Creating Their Own Enemy," democraticunderground.com.

33. John Young, "Accuracy in Media? Or Fabrication?" *San Francisco Chronicle*, March 20, 1991.

34. "Rush Limbaugh Is Foiled by Conservative Newsletter," *Orlando Sentinel*, April 30, 1995.

35. Joann Byrd, "Catching the Ear of the Media," *Washington Post*, August 14, 1994.

36. Michael Scherer, "Framing the Flag," *Columbia Journalism Review* (March–April 2002).

37. Jim Rutenberg and Bill Carter, "Network Coverage a Target of Fire from Conservatives," *New York Times*, November 7, 2001.

38. Scott Sherman, "David Horowitz's Long March," *The Nation*, July 3, 2000.

39. Jack E. White, "A Real Live Bigot," *Time*, August 30, 1999.

40. David Horowitz, "I Know a Thing or Two About College Protest—And This Time the Students Are Wrong," *Jewish World Review*, October 1, 2001.

41. White, op. cit.

42. Sander Hicks, "How Karl Rove Won the White House with David Horowitz and 'Compassionate Conservatism,'" www.sanderhicks.com.

43. Ibid.

44. Sherman, op. cit.

45. Ibid.

46. Ibid.

47. David Barsamian, "The Right-Wing Attack on Public Broadcasting," www.public eye.org/eyes/medi_pow.html.

48. Kurtz, op. cit.

49. Richard Reeves, "The Myth of Media Liberalism," *Denver Post,* June 1, 1997, D-02.

50. Barsamian, op. cit.

51. Jim Naureckas, "Study of Bias or Biased Study?" Fairness & Accuracy in Reporting, May 14, 1992.

52. James McCartney, "Used and Abused," *American Journalism Review,* April 1995, 34.

53. Jerry Landay, "Failing the Perception Test," *Current* (June 2001).

54. Jennifer L. Pozner, "Rally 'Round the Boys," *Extra!* (September–October 1999).

55. Chris Lehmann, "Bernard Goldberg's War," *Washington Post,* January 8, C09.

56. Jonathan Chait, "Victim Politics," *New Republic,* March 18, 2002.

Chapter Four. The Fifth Columnists

1. David Brock, "Capital Gangster," *George,* May 1998, 102.

2. Kathleen Sullivan, "Novak 'Has a History' As They Say," www.buzzflash.com, November 13, 2003.

3. Thomas Griffith, "Is It Fact or Opinion?" *Time,* January 14, 1985.

4. Eleanor Randolph, "George Will, the Oracle at Strict Remove," *Washington Post,* September 26, 1986, B1.

5. Eric Alterman, *Sound and Fury: The Making of the Punditocracy* (Ithaca: Cornell University Press, 1999), 71.

6. Steve Rendall and Jim Naureckas, "20 Reasons Not to Trust the Journal Editorial Page," *Extra!* (September–October 1995).

7. Robert L. Bartley, "The Press: Time for a New Era?" *Wall Street Journal,* July 28, 2003.

8. Dan Kennedy, "Who Was Robert Bartley?" *Boston Phoenix,* December 19–25, 2003.

9. Brock, *Blinded by the Right,* 246–249.

10. Graham, op. cit., 421.

11. Colman McCarthy, "Why the Washington Post Op-Ed Is So Dull," *The Progressive,* October 1, 2001.

12. George Will, "Her Potent Measuredness; Call It the Greenfield Effect," *Washington Post,* May 17, 1999, A19.

13. William Greider, "Washington Post Warriors," *The Nation,* March 24, 2003.

14. Todd Gitlin, "The Pro-War Post," *American Prospect,* April 1, 2003.

15. Edward Lazarus, "Truth and Consequences," *Washington Post,* July 28, 2002, T13.

16. Bruce Selcraig, "The Worst Newspaper in America," *Columbia Journalism Review* (January–February 1999).

17. Crawford, op. cit., 196.

18. Ibid., 194.

19. Doris A. Braber, ed., *Media Power in Politics* (Washington, D.C.: CQ Press, 2000), 120.

20. Don Oberdorfer, "From U.S. Officials, Denials and Uncertainty," *Washington Post*, November 1, 1980, A1.

21. Alterman, *What Liberal Media?*, 11.

22. Ben McGrath, "Balking," *The New Yorker*, November 17, 2003.

23. Bob Somerby, "Susan's Lament!" Daily Howler, www.dailyhowler.com, October 3, 2003.

24. Bagdikian, op. cit., 129–130.

25. Michael Tomasky, "Lib Liberation," *New York* magazine, June 23, 2003.

26. "Why Do We Need Media Beat?" excerpts of a speech by Norman Solomon to the Association of Opinion Page Editors, Fairness & Accuracy in Reporting, www.fair.org, November 1995.

27. Dave Astor, "SF Chronicle Won't Reinstate Columnist," *Editor & Publisher*, September 6, 2002.

28. Matthew Yglesias, "Boyer Plate," *American Prospect*, November 14, 2003.

Chapter Five. Scandal Sheets

1. George Thayer, *The Farther Shores of American Politics* (New York: Simon & Schuster, 1967).

2. Crawford, op. cit.

3. Thayer, op. cit., 291.

4. Brock, *Blinded by the Right*, 86–87.

5. Chris Potter, "Notes from the Blunder Ground," *Pittsburgh City Paper*, September 4, 2003.

6. Terry Krepel, "NewsMax by the Numbers," www.conwebwatch.tripod.com.

7. Ibid.

8. Sidney Blumenthal, *The Clinton Wars* (New York: Farrar, Straus & Giroux, 2003), 249.

9. Richard Pachter, "Linking News Sites, Matt Drudge Creates an Internet Success," *Miami Herald*, September 1, 2003, 7.

10. Ben McGrath, "Fit to Print?" *New Yorker*, September 10, 2003.

11. Francine Mayas, "Gore Ticket Scam: Anatomy of a Smear," www.mediawhoresonline.com, August 14, 2002.

Chapter Six. Toilet Papers

1. William Shawcross, *Murdoch: The Making of a Media Empire* (New York: Touchstone, 1997), 188.

2. Ibid., 100.

3. Neil Chenoweth, *Rupert Murdoch: The Untold Story of the World's Greatest Media Wizard* (New York: Crown Business, 2001), 158.

4. Patrick Barkham, "Murdoch on Murdoch," *The Guardian*, July 25, 2001.

5. Chenoweth, op. cit., 283–285.

6. Fred Clarkson, "Behind the Times: Who Pulls the Strings at Washington's No. 2 Daily?" *Extra!* (August–September 1987).

7. Robert Parry, "Moon's Billions and Washington's Blind Eye," www.consortiumnews.com, 1997.

8. Steven Alan Hassan, "A Christian Call to Protest the Moon Mass Wedding Festival," www.freedomofmind.com.

9. Carla Binion, "Why Is TV News Ignoring the Relationship Between Moon and the Bush Family?" www.onlinejournal.com, February 22, 2001.

10. "White House Official Promotes Faith-Based Plan at Moon Event," Americans United for Separation of Church and State, www.americansunited.org.

11. Binion, op. cit.

12. Nicholas Confessore, "Bad News: What the Right Doesn't Understand About Howell Raines," *American Prospect,* October 7, 2002.

13. Bob Somerby, "Wes Pruden—Anti-American," Daily Howler, www.dailyhowler. com, November 12, 2001.

14. Barbara Leiterman, "The Ascendancy of Conrad Black," *Extra!* (November–December 1996).

15. Hao Wang, "Sun Founder Lipsky Inspires Students at Tea," *Yale Daily News,* October 16, 2003.

16. "Ira Stoll Versus the Red Menace," *Smarter New York Sun,* May 2, 2002.

17. Timothy Noah, "Dissent Equals Treason," *Slate,* February 11, 2003.

Chapter Seven. Ministers of Propaganda

1. Edwin Feulner, "Salute to a Visionary Founder," *Washington Times,* March 19, 2003.

2. Dan Junas, "Report on the Religious Right in Washington State," www.aclu-wa.org/issues/religious/3.html, 1995.

3. Allan Sloan and Anne Bagamery, "The Electronic Pulpit," *Forbes,* July 7, 1980, 116.

4. Dennis Mazzocco, *Networks of Power* (Boston: South End Press, 1994), 34.

5. Hofstadter, op. cit.

6. Thayer, op. cit., 217–237.

7. Ibid., 244–245.

8. Ibid., 246.

9. Ibid., 149.

10. Junas, op. cit.

11. Chip Berlet, "The Right Rides High; Dogmatism and Religious Fundamentalism in U.S. Republican Party," *The Progressive,* October 1994, 22.

12. Howard Rosenberg, "Setting the Record Straight," *Los Angeles Times,* December 19, 1986.

13. Chenoweth, op. cit., 224.

14. Junas, op. cit.

15. Chenoweth, op. cit.,

16. "The Rise of the Religious Right in the Republican Party," www.4religious-right.info/religious_right_dominion_over_media2.html.

17. Stacey Michael, "Rev. Pat Robertson Hanging by a Thread," www.religiousconceit. com, October 12, 2003.

18. Ibid.

19. Jamie Doward, "U.S. Millionaire Bankrolls Crusade Against Gay Anglican Priests," *The Guardian,* October 12, 2003.

20. Eric Huebeck, "The Integration of Theory and Practice: A Program for the New Traditionalist Movement," www.freecongress.org/centers/cc/new_traditionalist.asp.

21. "MacNeil/Lehrer Sells Out," *Extra!* (February 1995).

22. Herman, op. cit.

23. Ibid.

Chapter Eight. Talking Heads

1. Mazzocco, op. cit., 40.

2. Harry F. Waters, "Ted Turner Tackles TV News," *Newsweek,* June 16, 1985, 58.

3. See "Quotations on Free Thought and Religion," www.atheism.about.com.

4. Ibid.

5. Ibid.

6. Julianne Malveaux, "Speaking of Education: How Many Sides to a Story?" EthnicNewsWatch, January 26, 1995, 40.

7. Chip Berlet, "Ashcroft Appearance on Schlafly's 1997 Conspiracist Video," www.publiceye.org, January 11, 2001.

8. David A. Vise and Thomas B. Edsall, "Battle for CBS Takes on Air of Mudslinging Contest; Network Cites Tie Between FIM, Controversial Group," *Washington Post*, March 31, A16.

9. Scott Shepard, "Turner Vows Continued Attempt at Network Takeover," Associated Press, June 27, 1984.

10. *Communications Daily*, July 2, 1985, 4.

11. "Turner Admits Role in Takeover Try," UPI, March 22, 1985.

12. Sally Bedell Smith, "CBS Criticizes Turner's Views," *New York Times*, May 3, 1985, D1.

13. "Pat Buchanan, Equal Opportunity Maligner," Fairness & Accuracy in Reporting, www.fair.org, February 26, 1996.

14. Hal Boedeker, "15 Loud Years of Annoying Blowhards; Crossfire Often Reduces Political Discussion to Name-Calling, Condescension and Theatrics," *Orlando Sentinel*, June 13, 1997, E1.

15. "Field Guide to Lukewarm Liberals," *Extra!* (July–August 1998).

16. David Brock, "Capital Gangster," *George* (May 1998).

17. "Field Guide to Lukewarm Liberals."

18. "A Tort Reply," *Washington Post*, October 1, 2002, C01.

19. Howard Kurtz, *Hot Air: All Talk, All the Time* (New York: Basic Books), 227–268.

20. Alterman, *What Liberal Media?*, 2.

21. Eric Boehlert, "CNN: Veering Right and Aiming Low," *Salon*, September 5, 2001.

22. Steve Rothaus and Andrea Elliott, "AOL Chief Case's Gift to Christian School Offends Gay Activists," *Miami Herald*, October 20, 2000.

Chapter Nine. Mort the Mouth

1. Adam Buckman, "The Mouth Roars," *Electronic Media*, May 9, 1988.

2. Paul Vitello, "Machismo for the Masses," *Newsday*, November 16, 1988, 6.

3. Dick Polman, "TV's Bad Boy Mort Downey Feels Right When He's Talking Up a Storm," *Chicago Tribune*, May 27, 1988.

4. Randall Rothenberg, "Morton Downey Jr. Is Taking His Abrasive Style Nationwide," *New York Times*, May 16, 1988, C15.

5. Alan Bunce, "Why Do People Watch?" *Christian Science Monitor*, October 15, 1988, 32.

6. Tom Shales, "Shriek! Chic! It's Morton Downey," *Washington Post*, July 6, 1988, D1.

7. A. Craig Copetas, "Lips of Fury," *Regardie's*, August 1988, 36.

8. Ibid.

9. Rebecca Johnson, "The Lives They Lived," *New York Times Magazine*, December 30, 2001, 45.

Chapter Ten. *General Electric Theatre*

1. Kurtz, *Hot Air*.

2. Bagdikian, op. cit., 209.

3. "Names & Faces," *Washington Post,* August 29, 2001.

4. Joe McGinniss, *The Selling of the President, 1968* (New York: Trident Press, 1969), 101.

5. The next fourteen paragraphs appeared in a somewhat different form in David Brock, "Roger Ailes: The Angriest Man in Television," *New York* magazine, November 17, 1997.

6. Alicia C. Shepard, "The Pundit Explosion," *American Journalism Review* (September 1995).

7. Chris Matthews, "Hail and Farewell," *San Francisco Chronicle,* September 1, 2002, D3.

8. Noam Scheiber, "Class Act: Chris Matthews and Bill O'Reilly v. the Working Man," *The New Republic,* June 25, 2001.

9. Ned Martel, "The Cable Guy," *New York* magazine, June 18, 2001.

10. David Rensin, "Chris Matthews," *Playboy,* July 1, 2001.

11. The author observed this exchange while standing on the *Hardball* set.

12. Peter Nichols, "But Could He Take It?" *Philadelphia Inquirer,* June 3, 2001.

13. Bob Somerby: "Memory Fails to Serve," Daily Howler, www.dailyhowler.com, January 8, 1999.

14. Bill Adair, "Rep. Scarborough Chooses Kinds Over D.C.," *St. Petersburg Times,* May 26, 2001.

15. Nikki Finke, "Behind Enemy Lines," *Los Angeles Weekly,* August 8–14, 2003.

16. Ibid.

17. Ed Henry, "No Ordinary Joe," *Roll Call,* June 30, 2003.

18. Don Kaplan, "Arnold Accuser Wants MSNBC Apology," *New York Post,* October 30, 2003.

19. Robert Stacy McCain, "Life in a Savage Nation," *Washington Times,* February 13, 2003.

20. Dave Ford, "Raging 'Savage' Could Use a Fix from His New Age Books," www.SFGate.com, July 11, 2003.

21. Frank Greve, "Pollster May Have Misled GOP on Contract," Knight-Ridder, November 10, 1995.

22. "Nevada: Luntz Loses Cool as He Declares—I'm Always Right," *Hotline,* February 23, 2003.

23. Dante Chinni, "Why Should We Trust This Man?" *Salon,* May 26, 2000.

24. Mark Francis Cohen, "Say the Magic Words," *Washingtonian,* October 2002.

25. See www.luntzspeak.com.

26. Chris Mooney, "The Most Partisan Journalist," *American Prospect,* January 15, 2002.

27. Amy Sullivan, "Sticks and Stones," *American Prospect,* December 3, 2002.

28. Anna Palmer, "Wyoming Man Out on Bail After Threatening Daschle," *Roll Call,* March 20, 2003.

29. Max Blumenthal, "California Confidential," *American Prospect,* August 19, 2003.

30. Ed Henry, "How About the Language of Truth-Telling?" *Roll Call,* November 19, 2003.

31. Rick Ellis, "The Surrender of MSNBC," www.commondreams.org, February 26, 2003.

32. Ralph Nader, "For Execution of Donahue, General Electric Supplied the Current," www.freelancestar.com, March 5, 2003.

33. Kurtz, *Hot Air,* 238.

34. Duncan Currie, "Dennis the Right-Wing Menace" *National Review,* June 27, 2003.

Chapter Eleven. Hate Radio

1. *Arkansas Democrat Gazette,* December 31, 1985.

2. Steven V. Roberts, "What a Rush!" *U.S. News & World Report,* August 16, 1993, 26–31.

3. Paul D. Colford, *The Rush Limbaugh Story* (New York: St. Martin's Paperbacks, 1994), 31–32.

4. Michael Arkush, *Rush!* (New York: Avon Books, 1993), 57.

5. Ibid., 100.

6. Ibid., 114.

7. Rush Limbaugh, "Voice of America: Why Liberals Fear Me," *Policy Review* (Fall 1994), 4.

8. David C. Barker, *Rushed to Judgment* (New York: Columbia University Press, 2002), 24.

9. Thayer, op. cit., 152.

10. Ibid., 154.

11. Ibid., 157.

12. Dan Wilson, "The Right of the Story," *Extra!* (September–October 1997).

13. Mazzocco, op. cit., 138.

14. Kurtz, *Hot Air,* 266.

15. Colford, op. cit., 44–47.

16. Kurtz, *Hot Air,* 231.

17. Colford, op. cit., 149.

18. Steve Rendall, "An Aggressive Conservative vs. a 'Liberal to Be Determined,'" *Extra!* (November–December 2003).

19. Ibid.

20. Katy Backman, "Inside Rush's Head," *Mediaweek,* August 11, 2003, 19.

21. Kathleen Hall Jamieson, "Call In Political Talk Radio," Annenberg Public Policy Center, August 7, 1996.

22. Edward Olshaker, "A Media Establishment in Denial over Hate Speech–Hate Crime Link," www.onlinejournal.com.

23. David Neiwart, "Rush, Newspeak, and Fascism: An Exegesis," Orincus.org, 7.

24. www.scoobiedavis.blogpsot.com, Wednesday, October 1, 2003.

25. Larry Keller, "Study Refutes Limbaugh's Take on Media," *Palm Beach Post,* October 2, 2003.

26. Kurtz, *Hot Air,* 262–263.

27. Pew Research Center Biennial News Consumption Survey, Pew Research Center for the People and the Press, June 9, 2002.

28. Barker, op. cit., 24.

29. Susan J. Douglas, "Letting Boys Be Boys," AlterNet.org, June 27, 2000.

30. Barker, op. cit., 19.

31. Ibid., 25.

32. David Limbaugh, "Talk Radio—Liberals Don't Have a Clue," WorldNetDaily, March 5, 2003.

33. Barker, op. cit., 19–20.

34. Ibid., 73–74.

35. Ibid., 53.

36. Ibid., 106–118.

37. Ibid., 118.

38. Ibid., 28.

39. Ibid., 93–94.

40. Richard L. Berke, "Limbaugh's Right-Hand Legman," *New York Times*, March 26, 1995, 33.

41. Kurtz, *Hot Air*, 294.

42. Ibid., 251.

43. Rich Lowry, "How the Right Rose," *National Review*, December 11, 1995.

44. Mike Hoyt, "Talk Radio, Turning Up the Volume," *Columbia Journalism Review* (November–December 1992), 44.

45. Kurtz, *Hot Air*, 233.

46. Ibid., 234–235.

47. Ibid., 241.

48. Roberts, op. cit., 26–31.

49. Neiwart, op. cit., 84.

50. Bob Somerby, "Truth Teller," Daily Howler, www.dailyhowler.com, September 30, 2002.

51. Kurtz, *Hot Air*, 289.

52. Megan Garvey, "Talk Radio Beats the Drum for Recall," *Los Angeles Times*, July 27, 2003.

53. Rekha Basu, "When Talk Radio Incites," *Des Moines Register*, April 20, 2003.

54. Kurtz, *Hot Air*, 291.

55. Douglas, op. cit.

Chapter Twelve. "Information Wars"

1. Blumenthal, op. cit., 125.

2. Bagdikian, op. cit., 84.

3. Jamieson, op. cit., 155.

4. Thom Hartmann, "Talking Back to Talk Radio," AlterNet.org, December 11, 2002.

5. Edward Monks, "The End of Fairness: Right-Wing Commentators Have a Virtual Monopoly When It Comes to Talk Radio Programming," *Register-Guard*, June 30, 2002.

6. Richard Hack, *Clash of the Titans* (Beverly Hills, Calif.: New Millennium Press, 2003), 217.

7. Ibid., 216.

8. Monks, op. cit.

9. Ibid.

10. "Hightower Gets Mickey Mouse Treatment," *Extra!* (December 1995).

11. Monks, op. cit.

12. Chenoweth, op. cit., 204.

13. Wil Lepkowski, "Policy Issues Permeate Efforts to Create Information Infrastructure," *Chemical & Engineering News*, March 27, 1995.

14. Chenoweth, op. cit., 203.

15. Frank Beacham, "New (Right) Technologies: In the Right Lane of the Information Superhighway," *Extra!* (March–April 1995).

16. Eric Boehlert, "Former FCC Chairman: Deregulation Is a Right-Wing Power Grab," *Salon*, May 31, 2002.

17. Robert W. McChesney, "This Communication Revolution Is Brought to You by U.S. Media at the Dawn of the 21st Century," *Third World Traveler*, 1998.

18. David Barsamian, "Media Power & the Right-Wing Assault on Public Broadcasting," *Z Magazine* (April 1995).

19. "MacNeil/Lehrer Sells Out."

20. Jenny Toomey, "Empire of the Air," *The Nation,* January 13, 2003, 28.

21. "One Thing Is Crystal Clear: Clear Channel Is a Subsidiary of Bush Inc.," www.buzz flash.com, April 18, 2003.

22. Dante Toza, "Clear Channel Rewrites Rules of Radio Broadcasting," *CorpWatch,* October 8, 2003.

23. Paul Fahri, "For Broadcast Media, Patriotism Pays," *Washington Post,* March 28, 2003, C1.

24. Toza, op. cit.

25. "Randi Rhodes, Liberal Talk Show Host," www.buzzflash.com, January 3, 2003.

26. Gordon Gregory, "KOPE Chasing National Audience," *Grants Pass Daily Courier,* December 22, 1993.

27. "Former Relative Denounces Grants Pass Evangelist," *Oregonian,* February 28, 1999.

Chapter Thirteen. "Fair and Balanced"

1. Neil Chenoweth, "The Untold Story of the World's Greatest Media Wizard," 163–170.

2. Neil Hickey, "Is Fox Fair?" *Columbia Journalism Review* (March–April 1998).

3. The next six paragraphs appeared in somewhat different form in David Brock, "Roger Ailes: The Angriest Man in Television," *New York* magazine, November 17, 1997.

4. "Wow! More Fox Bias!," www.the-hamster.com, October 4, 2002.

5. "The Most Biased Name in News," Fairness & Accuracy in Reporting, August 2001.

6. Ibid.

7. Alterman, *What Liberal Media?,* 209.

8. Rendall, op. cit.

9. David Folkenflik, "Fox News Defends Its 'Patriotic' Coverage," *Baltimore Sun,* April 2, 2003.

10. Shanya Grunewald, "Fox Anchor Is Big on Bush," *Star-Banner,* October 15, 2003.

11. Alessandra Stanley, "Threats and Responses: The TV Watch," *New York Times,* March 20, 2003.

12. "How Fox News, Owned by Rupert Murdoch and Managed by Roger Ailes, Tries to Trivialize the Death of Our Soldiers," www.buzzflash.com, August 29, 2003.

13. Alterman, *What Liberal Media?,* 178.

14. "Press Pass: GOP Activists to Take on Helen Thomas," *Hotline,* February 21, 2003.

15. Michael Klein, "O'Reilly Tells Why He Walked Out on NPR's 'Fresh Air,'" *Philadelphia Inquirer,* October 14, 2003.

16. Joel Connelly, "In the Northwest: The Hugely Self-Absorbed World of Bill O'Reilly," *Seattle Post Intelligencer,* October 3, 2003.

17. Peter Hart, *The Oh Really? Factor* (New York: Seven Stories Press), 120.

18. Ibid., 120.

19. Ibid., 72–74.

20. Ibid., 79.

21. Ibid., 47–49.

22. Ibid., 43–44.

23. Peter Hart, "The 'Oh Really?' Factor," Fairness & Accuracy in Reporting, www. fair.org, May–June 2002.

24. Hart, *Oh Really? Factor,* 115.

25. See www.hamster.com, June 5, 2003.

26. Brendan Nyhan, "O'Reilly Repeatedly Misquoted Glick," www.spinsanity.org, October 16, 2003.

27. Jack Shafer, "Bill O'Reilly Wants You to Shut Up," *Slate*, August 28, 2003.

Chapter Fourteen. Dirty Books

1. Crawford, op. cit., 31–32.
2. Brock, *Blinded by the Right*, 114–115.
3. Eric Alterman, "The Right Books and Big Ideas," *The Nation*, November 22, 1999.
4. Ibid.
5. Michael Wolff, "Judith's Untold Story," *New York* magazine, April 5, 1999.
6. Ben Fritz and Bryan Keefer, "The Blowhard Next Door," *Salon*, August 26, 2002.
7. Peter Bergen, "Armchair Provocateur," *Washington Monthly* (December 2003).
8. Brock, *Blinded by the Right*, 290–291.
9. "The Year in Hate," Southern Poverty Law Center, 2003.
10. Nicholas Confessore, "Hillary Was Right," *American Prospect*, January 17, 2000.
11. Brock, *Blinded by the Right*, 294.
12. Sam Tanenhaus, "A Vast Right-Wing Cry of Treason," *Slate*, July 24, 2003.

Chapter Fifteen. Sunday Morning

1. Bob Somerby, "Bend Living History (Part One)!" Daily Howler, www.dailyhowler.com, June 19, 2003.
2. David Brock, "Sunday, Bloody Sunday," *New York* magazine, May 18, 1998.
3. Eric Alterman, "Farewell My Cokie," *The Nation*, July 18, 2002.
4. Martin Plissner, "Flunking Statistics," *American Prospect*, December 30, 2002, 15.

Chapter Sixteen. *20/20*'s Vision

1. "Stossel Tampers with the Facts," Fairness & Accuracy in Reporting, July 17, 2001.
2. "The Stossel Beat," Fairness & Accuracy in Reporting, November–December 1996.
3. Ibid.
4. "Stossel's Shoddy Reporting on Government," Fairness & Accuracy in Reporting, February 7, 2001.
5. Peter Hart, "Give Us a Break: The World According to John Stossel," *Extra!* (March–April 2003).
6. Marianne Manilov, "More Underhanded Reporting from ABC News," TomPaine.com, June 26, 2001.

ACKNOWLEDGMENTS

I OWE AN ENORMOUS DEBT to the authors, writers, and commentators on whose published works I have drawn in writing *The Republican Noise Machine*. Books that enlightened me on the early history of the right-wing media include George Thayer's *The Farther Shores of American Politics*, Richard Hofstadter's *The Paranoid Style of American Politics*, Alan Crawford's *Thunder on the Right*, and Rick Perlstein's *Before the Storm*. Books and articles by media historians Robert W. McChesney, Ben H. Bagdikian, and Kathleen Hall Jamieson shaped my overall thoughts. I consulted various biographies of Rupert Murdoch, especially Neil Chenoweth's *Rupert Murdoch*. For more recent developments, I also relied heavily on two seminal books by media critic Eric Alterman, *The Sound and the Fury: The Washington Punditocracy and the Collapse of American Politics* and *What Liberal Media?*, on Howard Kurtz's *Hot Air*, and on Trudy Lieberman's *Slanting the News*. My chapter on talk radio owes a particular debt to the research of David C. Barker, author of *Rushed to Judgment*.

Research conducted by various writers for *Columbia Journalism Review*, *The Nation*, *The American Prospect*, *The Washington Monthly*, and *Salon* (especially the work of Eric Boehlert) was invaluable.

Nor could I have written this book while failing to regularly consult several media-focused Web sites and blogs, among them atrios.blogspot.com, BuzzFlash.com, ConWebWatch.com, DailyHowler.com, MediaWhores-Online.com, MediaTransparency.org, Poynter.org, rittenhouse.blogspot.com, rogerailes.blogspot.com, scoobiedavis.blogspot.com, Spinsanity.org, and The-Hamster.com.

Indispensable research done by Fairness & Accuracy in Reporting is cited throughout the book.

This is my second book with Crown Publishers, where I have enjoyed the unwavering support of publisher Steve Ross; of my editor, Doug Pepper; and of the entire Crown production and public relations teams. I thank Sona Vogel for careful copyediting.

This is also my second book with my terrific agent, Phillippa Brophy.

The indefatigable Amanda Fazzone helped line-edit and check the manuscript.

After publishing *Blinded by the Right,* I had the good fortune to meet several people whose encouragement and support enabled me not only to complete this work but also to continue it through the founding of a non-profit media watchdog organization in Washington, D.C. You know who you are. To my friends of longer standing, thank you all.

As always, my family, especially my mother, Dorothea, was supportive and understanding when the crunch of deadlines meant less time spent together.

Above all, I wish to thank James Alefantis, who makes it all worthwhile.

INDEX

Grateful acknowledgment is made to the following
for permission to reprint previously published material.

Columbia Journalism Review: Excerpts from "Seceding from the Union: Why I Quit" by Kathleen Salamon from *Columbia Journalism Review* (January/February 1991). Copyright © 1991 by Columbia Journalism Review. Excerpts from "In Review: Framing the Flag" by Michael Scherer from *Columbia Journalism Review* (March/April 2002). Copyright © 2002 by Columbia Journalism Review. Reprinted by permission of Columbia Journalism Review.

Copyright Clearance Center: Excerpts from "Behind the Green Screen . . ." by Mark Jurkowitz from *Boston Globe* (staff produced copy only). Copyright © 2002 by Globe Newspaper Co (MA). Reprinted by permission of Globe Newspaper Co (MA) in the format of Trade Book via Copyright Clearance Center.

Fairness & Accuracy in Reporting: Excerpts from "A Special FAIR Report: The Most Biased Name in News: Fox News Channel's Extraordinary Right-Wing Tilt" by Seth Ackerman (*Extra!*, August 2001). Reprinted by permission of Fairness & Accuracy in Reporting.

Dr. Paul Ginnetty: Excerpts from "Limbaugh's Fans Are Certain They're Right" by Paul Ginnetty from *Newsday* (November 12, 2003). Reprinted by permission of the author.

Joan Shorenstein Center on the Press, Politics and Public Policy: Excerpts from "Whispers and Screams: The Partisan Nature of Editorial Pages" by Michael Tomasky from *The Joan Shorenstein Center on the Press, Politics and Public Policy Research Paper Series* (July 2003). Reprinted by permission of the Joan Shorenstein Center on the Press, Politics and Public Policy.

Edward T. Monks: Excerpts from "Edward T. Monks Commentary" from *Register-Guard* (June 30, 2002). Reprinted by permission of the author.

The Nation: Excerpts from "A Teflon Correspondent" by Mark Dowie from *The Nation* (January 7, 2002). Reprinted by permission of *The Nation.* For subscription information call 1-800-333-8536. Portions of each week's *Nation* magazine can be accessed at http://www.thenation.com.